Historical Foundations of Education

BRIDGES FROM THE ANCIENT WORLD TO THE PRESENT

Janice B. Tehie
Immaculata University

PEARSON

Merrill
Prentice Hall

Upper Saddle River, New Jersey
Columbus, Ohio

Library of Congress Cataloging-in-Publication Data

Tehie, Janice B.

Historical foundations of education: bridges from the ancient world to the present/
Janice B. Tehie.—1st ed.

p. cm.

Includes bibliographical references and index.

Contents: Contents: Education in the Greek and Roman Empires, and the Middle Ages
—Rebirth of learning: Renaissance and Reformation—Formation of the American
educational system—Modern educational problems and reform movements (1930-present).

ISBN 0-13-061707-5

1. Education—History. 2. Education—Philosophy. I. Title.

LA11.T44 2007

370.9—dc22   2005058264

Vice President and Executive Publisher: Jeffery W. Johnston
Assistant Development Editor: Daniel J. Richcreek
Executive Editor: Debra A. Stollenwerk
Senior Editorial Assistant: Mary Morrill
Production Editor: Kris Roach
Production Coordination: Bookworks
Photo Coordinator: Maria B. Vonada
Design Coordinator: Diane C. Lorenzo
Cover Designer: Terry Rohrbach
Cover Image: Cristy Terry
Production Manager: Susan Hannahs
Director of Marketing: David Gesell
Senior Marketing Manager: Darcy Betts Prybella
Marketing Coordinator: Brian Mounts

This book was set in Helvetica by Pine Tree. It was printed and bound by R. R. Donnelley & Sons Company. The cover was printed by R. R. Donnelley & Sons Company.

Photo Credits: Francesca Yorke © Dorling Kindersley, p. 3; Corbis/Bettmann, p. 23; Mary Evans Picture Library/Photo Researchers, Inc., p. 42; Geoff Dann © Dorling Kindersley, Courtesy of the Wallace Connection, London, p. 67; Library of Congress, pp. 87, 139, 165, 193, 221; Private Collection, The Bridgeman Art Library Ltd., p. 111; Robert Kozloff/AP World Wide Photos, p. 247; Anthony Magnacca/Merrill, p. 265.

Pearson Education Ltd.
Pearson Education Singapore Pte. Ltd.
Pearson Education Canada, Ltd.
Pearson Education—Japan

Pearson Education Australia Pty. Limited
Pearson Education North Asia Ltd.
Pearson Educación de Mexico, S.A. de C.V.
Pearson Education Malaysia Pte. Ltd.

10 9 8 7 6 5 4 3 2 1
ISBN: 0-13-061707-5

This textbook is dedicated to my mother,
Frances Sydnor Tehie (April 16, 1926–April 15, 2003).
She always encouraged me to persevere,
no matter how difficult the task.

Preface

The purpose of this textbook is to show the connections (bridges) between education in past centuries and today's educational system in the United States. Many of the struggles in education today, such as literacy, have their roots in the past.

This book was written after I examined many textbooks while teaching courses in educational foundations and discovered that many of them did not adequately place education in the context of the times. Without that framework, students will not fully understand why these developments in education occurred.

Education does not develop in a vacuum; it always develops in response to religious, economic, political, and social conditions. For instance, students in colonial New England in the 1700s were allowed to read only religious-based texts such as the *New England Primer* because of their Puritan culture. Similarly, World War II spurred renewed emphasis on studying math and science, to bolster America's national defense.

Many of the current concerns with curriculum are not new; for example, the debate over whether students should study a liberal arts curriculum dates to the ancient Greeks. The type of education students receive in elementary school has roots in ancient Rome and the work of Quintilian, the Roman educator. The connections from modern education to the past are clearly explained in the "Bridges from the Past to the Present" section at the end of each chapter.

This text is suitable for either an undergraduate or graduate course in the history of education (foundations of education) or in the history of curriculum theory.

FEATURES OF THE TEXT

1. Discussion questions at the end of each chapter are ideal for students to work on in groups. These can be assigned as homework assignments to be turned in for a grade.

2. Activities are suggested at the end of each chapter to improve students' research skills in each topic area and to acquaint them with primary sources in the field. Students can work on these activities individually or in groups, for part of their course grade.

3. The "Shapers of Education" feature in each chapter summarizes the work of significant educators in the field. For instance, chapter 8 highlights the work of Horace Mann, founder of the American public school system.

4. Modern developments in education, such as the results of the *Third International Math and Science Study (TIMSS),* have been condensed into easy-to-understand tables.

5. This book is organized chronologically, and a timeline at the start of each chapter helps students place developments in education in context.

STRENGTHS OF THE BOOK

1. An easily readable text, reviewed by students in both graduate and undergraduate curriculum and foundations courses throughout its development

2. An opening photo or illustration representing the time period under study

3. Learning objectives for each chapter

4. Biographical notes on significant educators that discuss how their educational philosophy was shaped and that highlight their contributions to education

5. Annotated Web sites at the end of each chapter that can be used for further research on the topics or to help students complete the suggested activities in each chapter

6. Timelines that place the educational developments of each chapter in a political, social, economic, and religious context

7. Connections from the past to the present clearly spelled out

PEDAGOGICAL FEATURES

1. Chapter summary

2. Section at the end of each chapter, called "Bridges from the Past to the Present," clearly spelling out and summarizing the connections and contributions from each time period to the present

3. Timelines

4. Discussion questions and suggested activities at the end of each chapter

5. Suggestions for further reading, to encourage students to develop their research skills

6. List of annotated Web sites at the end of each chapter, to encourage further research

7. Boldface glossary terms

ACKNOWLEDGMENTS

I have been very fortunate to have had much support and encouragement from family, colleagues, and friends since I began working on this textbook about 5 years ago. Everyone at Prentice Hall has been very supportive, especially when some family issues and work responsibilities delayed some of the writing.

At Merrill/Prentice Hall, I would like to thank my editor, Debra Stollenwerk, who has proved to be a great mentor as well as a kindred spirit; Jan Hall, who helped with the design features; and Cheryle Gehrlich, the sales representative who submitted my manuscript to Debra several years ago, when I had made initial inquiries about writing a textbook.

I have appreciated the input of our reviewers: Judy Arnold, Lincoln Memorial University; Carolyn Babione, Indiana University Southeast; Malcolm B. Campbell, Bowling Green State University; Andriana Kalapothakos, Trinity University; Tom Kessinger, Xavier University; W. Thomas Jamison, Appalachian State University; Janet R. McNellis, Troy State University; Stephen D. Oates, Northern Michigan University; William G. Samuelson, Emporia State University; Patrick M. Socoski, University of Florida; Justin J. Wageman, North Dakota State University; and Karl G. Wolfe, Pepperdine University.

I would also like to thank my colleagues, past and present: Sr. Carol Anne Couchara, Sr. Anne Marie Burton, Joanne Burgert, Michael Stuckart, Carol Baker, Richard Frederick, Marietta Frank, Sheri Christjohn, Kimberley Hanold, Gloria Saar, and many other staff and faculty I have worked with, who are too numerous to mention.

I've been encouraged by many friends, including D. Scot Malay, DPM; Loretta J. Moore; Beth and Chris Fahr; Lindsey Britton; and Charles Wright Sydnor, Jr. (my cousin and a historian and author in his own right). Lastly, I especially want to thank my parents, Frances and John Tehie, who have always believed in me and encouraged me to do difficult tasks.

Brief Contents

Teacher Preparation Classroom

TEACHER PREP

MERRILL
PRENTICE HALL

See a demo at
www.prenhall.com/teacherprep/demo

Your Class. Their Careers. Our Future. Will your students be prepared?

We invite you to explore our new, innovative and engaging website and all that it has to offer you, your course, and tomorrow's educators! Organized around the major courses pre-service teachers take, the Teacher Preparation site provides media, student/teacher artifacts, strategies, research articles, and other resources to equip your students with the quality tools needed to excel in their courses and prepare them for their first classroom.

This ultimate on-line education resource is available at no cost, when packaged with a Merrill text, and will provide you and your students access to:

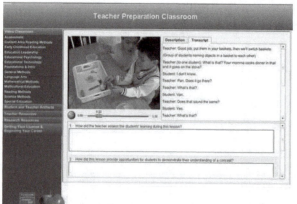

Online Video Library. More than 150 video clips—each tied to a course topic and framed by learning goals and Praxis-type questions—capture real teachers and students working in real classrooms, as well as in-depth interviews with both students and educators.

Student and Teacher Artifacts. More than 200 student and teacher classroom artifacts—each tied to a course topic and framed by learning goals and application questions—provide a wealth of materials and experiences to help make your study to become a professional teacher more concrete and hands-on.

Research Articles. Over 500 articles from ASCD's renowned journal *Educational Leadership*. The site also includes Research Navigator, a searchable database of additional educational journals.

Teaching Strategies. Over 500 strategies and lesson plans for you to use when you become a practicing professional.

Licensure and Career Tools. Resources devoted to helping you pass your licensure exam; learn standards, law, and public policies; plan a teaching portfolio; and succeed in your first year of teaching.

How to ORDER *Teacher Prep* for you and your students:

For students to receive a *Teacher Prep* Access Code with this text, instructors **must** provide a special value pack ISBN number on their textbook order form. To receive this special ISBN, please email **Merrill.marketing@pearsoned.com** and provide the following information:

- Name and Affiliation
- Author/Title/Edition of Merrill text

Upon ordering *Teacher Prep* for their students, instructors will be given a lifetime *Teacher Prep* Access Code.

Contents

PART 3   *FORMATION OF THE AMERICAN EDUCATION SYSTEM*   137

Chapter 7   **Puritan Life: Education in the New England and Virginia Colonies   139**

Introduction

This textbook has been designed with you, the student, in mind. Those of you taking a course in the history and philosophy of education, or in the history of curriculum theory, may wonder where some of the modern educational practices originated. Contributions from many time periods, including those of ancient Greece and Rome, can be found in our current educational system. For instance, much of what is done in elementary schools today can be traced to ancient Rome and the educator Quintilian, profiled in chapter 2. Quintilian discouraged teachers from using corporal punishment and talked about how to teach math and reading to elementary students—ideas that are still relevant today.

This text will help you place past developments in education into the context of the time in which they occurred. Education is influenced and affected by political, religious, economic, and social developments. For example, in medieval times, people did not think in terms of going to school to prepare for a career. Medieval thought held that it was sinful to try to better yourself, because God ordained the social class into which you were born.

Each chapter begins with a timeline that highlights the significant political, religious, economic, and social developments of the time period under discussion. Important terms in the text appear in boldface or italic print. Boldface terms are also found in the glossary.

At the end of each chapter, a "Bridges from the Past to the Present" feature summarizes the contributions from each time period to modern education, to emphasize the connections between the past and the present. As you read you will be surprised at how many modern educational problems have their roots in past history. Much of what people think is "new" in education is really not.

Each chapter also contains a list of annotated Web sites for further information on the topics presented in the chapter. You can also use these Web sites to help you complete the suggested activities at the end of each chapter. These activities will help you analyze the contributions from the past to the present more thoroughly. Suggestions for further reading in each chapter list both primary and secondary sources. Primary sources are those from the time period itself, for example, a book or lecture written by Horace Mann, who developed the concept of the American public (common) school.

This book has been developed with the help of students in the author's graduate courses, who have provided assistance and suggestions. They felt they learned a great deal and enjoyed the easy-to-read style in which it is written. It is the author's hope that you will find the text interesting, educational, and highly informative and that you will keep it as a reference to refer to again and again.

PART 1

Education in the Greek and Roman Empires, and in the Middle Ages

Chapter 1

Education in the Ancient World: Greek Contributions to Education (500–168 BC)

Learning Objectives

1. Describe the geography of ancient Greece and the economic, political, social, and educational system of each city-state.
2. Describe the contributions of Aristotle, Socrates, and Plato to today's educational system.
3. List the similarities and differences between the educational system in ancient Greece and today's educational system.

INTRODUCTION

Many contributions to education, such as age-grading practices, orginated in ancient Greece and Rome. Thus, we begin our study of the historical foundations of education with these two empires: this chapter discusses ancient Greece, and chapter 2 focuses on Roman culture. Greek and Roman influence can be seen in today's elementary schools as well as in institutions of higher education. The timeline gives the crucial dates in the development of Greece and Greek education.

The ancient Greeks studied philosophy, art, and literature, all of which are studied in liberal arts colleges and even in public universities today. This chapter discusses the many similarities between the ancient Greek system of education and our own, including the concept of regionalization (see Table 1-1). Today, the type of education a student receives may vary greatly from one state to another. This was also the case in ancient Greece. A person who moved from the **city-state** of **Athens** to the city-state of **Sparta** would receive a very different type of education in Athens from that offered in Sparta.

This chapter discusses the influence of the culture of Athens and Sparta, the two major Greek city-states, on education and teaching methods; and details about the daily schedule of an Athenian schoolboy illustrate what it was like to be in school in ancient Greece. There are many parallels between the types of subjects studied by young Athenian children and those studied by elementary school children today. Another similarity is that just as in modern times, parents could send their children to private schools if they chose.

This chapter also describes the contributions of the philosophers **Socrates, Plato,** and **Aristotle** to education. Their educational philosophies, which focused

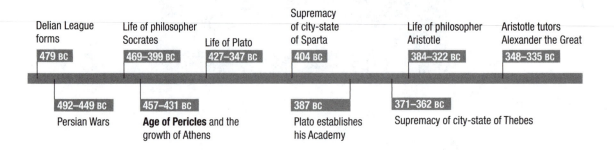

Delian League forms	Life of philosopher Socrates	Life of Plato	Supremacy of city-state of Sparta	Life of philosopher Aristotle	Aristotle tutors Alexander the Great
479 BC	469–399 BC	427–347 BC	404 BC	384–322 BC	348–335 BC

492–449 BC	457–431 BC	387 BC	371–362 BC
Persian Wars	**Age of Pericles** and the growth of Athens	Plato establishes his Academy	Supremacy of city-state of Thebes

Table 1-1 **Educational Philosophy: Greek Era Versus Modern Times**

GREEK EDUCATION	MODERN EDUCATION
Education was regionalized.	Education is regionalized.
Philosophy, art, and literature were studied.	Philosophy, art, and literature are studied in liberal arts colleges.
Private schools were an option.	Private schools are an option.
Education for women and girls was generally not approved of, except by Plato.	Education is provided for both girls and boys.
Liberal arts subjects were valuable in themselves.	The value of liberal arts subjects may be questioned in preparing for the job market and for teaching.
The Spartan educational system taught practical subjects.	Vocational education is available.
Citizenship was taught.	Citizenship is taught.
Fourth-century Athenian boys studied art as children.	Elementary school students have art classes.
Physical education was just as important as intellectual.	Physical education courses are part of U.S. school curricula.

on the question of how best to educate someone to be a good citizen as well as a moral human being, can clearly be seen in their teaching methods and the focus of their instruction. Plato, for example, advocated early childhood education as well as education for women; the latter was an idea generally unheard of in ancient Greece. His educational philosophy as well as his teaching methods at his school, the Academy, reflected his strong beliefs in the importance of these ideals.

In this chapter we briefly describe the culture and geography of Sparta and Athens so that you can understand the social, economic, and political context of the types of education available to Athenian and Spartan youth. As you read think about how your state's social, economic, and political issues are reflected in its public educational system.

ANCIENT GREEK EDUCATIONAL IDEALS

The ancient Greeks developed a system of education that reflected their culture and geographic location. It is impossible to identify a *single set system* of education for ancient Greece, because the type of education that students received depended on where they lived. If they lived in the city-state of Athens, then their education was more likely to reflect the Athenians' beliefs that a person needed to study art, literature, architecture, mathematics, and physical education to become a productive citizen of Athens. In the city-state of Sparta, however, the citizens were a militaristic people whose main educational focus and purpose was training and

readiness for war. The educational system of ancient Greece thus depended on location and culture.

A parallel situation exists in the United States today, for education is not the same in each state but varies according to the culture of each state. For example, schools in the Southern states, a region sometimes called the Bible Belt because of an emphasis there on religion, may prohibit the teaching of evolution because it contradicts biblical teachings, whereas schools in the Northeast may include the teaching of evolution in science classes. This does not mean that parents and/or students in the Northeast will not object to the teaching of evolution, but it is more common to find objections to this practice in areas that place a high emphasis on religion in the predominant culture.

To understand how education developed in ancient Greece we must first look briefly at the early history and government of ancient Greece. Its history is long and complicated and marked by many wars, the most notable of which were the Persian Wars, from 492 to 449 BC. The Greek victory over the Persians led to the growth of the Athenian Empire, with its focus on philosophy, literature, architecture, sculpture, music, and mathematics. Today, the study of these subjects is known as a *classical,* or *liberal arts,* education. The Greeks believed that the highest task was the formation of the individual, via the liberal education. True education, from the Greeks' perspective, was not to train an individual for a specific occupation in adulthood but to develop a person's nature and faculties as a whole.[1]

EARLY HISTORY AND GOVERNMENT OF ANCIENT GREECE

The early Greek city-states were settled by tribes in the central city, in farming and grazing areas in the countryside, and in coastal regions. The citizens of these areas made their living as farmers, livestock herders, and fishermen, and in urban occupations. There were about 20 city-states in ancient Greece, the most important of which were Boeotia, with its central city of Thebes; Attica, with its capital city of Athens; and Laconia, with its central city of Sparta.

Unfortunately, the city-states lacked cohesion; they functioned as individual entities without much interaction. Each city-state had its own agenda, and the type of education children received depended, as noted previously, on their city-state of residence. The lack of cooperation among city-states had crucial implications for education; it meant that there was no agenda for a centralized system of education.

This situation has a parallel in modern times: the debate over whether the U.S. educational system would function better under national rather than state standards is very strong. The 2001 No Child Left Behind Act is the modern attempt to address this issue and to enact national standards that all students, regardless of their state of residence, must meet.

Although most of the city-states were run as democracies, in which individual citizens could have some influence on governmental decisions, there was no centralized form of government in ancient Greece. Competition and rivalry among the various city-states meant they did not have shared goals or a shared sense of

identity. This lack of cooperation caused friction and discontent; however, historians surmise that in times of danger the city-states pulled together and worked cooperatively, such as when an invasion threatened. For example, a defensive league, the **Delian League,** was formed in 478 BC during the second Persian invasions, and it helped the lower classes incorporate into the Athenian socioeconomic structure.[2] The poor citizens of Athens were not normally found in positions of power, so the Delian League was an important step toward democratic participation by Athenian citizens.[3]

Before 509 BC foreigners were prohibited from voting, attending public assemblies, or owning land, and only Greek citizens could participate in religious festivals or religious rites. Citizenship in ancient Greece could be obtained only after the appropriate education and required military and/or political training. This created a system in which the ruling classes had educational advantages over the poor.[4]

In ancient Greece the type of education that individuals received was determined by two factors: their social status, and their city-state of residence. The poor, who usually worked as **helots,** or slaves, had a low social status and, consequently, a low level of education. Helots in Sparta, for example, had no rights, although ironically, they could not be sold.[5] As you read the following sections note the differences between Athenian and Spartan philosophies and systems of education.

ATHENS AND SPARTA: DIFFERENT CITY-STATES, DIFFERENT EDUCATIONAL SYSTEMS

The Athenian system of education reflected the belief that the ruling classes, to whom Plato referred as "philosopher kings," should be educated, especially in philosophy, a subject that was widely believed to be important for truly educated men to study.[6] Thus, the ruling classes were to be well-educated men who were capable of distinguishing between truth and fiction and who could guide the rest of the population into making the right or morally appropriate decisions. The Athenian system of education was greatly influenced by the works of Plato, Socrates, and Aristotle, philosophers who advocated that individuals learn to think critically about their surroundings, question what they saw around them, and understand the difference between morally correct and incorrect behavior. This system of education also included instruction in the art of debating, which is used today in political campaigns, especially presidential campaigns. Debating originated with the ancient Greek philosophers known as *Sophists* (wise men), who trained young Athenian men in this skill.[7]

Athenian education was only for boys; for women, any training beyond instruction in household management was considered unnecessary.[8] Athenian boys were trained in gymnastics, because physical education was considered an important part of a comprehensive educational system for youth.[9] However, unlike Spartan boys, Athenian boys also studied sculpture, architecture, music, drama, poetry, philosophy, and even science.

An Athenian boy from a wealthier family started school at the age of 6, but a boy from the family of an artisan (craftsman) started school somewhat later. Three subjects were studied by elementary school boys: music, which involved learning to play the lyre and sing; literature, or reading and writing; and gymnastics. In the fourth century BC, Athenian boys also studied drawing and painting. Similarly, current-day elementary school students participate in art classes.[10]

Although preparation for war was important to both Athenians and Spartans, the Spartans focused on it more. Boys were taken from home at the age of 8 and lived in public barracks, where their life was very rigorous and disciplined; they did not receive much food, had to sleep on hard beds, and were often whipped in public to develop courage and endurance, qualities necessary for an effective soldier. The course of study in Sparta was mainly physical training for war. Students learned military music and drill and were taught how to use a spear and to fight, to steal, to wrestle, and to box. By the age of 30, Spartan men were supposed to be married, to live in the public barracks, and to train other young boys and men in the same regimen they had experienced.

Education for Spartan women and girls consisted of training in domestic arts and in gymnastics. The gymnastic training was supposed to make them strong and prepare them to bear healthy children. Most girls were taught to read and write by their mothers and nurses, who themselves were taught at home.

Spartan society seemed to be rather unconcerned with art, literature, music, or philosophy, all of which were very important to the Athenians. Education for the Spartans was defined as readiness for war at any time, and outstanding military training was the chief means to this goal. Traditionally, Greek educational philosophy did not advocate sacrificing the interests of the individual to the state, except in the case of Sparta.[11]

Because the same types of subjects are taught in our educational system as in ancient Athens, this chapter focuses more on the Athenian than on the Spartan system of education. The next section looks at a typical Athenian school day and examines how Athenian schools were established and run in ancient Greece.

THE SCHOOL DAY OF AN ATHENIAN SCHOOLBOY

Learning to read was an important part of the school day for Athenian boys in elementary school. They began by learning the alphabet and how to spell. Children posed in the shape of the letter they were representing; for instance, a child who was assigned the letter alpha (equivalent to our letter *A*) might stand with his feet apart and his arms folded over his stomach, to represent the shape of the letter. The children then got in the correct order to "spell" out the word they were assigned.[12]

Athenian boys also learned to memorize, committing to memory parts from the works of Homer and Hesiod, among others. When the boys learned to write, they did so on a wax tablet hinged in the middle. The two waxed halves were folded so that the wax sides touched each other and were protected when the tablet was not

in use.[13] A stylus, a metal rod about the length of a pencil, was used to make indentations in the wax. One end was pointed, and the other was like a modern-day pencil eraser and was used for the same purpose: to smooth out the wax and delete unwanted work or mistakes.[14]

It is interesting to note that the elementary school teacher did not command much respect in Athenian times. The fees charged to pay the teacher were evidently not very high, because even the poorest parents in ancient Greece could afford to send their boys to school if they chose. Elementary schools in Athens were operated privately, much like private schools or charter schools do today. These schools varied according to the work that was assigned, the teacher's qualifications and abilities, and the fees charged. Just as parents today insist on choice of schools for their children, Athenian parents were able to choose which schools their boys would attend.[15]

The concept of year-round school, an issue debated today, was a reality in Athenian Greece. There were no weekends to relax, play with friends, or do homework. The only holidays for an Athenian schoolboy were the feast days and religious holidays.[16]

For many centuries, schooling for an Athenian boy stopped at the elementary level, when he was about 13 or 14 years old and became an apprentice to learn a trade. Secondary education, which we know as high school education, was found in the form of private schools, most of which did not last long because the teachers were itinerant, traveling from one city to another.[17] The subjects studied were mathematics, including plane and solid geometry, the theory of numbers, and arithmetic. Students also learned to use the **abacus** (for adding) and were instructed in weights and measures. Time was also spent on music and literature, rhetoric, composition, and oratory, or public speaking.[18]

Did Athenian young men get the chance for higher education? As you will see in the following section, higher education was available, but not to everyone. There was no system of colleges or universities in ancient Greece; however, a course of study that many liberal arts colleges still follow today was prescribed for those interested in advanced study.

HIGHER EDUCATION IN ATHENIAN GREECE: SOCRATES, PLATO, AND ARISTOTLE

Although no formal system of higher education, or established colleges and universities, existed in Athens, a form of "higher" education, consisting of instruction in philosophy, did begin during this time. The schools of philosophy operated by Plato, Socrates, and Aristotle were an equivalent form of higher education, or college/university education. Usually, the students were those who showed some interest in the subject and had some aptitude for it.[19]

The educational philosophies of Socrates, Plato, and Aristotle are summarized in the feature "Shapers of Education" on page 10.

SHAPERS OF EDUCATION		
Socrates (469–399 BC)	**Plato** (427–347 BC)	**Aristotle** (384–322 BC)
■ Educate about morals. ■ Define the "good" life. ■ Develop self-knowledge. ■ Think critically (the dialectic method). ■ Question everything.	■ Education should be for all, including young children. ■ Include physical education. ■ Do not use **corporal punishment** (spanking, for example). ■ Provide role models. ■ Draw out students' abilities; prepare for an occupation. ■ Question even the senses (idealism). ■ Train the mind with a curriculum of concepts, like math. ■ Educate women if they are physically and mentally capable.	■ Pay heed to previous research. ■ Scientific studies require proof. ■ Educate about citizenship. ■ Women lack intellectual ability to learn. ■ Study politics.

THE CONTRIBUTIONS OF SOCRATES: MORAL EDUCATION AND THE SOCRATIC METHOD OF TEACHING

As the biographical notes indicate, Socrates had many unusual ideas, which were reflected in his teaching. He believed in sticking to his ideals and would not back down even though many people believed he was wrong. This personality characteristic contributed directly to his philosophies of education and ideas about teaching methods.

Socrates contributed to our educational system in two major ways. First, he examined the question of morality; that is, he sought to understand what it meant to live the good or true life. He thought that a necessary condition of the good life was to "know oneself." In other words self-knowledge of one's own faults as well as one's positive attributes, was important in answering this question.[20] Today, we encourage children to do the right thing and to lead the good life. Moral education, or *character education* as it is also called, is often cited as being necessary for students today, because they do not possess the correct values or morals to behave properly and be good citizens.

The second contribution of Socrates to our educational system was the Socratic method, also called the *dialectic*. In this teaching method, some questions, such as whether God exists, may be debated. Today, Socrates might take a student who believed that God existed and question him until the student admitted the inconsistencies in his theory and decided what kind of evidence might prove or refute his claim that God did exist.[21] This type of teaching encourages students

Spotlight On ⟵ ————————————————————————————————

THE SKEPTICISM OF SOCRATES

Skeptical by nature, Socrates was the ideal person to instruct in the art of debating. He even questioned religion, as he did not believe in the gods and goddesses who were so important to the ancient Greeks. He stated his disbelief publicly at the expense of his reputation. In Athenian society, the chief goddess was Athena, patroness of Athens and the source of wisdom. The Greeks relied heavily on religion for guidance. Such everyday affairs as courtship, childbirth, planting the fields, and hunting and fishing were influenced by gods or goddesses. Every room in the home was presided over by a god or goddess, as was every school, gymnasium, or public building. It was expected that Greek citizens would revere these gods and goddesses, and Socrates did not.

Socrates alienated the Sophists because his reply to the questions he asked others was: "I know nothing." He did so because he thought he should impart knowledge to others, not because he was the author of the knowledge.

to think critically and forces them not to accept whatever they are told but to question it, especially when evidence shows that what they are told is not necessarily true.

Socrates' work was carried on by his disciple Plato, who established the Academy, the seminary of higher learning, in 382 BC.

PLATO'S EDUCATIONAL THEORIES: THE ACADEMY

Plato's Academy was funded through private donation. It was a seminary of higher learning established in 387 BC, after Plato had returned to Greece. Fresh from his experiences in the war, Plato had many ideas about the best type of education to offer someone so that he or she would be truly educated.

The entrance requirements of the Academy included a familiarity with geometry. The course of study in geometry was grounded in the theory of numbers and was one of the most important of all the course offerings in the Academy, which included music, literature, history, law, and philosophy.[22]

An advocate of early childhood education, Plato believed that play was an important component of early childhood experiences. According to Plato, children should enjoy their activities and not worry about being punished or threatened.[23] Childhood in ancient Greece, however, was different than our present-day conception of childhood, for childhood, as defined by the Greeks, meant living up to adult standards. The concept of childhood that we hold today was not formed until much later, as you will see in chapter 4 on education during the Renaissance.

Spotlight On

PLATO'S LIFE, EDUCATIONAL IDEAS, AND PHILOSOPHY

Plato was Socrates' disciple, and that he took up where Socrates left off shows the great bond between teacher and pupil. Born in 427 BC into an upper-class family in ancient Greece, Plato became a student of Socrates as a teenager. He was called Plato, or the "broad-shouldered one," because he displayed great physical endurance, whether he was yachting, riding on horseback, or being a soldier. Plato established the Academy in Athens. Plato strongly believed in the democratic style of education for all, even women, as long as they could physically and mentally participate.

Unlike his contemporaries, Plato was not against education for women. He admitted them to the Academy for study with men if they could hold their own mentally and physically. In the *Dialogues,* Plato wrote:

This ill-ordained treatment of women acts injuriously on nearly half the objects of human improvement. The pursuits of men and women should both be set on a common footing. Women do not differ from men simply because they give birth to children: why need there be any difference as respects the appointments of state?[24]

Clearly, Plato felt that women were able to compete with men in important matters, including being appointed to governmental positions. The viewpoint that because women were biologically able to have children was no reason to hold them in contempt or deny them opportunities for public service was radical for this time period.

Plato's Academy was run like a monastery, with strict timetables for study, work, and mealtimes. Plato was a virtuoso in the art of teaching, for he tailored his teaching methods to the purpose he had in mind at the time. His major written contribution is the *Republic,* the complete philosophy of his educational ideology. In the 36 *Dialogues* of the *Republic,* Plato forces the reader to think about where ideas come from rather than just accepting them at face value. In Plato's view, philosophers were the ideal rulers of society, for they had the training and ability to think through difficult questions and analyze issues. They also could think about moral issues such as how to behave, live a virtuous life, and be a good citizen. Plato stated that "unless communities have philosophers as kings, there can be no end to political troubles, or to human troubles in general."[25]

Plato's major contribution to our educational system today is the philosophy of **idealism,** which holds that our senses may fool us into believing in things that are not real and may not exist at all. He used the fable, or allegory, of the cave to prove his point. The reader of his *Dialogues* is asked to imagine that he was born in a cave and is kept chained there, unable to experience anything outside the cave. When he turns his head as far as the chains allow, he can see only the shadows on the cave walls, which are produced by the sunlight outside the cave, and he is accustomed only to dim light. Once he breaks loose and escapes from the cave, he comes out into the sunshine and experiences the "real" world of other people, the sea, farmland, and animals. Outside the cave, he is freed from all mistaken and vague ideas, because he sees things as they really exist. Having once seen the light, he can never again believe in the reality of the cave.[26]

The concept of the cave is a metaphor. The cave is supposed to represent ignorance, and the sunshine represents real knowledge and truth. The shadows the person sees while in the cave can be said to represent false ideas, and what is seen in sunlight is supposed to represent truth or reality. The idea is that education must lead to the highest order of knowledge about reality. For this reason Plato proposed that the curriculum include subjects that involved conceptual systems, such as mathematics, language, ethical studies, history, and science, to train the mind. The *idealist* philosophy of education, to which Plato subscribed, holds that there is a universal mind, and the individual's spiritual essence, or soul, is permanent.[27]

Plato explained that the task of the educator is to draw out the abilities that exist in the individual. He did not believe in the prevailing educational idea that teachers have to imprint everything on the student's mind, because it is blank. Instead, Plato believed that the individual already has the capacity and the power to learn, and natural means by which to do so.[28] Plato also was concerned that education provide students with good role models to imitate. He believed that "children should imitate people who are courageous, self-disciplined, just, and generous and should play only those kinds of parts."[29]

Another important part of education was physical training, which is defined as proper diet and regimen and a variety of competitive games.[30] It was thought that if education was exclusively intellectual or exclusively physical, it would not be balanced. Thus, the educational experience should include some type of physical training to allow the student to harmoniously balance the physical and the spiritual aspects of life.[31]

Plato believed it was the function of education to determine what each individual was best fitted by nature to do and then to prepare him or her for this occupation. This was the Greek ideal of a liberal education. Plato's practical influence is seen in his formation and direction of the philosophical schools of Athens as well as the development of a curriculum that has been influential for centuries. Today, students in high school and college continue to study languages, philosophy, mathematics, and science, all of which were subjects of study in Plato's Academy.

Plato was not the only Greek philosopher to make major contributions to our educational system. Aristotle, a student in Plato's Academy, began studying with Plato when he was 17 and was soon making remarkable progress. His major contribution was the establishment of the Lyceum, a school for those of the ruling classes who sought an education. He also had a great interest in science and scientific investigation.

ARISTOTLE: THE CONTRIBUTION OF SCIENTIFIC INVESTIGATION

Aristotle contributed greatly to modern-day scientific scholarship by insisting that previous information on a subject had to be consulted before any new project was undertaken. He said that one's predecessors had to be consulted before any subject was introduced.[32] In modern scientific investigations, familiarity with previous research on the subject matter is a must. Before pursuing a research agenda, scientists today first determine what other research was previously carried out in that area or on that specific problem.

Aristotle's writings, which focus on mathematics, physics, and metaphysics, are concerned with the techniques and the principles of proof. He also advocated the study of politics, stating that attention should be paid to "which of the sciences are to exist in states, and what branches of knowledge the different classes of the citizens are to learn, and up to what point."[33]

Aristotle's ideas on education for women are reflected in the scholarship of the Middle Ages. He believed that women were intellectually inferior. His writings, quoted by early Christian moralists in the Middle Ages, were taken to mean that the female is at the root of all evil, because Adam was tempted by Eve to eat the fruit of the tree of knowledge in the Garden of Eden. Aristotle believed that women were fit only to be housekeepers and to take care of children. He thought that education for women was useless because they lacked the intellectual capacity to learn. Education for women, according to Aristotle's theory, should consist only of physical education so that a woman would be able to withstand childbirth and bear strong and healthy children. He even proposed a diet for pregnant women so that they would not have sickly or deformed babies. Aristotle proposed that by the age of 18 a woman should be married and begin having children. Her goal was supposed to be to please her husband in every way and to obey him, and that was the extent of her function.

Spotlight On ←

ARISTOTLE'S SCIENTIFIC INVESTIGATIONS

Aristotle (384–322 BC) was not an Athenian by birth but was the son of a court physician to King Amyntas II, the King of Macedon. Aristotle was sent to Plato's Academy at the age of 17, at his father's insistence, and was Plato's student for 20 years, until his teacher died.

An avid interest in science led to Aristotle's work in collecting biological specimens from 348 to 335 BC, during which time he also tutored Alexander the Great. When he returned to Athens from Persia, he founded his school, the Lyceum. He maintained a great interest in biology, physics, economics, psychology, morality, logistics, metaphysics, and art. Aristotle's work was highly influential in the Middle Ages.

Although Aristotle's ideas on education for girls and women seem to us today to be hopelessly outdated, he did make some important contributions to our educational system. He advocated instruction in mathematics and science and insisted on scientific investigation and proof. Aristotle also believed in citizenship education, which is now part of social studies curricula in some states. Citizenship education teaches individuals the necessary skills to behave in ways that are for the good of many people, not just the individual. In the United States at the turn of the century, many immigrants came into U.S. classrooms without knowledge of U.S. laws and customs, which educators thought they should learn to become law-abiding citizens. Aristotle himself stated that "to secure the good of one person only is better than nothing, but to secure the good of a nation or a state is a nobler and more divine achievement."[34]

BRIDGES FROM THE PAST TO THE PRESENT: VALUE AND USES OF LIBERAL ARTS EDUCATION TODAY

Today, high school students read and study plays by ancient Greek writers such as Sophocles and Euripedes. The study of mathematics, including geometry and trigonometry, is a part of all college-preparatory programs in the United States. These subjects are also studied at the college and university level. High school students planning to go to college must study physics, biology, and chemistry and take courses in art and music to meet college entrance requirements.

The value of a liberal arts education in today's society, which places increasing emphasis on technology, much more than education did in the past, has been debated for a long time. In 1984, William Bennett, the chairman of the National Endowment for the Humanities, advocated a return to the study of the classics.[35] Bennett, who later became the U.S. Secretary of Education under President George H. Bush in 1989, said that students should study Western cultural tradition because that is the basis for the formation of our values. Critics, however, have stated that the classics do not accurately portray women or minorities in today's society, and to focus exclusively on the classics is to give students a prejudicial view.[36]

Liberal arts colleges in the United States still require that students take courses in art, music, political science, mathematics, and science. There is a consortium of 59 liberal arts colleges, including the well-known schools of Bryn Mawr College and Haverford College in the suburbs west of Philadelphia. Other well-known institutions include Mount Holyoke, Williams, and Wellesley Colleges, all of which are located in Massachusetts and offer a liberal arts education, with courses in the humanities, mathematics, science, social sciences, and fine and performing arts.

The number of liberal arts colleges, which are usually private and do not usually offer advanced degrees, has dwindled. A hundred years ago, 70 percent of college students attended liberal arts colleges, but this figure has dropped to below 5 percent, according to Richard Hersh, President of Hobart and William Smith Colleges.[37] Two-year associate-degree institutions now account for more than 40 percent of the college population.[38] Higher education is viewed exclusively as preparation for jobs in the twenty-first century.[39] Interestingly, parents and high school students are poorly informed about the nature of a liberal arts education. Only 27 percent of parents and 14 percent of high school students indicated familiarity with the concept of a liberal arts education.[40] Forty-four percent of high school students and 14 percent of parents could not give any answer when asked to respond to the question, "what does a liberal arts education mean to you?"[41] However, when forced to think about the value of a liberal arts education, people were willing to admit that problem solving, critical thinking, writing and speaking skills—critical attributes of a liberal arts education—were actually career skills and were therefore valuable after all.[42] If the liberal arts curriculum is to appear attractive to college students and their parents, liberal arts colleges and their faculty must clearly delineate the benefits of a liberal arts education for future employment and careers. This certainly holds true if liberal arts is to be a training background in teacher education programs.

LIBERAL ARTS BACKGROUND: THE IDEAL TRAINING FOR TEACHERS

Should teachers study the liberal arts? Critics of current methods of teacher preparation think so. In a 2002 article in *Education Week,* Lloyd H. Elliott stated that the preparation for teachers must be stronger and that a 4-year liberal arts education is a basic prerequisite for those wishing to teach. A strong fundamental knowledge of history, mathematics, and science is necessary preparation to impart the correct information to students. Teachers would feel more confident about teaching if their academic preparation were stronger, because they would have the necessary background to teach. The methods or teaching-skills courses should come later, in the fifth or even sixth years of the program, and should be integrated with actual classroom experience.[43]

Clearly, it is not enough for future teachers to have a knowledge just of teaching methods; they must also be thoroughly competent in the subject matter or content areas in which they will teach. A group of 14 selective liberal arts colleges in the Midwest, the Associated Colleges of the Midwest (ACM), founded in 1958, does not allow education students to major in education alone; they must have a double major, with the second major area in an academic discipline. For example, students at Lawrence University in Wisconsin preparing to teach in grades 6–12 take a third of their courses in their major, such as history, mathematics, or chemistry; two natural sciences and two social sciences; and a quarter of courses in education. The students at Lawrence University take fewer education courses than other students at similar liberal arts colleges but feel they are better prepared in the subject matter they are supposed to teach. Principals and supervisors agree with the students' evaluation of their abilities.[44]

Unfortunately, faculty at liberal arts colleges are often distrustful of teacher education programs. This makes it difficult to have a program in which liberal arts faculty join with teacher education faculty to train teachers. At the turn of the century, teacher training was done in "normal schools," which taught the instructional methods of teaching but not the content of the academic disciplines.[45]

It has been suggested that one way to improve the quality of teacher education programs is to include liberal arts faculty in planning the teacher education programs at liberal arts institutions. The Holmes Group and the Carnegie Commission on Education and the Economy made this recommendation in 1986. Liberal arts faculty also could teach courses in the discipline developed for education students as well as supervise students doing their practicum or student teaching in the school systems.[46] It has also been suggested that liberal arts faculty will be more attracted to working with teacher education students if they have a strong academic background and excellent skills. Because of the historical background of teacher education students from the normal schools, the stereotype of the teacher education student as rather nonacademic and of mediocre abilities has persisted and must be overcome. The academic institution must also show strong support for the teacher education program, so that the liberal arts faculty realize that the institution believes the program has validity and is of good academic quality.[47]

To become an effective teacher, preparation in the liberal arts is crucial if one is to acquire the necessary content area knowledge. Thus, the liberal arts education, although no longer as popular as it used to be,[48] still has validity.

In the next chapter we shall examine the further impact of the liberal arts tradition as we acquaint ourselves with the breakup of the Greek Empire, the world of the Roman Empire, and the contributions of the Roman educational system to our present educational system.

SUMMARY

The type of educational system in ancient Greece was shaped by the geographic location and environment of each city-state. City-states in ancient Greece functioned much as individual states do today, each with its own political and economic system. Some city-states were highly agricultural; others depended on fishing or other types of industry. The educational system of each city-state reflected its unique economic, political, and social systems.

In Athens, the capital city of Attica, the culture demanded a high level of literacy and instruction in music, philosophy, art, and architecture. Education was mainly for men, although women could participate in higher educational opportunities, but did so rarely. However, the idea that women could take part in advanced forms of education did take root, although it would be centuries before significant numbers of women would receive advanced education. Athenian civilization was very advanced, and the study of mathematics, physics, biology, astronomy, and metaphysics led to more abstract levels of thought.

In contrast, the Spartan educational system concentrated on preparation for war. Thus, there was little academic preparation beyond the teaching of math and reading. Education in the ancient Greek city-states thus centered on the question,

What is necessary for our citizens to learn to be good citizens? The idea of tailoring an education to the economic, political, and social needs of a specific geographical region thus became established. Socrates, Plato, and Aristotle were the main figures shaping education during this period.

QUESTIONS FOR DISCUSSION

1. In modern times, one major issue in education is national versus local control of schools. In ancient Greece, each city-state had its own system of education. We might say that they had local control of education. Would a national system of education have benefited the ancient Greeks? Why? Would it benefit the United States today? Explain.

2. Describe Spartan society and the attitudes of the Spartans toward life, culture, and education. Can you think of any cultural or socioeconomic group today that has similar attitudes about the practical purposes of education? Explain your answer.

3. Describe Plato's ideas on women's education. Do you believe women today receive enough education, and is there equality in education for women? Explain your answer.

4. Socrates was a very controversial figure in ancient Greece. Controversy and education often go hand in hand. In a 1989 controversy in education the chancellor of the New York City Board of Education proposed the Children of the Rainbow curriculum to teach children about various lifestyle choices, including homosexuality. If Socrates had been alive then, what do you think his reaction would have been to this curriculum? Explain your answer.

5. Define Plato's ideas on early childhood education. How do these compare and contrast with ideas on early childhood education from preschool to grade 2 today?

6. Describe Aristotle's scientific ideas and his contributions to scientific investigative practices today.

7. Describe Plato's philosophy of idealism. Do you agree that the subjects he proposed are the best way to teach students today how to deal with the world around them? Why or why not?

SUGGESTED ACTIVITIES

1. Assuming that you are Plato, Aristotle, or Socrates, write a letter to the governor explaining your views on education and present it to your classmates. Be prepared to argue your point of view. The points in the letter can be presented as a PowerPoint presentation.

2. You are a member of your local school board and also a professor of classics at a major university nearby. You would like high school students in your community to study the works of Plato in philosophy and the works of Sophocles and Euripedes in literature. Write a letter to your local school board explaining your viewpoint.

3. Research the current educational system in Greece and compare it with the educational system of ancient Greece. Do any vestiges of the past remain in today's Greek educational system? Present your findings as a PowerPoint presentation.

4. Research the history of a piece of Greek architecture or Greek art, and report on it to your classmates.

5. Develop a dialectic on a philosophical issue or specific problem such as abortion, the death penalty, or another current pertinent issue. Be prepared to conduct the dialectic with at least one other person in front of your class. Choose questions for the argument carefully, as Socrates would have chosen them, so you can make the other person(s) see the mistaken ideas in their thinking as you question them.

Bibliography

Baldwin, J. (2000, Summer) Liberal arts for a new millennium. *Carnegie Reporter, 1*(1).

Barrow, R. (1976). *Plato and education.* Boston: Routledge and Kegan Paul.

Bergen, T. J., Jr. (1994). The Greeks and the education of humanity. *Journal of General Education, 43*(1), 32–43.

Boyd, W., & King, E. J. (1995). *The history of Western education* (12th ed.). Lanham, MD: Barnes and Noble.

Cordasco, F. (1963). *A brief history of education.* Paterson, NJ: Littlefield, Adams.

Cubberley, E. P. (1949). *History of education.* Cambridge, MA: Riverside Press. This is an exhaustive history of early civilizations.

Day, A. (1870). *Summary and analysis of the dialogues of Plato. With an analytical index, giving references to the Greek text of modern editions and to the translation in Bohn's classical library.* London: Bell and Daldy.

Dodd, A. W. (1996, May). A very different kind of teacher education program: Professional Development Schools. *NASSP Bulletin, 8*(580).

Gross, R. E., & Moelman, A. H. (1962). Our debt to the ancients of the Western world. In R. E. Gross (Ed.), *Heritage of American Education.* Boston: Allyn and Bacon.

Hersh, R. H. (1997). Intentions and perceptions: A national survey of public attitudes toward liberal arts education. *Change* (March/April).

Littlefield, G. E. (1965). *Early schools and school books of New England.* New York: Russell and Russell.

Livingstone, Sir R. (1944). *Plato and modern education.* New York: MacMillan.

Lodge, R. C. (1947). *Plato's theory of education, with an appendix on the education of women according to Plato, by Rabbi Solomon Frank, PhD.* London: Routledge and Kegan Paul.

Losin, Peter. (1996). Education and Plato's parable of the cave. *Journal of Education, 178*(3).

Meyer, Adolphe E. (1965). *An educational history of the Western world.* New York: McGraw-Hill.

Suggestions for Further Reading

Burnet, J. (Ed. & Trans.). (1967). *Aristotle. Aristotle on education: Being extracts from the Ethics and Politics.* Cambridge: Cambridge University Press. 1903.

Lynch, J. P. (1972). *Aristotle's school: A study of a Greek educational institution.* Berkeley: University of California Press.

Scott, G. A. (2000). *Plato's Socrates as educator.* Albany: State University of New York Press.

Relevant Web Sites

Art History Resources: Ancient Greece and Rome—Dr. Chris Witcombe, Professor of Art History, Sweet Briar College, VA *http://witcombe.sbc.edu/ARTHgreecerome.html* A great site for researching art and architecture in ancient Greece and Rome.

Ancient Greece and Ancient Rome, Comparisons and Contrasts *http://ancienthistory.about .com/cs/greecevsrome* Great comparison of ancient Greece and Rome.

Education Week *http://www.edweek.org* Weekly updates on current news in education in an easy-to-read format.

National Center for Education Statistics *http://www.nces.ed.gov* Up-to-date information on types of colleges, student graduation rates, teacher preparation programs.

The Condition of Education 2002; National Center for Education Statistics *http:// nces.ed.gov/programs/coe* Information on postsecondary education and teacher preparation programs.

U.S. Department of Education *http://www.ed.gov* Information on federal policies and educational statistics for all states.

Endnotes

[1] Timothy J. Bergen, Jr. "The Greeks and the Education of Humanity," *Journal of General Education, 43,* no. 1 (1994), 33–34.

[2] Norman F. Cantor & Peter L. Klein, Eds. *Ancient Thought: Plato and Aristotle* (Waltham, MA: Blaisdell, 1969), 3.

[3] Ibid., 5.

[4] Ibid., 17.

[5] Adolphe E. Meyer, *An Educational History of the Western World* (New York: McGraw-Hill, 1965), 11.

[6] Robert Ulich, "Plato c. 928–c. 348 BC," in *Three Thousand Years of Educational Wisdom: Selections from Great Documents* (repr., Cambridge, MA: Harvard University Press, 1965), 53. See also Allan C. Ornstein and Daniel U. Levine, *Foundations of Education,* 8th ed. (Boston: Houghton Mifflin, 2003), 71.

[7] Elwood P. Cubberley, *History of Education* (Cambridge, MA: Riverside Press, 1949), 18–19. Cubberley's exhaustive history is very detailed and contains much important information on these early civilizations, for the student interested in the history of education.

[8] Luella Cole, *A History of Education: Socrates to Montessori* (New York: Holt, Rinehart and Winston, 1962), 26. An excellent summary and description of an Athenian boy's school day.

[9] Ulich, "Plato," 36–37.

[10] Ibid.

[11] S. Howard Patterson, Ernest A. Choate, & Edmund de Schweinitz Brunner, *The School in American Society* (Scranton, PA: International Textbook, 1936), 68.

[12] Ibid.

[13] Ibid., 27.

[14] Ibid.

[15] Ibid., 26.

[16] Ibid., 35.

[17] Ibid., 37.

[18] Ibid.

[19] Ibid., 38.

[20] Ibid.

[21] Ibid., 53.

[22] Meyer, *Educational History,* 30–31.

[23] Robin Barrow, *Plato and Education* (Boston: Routledge and Kegan Paul, 1976), 41.

[24] Alfred Day, *Summary and Analysis of the Dialogues of Plato. With an Analytical Index Giving References to the Greek Text of Modern Editions and to the Translation in Bohn's Classical Library* (London: Bell & Daldy, 1870), 526–27. This extract comes from two passages in Plato's *Laws*: 781a–b, and 454e and 455a.

[25] Peter Losin, "Education and Plato's Parable of the Cave," *Journal of Education, 178,* no. 3 (1996), 50.

[26] John D. Pulliam & James Van Patten, *History of Education in America,* 6th ed. (Upper Saddle River, NJ: Prentice Hall, 1995), 17.

[27] Barrow, *Plato and Education,* 18.

[28] Losin, "Education and Plato's Parable," 50.

[29] Ibid., 54.

[30] Ibid., 55.

[31] Ibid., 4.

[32] Cantor and Klein, *Ancient Thought,* 12.

[33] Ulich, "Aristotle 384–322 BC," in *Three Thousand Years,* 70.

[34] Ibid.

[35] Thomas Toch, "Chiefs Consider Humanities in Schools and Society," *Education Week* (May 9, 1984). Available on the Web archives at *http://www.edweek.org*

36 Ibid.

37 Richard H. Hersh, "Intentions and Perceptions: A National Survey of Public Attitudes Toward Liberal-Arts Education," *Change* (March/April 1997), 16–17.

38 Joyce Baldwin, "Liberal Arts for a New Millenium," *Carnegie Reporter, 1,* no. 1 (Summer 2000).

39 Ibid.

40 Ibid. See p. 18 for information on these statistics.

41 Ibid.

42 Ibid., 20.

43 Lloyd H. Elliott, "Restructuring American Education," *Education Week* (February 13, 2002). Available on the Web archives at *http://www.edweek.org*

44 Karin Sconzert, Demetria Iazzetto, & Stewart Purkey, "Small-Town College to Big-City School: Preparing Urban Teachers from Liberal-Arts Colleges," *Teaching and Teacher Education, 16,* no. 4 (2000), 467–68.

45 Jean A. King, "The Uneasy Relationship Between Teacher Education and the Liberal Arts and Sciences," *Journal of Teacher Education, 38,* no. 1 (1987), 6–7.

46 Ibid.

47 Ibid.

48 Baldwin, "Liberal Arts." See first page of article.

Chapter 2

Life and Education During the Roman Empire (168 BC–AD 476)

Learning Objectives

1. Describe the conditions that led to the takeover of ancient Greece by the Romans.
2. Characterize the society of ancient Rome—what social classes existed and how were these social classes educated?
3. Explain the Roman philosophy of education.
4. Describe the two periods of Roman education.
5. Describe the contributions of Quintilian to today's educational system.
6. What are the similarities and differences between the educational system of ancient Rome and today's educational system?

INTRODUCTION

Chapter 1 described the development of the Greek educational system in the context of ancient Greek civilization. The ancient Greek educational system reflected the lack of unity among the various city-states. Each city-state had its own style and system of education, which reflected the local cultural and social history.

Like the ancient Greeks, the ancient Romans developed a system of education that reflected the unique aspects of their culture as well as their educational philosophy. The social hierarchy in ancient Rome also determined the educational opportunities for its citizens. Although the Romans conquered ancient Greece, they retained great respect for the Greeks' accomplishments and civilization, as evidenced by their interest in learning Greek and reading the Greek plays and other forms of literature. Like the Greeks, the Romans had specific beliefs about what it meant to be an educated person and the type of education necessary to achieve this goal.

Education in the Roman Empire will be examined in the context of ancient Roman civilization. Education was not readily available for many who were not in the two highest social strata.

This chapter begins by examining how the Romans adapted Greek ideas during their takeover of the Greek Empire, to help formulate their own system of cul-

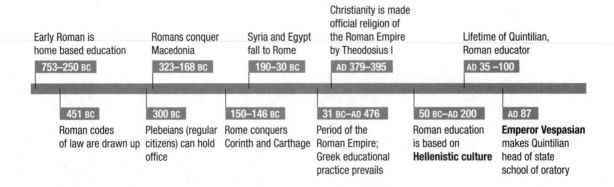

| Early Roman is home based education | Romans conquer Macedonia | Syria and Egypt fall to Rome | Christianity is made official religion of the Roman Empire by Theodosius I | Lifetime of Quintilian, Roman educator |
| 753–250 BC | 323–168 BC | 190–30 BC | AD 379–395 | AD 35–100 |

| 451 BC | 300 BC | 150–146 BC | 31 BC–AD 476 | 50 BC–AD 200 | AD 87 |
| Roman codes of law are drawn up | Plebeians (regular citizens) can hold office | Rome conquers Corinth and Carthage | Period of the Roman Empire; Greek educational practice prevails | Roman education is based on **Hellenistic culture** | **Emperor Vespasian** makes Quintilian head of state school of oratory |

Table 2-1 **Roman Education Versus Modern Education**

ROMAN-STYLE EDUCATION	MODERN EDUCATION
Education only for individuals at top of social hierarchy	Education for all
Homeschooling only from 753 to 250 BC	Home schooling is a trend.
Formal schools after 250 BC	Formal schools
Primary school ages 6–12	Primary school grades K–3
Secondary school ages 12–16	Middle school grades 6–8
Collegiate ages 16–19	High school grades 9–12
University ages 19–21+	College age 18–22+
Not all went to university.	Not all go to college.
Learn what you will do as an adult.	Vocational education is available.
Learning was developmental.	Learning is developmental.
Schools promoted majority's religion.	There is separation of church and state.
Schools were independently run.	Schools are run by the government.
There was no formal teacher training.	There is formal teacher training.
Early grades focused on reading, writing, math.	Early grades focus on reading, writing, and math.
Later grades studied advanced topics (history, geography, higher math).	Later grades study advanced topics (history, literature, science, math).

ture and education. Roman education went through two periods. In the first period, education took place primarily in the home, much like homeschooling in the twenty-first century. This initial period of home-based education was followed by a movement to formalize Roman education, although a public school movement in Rome was never developed.

The major contribution from the Roman Empire to today's educational system comes from the educator Quintilian, who wrote at length about the nature of children, how they should be taught, and what they should study.

Table 2-1 lists the contributions of the Roman educational system to today's system of education.

ANCIENT ROMAN CIVILIZATION AND CULTURE: USE OF GREEK IDEAS

How did the Romans use the Greeks' ideas? Despite having very different ideas about the type of civilization they wanted to develop and the type of education they wanted their youth to receive, Romans were quite open to Greek culture and Greek educational philosophy. The Greek Empire had broken apart by 150 BC, when the Romans were conquering the whole of Greece as well as Sicily and Macedonia.[1] The entire Greek world had been subdued by 27 BC.[2]

The Romans incorporated many of the ideas from the Greek Empire into their own civilization and into the development of their educational system. For instance, the study of the Greek language had become a part of the Roman educational system by the third century AD.[3] By the time of Augustus Caesar, Greek intellectuals were being awarded Roman citizenship.[4]

The Roman Empire was divided into two parts, the East and the West, which differed in social and economic structure. In fact, the western part of the Roman Empire fell before the eastern part did.[5] This chapter concentrates on the civilization of the western Roman Empire, where the capital city, Rome, was located.

Although the Romans respected the accomplishments of the Greeks, they did not incorporate all of them into their own culture and civilization, for the Romans did not attach the same significance to some of the ideas that the Greeks believed were important in educating their citizens. For instance, it has been suggested that the Romans regarded the Greeks as somewhat frivolous and inept, perhaps because of their love of music, philosophy, art, and literature.[6] The Romans concentrated on practical considerations, such as gearing a Roman boy's education to what he would be doing as an adult. Thus, the types of subjects a Roman would study might differ from the ones studied by a citizen of Greece.

We begin our study of the Roman contributions to our educational system by first surveying life and culture in ancient Rome. What were the forces inherent in Roman life and culture that influenced the development of their educational system? How did the social structure affect the educational opportunities available to those in ancient Rome? These questions are addressed in the following section.

CULTURE, GOVERNMENT, EDUCATION, AND SOCIAL CLASSES IN ANCIENT ROME

Rome was notable because it was a republic by 510 BC; that is, its system of government comprised a senate and two consuls. By 300 BC, the **plebeians,** or regular citizens as opposed to aristocrats, were allowed to hold office.[7]

The Romans' emphasis on political organization was a hallmark of their civilization, as was their system of law. In 451 BC, a code of law was drawn up.[8] The Romans elevated law to the honor and dignity of a science.[9]

The Roman Empire was also known for a well-developed system of communications, the growth of trade and industry, and the use of Latin as a universal language.[10] Latin became widely used after the first century BC. Although authors such as Cicero and Catallus translated Greek works, they are notable for their own independent contributions to Roman literature.

Like the Greeks, the Romans had an elaborate system of religion that involved the worship of various gods and goddesses. These deities were responsible for the physical health and safety of family members, who felt the responsibility to worship daily, and at every meal. At certain times during the year, such as at harvest time, the families of a **pagus,** or district, would join together in religious festivities, an important part of daily life in ancient Rome.[11]

Christianity, which was not tolerated until AD 313, was officially recognized and made the official religion of the empire by Emperor Theodosius I in AD 380.[12]

The beginnings of Christianity greatly affected Roman life and caused great fear among new believers, who were afraid of being found out and punished. Christianity also affected the schools. From approximately AD 150 to 230 a Roman child who was being raised in a Christian home would struggle in school, for all the schools were pagan.[13]

The festivals of **Minerva,** the Roman goddess of schools, pupils, and teachers, were held regularly, and Christian children had to participate.[14] This certainly must have been difficult for them, for these teachings were contrary to those they were taught at home. Similarly today, children who are being raised in fundamentalist Christian homes are told not to believe what they are taught in school, such as the theory of evolution, which is contrary to fundamentalist Christian teaching. Thus, some children today, facing the same situation as Roman children did many centuries ago, are home-schooled by their parents, because they prefer not to have their children exposed to contrary beliefs.

ROMAN SOCIAL CLASSES AND EDUCATIONAL OPPORTUNITIES

Roman society was divided into distinct social classes, each with its own privileges. The highest social class in the Roman Empire, in the second and third centuries, was the **honestiores,** which consisted of Roman senators and knights, soldiers, and veterans with children. Also included in this category were men who had served in public municipal offices in towns and cities outside Rome.[15]

Senators and knights were the two highest groups among the *honestiores.*[16] The exact social stratum into which these two groups were placed depended on their wealth. Members of the senatorial order, the highest social stratum, had to own at least the equivalent of $40,000 in property.[17] A member of the senatorial order might be assigned by the emperor to be a chief administrator in the city of Rome. He might also be appointed to a high-ranking post in the priesthood.[18]

On the other end of the social scale, the **humiliores,** also known as *plebeii* or *tenuiores,* seem to have been viewed as expendable. This was the poorest of the social classes in Rome. *Humiliores* were punished severely for minor infractions of the law. Punishments might include being sent to the mines, thrown to the beasts in a roman amphitheater, or even crucified.[19] In contrast, the *honestiores* could avoid punishment for the most part, because it would affect their position. They usually received lesser punishments, for instance, banishment or loss of their property.[20]

The Romans also had many slaves. It is uncertain how many were treated well and how many suffered cruel treatment. It is known, however, that the Emperor Claudius decreed that sick slaves abandoned by their master should be freed.[21] The Emperor Nero later drew up a document that allowed slaves who had complained about unjust treatment to have their complaints officially investigated.[22] Evidently, some humanitarian legislation was passed regarding the treatment of slaves in ancient Rome; however, they were still slaves, not free men. For instance, it is reported that slaves attended to every aspect of the emperor's existence: from washing his eating utensils, helping him bathe, cutting and dressing his hair, cooking and serving his food, to tasting his food to make sure it was not poisoned.

Although the emperor bestowed many favors on a few individuals, many in ancient Rome lived on the fringes of poverty. It is reported that in the second century the number of Romans receiving public assistance increased from 150,000 to 175,000. It is believed that approximately one third or even half the city lived on public assistance during this period.[23] It was necessary for a Roman citizen to have a minimum yearly income equivalent to $800 to live comfortably.[24]

The economic and social-class discrepancies in ancient Rome led to very different educational opportunities for the rich and the poor. Similarly, in the twenty-first century we find wide discrepancies between the educational opportunities and advancement possibilities available to the wealthy versus the poor. For instance, children living in public housing areas usually experience a poorer quality of education. Their schools often hire fewer certified teachers and have less modern facilities than those in wealthier districts with a higher property tax base.

The following section examines the first stage of Roman education: home-based schooling, and the text box gives some background information on daily life in ancient Rome.

Because the Romans believed strongly in family, it is natural that they believed that parents should be their child's first teachers and that a child's first educational experiences should ideally occur at home. In the first period of Roman educational history (753–250 BC) education took place entirely at home, where children were isolated from outside influences and could learn what it meant to be a virtuous individual.[25] The family was the chief educational unit from infancy to the ages of 16 or 17. The mother served as the primary teacher for the daughters, instructing

Spotlight On

EVERYDAY LIFE IN ANCIENT ROME

The type of housing available to Romans depended on their social class. The middle classes appear often to have lived in apartment buildings. Slaves had to hustle up and down stairs, hauling water, coal, and buckets of waste from the chamber pot. Light was provided by oil lamps. Romans went to bed early and arose early. Their morning routine was simple: they slept in their undergarments and in the morning draped themselves in their togas after quickly splashing water on their faces. Women had their hair dressed by their slaves and had to apply makeup, but men, after quickly dressing, went on about their day's business. They went to the baths later, to be bathed and shaved.

Wealthier Romans lived in mansions and had large and elaborate households to maintain.

Fortunately, Rome developed its own water supply, sewage, street maintenance and cleaning, fire and police departments, food supply, and public recreation systems. Without the sewage system, which lacked modern safety standards, the problem of disease would have been much worse.

them in techniques of household management and spinning and weaving. The fathers gave instruction in farming methods and practices and also taught basic reading and writing—skills necessary for their future adult roles. The education advocated by the Romans during this early period was a father-son, mother-daughter type of apprenticeship.[26] Despite a patriarchal culture, in which the father and husband had absolute power in the household, the Romans believed strongly in the marriage bond, and women were thought generally to have been well treated. Boys were prepared for adult roles by their fathers. Education for boys was based on what the Roman boy's eventual adult role would be. In keeping with the Romans' interest in law, Roman fathers insisted that their sons learn about the subject. In 450 BC the Romans inscribed their laws in the **12 Tables.** Subsequently, boys were extensively schooled in law, including the subjects of torts, real and personal property, summonses, and judicial proceedings. They also learned about the rights of fathers. The 12 Tables were used to teach reading and writing as well as law.

The educational system that developed in ancient Rome reflected the Romans' desire for practicality. Similarly, it has been suggested in modern times that a student's course of study should be planned around his or her eventual profession, as sometimes students see no value in learning a subject they never expect to use. Roman boys studied certain subjects for practical purposes rather than for the sake of knowledge itself. For instance, although the ancient Greeks believed that the study of music was appropriate for boys, Roman boys did not study the subject. Music was used in Roman times only during worship services to thank the many Roman deities for their generosity and goodness.[27] Likewise, the Greek idea of using gymnastics to prepare young men physically for war was not enthusiastically received. The Greeks believed that mathematics, specifically the study of geometry, was important to develop a young boy's intellect. Although the Romans learned mathematics, they had difficulties with the Roman numeral system.

The following section focuses on the formation of primary (elementary) schools and grammar (secondary) schools in ancient Rome and examines the subjects taught and the teaching methods used.

THE ROMAN SYSTEM OF FORMAL EDUCATION

After 250 BC the Romans relied less on home-based education as their system of education became more formalized and adopted some Greek educational methods and ideals. The Romans were heavily influenced by Greek culture, and both Greek and Latin were taught and spoken by about 150 BC.[28]

Did the government play a role in education, as it does today? The Roman emperors did not establish a school system, and for the 150 years before the birth of Christ, the Roman schools were independently operated.[29] In the later years of the Roman Empire, the emperors exerted some indirect control over schools by appointing teachers, especially in the schools they opened by imperial decree. The majority of the schools in ancient Rome, however, were operated independently.[30] Thus, there was no formally established system of public education in ancient Rome.

As Christianity became accepted and established throughout the Roman Empire the pagan schools closed. Children raised in a Christian household were required to take part in a curriculum that taught worship of pagan gods and goddesses because this conflicted with what they were being taught at home. Generally, the early Christians disliked pagan learning.[31] The early Christians examined the classics of Greece and Rome in a skeptical manner, because they did not focus on the salvation of the soul.[32] For the early Christians in the Middle Ages, the subject of chapter 3, theological concerns were more important than the preservation of culture.

The primary schools in ancient Rome were known as **ludi** (sing., **ludus**), and their schoolmaster was the **ludimagister.** These primary schools were similar to our own elementary schools, especially in the primary grades (K–3), as boys received instruction in the rudiments of reading, writing, and arithmetic. Anecdotes and poetry were used to teach history and literature.[33] Boys entered the *ludus* when they were approximately 7 years old.[34] One can only imagine how difficult it must have been for 7-year-old boys to learn, considering the teaching methods used at that time. Learning to read, for instance, required that students memorize the names of the letters and *all* the possible combinations of syllables.[35] Students were taught to write on wax tablets, just as in ancient Greece. Students carried long manuscripts rolled up in a container. These were known as manuscript books.[36] Roman teachers taught writing by steering the student's hand as he used the stylus on his wax tablet to form the letters. The teacher often dictated what he wanted the students to learn, and they read the dictation aloud and memorized it.

Learning arithmetic also posed difficulties because of the Roman system of writing numbers. Because of the difficulty of deciphering Roman numerals, students learned to use the abacus for counting. They were also allowed to use their fingers,[37] and there was no stigma attached to doing so. If you have ever struggled with advanced Roman numerals, you can imagine how difficult it was for young students to add or subtract larger Roman numerals!

The biggest problem in the Roman schools, however, was the lack of teacher training and understanding of how to motivate students to learn. Teachers also did not know how to make learning relevant to students' daily life, thus causing even more boredom and frustration among students, just as students today become upset when they think they are being forced to learn useless material. Teachers in ancient Rome, just as teachers do today, became angry with their students when they would not behave; however, Roman teachers could punish their students if they chose, whereas teachers today cannot use corporal punishment because most states have outlawed it. In ancient Rome, as in Colonial America, a student's hand was hit with a ruler if he did not do as he was told. For more serious offenses, students were whipped. The writer Cicero showed a complete lack of understanding of how children learn when he wrote that those who were quicker to learn and understand would teach at a faster pace and would become irritated if children did not understand them right away.[38]

Once boys were able to read ordinary prose, they transferred to one of two types of higher school: a grammar school (**grammaticus**) or a school of rhetoric (Greek language). The grammar schools taught Latin and were especially important and found in every part of the empire. In fact, they remained the most persistent part of Roman civilization until Rome was overthrown by the invasions from the north, which marked the beginning of the Middle Ages.

Grammar school students studied the works of Homer and Virgil and read the *Odyssey* and the **Aeneid,** which not only were literary sources but also served as teaching aids in history, geography, religion, customs, and morals. The grammar schools also taught mathematics, music, and rudimentary dialectics, or debating, but never included the subjects of gymnastics and dancing as the Greek schools did.

Boys might enter a school of rhetoric at about age 14 and stay until they were young men of about 25. This higher level school originated as a Greek institution and was adopted by the Romans.[39] Here boys were trained to become effective speakers. The importance of the schools of rhetoric was that they trained future leaders of the state. Cicero, one of the state speakers, or orators, believed that the training to become an orator consisted of instruction in "the sciences and of all the great problems of life."[40] The original objective of the study of oratory was to persuade others into action, but by Quintilian's time (AD 35–100), the study of oratory had a different purpose, which was to please and interest the audience. The famous men of Rome were noted as brilliant orators who could influence public opinion.[41]

Just as in our own educational system, the early years of a student's education were devoted to learning the basics: reading, writing, and arithmetic. Students in the upper levels were given instruction in more advanced subjects and specific areas, such as rhetoric and mathematics.

Although there are many similarities between the educational system and practices of ancient Rome and those of today, the most significant contribution from the Roman system of education comes from the humanistic educator **Quintilian,** whose work and educational ideas are discussed next.

QUINTILIAN: HUMANISTIC EDUCATIONAL PRACTICES IN EARLY CHILDHOOD

The traditional method of teaching in the ancient world seems to have involved heavy doses of discipline. Students were whipped, humiliated, and otherwise punished if they did not obey their teachers. The idea of educating children based on developmental practices appears to have been unknown. This is one area that Quintilian brought to the attention of many in the ancient world (see "Shaper of Education," p. 32). His landmark, 12-volume work, *Institutio Oratoria* [Education of an Orator], written in AD 93, puts forth many of his ideas about education, including the idea that education should be *humanistic* in nature. This meant that students have to be motivated to learn in a nonthreatening environment.

Quintilian was born in Caligurris, Spain, in AD 35. He was the son of a rhetorician and established a school in Rome in which he taught for 20 years. The Emperor Vespasian subsidized his school in AD 72, then made Quintilian head of a state school of oratory in AD 87.

We focus on two major themes of Quintilian's work: the importance of early childhood education, including moral education, and the problem with using corporal punishment to instill discipline in children.

SHAPER OF EDUCATION

Quintilian
(AD 35–100)

- Early childhood education is very important.
- Subject matter should be sequenced for students.
- Education fosters moral maturity and builds character.
- Corrective feedback should be used with students, not corporal punishment.
- Children should be exposed to proper speech from birth.
- Children can be corrupted at home if they are taught improper behavior before they begin school.
- Different character traits affect behavior.
- Corporal punishment eventually becomes ineffective.
- Corporal punishment may cause psychological harm.

QUINTILIAN ON EARLY CHILDHOOD EDUCATION: MORAL EDUCATION AS PART OF THE CURRICULUM

Quintilian was a believer in early childhood education. Just as parents today attempt to socialize infants by talking to them and providing them with stimulation to encourage learning, Quintilian believed that a child's first exposure to proper speech, and adequate environmental stimulation, was highly important in developing healthy children. Quintilian recommended that after the birth of a son, a father should "conceive, first of all, of all the best possible hopes for him," so that the child would become a "future orator."[42]

Quintilian strongly believed that children should be exposed to proper grammar and speech as infants and recommended that even the child's nurses be selected carefully so that they would speak properly. He understood that infants would imitate the sounds they were exposed to and wanted the sounds to be correct, so that the child would learn to speak properly. He did not want young children, who were developing early language skills, to have to be retaught, stating, "let the child not be accustomed, therefore, even while he is yet an infant, to phraseology which must be unlearned."[43]

Quintilian also believed that **moral education** should begin at an early age, as "there is no age so tender that it may not readily learn what is right and wrong."[44] The development of self-control was also highly important and should be acquired as a habit. Quintilian wrote that "a child is as early as possible to be admonished that he must do nothing too eagerly, nothing dishonestly, nothing without self-control."[45] He pointed out that although people thought that schools corrupt children, they can be corrupted at home, long before they enter school. He wrote that children "see our mistresses, our male objects of affection . . . things shameful to be told are objects of sight."[46] Quintilian believed that "it is the disposition of the individual pupil, and the care taken of him, that make the whole difference."[47] Thus, to address the question of moral education, the teacher must carefully evaluate the student's personality, for certain personality types may be more prone to forming bad habits than others. However, if more attention is paid to these students, if they are shown how to behave by example, then they may be less likely to develop an immoral character. Quintilian thought that many children learned immoral behavior at home, by seeing immoral behavior of the adults around them, before they even were aware that the behavior was immoral, and they transferred that behavior into schools.[48]

How do these ideas resonate with our present-day conceptions of early childhood education? Early childhood educators are concerned not only with the development of proper speech and grammar but also with the development of self-control and discipline. Modern-day day-care centers and nursery schools attempt to teach self-control and discipline. Students are taught rules such as not to push or shove each other, to say please and thank you, and to wait their turn in line.

Today, educators recognize the importance of moral education, also referred to as "character education," which is defined as a type of moral training to help children become good people who make the right decisions.[49] Fifteen states require character education programs in their schools, and the U.S. Department of Education has given grants to support this movement.[50]

A central theme of character education appears to be that children, like adults, can behave very badly indeed and can be very immoral. They have to be taught to be good. Character education deals with teaching values and moral virtues. The term *character* refers to internal qualities that include goodness, moral maturity, and virtue.[51] Any type of activity or program that schools use to help children and adolescents learn appropriate ways of behaving can be thought of as character education. Character education has become more prevalent in schools in the last few years.[52] The approaches used to teach character education include instruction in conflict resolution and values education.[53]

QUINTILIAN ON CORPORAL PUNISHMENT AND HARSH PHYSICAL AND PSYCHOLOGICAL TREATMENT OF STUDENTS

Quintilian believed that using physical force to discipline students was a mistake. He stated that the use of force on children was "a disgrace," not the least because force was used as "a punishment for slaves."[54] He recognized that the use of physical force would make boys "hardened, like the worst of slaves, even to stripes."[55]

An even more pertinent point, which we can identify with today, is that physical punishment cannot be relied upon to change behavior into adulthood. Over time, corporal punishment appears to lose its effectiveness; however, that is the least of the damage that it causes. The process of physical punishment may do a student great psychological harm, which we recognize just as Quintilian did in ancient Rome. He wrote that physical punishment causes shame, which "enervates and depresses the mind, and makes them shun people's sight and feel a constant uneasiness."[56]

Quintilian also admonished teachers against using too harsh a tone in correcting students' mistakes or behavior. He pointed out that "the powers of boys sometimes sink under too great severity in correction."[57] He believed that boys would become despondent and "grieve, and at least hate their work, and while they fear everything, they cease to attempt anything."[58] Quintilian recommended that teachers encourage their students as much as possible and not try to correct all their faults at once, for some of what they are doing is excellent, some is mediocre, and some is poor. He said that the teacher "ought to praise some parts of his pupils' performances, to tolerate some, and to alter others, giving his reasons why the alterations are made."[59] Quintilian wisely wrote that "study is cheered by nothing more than hope."[60] Thus, if students are provided with a supportive environment in which they are not harshly punished for mistakes but are encouraged to keep trying, they will want to continue learning and will not give up hope, thinking they are incapable of doing the task at hand.

In the twenty-first century, educators of elementary, middle school, and high school students follow Quintilian's recommendations on constructive criticism and try to encourage students to perform as well as possible. They provide feedback on the parts of the students' work that need revision while recognizing those parts that are of good or excellent quality.

Modern studies recognize that the effects of psychological harshness can be just as harmful as the effects of corporal punishment. Murray A. Straus, a social scientist who has researched the psychological and physical effects of corporal punishment on schoolchildren, points out that the psychological effects of corporal punishment are parallel to the harmful effects of physical abuse.[61] Children who are hit or slapped or punished in other physical ways may act out later in life, using physical violence as a way to resolve psychological conflicts with others. Straus recounts data from a longitudinal study done in 1997, in which 1,112 children ages 4 through 7 and 8 through 11 were studied. Parents were interviewed in 1987–88 and then again 5 years later. The study found that the more corporal punishment the children encountered at home in 1987–88, the more likely they were to fight in school 5 years later.[62]

Straus cites a major benefit of never using corporal punishment: above-average cognitive growth in children.[63] Neural pathways in the brain that are involved in the formation of language can be disrupted by the use of physical force. The National Longitudinal Study of Youth studied corporal punishment in 806 children 2 to 4 years of age and found that children whose mothers used less spanking or other forms of corporal punishment were likely to have higher cognitive growth, as measured by the Peabody Picture Vocabulary Test, used to measure cognitive growth in preschool-aged children.[64]

Despite the research, corporal punishment continues to be used in our society against children and adolescents. In 1999, Arizona and Arkansas passed laws that allowed teachers and parents to use corporal punishment if they thought it necessary.[65] Straus points out in his book *Beating the Devil Out of Them* that students who are subjected to corporal punishment are more likely to engage in domestic violence and masochistic sex and are also more prone to become violent as juveniles.[66] Thus, the effects of corporal punishment, whether it occurs at home or in the school setting, can be long lasting and have far-reaching consequences in the lives of children and adolescents.

A statement by the National Association of School Psychologists notes that although more than half of the states ban the use of corporal punishment, over 250,000 children are hit each year in public schools. Most of them are members of minority groups or are children with disabilities.[67] Unfortunately, the laws are made to favor the school and the state, rather than the student. In the *Hall v. Tawney* case (1980), a sixth-grader was shoved against a desk and beaten by a male teacher with a hard, thick rubber paddle, causing a hospital stay of 10 days and possible permanent spine injury.[68] The courts recognized a constitutional violation in this case, because the student was so severely beaten. For action to be taken against the state, the punishment must be considered "shocking to the senses."[69] Children should be given higher levels of protection against corporal punishment. Students are not supposed to experience excessive physical punishment, and the government and state should abide by this finding.[70]

BRIDGES FROM THE PAST TO THE PRESENT: VALUE AND USES OF ANCIENT ROMAN IDEAS TODAY

The major contribution from ancient Roman times to today's system of education is age grading. Early instruction focused on the basics of reading, writing, and arithmetic, subjects that still receive much attention in elementary grades today.

The school of rhetoric, in which boys were trained to be orators, was the ideal goal of education for boys, according to Quintilian, but he recognized that not all boys were interested in or suited for this type of study. The school of rhetoric was the highest level of study in ancient Rome and parallels college education today. Not everyone today is interested in college or has the academic ability or work ethic to attend, but it is the ideal to which many aspire.

A problem common to both systems of education was student motivation. In Rome, there was little mention of ways to motivate students. Today, teachers of all age groups learn methods to motivate their students as part of their training.

As you have already seen, educators today are indebted to Quintilian, the humanistic educator who described developmentally appropriate ways of teaching and sequencing subject matter for students, pedagogies that are used today in elementary, middle, and high schools. In our society we believe that early childhood education is important and have developed programs such as Head Start to maximize the benefits children get from early intervention in childhood. The idea of moral education, which also comes from Quintilian, includes a focus on self-control, which is encouraged among students today. Character education, which includes teaching students to develop qualities such as goodness and moral maturity, is often used today in schools, either incorporated into lessons or as a separate program.

Finally, the ideas on discipline and punishment, with which we still struggle today, have deep roots in the past. You will recall that Quintilian called physical punishment disgraceful, but he also recognized that pupils had to be corrected when they made a mistake or misbehaved. Just as we do, he struggled with the amount of discipline to use. Knowing the psychological effects of corporal punishment and verbal reprimands, educators today follow Quintilian's teachings in using corrective feedback and establishing a supportive environment in which students are not penalized for failure but are encouraged to keep trying until they succeed.

In the next chapter you will see that some of Quintilian's ideas persisted into the Middle Ages, although they were not widely used; and you will learn about the status of society and education after the fall of the Roman Empire.

SUMMARY

Although the ancient Romans recognized the value of some of the Greek educational methods and subjects of study, they did not duplicate the Greeks' educational system, because it did not fit in with their culture or conception of the purposes of education. Whereas the Greeks believed that the study of subjects was valuable for the sake of knowledge itself, the Romans were more concerned with the practicality of subjects and in preparing boys for their adult roles.

Because the Romans believed that parents were a child's first teachers, the first period of Roman education (753–250 BC) consisted of homeschooling. The idea of sending children to a school was unknown until after 250 BC. Even then, there was no formal, public system of education such as we have today. Schools were independently operated.

Decline of the Roman Empire

The reasons for the fall of the Western Roman Empire are too lengthy to explore in this chapter. Briefly, the western part of the Roman Empire collapsed first, while the eastern part remained more politically stable and had fewer civil wars.[71] The western Roman Empire had many problems with taxation. Landlords owned a high percentage of the land, and the peasants living on that land had to pay rents that were higher than their taxes. The social structure was further eroded when the landed aristocracy refused to tax members of their own class; in fact, landowners often were granted reductions in taxes.[72]

The Roman Empire also suffered from the effects of primitive agriculture methods, lack of transportation, and poor methods of industrial production. Great effort was needed to feed, clothe, and transport the 300,000 soldiers who guarded the Roman Empire against invaders, so to support the army, taxes had to be increased.[73] The empire suffered economically because there were too many idle rich, such as

the senators, who had huge households that were very expensive to maintain; civil servants; lawyers; soldiers; and clergy. The Roman population appears to have been apathetic during this time, offering little resistance to the barbarian invaders who were marching in. This was the situation at the close of the Roman Empire and the beginning of the Middle Ages.

QUESTIONS FOR DISCUSSION

1. Describe the class and economic systems as they existed during the Roman Empire and how they contributed to its decline.
2. How did educational opportunities for the masses in the Roman Empire mirror its class and economic systems? Does this problem still exist today?
3. What do you think would happen to the current educational system if our government and economic, political, and military security collapsed? What does this tell you about the primacy of education in society when the economic, religious, and political systems are in turmoil, and military security is jeopardized?
4. How did the decline of ancient Rome parallel the previous decline of ancient Greece?
5. Of all Quintilian's ideas presented in this chapter, which do you believe are most valuable and why? Give evidence to support your answer.

SUGGESTED ACTIVITIES

1. Interview an early childhood teacher about his or her beliefs regarding the positive and negative aspects of early childhood education. Present a summary of the interview findings to your class in a PowerPoint presentation, *or* write it up as a 5- to 10-page paper and hand it in.
2. Choose a day-care center. Observe the activities the children participate in, and take notes on what you observe. Do any of the activities correspond to the type of education Quintilian advocated? Explain your findings in a three- to five-page paper.
3. Interview a teacher and a principal about their beliefs regarding corporal punishment. Do they feel it is appropriate? What is their district's policy regarding corporal punishment? Present your findings in a PowerPoint presentation of approximately 20 minutes.
4. Assume that you are a principal of a school formulating new policies relating to discipline issues. Write a letter to the parents of your school district explaining

why you feel corporal punishment is not appropriate (assume that this district has used corporal punishment in the past).

Bibliography

Carcopino, J. (1940). *Daily life in ancient Rome: The people and the city at the height of the empire*. (E. O. Lorimer, Trans., H. T. Rowell, Ed.). New Haven, CT: Yale University Press.

Cole, L. (1962). *A history of education: Socrates to Montessori*. New York: Holt, Rinehart and Winston.

Fowler, W. W. (1965). *Rome* (2nd ed.). (M. P. Charlesworth, Rev.) New York: Oxford.

Gross, R. E., & Moelman, Arthur H. (1962). Our debt to the ancients of the Western world. In R. E. Gross (Ed.), *Heritage of American education*. Boston: Allyn and Bacon.

Hodgson, G. (1906). *Primitive Christian education*. Edinburgh: T&T Clark.

Jones, A. H. M. (1966). *Decline of the ancient world*. New York: Holt, Rinehart and Winston.

Meyer, A. E. (1965). *An educational history of the Western world*. New York: McGraw-Hill.

Murphy, J. J. (Ed.). (1987). *Quintilian on the teaching of speaking and writing. Translations from books one, two, and ten of the* Institutio Oratoria. Carbondale: Southern Illinois University Press.

National Association of School Psychologists. (n.d.) NASP position statement on corporal punishment in schools. Retrieved 2003, from *http://www.nasponline.org*.

Rawson, E. (1985). *Intellectual life in the late Roman Republic*. London: Duckworth.

Robinson, K. D. J., & Hayes, B. G. (2000). Humanistic education to character education: An ideological journey, *Journal of Humanistic Counseling, Education and Development, 39*(1).

Roy, L. (2001). Corporal punishment in American public schools and the rights of the child. *Journal of Law and Education, 30*(3).

Straus, M. A. (2001, September/October). Social science and public policy: New evidence for the benefits of never spanking. *Society*.

Treadgold, W. (Ed.). (1984). *Renaissances before the Renaissance: Cultural revivals of late antiquity and the Middle Ages*. Stanford, CA: Stanford University Press.

Watson, Rev. J. S. (Trans.). (1873). *Quintilian's Institutes of oratory: Education of an orator. In twelve books*. London: Bell and Daldy.

Suggestions for Further Reading

In addition to the works cited in the bibliography, the following are suggested for further reading.

Dill, S. (1905). *Roman society in the last century of the Western Empire* (2nd ed, rev.). London: Macmillan.

Gibbon, E. (1804–5). *The history of the decline and fall of the Roman Empire*. Philadelphia: William Y. Birch & Abraham Small.

Hodgson, Geraldine. (1906). *Primitive Christian education*. Edinburgh: T&T Clark.

Jones, A. H. M. (1966). *The decline of the ancient world*. New York: Holt, Rinehart and Winston.

Marrou, H. I. (1956). *A history of education in antiquity*. (George Lamb, Trans.). New York: Sheed and Ward.

Relevant Web Sites

Civilizations: Greece and Rome: Voyage Back in Time: Ancient Greece and Rome *http://www.oncampus.richmond.edu* This site introduces third-grade students to the ancient Greek and Roman civilizations and can be useful for lesson planning.

Art History Resources: Ancient Greece and Rome—Dr. Chris Witcombe, Professor of Art History, Sweet Briar College, VA *http://witcombe.sbc.edu/ARTHgreecerome.html* This Web site is maintained by a professional art historian and offers valuable insights on the art and architecture of ancient civilizations.

Ancient Greece and Ancient Rome: Comparisons and Contrasts *http://ancienthistory.about.com/cs/greecevsrome* Updated, easy-to-follow format that compares civilizations of Greece and Rome.

Education Week *http://www.edweek.org* Current news pertaining to federal and state educational policies, grading systems, and so on.

Humanistic Education *http://chiron.valdosta.edu/whuitt/col/affsys/humed.html* Work of W. Huitt at Valdosta State University, Valdosta, GA. Explains the implications of humanistic education.

Metropolitan Museum of Art *http://www.metmuseum.org/* Web site of the famous museum in New York City, to educate about civilizations of ancient Greece and Rome.

National Center for Education Statistics *http://nces.ed.gov/* Web site on federal and state educational policies, test scores, comparative education, and other data.

U.S. Department of Education *http://www.ed.gov.* U.S. Department of Education home page, for research on all aspects of modern education.

Endnotes

[1] Richard E. Gross & Arthur H. Moelman, "Our Debt to the Ancients of the Western World," in *Heritage of American Education,* ed. Richard E. Gross (Boston: Allyn and Bacon, 1962), 50.

[2] *Larousse Illustrated International Encyclopedia and Dictionary* (New York: World, 1972), 399 in encyclopedia section.

[3] Luella Cole, *A History of Education: Socrates to Montessori* (New York: Holt, Rinehart and Winston, 1962), 58.

[4] Elizabeth Rawson, *Intellectual Life in the Late Roman Republic* (London: Duckworth, 1985), 3.

[5] A. H. M. Jones, *The Decline of the Ancient World* (New York: Holt, Rinehart and Winston, 1966), 363–64.

[6] Ibid., 13.

[7] *Larousse,* 399.

[8] Ibid.

[9] Adolphe E. Meyer, *An Educational History of the Western World* (New York: McGraw-Hill, 1965), 43.

[10] *Larousse,* 399.

[11] W. Warde Fowler, *Rome,* 2nd ed., rev. M. P. Charlesworth (New York: Oxford, 1965), 40–41. An excellent revision of a classic book that, although quite a small volume, is filled with knowledgeable information about lifestyles in ancient Rome, including education.

[12] *Larousse,* 399.

[13] Geraldine Hodgson, *Primitive Christian Education* (Edinburgh: T&T Clark, 1906), 188.

[14] Ibid.

[15] Jerome Carcopino, *Daily Life in Ancient Rome: The People and the City at the Height of the Empire,* trans. from the French by E. O. Lorimer, ed. Henry T. Rowell (New Haven, CT: Yale University Press, 1940). See pp. 52–53 for an excellent explanation of the various social classes in ancient Rome.

[16] Ibid.

[17] Ibid.

[18] Ibid.

[19] Ibid.

[20] Ibid.

[21] Ibid., 57.

[22] Ibid.

[23] Ibid., 65–66.

[24] Ibid., 66.

[25] Warren Treadgold, ed., *Renaissances Before the Renaissance: Cultural Revivals of Late Antiquity and the Middle Ages* (Stanford, CA: Stanford University Press, 1984), 4.

[26] Gross and Moehlman, *Debt to the Ancients,* 50.

[27] Ibid.

[28] Gross and Moehlman, *Debt to the Ancients,* 53.

[29] Cole, *History of Education,* 61.

[30] Ibid.

[31] Hodgson, *Primitive Christian Education,* 7.

[32] Ibid., 10.

[33] Cole, *History of Education,* 62.

[34] Ibid.

[35] Ibid.

[36] Ibid.

[37] Ibid., 63.

[38] Ibid.

[39] Ibid., 64.

[40] Ibid., 44.

[41] Ibid., 45.

[42] Rev. Selby Watson, trans. *Quintilian's Institutes of Oratory: The Education of An Orator. In Twelve Books.* (London:.Bell and Daldy, 1873), bk. 1, chap. 1, p. 9.

43 Ibid., 10.

44 Ibid., 27.

45 Ibid.

46 James J. Murphy, ed., *Quintilian on the Teaching of Speaking and Writing: Translations from Books One, Two, and Ten of the* Institutio Oratoria (Carbondale: Southern Illinois University Press, 1987), 20–21.

47 Ibid.

48 Ibid.

49 E. H. Robinson, Karyn Dayle Jones, and B. Grant Hayes, "Humanistic Education to Character Education: An Ideological Journey," *Journal of Humanistic Counseling, Education and Development, 39,* no. 1 (2000), 22.

50 Ibid.

51 Ibid., 23.

52 Ibid., 24.

53 Ibid.

54 Ibid.

55 Ibid.

56 Ibid., 28.

57 Murphy, *Quintilian,* 100.

58 Ibid.

59 Ibid.

60 Ibid.

61 Murray A. Straus, "Social Science and Public Policy: New Evidence for the Benefits of Never Spanking," *Society* (September/October 2001), 53.

62 Ibid., 54.

63 Ibid., 56.

64 Ibid.

65 Ibid.

66 Ibid., 59.

67 National Association of School Psychologists, "NASP Position Statement on Corporal Punishment in Schools," http://www.nasponline.org (retrieved June 2005).

68 Lynn Roy, "Corporal Punishment in American Public Schools and the Rights of the Child," *Journal of Law and Education, 30,* no. 3 (2001), 561.

69 Ibid.

70 Ibid., 562.

71 Jones, *Decline,* 363.

72 Ibid.

73 Ibid., 366.

Chapter 3

The Middle Ages
(AD 476–1200)

Learning Objectives

1. Describe how education was affected by the fall of the Roman Empire.
2. List and describe the types of education available during the medieval period.
3. Develop a chronological understanding of events pertaining to education in the Middle Ages, including the rise of the universities.
4. Compare and contrast higher education in the Middle Ages with higher education for students today.
5. Describe methods of teaching in the Middle Ages, in the cathedral and grammar schools.
6. Describe the similarities and differences between education in the Middle Ages and education today.
7. List and explain the contributions from the medieval period to today's educational system.

INTRODUCTION

The Middle Ages was the period between the fall of the Western Roman Empire in AD 476 and the middle of the fifteenth century. Although there is disagreement about the exact dates when the Roman Empire fell and the Middle Ages began, what is known is that the foundations of Roman society were shaken by the influx of barbarian tribes from the north.[1] At this time the Roman Empire was vulnerable in many crucial areas, including education. Because Roman society had become largely Christianized, Roman citizens were becoming distrustful of pagan schools, which continued to teach about the Roman gods and goddesses. The pagan schools eventually closed because Christian parents hesitated to send their children there. Overall, public support for the educational system in ancient Rome was dwindling, and the turbulent political, economic, and social conditions of the empire meant that it was not long before the schools permanently closed their doors.

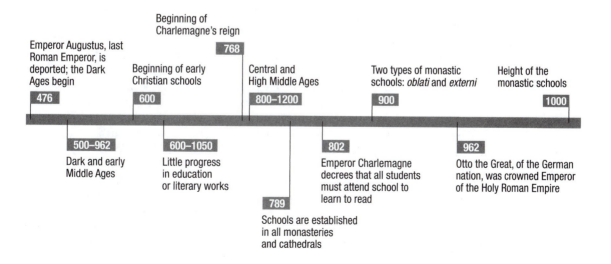

Emperor Augustus, last Roman Emperor, is deported; the Dark Ages begin
476

Beginning of early Christian schools
600

Beginning of Charlemagne's reign
768

Central and High Middle Ages
800–1200

Two types of monastic schools: *oblati* and *externi*
900

Height of the monastic schools
1000

500–962
Dark and early Middle Ages

600–1050
Little progress in education or literary works

789
Schools are established in all monasteries and cathedrals

802
Emperor Charlemagne decrees that all students must attend school to learn to read

962
Otto the Great, of the German nation, was crowned Emperor of the Holy Roman Empire

Invading tribes from the north succeeded in settling kingdoms for approximately three centuries after Rome fell. Although these invaders had some respect for the Roman government and laws, since they permitted Roman governmental agencies to keep operating under the protection of the larger towns, the Roman civilization and its educational system were permanently altered.

Education was in a state of flux owing to frequent civil wars and economic change. At the end of the Roman Empire, as the Roman schools closed, education had to be conducted in other ways besides the traditional school-based setting. In the Middle Ages, youth were often educated in monasteries and convents. For many in the Middle Ages, opportunities for education were found just by going through daily life.

The monastic educational system in the Middle Ages was crucial to keeping learning alive at this time of economic, political, religious, and social turmoil. This church-related system of education has parallels in the present day. Christian schools today have their roots in the Christian schools of the medieval period, in which the study of the Psalter and the New Testament were required reading.

Because the type of education available depended on the socioeconomic and political circumstances at the time, this chapter is divided according to the developments of various parts of the Middle Ages. The first part focuses on education during the Dark and early Middle Ages, from approximately AD 500 until approximately AD 962. This encompasses the period during which time education experienced a revival, at about AD 800, thanks to the efforts of Charlemagne and his chief scholar, Alcuin. The second part of the chapter focuses on the development of education in the **central and high Middle Ages,** from approximately AD 800 until approximately AD 1200, when cathedral schools were established. The revival of learning in the later part of the Middle Ages led to the establishment of universities in Europe and corresponding improvements in trade and commerce, which helped foster the economic development of society and an increase in the educational opportunities available.

EDUCATION IN THE DARK AGES

The **Dark Ages** began about AD 476, after the dissolution of the Roman Empire, and lasted until AD 962, when **Otto the Great,** of the German nation, was crowned Emperor of the Holy Roman Empire.[2] The period after Otto's coronation is traditionally referred to as the Middle Ages, when Europe developed a unique civilization that provided the cultural milieu in which the Renaissance and subsequent Reformation periods developed.[3]

After the Roman Empire fell, the civilization was in chaos. It is hard to picture what the schools and the educational system were like as the economic and political system verged on collapse. Barbarian tribes invaded the countryside, and civil wars and assassinations became frequent occurrences. In Britain, the fifth century was marked by violence as barbarian invasions intensified. The term **barbarian** comes from the Greeks, indicating someone who is a foreigner and of inferior culture.[4] All the former Roman territories, including Britain, were seized by Germanic invaders, and there was a complete breakdown of Roman life. The schools, as they had been, completely disappeared.[5] This situation was much the same over the rest of Europe.

However, a few vestiges of learning remained. Despite the barbarian invasions, some grammar was still being taught in Rome until the middle of the sixth century. Law and medicine were also being taught, with teachers' salaries paid by the State.[6] Gradually, however, Italy and the Roman people were besieged by the barbarian invasions, and from the end of the sixth century to the end of the seventh century AD, education as we think of it, conducted in the formal sense in schools, disappeared. The only education that remained was almost entirely religious in nature, conducted by monks.[7] The Episcopal school, a second type of Christian school, also arose at this time.

What were the effects of frequent barbarian invasions, a lack of centralized government, and economic and political turmoil on the society? Cities and villages disappeared, and ancient culture quickly deteriorated. The nobility, or those of wealth, had great amounts of land, known as **estates** or demesnes, cultivated by peasants, or serfs, who were bound to the land and deprived of their civil rights. This system arose because wealthy townsmen bought agricultural estates, which allowed them to become part of the privileged class of the Empire. The middle class, traditionally a stabilizing force in any social order, had vanished.[8] Western Europe settled into a routine of religious devotion, local and personal government, and farming, all of which formed the basis for the rise of commerce, cities, parliaments, and the constitutional monarchy of the later Middle Ages. The invading barbarian tribes, who were mostly illiterate and uninterested in education, did not wish to perpetuate the Roman school system, so it fell into decline.[9] Schools and literary works made almost inconsequential progress in Europe between AD 600 and 1050.[10] By the tenth century, the monastic schools were of two types: the ***oblati,*** for those who intended to take vows, and the ***externi,*** for those not intending to go into the Church.[11]

Because of the difficulties of conducting historical research on a period when education was not widespread, and the society was in political, economic, religious and social turmoil, the educational historian cannot give an exact picture of what education was like during this early part of the Middle Ages. Different schools of historians have developed vastly differing views as to the state of society and

Spotlight On ←————————————————————————————————

THE FEUDAL ECONOMIC SYSTEM: THE MANORIAL ECONOMY

The economic system in the Middle Ages was known as the feudal system. A member of the nobility, usually a lord, controlled a large portion of land. Those who worked the land were called serfs and usually lived under poor conditions, in small huts shared with animals. Medieval society was interested in preserving the status quo. The medieval perception of life was based on a Christian philosophy of life that appears to have been widely accepted, namely, that life on earth was preliminary to an eternal existence. Medieval thinkers believed that if a man climbed the ladder into a higher social class, it would disturb the divinely appointed order. This idea is in direct contrast to our present-day belief that if we work hard enough, we can make a better life for ourselves. Furthermore, until the rise of industry and trade and commerce in the High Middle Ages, there were few other opportunities for advancement, as medieval life was agrarian in nature. Insufficient land-use policies and poor harvests contributed to disease and famine.

education during the early part of the Middle Ages. Some historians believe that the Dark Ages really lived up to their name, because the society was in such turmoil that education was out of the question; it was a luxury.[12] However, other historians do not believe that this name is accurate, since some foundations for the developments of the High Middle Ages were being established.[13] For example, the **manorial economy** was a basis for an economic system based on trade.[14]

Although historians may debate about whether an active system of learning existed in the Dark and Early Middle Ages, we know that learning during this period was not very widespread. Education is the first element in a society to be neglected when a society is at war or in turmoil. Such is the case currently in third world countries, such as Afghanistan, where schools have been dismantled in record numbers and women are not allowed to attend school.

During the Dark and early Middle Ages, culture and learning were maintained in monasteries despite the outside turmoil from invasions and the collapse of the Western Roman Empire. All monasteries, in addition to teaching those who enter the order, made provisions for educating laypeople who did not intend to take vows.[15]

MONASTIC EDUCATION

Because **monastic education** was so important in maintaining literacy in the Dark and Middle Ages, its value cannot be overstated. The type of learning, however, was not the type of education we have today, which tends to be secular, or not affiliated with any religious group. The Church in the Dark and Middle Ages was antagonistic to any sort of pagan worship, and the type of secular stories that children read today would never have been allowed at that time. The Church banned any literature in which the pagan gods and religions were honored.[16] Children's books such as the *Harry Potter* series would never have been allowed during the Dark or Middle Ages

Spotlight On ←————————————————————————

MEDIEVAL THEORIES ABOUT CONCEPTION

Medieval science was inextricably intermixed with superstition. Theories about conception are an example of superstitious belief. Medical experts believed that the female produced semen, and the character of the child was determined according to the substance of both mother and father. When the blood in the father's semen was predominant, the fetus resembled him in character traits, but if the mother's blood was predominant, the fetus resembled her. For noble parents, the mother's blood was considered as important as the father's. The blood in the mother's semen was supposed to transmit nobility and the accompanying genetic traits. This theory was used to justify the existence and the exclusivity of the nobility.

because they deal with witchcraft. Medieval people were very superstitious; books about medieval history all mention the superstitions that medieval people held.

PURPOSE OF MONASTIC EDUCATION

The Church had as its major purpose the study and interpretation of the Bible, which was written in Latin. This meant that anyone studying the Bible had to be fluent in Latin. Medieval education was organized and controlled by the Church, through monastic institutions, cathedral schools, and later, by universities.[17] The monastic schools, especially those which followed the rule of St. Benedict, were numerous. In the sixth century, with the Roman Empire under attack, and frequent barbarian invasions, the **Benedictine** monks turned to farming, preserving literature and teaching, under the rules of their order. Monastic schools were run by Benedictines in England, and later in Ireland. The discipline of St. Benedict continued to control the monasteries of Western Europe largely because of the popularity of Pope Gregory I (AD 590–604), who was a former monk of that order. It gained full approval in England and thus prospered.[18] From AD 600 to 1066, the monks intended to preserve education from the Greeks and Romans, as well as that of the early Christians. This was especially prevalent in England, where education was greatly influenced by monastic achievements from AD 600 to 1540[19].

The Benedictine monks made economic as well as cultural contributions. They drained swamps and cleared forests. They helped train peasants in agricultural methods that would yield better quality crops and feed more people. Large resident communities of monks prospered, and grew in numbers, especially in the late twelfth and thirteenth centuries.[20]

Christianity was introduced in England in AD 597, and it greatly influenced education. English boys and girls were admitted to monasteries and nunneries to be trained for the religious life. This training emphasized literacy and memory. Teaching consisted largely of the question-and-answer method. The printing press had not yet been invented, so students used manuscripts on scrolls. Teachers often dictated their lessons, and the pupils wrote the passages on their tablets and memorized them.[21] The Western Church used Latin for speaking and writing, so students had to learn that language.

Early monastic education began with elementary reading, introduced Latin grammar, and extended to the study of liberal arts and theology. Religious works, secular poems, laws, and charters to grant land, were written in English, so a **vernacular** literature, or a literature not in Latin, was created. Thus, although many children learned only the Latin alphabet, they went on to read and write English later.[22]

The study of the **seven liberal arts** from ancient Greece and Rome became an important part of the curriculum in the Middle Ages in the monastic schools, and later in the cathedral schools. The seven liberal arts consisted of the verbal arts, known as the *trivium,* which was the study of the sciences of language, oratory, and logic, and the *quadrivium,* which was the study of arithmetic, music, geometry, and astronomy.[23] Two important texts used in the study of grammar were

De partibus orationis, an introduction to the parts of speech, and *Ars grammatical,* a more intense and advanced study of grammar.[24]

Although the monasteries played an important role in educating children, only a fraction of the population in the Dark and Early Middle Ages received an education there. Although nearly all monastic houses had schools for children in nearby communities by the ninth century,[25] there is little information available about how many children attended them. It seems likely that although the monastic schools offered opportunities for education, many individuals did not or were not able to take advantage of them.

Rather, most education in the Middle Ages took place at home. The education was primarily domestic and social and included learning to walk and eat, speak, dress oneself, cope with one's surroundings, and interact with others.[26] By closely interacting with their elders, children absorbed their customs and beliefs. Medieval homes were also training places for work. Boys and girls shared in parents' tasks and received instruction in the skills their parents knew. At this time, it was not necessary to attend school in order to learn. Most people in the Middle Ages learned by practical experience. Traveling also provided opportunities for learning.[27]

Formal education in the Middle Ages was limited to the nobility. In noble families, some of the younger sons who were not destined to inherit, or daughters who would not marry, were sent to be educated in monasteries or convents. Orphaned children also were put in the care of priests and nuns to guarantee their future, for they would be prepared for a career in the Church. Until the twelfth century, noble families often encouraged sons who were unsuited to the physical demands of knighthood, which included jousting and horseback riding, to go into the monastic life. Monasteries were also excellent repositories for the physically handicapped. Although the abbots of many of these monasteries disliked this practice, it was never completely stopped.[28]

Few sons of the lower social classes reached the higher ranks in the secular church or in the monastery, and the number of girls from the lower social classes who became nuns was dismally low, because girls were required to bring a dowry to the convent. Poorer girls were not accepted. The same situation applied to boys. The mendicant orders accepted more boys and young men from the lower social classes, but girls from those classes usually were not accepted. In fact, girls placed in Benedictine convents were almost all of noble birth.[29]

In the Middle Ages, the adoration of Mary, the Virgin Mother, was an important part of the religious mysticism. It was believed that if women were formally educated, they would be exposed to corrupting influences that would make them impure. Thus, to preserve their purity, it was safer to shield women from the outside world, which meant that it was better not to educate them.[30]

In the twelfth and thirteenth centuries, coeducational village schools provided instruction in reading and writing. Girls were not usually admitted to the **song schools,** which prepared children to participate in religious services. However, apprenticeships, especially in the later Middle Ages, were available to women in the trades of brewing, tailoring, metal working, embroidering, grinding corn, and silk manufacturing.[31]

The philosophy of education in the Middle Ages held that its purpose was to prepare a child for his or her role in society. Teaching a child to accept the social order to which he or she belonged was part of the medieval educational philosophy, and it was believed that social class was divinely appointed. Three classes existed, and it was not possible to move out of a lower class into a higher one. These three classes were those who fought and governed, or the nobility; those who prayed, or the clergy; and those who toiled with their hands, or the peasants. The amount of education someone received in the Middle Ages was determined not only by gender but also by social class.[32] For instance, children of the peasantry rarely received any education. Formal education as we think of it, involving a specific curriculum in a school setting, did not occur in the Middle Ages.

MORAL EDUCATION IN THE MIDDLE AGES

A crucial component of education in the Middle Ages was moral education. Children were considered to be born under the weight of **Original Sin,** necessitating baptism.[33] Raising a Christian human being was a vital part of educational philosophy. Medieval scholars who spoke of "being a good Christian" defined this as observing the rules of worship, including the observance of fast days, following the Ten Commandments, and refraining from the seven deadly sins: pride, covetousness, lust, envy, gluttony, anger, and sloth. Certain character traits, such as demonstrating faith, hope, charity, reason, moderation, and fortitude, were crucial in

Spotlight On ←

THE MEDIEVAL PERCEPTION OF CHILDHOOD

In modern times, we think of childhood as a separate period of human development. This was not the case in medieval times. The idea of childhood as a separate and unique time of development did not originate until after the 17th century. In the Middle Ages, children were considered to be adults when they started school. The historian Philippe Aries, in his landmark work *Centuries of Childhood*, tells us that as soon as a child no longer needed constant attention from his nanny, nurse, or mother, he was part of adult society.

Because the knowledge of medicine and the causes of disease were primitive, child mortality was high in the Middle Ages. From *Childhood in the Middle Ages*, we learn that of every 1,000 infants, 200 to 300 died in their first year. Only half of the 1,000 reached the age of five.

establishing a good Christian character. Being a good Christian also meant visiting the poor and sick, giving money to the Church, and comforting prisoners.[34]

Parental discipline was also important in raising a child of good Christian character in the Middle Ages. Childish mischief was considered to be evil, and it was recommended that parents not ignore it. Parents had to conduct themselves in a proper fashion, because children imitated their parents.[35] The idea of educating the young in a system that taught moral values goes as far back as AD 375, when **St. John Chrysostom** prevailed upon Christian parents to have their children educated after they were ten by the monks, so they would be removed from dangerous worldly influences.[36]

Medieval writers who focused on parenting said that parents of the nobility, or middle-class parents, should raise their children as the Spartans in earlier Greece did, so that children should be raised under harsh conditions (lack of food and water, exposure to cold) to increase their physical and mental strength.[37]

The emphasis on moral education in medieval times is mirrored in our society today. Today, moral education is a part of the curriculum in many parochial and Christian schools, and it is incorporated into the curriculum in public schools in many states.

Educators recognize that the behavior a child or adolescent brings to the classroom setting often mirrors what he or she sees at home. Parenting skills in modern times are often considered to be lacking, and teachers and other educators are increasingly called upon to teach appropriate behavior. Thus, the advice of educators to parents in medieval times: to teach their children appropriate behavior by modeling it to them on a regular basis is equally applicable today.

Formal moral education in the school, was not widespread in the medieval period, because there was scarcely any basic education in formally established schools. By the eighth century, when Charlemagne was crowned king of the Franks, it was seen as important to revive learning by a common language, culture, and set of ideas and values.

THE CONTRIBUTIONS OF CHARLEMAGNE AND ALCUIN

Charlemagne was a great learner and worked closely with **Alcuin,** his chief scholar, whom he appointed his minister of education. Formerly the head of the cathedral school at York, Alcuin was given the task of reestablishing the school of the royal palace at Aachen, begun by Charlemagne's father. Students in the cathedral school were taught Latin, composition, mathematics for the study and understanding of arithmetic, and astronomy, so that they could understand the calendar year of the Church.[38] Students also studied the natural sciences to understand such phenomena as the eclipses of the sun and moon, the tides, and earthquakes as well as the natural laws that governed men and animals, as explained in the works of Pliny, the Roman writer, and **Bede,** the monk who wrote *Church History of the English People.*[39] Alcuin advocated the Socratic style of teaching, although he did not conduct it exactly as Socrates himself had. Alcuin was interested in finding out what students believed and why they believed it to be so. When he arose daily at dawn he wrote down the questions and answers he would dictate to his pupils for them to memorize because recitation was considered the best method of teaching. Alcuin himself knew the contents of 40 books by heart, as was the custom of the time.

One of the problems that concerned Charlemagne and Alcuin was the illiteracy of priests. Alcuin thought that the priests had an important role to play, since they had to advise the people, who had to listen in humility.[40] However, because many village priests could not read or write, Charlemagne wondered how they could possibly be in a position to give moral advice, or instruct the people. Thus, in AD 789, he issued an edict that the clergy must establish schools in all monasteries and cathedrals. Charlemagne envisioned education becoming highly important once again in the lives of the people, just as it had been in ancient Greece and Rome. Charlemagne wanted the priests to become better educated, so that they could teach lay people.[41] The priests were not supposed to ask fees for teaching children, and Charlemagne declared that they should not "receive anything from them, save what the parents may offer voluntarily and from affection."[42] In AD 791, he issued an order that urged every freeman to enroll his son in school so that he might become educated. This order resulted in the establishment of schools in various monasteries, cathedrals, and villages. In Charlemagne's kingdom, at least, elementary education was almost compulsory; a decree in AD 802 said that all children must be sent to school to learn to read and that they must stay there until they had mastered reading and writing.[43] This represented the first organized attempt at compulsory education, a precursor to our modern-day compulsory education law, passed in 1916.

When Charlemagne died, his successors could not keep his kingdom together, and it soon separated into the three countries known today as France, Italy, and Germany.[44] Without Charlemagne's influence and the stability of his kingdom, the educational situation destabilized, demonstrating how influential just one individual can be in the development and perpetuation of education. Further invasions, from the Magyars (Hungarians) and the Norsemen, continued from the sixth to the eighth centuries, ending about AD 933. By the eleventh century, however, the Norsemen had been Christianized and absorbed into the general population, and the Magyars had been driven out.

As the history of Charlemagne's ideas on education, and chief scholar Alcuin, demonstrates, it is very important to have some type of legislation that encourages individuals to send their children to school to make education more widespread. If Charlemagne had not decreed that all freemen had to send their children to school, it is doubtful that children would have attended. Today, the government has great influence on educational developments. One example is the No Child Left Behind Act of 2001.

STATE OF LEARNING AND SOCIETY IN THE HIGH MIDDLE AGES

During the period known as the High Middle Ages, which runs roughly from the twelfth century to the fifteenth century, medieval society was undergoing change. These changes also included the expansion of education. Although education was

SHAPERS OF EDUCATION

Charlemagne (742–814)	Alcuin (735–804)	Gerbert (950–1003)
■ Decreed that government should provide a free education ■ Declared that government should require schooling ■ Believed that teacher education is important ■ Ordered clergy to establish schools in all cathedrals and monasteries ■ Ordered all freemen to enroll their sons in school by AD 791	■ Used recitation as a means of learning ■ Helped Charlemagne reestablish schools ■ Advised students to question why they held certain beliefs as true	■ Made math easier by using Arabic numerals ■ Encouraged use of abacus ■ Showed students the value of each subject ■ Used lecture method of teaching ■ Encouraged students to study public speaking

still by no means universal, or available to all individuals regardless of social class, education had nonetheless become a more accepted part of society, and was considered to be important for individual growth and development. In the twelfth century, a network of schools was established, some of which became universities.[45] Vocational education existed in thirteenth-century Paris, in the apprenticeships available to youth in the wool trade.

Feudalism, which had been the mainstay of the economic system in the Middle Ages, began to disintegrate. Improvements occurred, but not steadily. However, commerce became increasingly important in the thirteenth century as the continental trade of Europe connected different regions and gave a sense of economic coherence to an area that had been politically divided. Trade moved from the land to the sea as goods began to be transported from farther away. Bad road conditions limited the distances that goods could be transported on land. Roman roads, though they still existed, had not been kept in good repair. Craftsmen, who worked in guilds in the medieval towns, needed raw materials such as wool, to manufacture their products, such as clothing. Roads were improved during the thirteenth century, and canals were widened to accommodate an increase in waterway traffic.[46]

By the fourteenth and fifteenth centuries, however, there was insufficient arable land in Europe to grow enough food to feed everyone; as a result, after 1300 the population of Europe declined, owing to famine and disease. This scarcity of land had devastating effects on the population. Without sufficient food, mortality increased. Then in 1348, the Bubonic plague, also known as the **Black Death,** struck. Black rats carried fleas that bit people and spread the disease, which killed people in record numbers. Epidemics recurred frequently, causing great fear among the population. The Black Death even affected education. Parents who sent their children to the universities often found that they had died from plague. At Winchester College, 23 students died from bubonic plague between 1401 and 1410, and 11 of the students admitted to Winchester in 1401 did not survive. When outbreaks of plague were reported, the students and their masters packed up and moved to rural manors to continue the school year, where they felt they would be safer than in the more crowded areas.[47]

It was in this atmosphere of fear and uncertainty that economic and social changes developed. The peasantry, formerly the backbone of the medieval economy, revolted against the scarcity of land and poor wages. Peasant revolts occurred in Europe; three of the major revolts occurred in Flanders in 1323 and 1328, in Northern France in 1358, and in England in 1381.

The peasant revolts were but one symptom of economic and social change in the Middle Ages, which are too numerous and complex to describe in this chapter, but they even affected education. The members of the aristocracy were accused of using education to perpetuate their social class. In the later part of the Middle Ages, after 1200, education was viewed as being important, as evidenced in the many forms in which it was available. For instance, children of nobility were taught by professional schoolmasters in their own homes. Furthermore, monasteries expanded their offerings to include boys from the lay population, who were taught in monasteries up until the Reformation.[48,49] Towns in the later Middle Ages had their town-centered, fee-paying schools and added one or two schoolmasters, who taught classes in private houses. Even women, who formerly did not have access to education outside the home, benefited from the newfound awareness of education, as a local priest, clerk, or lay person could teach them to read and write.[50]

By 1348, the number of elementary and grammar schools in medieval England had increased. Elementary and grammar education had expanded noticeably by the fourteenth and fifteenth centuries, first in Italy, then in France, Germany, and Spain.[51] Education in England expanded in the 50 years before the English Reformation, from approximately 1480 to 1530.[52] In Italy, France, Germany, and Spain, it is believed that education was supported, especially in the towns, because it provided certain benefits, such as promoting future civil servants as well as preparing the young for future leadership positions.[53] The English, however, were more interested in supporting education because the schools would provide priests to replace those who had died of the plague, and because chantries were growing. It is clear that education is supported when it can provide instruction for specific purposes, such as to produce priests or civic leaders. The next section examines the growth of cathedral schools.

CATHEDRAL SCHOOLS

The monastic schools in the eleventh century had reached their prime.[54] They had disregarded intellectual knowledge, so classical studies were not encouraged. Education was taken over by the secular clergy, and schools developed in the cathedrals under the control of their bishops.[55] **Cathedral schools** played an important role in providing royal chaplains and bishops for the church; and a cathedral school education was almost required for higher office in the imperial church and was a prerequisite for service, either in the secular court, or in the church.[56] Overall, 12 cathedral schools were established over 60 years. One of the most famous was that of Chartres, in France. It was referred to as a "second Athens" because of the leadership of its teachers, such as the famous Bishop Fulbert.[57] Chartres and other cathedral schools were responsible for laying the foundation for our entire scholastic system.[58] Students learned the Psalms and to chant in **plainsong,** and also received instruction in the *trivium* (grammar, rhetoric, dialectics) and the *quadrivium* (geometry, arithmetic, astronomy, music), and in theology, which was a study of the scriptures and canon law.[59]

Cathedral schools became prominent beginning in the mid-tenth century in Germany and France. Another very important school was in Cologne, Germany. By 953 it had an excellent reputation and produced many intellectuals, statesmen, educators, and bishops.[60]

The cathedral schools used as their model the classical education of the Greeks and Romans to train individuals to care for the state and defend its interests.[61] Quintilian, Cicero, and Seneca, of ancient Rome, had written about how to teach future leaders who would take part in an active life and in secular affairs, and who would serve the state. Education in the cathedral schools consisted of instruction in the liberal arts as well as in moral values. Such cathedral schools as Wurzburg, in Germany, taught rhetoric, oratory and poetry, to teach students how to speak properly, and ethics, to teach them how to live properly.[62]

In the cathedral school at Rheims, France, **Bishop Gerbert,** a brilliant teacher, introduced new methods to make learning more interesting for students. For instance, when he taught arithmetic he used the nine Hindu-Arabic numerals 1 through 9, instead of Roman numerals, to make writing problems easier for children. He also allowed students to use the abacus, which is a rectangular device of counters that can be manipulated to solve arithmetic problems. He taught students to represent a three digit number, for example, by manipulating the correct number of counters into the hundreds, tens, and ones digit columns of the abacus.[63]

Gerbert strongly advocated that the value of each subject be demonstrated to students so they would understand why they were learning it and appreciate it more fully. For instance, when he taught astronomy, Gerbert demonstrated what the earth and the heavens looked like by using spheres on which the stars' movements could be shown. He also invented the prototype of the telescope.[64]

As was noted earlier, one of the main subjects studied in cathedral schools, was the study of public speaking, or logic and rhetoric. Gerbert insisted that public speaking be part of the curriculum because it was necessary for a career in public affairs. He wrote that "to be able to persuade and restrain with words the wills of lawless men is useful in the highest degree."[65]

The lecture method of teaching, which is still used today, became common in the twelfth century.[66] Students read the assigned text, which might have been the Bible, a historical work, or a medical volume, and answered questions posed by the teacher. Unlike lectures today, students were not allowed to take notes but had to remember much of what the teacher discussed. Students had to recite what they had learned from memory each day.[67] Over time, however, students were allowed to take notes, and lecturers even circulated their own notes among the students, to be taken home.[68]

The cathedral schools grew away from their ecclesiastical beginnings after the 1170s when any man who wanted to teach in the cathedral schools was allowed to do so. This individual did not have to take any tests or pay any fees and did not have to be concerned primarily with preparation for worship as the main goal of education. Learning became important for its own sake.[69] This secularization of education in the Middle Ages mirrors the development of public schools in America in the colonial period. They had strong religious roots in the 1600s but grew away from those under the influence of Horace Mann and the growth of the American "common school."

RISE OF THE UNIVERSITIES

Cathedral schools developed during the intellectual expansion of Europe, from 1240 to 1270, and 1300 to 1325. Intellectuals such as Abelard, Otto of Freising, and John of Salisbury took advantage of Europe's new social order to turn their attention from matters of mere survival to such questions as the nature of man and the nature of the world.[70] With the new emphasis on education, cathedral schools soon grew into universities. This change was easy because all that was necessary was that the schoolmasters of the cathedral school incorporate themselves into a guild, or a *universitas*.[71]

The former feudal world of the Middle Ages, in which superstition and ignorance were widespread, gave way to an intellectual revolution.[72] Learning, for its own sake, had gained acceptance.

The life of a university student in the Middle Ages was similar in some ways to the life of a college or university student today. The instructors determined the length of time a student had to be in a program of study and serve as an apprentice and the criteria necessary to pass and receive the degree, either the master's or the doctorate. Essentially the degrees were all technically licenses to teach.[73] The standards to be met were very stringent, so medieval students took as long, or even longer to train for a profession as it takes students today.[74]

The masters in the northern universities were licensed to teach by the bishop in the city in which the school was located. The bishop had the power to interfere if he felt that what a professor said or wrote might have negative implications, so many professors kept quiet for fear of retribution. Just as professors today compete for departmental honors, grants, and special distinctions, medieval faculty members also competed with one another. Thus, it might be said that the modern university, in some respects, resembles the medieval university.

College and university students today often have to work and attend school, due to the high cost of tuition, living expenses, and books. The medieval student's life was just as difficult in many ways. Medieval students usually came from families with less money, such as those of burghers or lesser knights.[75] Housing and food were expensive and inadequate. The relationship between townspeople and students was often strained, and fights occurred as a result. Students were often unhappy not only because their course of study was so long and the discipline severe but because they had no money and had to struggle on a daily basis for many years. This unhappiness resulted in their getting involved in fights, drinking too much, and even gambling.[76] Students in universities today are disciplined for many of the same infractions!

Students in medieval universities chose subjects such as law, which was a means to a good job in either the church or the state.[77] Studies such as theology, thought to be the ultimate of the sciences, took too long to complete and offered little in the way of jobs. Medieval university students, like today's university students, looked for a course of study that would provide some economic and career stability when they had completed their training.[78]

It was said that students in the Middle Ages who spent long years of study at the university were of no use to society. Rather, they were supposed to be acquiring knowledge to apply to areas needed by society, such as medicine to cure the sick. Another argument was over the types of careers that were acceptable. Doctors, lawyers and notaries were respectable careers, but teaching was not. Those of low social status were likely to go into teaching. Even in the Middle Ages, the question of whether teaching was a profession was a concern, just as it is today.[79] Owing to the high graduation fees, many students who were studying for an arts degree did not finish. Despite their lack of qualifications, they were able to get teaching jobs, especially in municipal schools. As the educational demands increased, the standards were raised, and candidates for such positions were expected to have earned a Master of Arts degree, at the minimum. Working conditions for municipal schoolmasters, however, led candidates to take the job only for a short period and take a better position later on. Those who had higher degrees did not face the discrimination that teachers faced. Students who intended to teach were often isolated; rather than form relationships with faculty, who could help them locate faculty appointments through personal contacts, they kept to themselves. This isolation kept them from taking advantage of the learning and career opportunities experienced by the elites in academic life.[80]

Today, a frequent criticism of teaching is that it is not a profession. To counteract that criticism, many states have raised the criteria for admission to teacher education programs. Many colleges and universities that offer teacher education programs have raised admissions standards, and states are now requiring that candidates for a teaching certificate pass a state-mandated examination, both for elementary and secondary teaching certification. Colleges of teacher education, higher education faculty, and state legislatures are working together to change the misconception that you teach if you aren't fitted for anything else.

BRIDGES FROM THE PAST TO THE PRESENT: VALUE AND USES OF CONTRIBUTIONS FROM EDUCATION IN THE MIDDLE AGES TODAY

Table 3-1 gives several very important contributions from the medieval period to today's educational system. First, the recognition that not all parents provide adequate moral examples to their children in the home, so that moral values need to be taught in the school, applies today. In 2002, First Lady Laura Bush announced that $16.7 million in grants was awarded to five states and 34 school districts, to help develop lesson plans to promote high moral character.[81] She stated that children need

Table 3-1   **Educational Philosophy: Medieval Versus Modern Thought**

MEDIEVAL EDUCATION	MODERN EDUCATION
Moral values were taught.	Moral values are taught.
Vocational education was taught.	Students take vocational education courses.
Education was not compulsory until Charlemagne's reign.	Compulsory education laws exist.
Arabic numerals were introduced.	Arabic numerals are used.
Students struggled to survive a long university program.	Students often must work while attending college.
Students looked for course of study that would enable them to find a job.	Students want a career when they finish college.
Training period for a profession was very long.	Students want to finish college in 4 years or less.
Lecture method of teaching was primarily used.	Other methods of teaching are used to get students more involved in learning.
Recitation was important and memorization was often used.	Students can take notes, tape lectures, and use laptop computers in class.
Education initially was not seen as a way to advance oneself.	Education is believed to be the way to a better future.

to be taught good moral values just as much as they need to be taught reading and writing. If children are taught good moral values, they will become responsible citizens. Character education programs for youth focus on civic virtue and citizenship, caring, justice and fairness, respect, responsibility, and trustworthiness.[82]

Second, the concept of vocational education, which began in the Middle Ages, continues today, as students train for careers as computer repair persons, graphic artists, and others. In 2002 the U.S. Department of Education reported that 77 percent of public high schools offered career majors or pathways, and 50 percent of such schools required that all students participate in them.[83] Further information from the National Center for Education Statistics reveals that despite a decline in vocational courses from 1982 to 1988, vocational education continues to occupy a steady place in the high school curriculum.[84] In 1998 it was shown that graduates of vocational/technical programs were more likely to be members of disadvantaged groups, were more likely to be male, and were more likely to come from rural schools than from urban or suburban schools.[85] Vocational and/or technical programs appear to be more attractive to members of lower socioeconomic groups, probably because they provide specific training to allow students to train for jobs already available in the labor force, which is important, because they need to earn money right away. Students in the Middle Ages who went into vocational training were also more likely to be members of the lower socioeconomic groups.

Third, Charlemagne's edicts that parents must send their children to school were a precursor to modern-day compulsory education laws. Charlemagne recognized the importance of establishing schools and also making certain that the priests, who did the teaching, were educated enough to be entrusted with this task.

The work of Bishop Gerbert at Chartres, the renowned French cathedral school, is remarkable for its insistence on innovative ways of teaching children, particularly in arithmetic; for instance, by using Arabic numerals and allowing students to use the abacus. Students today use math manipulatives in learning about numbers.

Many of the dilemmas that educators struggle with on a daily basis, from how best to educate students in appropriate behavior, including moral behavior, to the question of how college and university students struggle to pay their tuition and what majors they choose in the higher educational system, have their roots in the medieval period.

SUMMARY

This chapter described the economic, social, and political situation in Europe after the fall of the western part of the Roman Empire and the implications of the barbarian invasions on education in the period known as the Middle Ages. Contributions from this period to today's educational system include the rise of the universities and the concept of vocational education.

In Chapter 4 we move from education during the Middle Ages to education during the Renaissance, which began in Italy in the thirteenth century and developed in England in the fourteenth to the fifteenth centuries.

QUESTIONS FOR DISCUSSION

1. Many parents today feel that the public schools, like the pagan schools at the beginning of the Dark Ages, don't teach moral values. As in the Dark Ages, aspects of our society are in turmoil: the divorce rate is high, the economy has been faltering, and there are many single-parent families living in poverty. How important is moral education of the young when the society is in turmoil?

2. Describe the development of the monastic schools and their uses by the nobility. How does this type of class-conscious education compare or contrast with the sorts of education advocated by the wealthy today?

3. How did the monastic schools inadvertently help reinforce the class system that existed during the Middle Ages? Do schools today perpetuate the class system? Explain your answer with at least one example.

4. Charlemagne had an avid interest in education and contributed to improvements in education during his 50-year reign. In any country, the importance of education often is related to how seriously education is taken by its leaders. How seriously do you think the leaders of the United States take education today? Explain your answer by providing at least one example.

5. Compare and contrast Alcuin's methods of teaching, as well as the subjects he chose for study, to the methods of teaching and the subjects studied today.

6. Were the improvements made during Charlemagne's reign widespread in Europe? Why or why not? How does this situation parallel the situation today, in terms of local versus national control of education?

7. Describe the political, economic, and social situation at the beginning of the Dark Ages and early Middle Ages after the Roman Empire fell and how these affected education. What do you think would happen to the U.S. educational system if similar circumstances existed? Explain.

8. Education for the lower classes was neglected in the Middle Ages. Compare and contrast this situation with educational opportunities for the lower socioeconomic classes today.

SUGGESTED ACTIVITIES

For help with these activities, utilize the books and resources listed in the Suggestions for Further Reading.

1. Research the living conditions of the serfs (peasants) as compared with those of the nobility in the Middle Ages. What conclusions can you draw about the effect of socioeconomic status on educational opportunities for nobles versus peasants? Present these findings to your classmates as a 15- to 20-minute PowerPoint presentation.

2. The Middle Ages were a time of great superstition. Choose a book on the popular culture of the Middle Ages, and write a 5- to 6-page report on one or two of the superstitious beliefs described. What conclusions can you draw about the role that ignorance plays in superstition today, and how can educators address this problem? For example, some teenagers have superstitious beliefs about birth control and conception.

3. Poor medical care and inadequate hygiene shortened the lives of many people in the Middle Ages. For instance, many women died in childbirth. Develop a PowerPoint presentation of at least 15 to 20 minutes on childbirth practices in the Middle Ages, their effect on mortality, and the attitudes about childhood in the Middle Ages.

4. Write a short paper of approximately 5 to 8 pages on Charlemagne's role in the revival of learning in the Carolingian Empire. State your conclusions about the potential impact one person can have in bringing about improvements in education. Also, discuss anyone in the present day who has had a significant impact on education.

5. Research the causes, symptoms, and effects of the bubonic plague on individuals in the Middle Ages. How do the effects of the plague compare to the effects of the current AIDS epidemic? Explain your findings and conclusions in a PowerPoint presentation of at least 15 minutes.

6. Compare and contrast the curriculum and teaching methods used in the universities of the High Middle Ages with those used in colleges and universities today. Present your findings in a PowerPoint presentation of at least 15 minutes.

Bibliography

Aries, P. (1962). *Centuries of childhood: A social history of family life* (R. Baldick, Trans.). New York: Knopf.

Cantor, N. F. (1993). *Civilization of the Middle Ages.* New York: Harper Perennial.

Clabaugh, G. K. (1986). A history of male attitudes toward educating women. *Educational Horizons, 64*(3), 127–135.

Classen, P. (1981). Associations of teachers and learners: The medieval view of the university. *Western European Education, 13*(3), 28–37.

Contreri, J. (1989). Education and learning in the early Middle Ages: New perspectives and old problems. *International Journal of Social Education, 4*(1), 9–25.

Coulton, G. G. (1915). *Medieval studies, first series* (2nd rev. ed.). London: Simpkin, Marshall, Hamilton, Kent.

Courtenay, W. J. (1980). The effect of the Black Death on English higher education. *Speculum, 55*(4), 696–714.

Courtenay, W. J., & Miethke, J. (Eds.). (2000). *Universities and schooling in medieval society.* Leiden, The Netherlands: Brill.

Fercozo, G., & Muessig, C. (Eds.). (2000). *Medieval monastic education.* London: Leicester University Press.

Graves, F. P. (1970). *A history of education during the Middle Ages and the transition to modern times.* Westport, CT: Greenwood Press.

Gurevich, A. (1988). *Medieval popular culture: Problems of belief and perception.* (J. M. Bak & P. A. Hollingsworth, Trans.) New York: Cambridge University Press.

Hay, D. (1966). *Europe in the fourteenth and fifteenth centuries.* New York: Holt, Rinehart and Winston.

Jaeger, C. S. (1994). *The envy of angels: Cathedral schools and social ideals in medieval Europe, 950–1200.* Philadelphia: University of Pennsylvania Press.

Kersey, S. (1980). Medieval education of girls and women. *Educational Horizons, 58*(4), 188–192.

Knowles, D. (1943). The cultural influence of English medieval monasticism. *Cambridge Historical Journal, 7*(3), 146–160.

Orme, N. (1989). *Education and society in medieval and Renaissance England.* London: Hambledon Press.

Pannabecker, J. R. (1989). Industrial education in the Middle Ages: Apprenticeship in the wool textile industry in thirteenth-century Paris. *Journal of Industrial Teacher Education, 26*(4), 39–52.

Piltz, A. (1981). *The world of medieval learning.* (D. Jones, Trans.) Totowa, NJ: Barnes and Noble.

Rowling, M. (1973). *Life in medieval times.* New York: Berkley.

Shahar, S. (1990). *Childhood in the Middle Ages.* New York: Routledge.

Wagner, D. (Ed.). (1983). *The seven liberal arts in the Middle Ages.* Bloomington: Indiana University Press.

Wood, M. (2001). *In search of the Dark Ages*. New York: Checkmark Books. (Originally published 1987).

Suggestions for Further Reading

In addition to the works cited in the bibliography, the following are suggested for further reading.

Holme, G. (1992). *Oxford history of medieval Europe*. Oxford: Oxford University Press.

Pirenne, H. (1925). *Medieval cities: Their origin and the revival of trade*. F. D. Halsey, Trans. Princeton, NJ: Princeton University Press.

Sears, W.P. (1931). *The roots of vocational education*. New York: John Wiley.

Relevant Web Sites

European Middle Ages *http://www.wsu.edu* Michael Delahoyde's introduction to the Middle Ages, at Washington State University. Excellent site for researching this era, checking facts, and so forth.

The Medieval Research Library at Questia.com *http://www.questia.com* Site which contains many research sources from articles, books, magazines, and newspapers on the Middle Ages.

Annenberg/CPB learner.org *http://www.learner.org/exhibits/middleages/* Interactive site on the Middle Ages. Covers feudal life, home, religion, clothing, and the like.

Education Week *http://www.edweek.org*. A weekly newspaper that covers all aspects of modern education.

National Center for Education Statistics *http://nces.ed.gov/* Web site for investigating federal and state data on education.

U.S. Department of Education *http://www.ed.gov* Home page of the U.S. Department of Education.

American Council on Education *http://www.acenet.edu//AM/Template.cfm?Section=Home* All about higher education, courses of study, opportunities for lower-income college students, and more.

Endnotes

[1] Boyd, *History of Western Education,* 95.

[2] Robert Holmes Beck, *A Social History of Education. Foundations of Education Series,* Volume 1. (Englewood Cliffs, NJ: Prentice-Hall, Inc. (2005), 20. This chapter, entitled "Education in Western Europe, A.D. 476–1000," is an excellent reference. It has a clear explanation of the division between the Dark and Middle Ages, and why they were so named.

[3] Henry S. Lucas, *The Renaissance and the Reformation, Second Edition.* New York: Harper and Row, 2005), 7.

[4] Norman F. Cantor, *Civilization of the Middle Ages, Revised and Expanded* (New York: Harper Perennial, 1993), 89.

[5] Henri Irenee Marrou, *A History of Education in Antiquity,* translated by George Lamb (New York: Sheed and Ward, 1956), 343–344.

[6] Ibid., 346.

[7] Ibid., 347.

[8] Charles Flinn Arrowood and Frederick Eby, *The History and Philosophy of Education: Ancient and Medieval* (Englewood Cliffs, NJ: Prentice Hall, 1940), 575–576. This book is an excellent and easily readable source, for those who are unfamiliar with the complexities of the Roman Empire and how it disintegrated due to political, economic, and social forces that are not easily understood.

[9] J. F. Dobson, *Ancient Education and Its Meaning to Us.* (New York: Cooper Square Publishers, 1963), 163.

[10] Arrowood and Eby, *History and Philosophy of Education,* 606.

[11] Francesco Cordasco, *A Brief History of Education* (Paterson NJ: Littlefield, Adams and Co., 1963). See p. 24.

[12] Joel Rosenthal, "Dark Age Education: Our Latest Survey," *History of Education Quarterly, 21* (1), Spring 1981, 118.

[13] Ibid.

[14] Ibid.

[15] Ibid.

[16] Ibid.

[17] Ibid.

[18] Frank Pierrepont Graves, *A History of Education During the Middle Ages and the Transition to Modern Times* (Westport CT: Greenwood Press, 1970). Originally published 1920 by Macmillan. See pp. 8–9.

[19] David Knowles, "The Cultural Influence of English Medieval Monasticism," *Cambridge Historical Journal, 7, 3* (1943), 146–147.

[20] M. M. Postan, *The Medieval Economy and Society: An Economic History of Britain 1100–1150* (Berkeley, CA: University of CA Press, 1972), 91.

[21] Graves, *History of Education,* 19.

[22] Nicholas Orme, *Education and Society in Medieval and Renaissance England* (London: The Hambledon Press, 1989), 2–3.

[23] David L. Wagner, "The Seven Liberal Arts and Classical Scholarship," in *The Seven Liberal Arts in the Middle Ages,* edited by David L. Wagner (Bloomington, IN: Indiana University Press, 1983), 1.

[24] Ibid., 18.

[25] Graves, *History of Education,* 12.

[26] Ibid., 1.

[27] Arrowood and Eby, *History and Philosophy of Education,* 734.

[28] Shulamith Shahar, *Childhood in the Middle Ages* (New York: Routledge, 1990). See pp. 184–185, which have a wonderful explanation of the uses of monasteries and convents for educational purposes for the nobility.

[29] Ibid., 186.

[30] Gary K. Clabaugh, "A History of Male Attitudes toward Educating Women," *Educational Horizons, 64* (3), Spring 1986, 132.

31 Shirley Kersey, "Medieval Education of Girls and Women," *Educational Horizons, 58* (4), Summer 1980, 190.

32 Marjorie Rowling, *Life in Medieval Times* (New York: Berkley, 1973), 136.

33 Shahar, *Childhood in the Middle Ages,* 162–163.

34 Ibid, 172.

35 Ibid.

36 Marrou, *History of Education in Antiquity,* 332. See the chapter on "Appearance of Christian Schools."

37 Ibid.

38 Eleanor Shipley Duckett, *Alcuin, Friend of Charlemagne: His World and His Work* (New York: Macmillan, 1951), 7.

39 Ibid., 3.

40 Luitpold Wallach, *Alcuin and Charlemagne: Studies in Carolingian History and Literature* (Ithaca NY: Cornell University Press, 1959), 3.

41 Anders Piltz, *The World of Medieval Learning,* translated by David Jones (Totowa NJ: Barnes and Noble, 1981), p. 12.

42 Graves, *History of Education,* 32.

43 Ibid., 31–32.

44 Boyd, *History of Western Education,* 125.

45 Aries, P. (1962). *Centuries of childhood: A social history of family life.* R. Baldick, Trans. New York: Knopf. 140.

46 Denys Hay, *Europe in the Fourteenth and Fifteenth Centuries* (New York: Holt, Rinehart and Winston, 1966), 360–364.

47 Orme, *Education and Society,* 12.

48 Ibid., 6.

49 Ibid.

50 Ibid.

51 JoAnn Hepner Moran Cruz, "Education, Economy, and Clerical Mobility in Late Medieval Northern England," in *Universities and Schooling in Medieval Society,* edited by William J. Courtenay and Jurgen Miethke (Leiden: Brill, 2000), 182.

52 Ibid.

53 Ibid.

54 Piltz, *World of Medieval Learning,* 49.

55 Rowling, *Life in Medieval Times,* 66.

56 Jaeger, 47.

57 Ibid., 48.

58 Aries, 139.

59 Ibid.

60 Jaeger, 47–48.

61 Ibid.

62 Ibid.

63 Rowling, *Life in Medieval Times,* 139–141.

64 Ibid.

65 Ibid.

66 Piltz, *World of Medieval Learning,* 85.

67 Ibid., 86.

68 Ibid.

69 Ibid., 50–51.

70 Cantor, *Civilization of the Middle Ages,* 319–320.

71 Ibid.

72 Ibid., 321.

73 Ibid., 440.

74 Ibid.

75 Ibid., 441.

76 Ibid., 441–442. See also Frank Rexroth, "Ritual and the Creation of Social Knowledge: The Opening Celebrations of Medieval German Universities," in *Universities and Schooling in Medieval Society,* 67.

77 Ibid.

78 Ibid.

79 Martin Kintzinger, "A Profession but Not a Career? Schoolmasters and the Artes in Late Medieval Europe," in *Universities and Schooling in Medieval Society,* 167.

80 Ibid., 181.

81 U.S. Department of Education, "16.7 Million in Character Education Grants Go to States and School Districts," October 23, 2002. Available on the Web at: *http://www.ed.gov.*

82 Ibid.

83 National Center for Education Statistics, Data on Vocational Education (DOVE) Newsletter, January 3, 2004, available on the Web at *http://www.nces.gov/surveys/dove/index.asp.*

84 National Center for Education Statistics, "Trends in High School Occupational Course-taking," available on the Web at *http://www.nces.ed.gov/programs/coe/2001/.*

85 Ibid.

PART 2

Rebirth of Learning: Renaissance and Reformation

Chapter 4

The Renaissance: New Consciousness and Love of Learning (1150–1517)

Learning Objectives

1. Understand the forces (social, economic, political) that led to the start of the Renaissance in Italy.
2. Explain why and how the Renaissance led to a new interest in learning and education.
3. Describe and discuss the philosophy of humanism and its implications for learning.
4. Discuss the types of schools found during the Renaissance and the teaching methods used in these schools.
5. Describe the educational and teaching philosophies of Vittorino da Feltre and Juan Luis Vives and how they are still used today.
6. List and describe the contributions from Renaissance Italy to today's educational system.

INTRODUCTION

In chapter 3 you learned that during the Middle Ages education received a low priority because of the economic, political, religious, and social conditions in Europe after the Roman Empire fell to barbarian invasions. Medieval people did not think, as we do, of going to school to get an education to make more money or to have a better life. You will recall that medieval society did not encourage people to rise above the station in life to which they had been born, because of the belief that it was sinful to better oneself. The church also preached against self-improvement and was distrustful of business practices.

This mind-set changed when the feudal economic system of the Middle Ages began to disintegrate. Economic development occurred when continental trade increased, and large-scale commerce left the land and took to the ships.[1] Guilds of craftsmen in medieval towns needed raw materials to manufacture their products, and town councils and urban republics needed their supplies, so roads were improved and canals widened to accommodate an increase in waterway traffic.[2] Society changed in other ways as well. Travel for both business purposes and pleasure increased. University students in Paris and Bologna traveled in order to attend

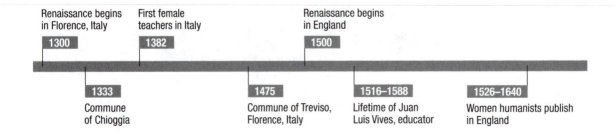

Renaissance begins in Florence, Italy	First female teachers in Italy		Renaissance begins in England		
1300	1382		1500		
	1333	1475	1516–1588	1526–1640	
	Commune of Chioggia	Commune of Treviso, Florence, Italy	Lifetime of Juan Luis Vives, educator	Women humanists publish in England	

school. Masons traveled to erect new buildings, and bankers, kings, and town councils who escorted high-ranking ambassadors from one court to another also traveled for business purposes and for pleasure.[3] This period of time at the end of the Middle Ages is known as the **Renaissance,** meaning "rebirth." In this chapter we concentrate on the rebirth, or renewal, of education in the Renaissance, which occurred within the context of new economic, social, and political developments in society.

The main focus of this chapter is the Renaissance contribution of humanism, which can still be seen in our educational system today.

TIMELINE: SPECIFYING THE DATES

When exactly was the Renaissance? The dates we are using, AD 1150 to 1517, are approximate. The Renaissance also overlapped the Reformation, the subject of chapter 5. The Renaissance began and ended in different parts of Europe depending on the cultural background and social, economic, and political circumstances. In Italy it is believed that the Renaissance began about 1300, and in England, it began in the 1500s and ended about 1660. These dates vary depending on the scholar's discipline. Political historians look for the crucial stages in Europe's transition from medieval forms of political and social organization to those characteristic of the modern world, such as the growth of a civil bureaucracy.[4] The Renaissance reached its peak about 1500 in Italy, which led the way in European cultural life and thought.[5] This chapter focuses primarily on the educational contributions from Renaissance Italy, particularly from Florence, which had an important role as the leading cloth-trading and banking center in Italy.[6] The economic and social growth created by the Florentines' knack for business also extended to growth in education. Furthermore, the Florentines had a great love of art and architecture. Rich Florentines built magnificent villas and adorned their churches and private homes with sculptures and paintings.

Why did the Renaissance begin in Italy, rather than in other parts of Europe? The answer appears to lie in Italy's culture, which was more secularized, despite having more priests and monks than other European countries.[7] This secularized culture freed the study of literature, for instance, from some of the constraints imposed by medieval theologians. Florentine Renaissance scholars also questioned the role of divine intervention in men's lives, contrary to medieval scholars, who believed that most of life's events were preordained. For example, Albertino Mussato, who translated Aristotle's *Politics,* stated that political development in society had nothing to do with divine intervention. It was directly due to men's own actions.[8] Italian scholars also looked at Rome's decline in sociological perspective, believing that it was an example of municipal growth and decay, rather than thinking the decline was divinely ordained.[9]

The Florentines played an important role in shaping Renaissance thought in economics, sociology, politics, and, of course, education. A summary of their achievements is found in the text box.

Because the philosophy of humanism is such an important contribution from the Renaissance, we begin with an examination of its origins.

Spotlight On ◄──

THE RENAISSANCE IN FLORENCE

The Florentines' high level of culture during the Renaissance led to the study of the architecture, art, and sculpture of the classical Greek and Roman artists. Wealthy people sponsored architects to build luxurious villas for them.

Florentines believed they were living in a golden age. The Roman Catholic Church benefited from this renewed interest in art. For instance, Pope Julius II commissioned Raphael to paint *Parnassus* in the Vatican. The guild patronage of early fifteenth-century Florence was very influential in commissioning works of art and sculpture for cathedrals.

PETRARCH

Petrarch is known as the Father of Humanism. He studied the important writings of **St. Augustine,** the author of the *Confessions,* who had been important to medieval theologians. Augustine's theory was that the best way for a man to understand himself and the world around him was to lead a solitary life. Petrarch, however, said that it was not wise to lead an ascetic life of solitude and poverty to attain knowledge. He redefined the ideas of Augustine and Aristotle and propounded the theory that humans are social creatures who cannot fully realize their potential by living solitary lives. They have to interact in groups and have social responsibility and activity.

The answer to the age-old question, What is a truly educated man? changed with the advent of humanism, from an idealized version of a solitary monastic living the contemplative life to a man educated for participation in a social environment. Education, virtue, and civic action became linked, as they had a firm base in the economic, political, and social life of the community.[10]

Petrarch, as well as other humanists such as Pier Paolo Vergerio, Leonardo Bruni, and Maffeo Vegio, who all wrote about the type of education children should have to promote character and an understanding of literary studies, advocated a thorough study of the classics. They felt that by looking at causes of past events, students could learn how to avoid dealing with such events in the future. If they read about a war, for example, and its root in economic problems, they might be able to figure out how to prevent a war in the future by addressing similar existing economic problems. The humanists said that if students were to develop a comprehensive knowledge of the past they had to withdraw from the world to avoid its distractions. This withdrawal from society would be temporary, however, because students were expected to put what they had learned about the past to use in their lives as active men in civic affairs.[11]

Today, the concept of humanism is used in teaching students. For instance, instruction in world history and American history is given so that students understand not only how events of the past shaped the world they live in today but also how to prevent them from happening again. For instance, if World War II and the Nazi Holocaust are studied so that students understand the terrible consequences of intolerance and racist beliefs, they should be encouraged to think about how those concepts are present in their daily lives.

HUMANISM AND THE NATURE OF CHILDHOOD

Humanism was responsible for revised ideas about the nature of childhood. You will recall that children were viewed as "little adults" in the medieval period. The Florentines, particularly, held a different view of the child and the nature of childhood, which translated into new ideas on child-rearing practices as well as educating children. Children were to be educated for a life of civic duty, pleasure in literature, and in the arts, sports, and social gentility.[12] Educators today teach about civic responsibilities and encourage children and adolescents to read literature. Furthermore, sports and the arts are also present in today's schools.

During the Renaissance, children were revered, particularly in Florence. The Florentines had a great desire for children, especially those in the merchant and ruling elite. Large families were common; by 1427, 11 percent of Florence's population lived in households with 10 or more members, and 50 percent lived in households with 6 or more individuals.[13] Books on child-rearing practices were written. A notable one was that of Francesco Barbaro (1390–1454), who wrote a guide on family life for the new wife of Lorenzo de' Medici.[14] This guide contained information on the practice of wet-nursing, or sending the new baby out to be fed by a woman who produced a great deal of milk, to ensure a healthier baby.[15] It was thus recognized that certain practices were necessary to ensure the survival of an infant, at a time when child mortality was high. In fact, books on methods of child rearing and pediatric medicine were composed in the sixteenth century.[16]

During the Florentine Renaissance, Italian medical authors led European scholars in the study of childhood diseases, which often killed children at a very young age. Unfortunately, premodern hygienic practices contributed to these diseases, but there was little recognition of that fact. Nonetheless, that childhood diseases were being studied shows an awareness that certain conditions were specific to childhood.

In the fifteenth century it was recognized that children had certain physical attributes that made it difficult for them to perform in the same way as adults. Medical authors realized that children developed at different rates and that they should not be forced to walk or sit before they were ready.[17] An important recommendation included using child-sized seats, which were available in the fifteenth century.[18] Information was also provided on how to teach children to walk and to prevent accidents. Wet nurses, who played an important role in raising young children, were told to dress children in padded bonnets so that they wouldn't hurt themselves if they fell. The connection between the emergence of teeth and the beginnings of speech was also recognized. Renaissance authors believed that children at the age of 2 should be able to speak because that was when the teeth had appeared; however, they did not understand speech as a developmental progression through phases.

Although late medieval and Renaissance authors realized that childhood was a separate stage, they did not have the specific theoretical constructs that we have today about child development. The prevailing theory of childhood was that children were weak, tender, and vulnerable.[19] It was believed that children under the age of 7 were unable to learn science or morals, subjects that required the use of reason.[20] Instead, they were to be taught the vernacular language. The concept of children as vulnerable doubtless was a consequence of the high child mortality. It was more important to pay attention to the child's physical health than to worry about what he or she was learning at so young an age. Thus, child-rearing practices in the late Middle Ages and the Renaissance differed from ours in that they did not focus as much on the importance of early childhood education.

If children lived to the age of 7, they begin to acquire an education. In elementary schools today, children in the first grade are generally 6 to 7 years old. A major goal of education for boys was to become good businessmen. Early exposure to business practices was a valuable experience for Florentine children. Both boys and girls might act as messengers, delivering payments and other goods to recipients. These experiences gave them an idea as to what a successful worker must be able to do. Boys went into the trades after about the age of 7. Fathers enrolled sons into the guilds and brought them to guild meetings to introduce them to the political, economic, and social structures of Florence.[21]

APPRENTICESHIPS

During the Renaissance, **apprenticeships** were commonly held, especially by urban children. Apprenticeships were considered to be a type of preprofessional training.[22] Girls as young as 8 went into domestic service, and this practice was common in Florence in 1427.[23] They stayed in domestic service until the age of 18, when they usually married. It was also common practice in England to employ girls as household servants beginning at a very young age. Employers were forced to parent such young children as well as serving as their employers, thus taking on a double role.[24] Domestic service was not strictly considered an apprenticeship; the terms of service were negotiated by work contracts determined by the parent or guardian.[25]

Apprenticeships became more popular after the thirteenth century, to limit outsiders. The guilds were influential in this respect, because they wanted to regulate the terms of apprenticeship. In the fourteenth century, as guilds gained political power and developed stricter professional standards, apprenticeships were more commonly required.[26] By the late fifteenth century, a typical requirement of the guilds was that the apprentices be literate. Guilds also required longer periods of apprenticeship and stipulated that children had to be a certain age before they started training.[27]

In France, between 1380 and 1450, in the city of Orleans and its suburbs 63 percent of the 376 apprentices were orphans lacking one or both parents. This condition was even more common among those aged 13 to 15, as 85 percent of them were orphans. Typically, the mother had died, and many of these teenagers arranged

their own apprenticeships. Many came from broken homes in which remarriage may have made their position uncomfortable, and they chose to leave because proper provisions could not be made for them by their families.[28]

Socioeconomic status as well as family stability were crucial factors in determining whether the individuals aged approximately 8 to 15 would enter into apprenticeship training. In the "Bridges" section at the end of this chapter we will examine how the socioeconomic status and family situations of modern youth determine their career choices.

WOMEN HUMANISTS IN THE RENAISSANCE: THE FEMININE VOICE

Although most of the humanists were men, there were some women humanists writing during the Renaissance. From 1526 to 1640, women humanists from England composed or translated more than 100 works that were printed.[29] These women humanists translated religious works, including meditations and prayers. They also translated or composed manuals, such as those intended for expectant mothers. Further literary efforts included books of songs, sonnets, dream visions, or rhymed history. Sixty percent of the works published by female humanists in the Renaissance were prose, and 40 percent were poetry.[30] In general, these female humanists were members of the upper classes, whose families supported education for girls. Their writing styles often lacked self-confidence and were otherwise consistent with their awareness of women's social identity within a highly patriarchal culture.[31] The women humanists who wrote during the time period 1526–1640 were trying to find out how much education they could obtain without being penalized for it. That their works were published is a tribute to their persistence in wanting to learn and in pursuing education as a valuable resource for their lives. The noted woman humanist Christine de Pisan advocated education for girls and women of the nobility.

How best to educate girls in a general sense was considered by two humanist educators, **Vittorino da Feltre** and **Juan Luis Vives,** whose ideas are discussed in the next section. Although there were other humanists of note, such as Guarino and Vergerius, da Feltre and Vives were chosen for inclusion in this chapter because of their ideas on the education of girls (see "Shapers of Education" on page 74).

HUMANIST EDUCATORS VITTORINO DA FELTRE AND JUAN LUIS VIVES

Vittorino da Feltre began the first Italian humanist school during the Renaissance, under the patronage of the Gonzaga court. Keep in mind that during this period most people could not send their children to school, because education was a luxury for the wealthy. The poor did not send their children to school.[32] The schools established by da Feltre focused on training young men in the humanities, defined as a study of the Latin classics, history, rhetoric, grammar, poetry, and moral philosophy. The aim of such a curriculum was to develop the individual's potential for life and for public service. Da Feltre stated that education had to "encourage the life

SHAPERS OF EDUCATION

Juan Luis Vives
(1516–1588)

- Advocated progressive education
- Believed in memory exercises
- Taught study skills and organization
- Held that each student is unique
- Advocated patience with beginning learners
- Propounded education and exercise for both girls and boys

Vittorino da Feltre
(1378–1446)

- Believed education should prepare student for life and public service
- Saw education of girls as highly important
- Believed in exercise for girls as well as boys
- Used manipulatives to study math and the alphabet
- Made subjects relevant to learners to increase their attention and meet their needs

of social duty, all of us are responsible for the personal influence which goes out from us."[33] Students taught at these schools became secretaries, councillors, and ambassadors. Schoolmasters and professors who were interested in learning the humanities also were students at these schools. Italian universities, unlike universities in other places, which had unyielding divinity schools, were quick to accept the new humanistic curriculum.[34]

Although not much information is available on the work of Guarino with regard to education for girls, both da Feltre and Vives were advocates of female education. Da Feltre believed that women and girls should receive a liberal arts education and should be "brought up with all the aids of religion and good example."[35] Girls learned the Psalms and Gospels in class and attended daily Mass with da Feltre, to establish a firm foundation in Christian attitude and habits.[36]

Vittorino da Feltre believed that girls should have physical as well as mental exercise. He believed that exercises increased mental functioning, so girls exercised outdoors for 2 hours daily. They rode horses and did exercises to increase aerobic capacity, such as fencing, leaping, running, and catching balls.[37] His curriculum also included music and the study of Greek and Latin. While teaching Greek and Latin he gave a summary of the author's life to increase students' understanding of and interest in the material.[38] Students in da Feltre's classes read aloud their original essays in Greek or Latin, and they discussed the meaning of their composition when they did so.[39] When teaching arithmetic, da Feltre used colored beads to teach adding and subtracting, and he made alphabet letters from ivory to teach his students the letters of the alphabet in teaching them to read. He also played mathematical games to challenge them and keep them interested. He understood that students could not sit still an entire day without a break and be able to pay

attention, so he alternated 2 hours of study with 2 hours of exercise, with a meal period serving as a break between morning and afternoon classroom routines.[40]

Da Feltre by no means abandoned the traditional rote memorization method of teaching but added other methods to his repertoire, making his approach a more humane and comprehensive one. In addition to using unusual teaching methods, da Feltre did not believe in corporal punishment, which was traditionally used to discipline students. He tried to make learning interesting, enjoyable, and relevant to the students, which is just as important a goal for educators today. Da Feltre may be said to be a humanist educator because he was concerned with the simultaneous development of body, mind, and character, which must occur in harmony.[41] Humanists such as da Feltre believed that subject matter such as the literature of ancient Greece and Rome was important, but they wanted to adapt the study of the past to meet the needs of the present.[42]

Another educator of note was Juan Luis Vives (1516–1588), a Spaniard who was entrusted with the education of Mary Tudor, daughter of King Henry VIII. Vives said that "learning is the truest food of the mind."[43] Considered to be one of the most progressive educators of the Renaissance, Vives advocated that students do what he called "memory exercises" to improve their memory. Students were supposed to do two things before they retired each night, the first being to recall everything they had heard, read, or seen that day. The second was to learn a passage or specific lesson by repeating the words at bedtime and again first thing in the morning. Without such continual exercise of the mind, Vives thought that memory would be lost.[44]

Vives had some interesting ideas that we use today, in terms of teaching study skills and organization. For instance, he told students to carry a notebook with them at all times to assist in memorizing and learning information.[45] Today, we remind students to write everything down, such as their homework assignments, projects, or anything due, in a notebook or homework folder. Vives also recognized, just as we do today, the individual differences among pupils. He wrote that some students are "made and fitted for some things, and very little fitted for others."[46] Vives also admonished teachers not to have too high expectations of students who were just learning. He recommended patience and stated that "he cannot require from a boy, who is beginning, that which he expects from a youth, who has made progress in self-control and moral character."[47] Vives further recommended that "the wise teacher will remember what a difference there is between the beginner, one who is getting on, and the one who is fully accomplished."[48] Teachers today understand the differences in skill levels among beginners, those of intermediate skill, and those of advanced levels and do not have the same expectations of each group. Many centuries later, teachers still use Vives's ideas, although they may not be aware that they do.

Vives had specific ideas for the education of girls. His plan for Mary Tudor emphasized a study of the classics, including the works of Plutarch, Cato the Elder from Rome, Seneca, Erasmus, and Melanchthon.[49] He chose these authors for study because they lived a moral life and could be held up as virtuous role models by an impressionable young girl. Vives's instructional plan also called for lessons

in penmanship, grammar, pronunciation, memorization, vocabulary, and Latin conversation.[50]

Did girls from poorer families receive instruction in such a wide range of academic subjects? No, they did not. Girls from wealthy families were educated in this way because they were to be prepared to be of sound moral principle and to become women who were well suited to matrimony and motherhood as well as intelligent and thoughtful companions. Like Vittorino da Feltre, Vives also thought exercise for girls was important and advocated a strict diet of vegetables and cold water to drink to make them physically strong.[51] Today, physical education is considered just as important for girls as for boys and is a well-established part of the school curriculum.

TYPES OF SCHOOLS IN RENAISSANCE ITALY

The major similarity between schools in Renaissance Italy and schools today is seen in the **communal schools** of Italy, which were sponsored by towns or city governments, much like the federal government is involved in education in today's public schools. In Renaissance Italy the government officials selected the teacher and paid his salary. Government officials also supervised curriculum development. Individual, or private, schools were also found in Renaissance Italy, in which teachers joined with parents to develop a school.[52] An equivalent situation exists in the charter school movement.

Another type of educational situation in Renaissance Italy was home-based schooling. Independent schoolmasters made a living as daily tutors or live-in tutors.[53] Today, school districts provide tutors to instruct home-bound students who are unable to attend school owing to accident or illness. Independent schoolmasters also established their own boarding schools. The humanistic schools of Gasparino Barzizza and Guarino Guarini were famous schools of this type.[54]

Ecclesiastical schools were another form of school in Renaissance Italy. These were sponsored by bishops who acted through cathedral chapters. Religious orders in monasteries also supported such schools, in which clergymen taught lay students as well as clerics. However, as the society became increasingly urbanized and secularized, and its needs changed, monks and nuns were not needed to educate the young. For instance, secretaries, notaries, and public officials were needed in public life. It was thought that the monastic and cathedral schools would not provide students with the proper education to perform such jobs, because these schools had as their major purpose the training and education of novices and future members of the religious order.[55]

The influence of the church declined in society as people began to see the church's teachings as narrow in scope. As we learned in the section on humanism earlier in this chapter, people were learning about their own responsibility in creating their environment and were seeking to solve their problems on their own. This change in thought occurred because the idea that men's lives were not solely predetermined by theological forces took hold.[56]

Communal schools became highly important in the education of professionals in the society of Renaissance Italy. Concern over the literacy of professionals led to the decree of the Commune of Chioggia in 1333, which stated that judges and other civic officials must be able to read and write to secure employment. This requirement greatly increased the importance of obtaining a formal education in Renaissance Italy to acquire the necessary skills to become a professional. Although the use of daily tutors or live-in tutors did not disappear, it became less common as large communal schools were established.

The civic officials in Florence also decided that they could not run schools without qualified teachers. This decision led the **Commune of Treviso** in 1475 to decree that they had to provide capable and well-trained teachers for the good of the city and the children. The common good, seen in civic and moral terms, quickly became the justification for spending communal funds on a teacher. Grammatical instruction for boys was thought to be very important, because knowledge of Latin grammar would benefit the city. The rationale for spending money on training boys this age was that if boys were taught properly, they would not make mistakes when they became businessmen but would have well-established habits of virtue, knowledge, and good behavior.[57]

Discrepancy in educational opportunity existed in Renaissance Florence, just as it does today. Whereas communal schools were concerned mostly with the education of the sons of prominent citizens of Italy, who would govern and administer in future, the majority of students were taught at independent schools or else were not taught at all and were illiterate. The growing working classes, which consisted of artisans, laborers, and small merchants, were viewed as threats to the existing political and social order; the poor were traditionally relegated to an extremely low socioeconomic status. It was impossible to have universal education at this time because of the economic inequalities in society.[58] Today, educators wonder if education is universal, because of the social and economic inequalities in society that are mirrored in the schools.

One important similarity between the schools of Renaissance Italy and modern-day schools lies in the educational philosophy that a well-trained, virtuous teacher will make a great difference in the lives of youth. Certain essential qualities and qualifications are needed to teach. Just as the credentials of teachers today are scrutinized, so were those of schoolmasters in Renaissance Italy, especially if they were from out of town, before they were allowed to teach. Renewable contracts, known as the **condotta,** were given, for terms of 1, 2, 3, or 5 years. As in modern times, teachers were not paid as well as other professionals in society, such as lawyers, physicians, or university professors. Even wealthy merchants during the Renaissance had higher incomes than teachers, earning hundreds of thousands of ducats, much more than teachers could ever hope to make.[59] Teachers today who are concerned about salaries should realize that such concern dates to the Renaissance!

Another important similarity between today's schools and those of Renaissance Italy lies in the use of female teachers, which began, to a limited extent, during the Renaissance. Table 4-1 summarizes the educational philosophy in the Renaissance compared with that today.

Table 4-1   **Educational Philosophy: Renaissance Education Versus Education Today**

RENAISSANCE EDUCATION	MODERN EDUCATION
Philosophy of humanism was used to teach students to be active and to apply what they had learned.	Fosters students' problem-solving skills.
Communal schools	Public schools
Condotta (renewable contracts)	Teacher contracts
Apprenticeships	Vocational training
Education for girls and women was debated.	Girls and women are educated.
Forbade corporal punishment in schools.	Corporal punishment is not allowed in schools.
Promoted character education through study of the classics.	Moral education and values clarification are part of curriculum.
Studied history to avoid making same mistakes as predecessors.	History is studied to help prevent intolerance and prejudice.
Civic responsibility	Citizenship education
Made education relevant to students.	Relevancy is needed to keep students interested.

FEMALE TEACHERS IN THE RENAISSANCE

Today, the overwhelming number of elementary school teachers are female. In the Renaissance, women also taught in the elementary grades. In late 1585 or 1586 a Venetian woman named Marieta opened a school. She taught elementary Latin grammar, some abbaco (math skills), and vernacular texts to a small group of eight boys and girls.[60]

Tax records show that female teachers existed for more than 300 years, with the first female teachers in Italy documented in 1382 and 1383. About 20 other female teachers declared taxes between 1409 and 1585. They ranged in age from 18 to 87 and were usually unmarried. In Verona in 1555, women made up 24 percent of all teachers. Because salaries were so low, some female teachers might not have been counted among the teaching population and escaped taxation, so it is possible the figure was higher.[61] The female teachers in Renaissance Italy, France, and England were all from the middle or upper classes, and they acquired an education in the vernacular language that was sufficient to prepare them for their expected roles as wives and mothers; they did not receive a classical Latin education. They taught reading and writing in the vernacular language, not in Latin, to their students.[62]

Today, more elementary school teachers are male, but the ratio of females to males in elementary school teaching is still highly skewed in favor of female teachers. Educational administrators and education policy makers are concerned that the lack of male elementary teachers during a child's formative years may deprive children of important male role models lacking in a child's life and are highly in favor of hiring more male teachers for elementary school children.[63]

BRIDGES FROM THE PAST TO THE PRESENT: VALUE AND USES OF CONTRIBUTIONS OF THE RENAISSANCE TO EDUCATION TODAY

The major contribution to education from the Renaissance is the philosophy of humanism. The noted Renaissance scholar Paul Oskar Kristeller has commented that the philosophy of humanism left a lasting impression. It established the *humanities,* which is defined as a broad area of secular learning and thought based on the classics, which are independent of, but not necessarily contrary to, both theology and the sciences.[64] Kristeller also points out that the Renaissance humanists provided us with a professional background on which to build as educators.[65] Students in high schools today study history, philosophy, and literature. Reading the Greek plays and studying the sciences and mathematics are part of the high school curriculum for college-bound students.

Educators and physicians today recognize that children develop at different rates, and that certain physical attributes make it impossible for children to do some of the things adults do. This is a direct contribution from the Renaissance humanists of the fifteenth century. They lacked the theoretical understanding we have today about child development as being a progression of stages, but they nonetheless had some of the same ideas we have about rearing young children, such as using child-sized seats and protecting young children from falling.

One major difference between the child-rearing ideas of the humanists of the Renaissance and our ideas today is the emphasis on early childhood education. Renaissance thinkers were more concerned about children's physical health than their learning, because the child mortality rate was so high that keeping them alive was the most important concern. Today, parents are concerned with learning from an early age. In fact, specific tests to determine problems with learning in infancy, such as the Bayley Scales of Infant Development, first developed in 1969, are used to test infants whose development seems to be lagging.

Humanists such as da Feltre and Vives made important contributions to today's education, such as varying teaching methods to increase interest and student understanding of the material, and having students write compositions and present them. Da Feltre also introduced the use of manipulatives such as colored beads in teaching arithmetic, and alphabet letters from ivory in teaching reading.

Educators today are concerned that students learn how to study. This was an issue for Renaissance educators such as Vives, who, as you recall, had students write information to be learned in a notebook, to aid in recalling it. Today, teachers incorporate the teaching of study skills into their lesson plans.

Physical education is another contribution from the Renaissance humanists. Da Feltre and Vives, as you learned, thought that exercise would strengthen the body, and educators today recognize that physical education is an important part of an integrated curriculum. It is believed today that girls should be given experiences in physical education that emphasize their potential for physical fitness and bodily competence.[66]

The idea of apprenticeship, in which a student studies a trade such as carpentry under a master, is reflected in today's vocational curricula, which are important in preparing students to find productive jobs. For example, the U.S. Department of

Labor predicts that 1 million new jobs will be available for skilled construction workers by 2005.[67] To prepare students for jobs in the construction industry, the National Center for Construction Education and Research (NCCER) has developed standardized curricula for training in construction. A workforce career path is available for youth who want to go into construction work. Apprenticeships are available at both the high school and technical college level in this field.[68] For students who cannot afford to attend college and want to get a job without amassing student loan debt, apprenticeship training can be a valuable investment in their futures.[69]

SUMMARY

This chapter focused on the contributions to our educational system from Renaissance Italy, a country that was more culturally advanced than other parts of Europe, partly because of its more secularized and urbanized society. Florence in particular had great success in developing a literate and cultivated society that prized art and saw great achievements in architecture, medicine, and law. An educated person in Florence was knowledgeable in all these areas.

The secularization of society, emphasis on literacy, and an understanding of child-rearing practices and individual differences in learning and child development all significantly affected education. A decline in the number of monastic schools and the emphasis on secularized learning are reflected in our current educational system, which is largely secularized, with a separation of church and state in the public schools. The communal schools of Italy, sponsored by the town or city governments, and the involvement of the state in education are reflected in today's educational system, in which there is federal, state, and local control of education.

With an increasingly secularized society, and an emphasis on learning, a new critical consciousness arose. People during this time were more willing to criticize the injustices they perceived in society, including the socioeconomic discrepancies they felt were unfair. Chapter 5 discusses how this new awareness influenced the educational system during the time period known as the Reformation.

QUESTIONS FOR DISCUSSION

1. Discuss the role of secular values in Renaissance society and how they perpetuated social change. What kinds of values are present in our society, and how have they contributed to social change?

2. How did the change in economic base shape the view of education in Florence during the Renaissance?

3. The Renaissance scholars learned to view past events differently. Rather than think of the decline of Rome as preordained, they looked at it in terms of mu-

nicipal decay. How do we attribute events in our world today, to divine intervention or to human error? Give at least one example to back up your opinion.

4. Discuss the attitudes of Florentine parents toward their children. Do you believe parents today have this attitude toward their children? Why or why not?

5. Discuss the educational philosophies of Vittorino da Feltre and Juan Luis Vives on education for girls. How do these philosophies compare/contrast with today's education for girls? Do you believe that girls today need a special type of education to succeed, because of gender inequalities? Why or why not?

6. How did the concept of a "truly educated man" change from the medieval period to the Renaissance? Do we have this same concept of a "truly educated man" today? Why or why not?

7. Humanistic learning was intended to enhance people's understanding of everyday problems. Do you believe that today's school curricula enable students to do this? Why or why not? Give at least one example to support your answer.

SUGGESTED ACTIVITIES

1. Choose one of the humanistic theorists (Erasmus, Petrarch, Ascham, da Feltre, or Vives) and assume the personality of that theorist. Based on the beliefs of the character you assume, write a letter explaining your beliefs about education, and why you feel a certain type of education is necessary.

2. As a Renaissance schoolboy (or girl who is receiving an education) write a diary entry about what you are studying and your feelings toward it. Be sure to remember that you are writing during the Renaissance, *not* the present day!

3. As a Renaissance parent, write a letter to your son who is about to go off to school, explaining the importance of studying the classics (the humanists' works) and how they will benefit him in future.

4. Research the life and works of Michelangelo or one of the other important artists during the Renaissance. Prepare a short (3–4 pages) report with the highlights of that person's life, and how he or she contributed to education and culture during the Renaissance. Present the report in the form of a 15- to 20-minute PowerPoint presentation.

5. List all the differences and similarities you can think of between the Renaissance and medieval periods. Be prepared to share the list with your classmates.

6. Compare and contrast Renaissance accomplishments and developments in Italy with those in England. In a 15- to 20-minute PowerPoint presentation, explain to your classmates the similarities and differences between these two countries, specifically the differences in art, architecture, medicine, and education. Explain how the culture and society of each country contributed to the developments in that country.

Bibliography

Blade, M. K. (1983). *Education of Italian Renaissance women.* Mesquite, TX: Ide House.

Diefendorf, B. (1987). Family culture, Renaissance culture. *Renaissance Quarterly, 40*(4), 661–81.

Charlton, K. (1965). *Education in Renaissance England.* London: Routledge and Kegan Paul.

Clements, R. J., & Levant L. (Eds.). (1976). *Renaissance letters: Revelations of a world reborn.* New York: New York University Press.

Cook, J. (1994, March) The curriculum conundrum. *Teaching K–8,* 32–33.

Cutshall, S. (2001). Practical applications. *Techniques: Connecting Education and Careers,* 76(8), 22–25.

Green, V. H. H. (1965). *Renaissance and Reformation: A survey of European history between 1450 and 1660.* London: Edward Arnold.

Grendler, P. F. (1990). Schooling in Western Europe. *Renaissance Quarterly, 43*(4), 775–87.

Gundersheimer, W. L. (Ed.). (1965). *The Italian Renaissance.* Upper Saddle River, NJ: Prentice Hall.

Hay, D. (1962). *Europe in the fourteenth and fifteenth centuries.* New York: Holt, Rinehart and Winston.

Hill, D. (1996, September 11). Odd man out. *Education Week.*

Honeyman, K., & Goodman, J. (1991). Women's work, gender conflict, and labour markets in Europe, 1500–1900. *Economic History Review, 44*(4), 608–28.

Kallendorf, G. (1987). Ancient, Renaissance, and modern: The human in the humanities. *Journal of General Education, 39*(3), 133–51.

Kristeller, P. O. (1962). Studies on Renaissance humanism during the last twenty years. *Studies in the Renaissance, 9,* 7–30.

Mazzeo, J. A. (1965). *Renaissance and revolution: The remaking of European thought.* New York: Pantheon Books.

Mee, C. L. (1969). *Lorenzo de' Medici and the Renaissance.* New York: Harper and Row.

Nicholas, D. (1995). Child and adolescent labour in the late medieval city: A Flemish model in regional perspective. *English Historical Review, 110*(439), 1103–31.

Satina, B., & Hultgren, F. (2001). The absent body of girls made visible: Embodiment as the focus in education. *Studies in Philosophy and Education, 20,* 523–24

Shahar, S. (1990). *Childhood in the Middle Ages.* New York: Routledge.

Tebeaux, E., & Lay, M. M. (1995). The emergence of the feminine voice, 1526–1640: The earliest published books By English Renaissance women. *Journal of Composition Theory, 15*(1), 53–81.

U.S. Department of Education, Entering the teacher pipeline. Report on the demographics of prospective teachers. Retrieved from http://www.nces.ed.gov 2003–2004.

U.S. Department of Education, *Education Statistics Quarterly* Vol. 2, Issue 1. Progress through the teacher pipeline: 1992–93 college graduates and Elementary/Secondary School Teaching as of 1997. Robin R. Henke, Xianglei Chen, Sonya Geis, Paula Knepper. Retrieved from website 2004. http://www.nces.ed.gov

Watson, F. (1913). *Vives on education: A translation of the* De Tradendis Disciplinis *of Juan Luis Vives* (F. Watson, Intro. & Trans.) Cambridge: Cambridge University Press.

Weinstein, D. (Ed.). (1965). *The Renaissance and the Reformation 1300–1600.* New York: Free Press.

Weller, A. S. (1983). "Humanism and humanitarianism before the Renaissance. *Journal of Aesthetic Education,* 17(4), 13–40.

Suggestions for Further Reading

In addition to the works cited in the bibliography, the following are suggested for further reading.

Black, R. (2001). *Humanism and education in medieval and Renaissance Italy: Tradition and innovation in Latin schools from the twelfth to the fifteenth century.* Cambridge: Cambridge University Press.

Grendler, P. F. (1989). *Schooling in Renaissance Italy: Literacy and learning, 1300–1600.* Baltimore: Johns Hopkins University Press.

Haas, L. (1998). *The Renaissance man and his children: Childbirth and early childhood in Florence, 1300–1600.* New York: St. Martin's Press.

Woodward, W. H. (1963). *Vittorino da Feltre and other humanist educators.* New York: Teachers College Publications.

Relevant Web Sites

Annenberg/Learner.org *http://www.learner.org/exhibits/renaissance/* Interactive Web site on the Renaissance in Italy.

Education during the European Renaissance *http://education.umn.edu/EdPA/iconics/reading%20room/6.htm* A wonderful site with many resources on education in the European Renaissance, geographic information, maps, and the like.

Education Week *http://www.edweek.org* Weekly periodical that provides updated information on education, federal, and state policies, and so forth.

Web Museum, Paris *http://www.ibiblio.org* Explanation of the Renaissance as a historical period, information on Renaissance social thought, philosophy, and science, and resources.

Renaissance and Reformation: A Survey of European History between 1450 and 1660 *http://www.questia.com/library/history/european-history/medieval-&-renaissance-europe/renaissance.jsp* Links to books such as William Henry Hudson (1912) on the Renaissance. All books/resources are online.

National Center for Education Statistics *http://www.nces.ed.gov* Federal and state data on education.

U.S. Department of Education *http://www.ed.gov* Home page of the U.S. Department of Education.

Endnotes

[1] Denys Hay, *Europe in the Fourteenth and Fifteenth Centuries* (New York: Holt, Rinehart and Winston, 1962), 360.

[2] Ibid.

[3] Ibid., 374.

[4] Joseph Anthony Mazzeo, *Renaissance and Revolution: The Remaking of European Thought* (New York: Pantheon Books, 1965), 4.

[5] Ibid.

[6] Charles L. Mee, *Lorenzo de' Medici and the Renaissance* (New York: Harper and Row, 1969), 15–16.

[7] Vivian H. H. Green, *Renaissance and Reformation: A Survey of European History between 1450 and 1660* (London: Edward Arnold, 1965), 29.

[8] Donald Weinstein, Ed. The Renaissance and the Reformation, 1300–1600 (New York: Free Press, 1965), 6.

[9] Ibid.

[10] Kenneth Charlton, *Education in Renaissance England* (London: Routledge and Kegan Paul, 1965), 26.

[11] Greg Kallendorf, "Ancient, Renaissance, and Modern: The Human in the Humanities," *Journal of General Education, 39,* no. 3 (1987), 135–38.

[12] Werner L. Gundersheimer, Ed. *The Italian Renaissance* (Upper Saddle River, NJ: Prentice Hall, 1965), 7.

[13] Louis Haas, *The Renaissance Man and His Children: Childbirth and Early Childhood in Florence, 1300–1600* (New York: St. Martin's Press, 1998), 12.

[14] Ibid., 20.

[15] Ibid.

[16] Shulamith Shahar, *Childhood in the Middle Ages* (New York: Routledge, 1990), 77.

[17] Ibid., 92.

[18] Ibid.

[19] Ibid., 100.

[20] Ibid.

[21] Grendler, 179. See *Schooling in Renaissance Italy: Literacy and Learning, 1300–1600.*

[22] David Nicholas, "Child and Adolescent Labour in the Late Medieval City: A Flemish Model in Regional Perspective," *English Historical Review, 110,* no. 439 (1995), 1103.

[23] Ibid., 1105.

[24] Ibid.

[25] Ibid., 1106.

[26] Ibid., 1107.

[27] Ibid., 1108.

[28] Ibid., 1109–10.

[29] Elizabeth Tebeaux & Mary M. Lay, "The Emergence of the Feminine Voice, 1526–1640: The Earliest Published Books By English Renaissance Women," *Journal of Composition Theory, 15,* no. 1 (1995), 53–54.

[30] Ibid.

[31] Ibid., 56–57.

[32] Gundersheimer, *Italian Renaissance, 7.*

[33] Hay, *Europe, 351.*

[34] Ibid., 352.

[35] Melinda K. Blade, *Education of Italian Renaissance Women* (Mesquite, TX: Ide House, 1983), 43. Blade also includes some excellent quotes from da Feltre and Vives.

[36] Ibid.

37 Ibid., 44.

38 Ibid.

39 Ibid., 45.

40 Ibid., 45.

41 William Harrison Woodward, *Vittorino da Feltre and Other Humanist Educators* (New York: Teachers College Publications, 1963), 36–37.

42 Ibid., 37–38.

43 Ibid., 48.

44 Ibid., 49.

45 Ibid., 50–51.

46 Foster Watson, *Vives on Education: A Translation of the* De Tradendis Disciplinis *of Juan Luis Vives,* intro. and trans. Foster Watson (Cambridge: Cambridge University Press, 1913), 79. This is part of chapter 3, book 2.

47 Ibid., 118.

48 Ibid.

49 Erasmus and Melanchthon are mentioned in detail in chapter 5.

50 Blade, *Education,* 52–53.

51 Ibid.

52 Paul F. Grendler, *Schooling in Renaissance Italy: Literacy and Learning, 1300–1600* (Baltimore: Johns Hopkins University Press, 1989), 3.

53 Ibid.

54 Grendler, "Education in the Renaissance and Reformation," *Renaissance Quarterly, 43,* no. 4 (1990), 775.

55 Grendler, *Schooling in Renaissance Italy,* 7–9.

56 Ibid., 11. See also Hay, *Europe,* 33.

57 Grendler, *Schooling in Renaissance Italy,* 18.

58 Ibid., 21–22. This book has been cited extensively because it is such an excellent source for understanding how schools and education developed in Renaissance Italy and what contributions they made to today's education. See also Grendler, "Education in the Renaissance and Reformation."

59 Ibid., 18.

60 Ibid., 91.

61 Grendler, *Schooling in Renaissance Italy,* 92.

62 Grendler, "Education in the Renaissance and Reformation," 784–85.

63 David Hill, "Odd Man Out," *Education Week* (September 11, 1996). Available on the Web at http://www.edweek.org Hill notes that most secondary school teachers are men, whereas most elementary school teachers are women. This gender discrepancy dates to the feminization of the teaching profession, which began in the United States when the common school movement began in the nineteenth century.

[64] Paul Oskar Kristeller, "Studies on Renaissance Humanism during the Last Twenty Years," *Studies in the Renaissance 9* (1962), 22.

[65] Ibid., 23.

[66] Barbara Satina & Francine Hultgren, "The Absent Body of Girls Made Visible: Embodiment as the Focus in Education," *Studies in Philosophy and Education, 20,* 6(2001), 523–24.

[67] Sandy Cutshall, "Practical Applications," *Techniques: Connecting Education and Careers, 76,* no. 8 (2001), 23.

[68] Ibid.

[69] Ibid.

Chapter 5

The German Reformation: Social Enlightenment and Reform (1517–1537)

Learning Objectives

1. List and discuss the conditions in society that led to the Reformation in Germany.
2. Describe how new inventions such as the printing press led to an increase in learning.
3. Describe the work of Martin Luther, Philipp Melanchthon, and John Amos Comenius in promoting education.
4. Explain how the concern with literacy in Reformation Germany parallels modern-day concern with literacy.
5. List the similarities and differences between education in Reformation Germany and education today.

INTRODUCTION

This chapter focuses on the educational contributions from Germany during the time of the Reformation. This period in European history, characterized by religious fervor as well as a critical examination of the problems of the Church, was one of many changes. People began to question whether the practices of the Church benefited the population or only those in power. They also began to express dissatisfaction with the problems in society. The printing press was invented, and documents criticizing the Church were published in the people's native language and made widely available. The invention of the printing press also made universal public schooling a practical reality. The comprehensive system of compulsory education that we have today largely owes its beginnings to the printing press, which allowed for the distribution of knowledge.[1]

Martin Luther, whose criticism of Church practices and insistence on literacy for all, was a leader in the German Reformation. With his insistence on schooling for all, children received the basic skills, especially literacy, that they needed to succeed. The contributions of two other important educators to our educational system, Philipp Melanchthon and John Amos Comenius, are also described. Melanchthon was a colleague of Luther's, and John Amos Comenius was a Czech

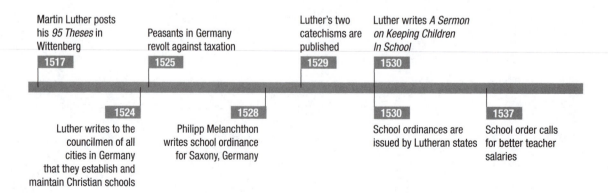

Martin Luther posts his *95 Theses* in Wittenberg
1517

Luther writes to the councilmen of all cities in Germany that they establish and maintain Christian schools
1524

Peasants in Germany revolt against taxation
1525

Philipp Melanchthon writes school ordinance for Saxony, Germany
1528

Luther's two catechisms are published
1529

Luther writes *A Sermon on Keeping Children In School*
1530

School ordinances are issued by Lutheran states
1530

School order calls for better teacher salaries
1537

who insisted upon educational reform to improve the lives and educational possibilities available for youth.

Comenius also wrote about the importance of early childhood education, which educators today believe is vitally important in helping children learn to read at early ages, and in preparing them for kindergarten and first grade in school.[2]

Insistence on mandatory educational practices in the pro-Lutheran territories was supposed to have a socially and religiously unifying effect on German society.[3] The form of compulsory education mandated by the German government was a precursor to modern-day compulsory education laws imposed by the federal government.

The Reformation later spread to England and also affected education there. The impact of the Reformation on England and the contributions from the English Reformation to today's educational system are the subject of chapter 6.

The Reformation was caused by a shift in thinking and a rise in critical consciousness. We now examine exactly why this change in thought occurred.

DEFINITION OF THE REFORMATION: ROOTS OF DISCONTENT

Although the Reformation is popularly thought to have begun in Germany, discontent with the discrepancies between the lives of the rich and the poor in society had its roots in the High Middle Ages. At that time, you will recall, some of the basic medieval concepts, such as not trying to improve one's station in life because it was predestined, began to disappear. Calls for reform in society may date to the year 1200.[4]

SHAPERS OF EDUCATION

Martin Luther (1483–1546)	Philipp Melanchthon (1497–1560)	John Amos Comenius (1592–1670)
■ Insisted on literacy for all, including clergy. ■ Superstition did not belong in an age of advancement. ■ Instruction had to be short and simple, and subject matter had to be sequenced appropriately, from simple to more advanced. ■ The most talented students should go on to university and then to a position in law or government. ■ General education was necessary for those not intended for higher education. ■ Recommended play for children. ■ Did not believe in corporal punishment.	■ Mandated qualifications for teachers and recommended that schools be visited and supervised by authorities. ■ Learning goals should be standardized. ■ Curricula should be supervised by the government. ■ Humanistic studies, including Latin and Greek, should be part of the university curriculum. ■ Parents were incapable of educating their children; children must be educated by professionals.	■ Children and youth will suffer if taught by incompetent teachers. ■ The way to realize children's potential is through early childhood education. ■ Advocated training in diet, hygiene, kindness, and respect towards elders. ■ Children, before the age of 6, should be able to understand the difference between a question and an answer.

The hallmark of the Reformation was the new awareness of the corruption in the Roman Catholic Church. It was recognized that clergy were often very wealthy and held multiple offices. Some priests might have had as many as three or four separate offices, to which they were appointed through influential connections, not because of academic background and training. For example, an illiterate priest who did not know Latin, the language in which Mass was said, was heard mumbling incoherently through his prayers at the altar. Despite his lack of knowledge of Latin, he had been ordained to the priesthood.[5] Thus, the idea that a person must have the proper qualifications for a job arose in the Reformation. Today, this idea has taken firm root in education. Teachers, for instance, must provide their college transcripts to prospective employers before being offered a teaching position, to verify that they do indeed have the appropriate training.

In pre-Reformation Germany, Martin Luther made tremendous efforts to stop corrupt practices in the Church and to increase literacy among the lay population. One particular practice he thought was highly corrupt was the selling of **indulgences,** or prayers for forgiveness; one could thus "buy" forgiveness, so that one's soul would not go to purgatory. Luther was so outraged at this practice that he posted his *95 Theses* on the door of the Wittenberg castle church in 1517.[6]

Luther certainly had much to be upset about, with the many reports of corrupt behavior that had surfaced. Such behavior as public drunkenness and breaking the vow of celibacy were unacceptable among the clergy. Clergy members were even known to keep concubines.[7]

A further issue on Luther's mind was literacy. Many priests during this time were poorly educated, knowing only the elements of Latin and basic catechismal theology. This situation gave even more credibility to the idea that the church was no longer a good role model. People looked up to clergy members as those who did the right thing and always had exemplary conduct, and reports of improper behavior fueled the discontent people felt during the Reformation. The Reformation was, above all,

Spotlight On ◄─────────────────────────────────

SUPERSTITIONS OF THE PEASANTRY

The peasants in both Germany and England were very dependent on the Church for advice on how to live their lives. Asking priests to pray for their souls and donating gifts to churches or guilds were ways in which people, afraid of what would happen after death, could be reassured about the state of their souls. Gilded, painted, or clothed images of the Madonna were reassuring to those who believed that they could have contact with the spiritual world if three-dimensional images of wood or stone were provided in the church.

Reformers complained that money was spent lavishly on crosses, holy-water sprinklers, vestments, altar cloths, chalices, crosses, and candlesticks and that these objects were a way of practicing a superficial form of religion; however, Reformation historians believe that such items may have served as visual images for the illiterate.

a rejection of papal and priestly authority.[8] Papal authority was already in jeopardy; it had diminished after the Roman Empire fell, and the government of the Church was controlled by kings and the aristocracy of nobles and bishops. Enormous wealth was concentrated in the hands of a few, and religious matters were of less importance than accumulating wealth and the pursuit of self-interest.[9]

Reformers such as Martin Luther were disturbed because they saw that although society was growing more advanced, with such inventions as the magnetic compass and gunpowder, many individuals were still clinging to the old ways. Despite new knowledge and a rediscovery of the value of classical works, the peasantry continued to follow superstitious beliefs in their daily lives. They believed in witches and went on grueling pilgrimages to saints' shrines. It is even reported that some of them went so far as to consume the dust from saints' tombs.[10] Middle-class humanists during the Reformation, who were more literate, were horrified at the lack of education and superstition among the peasantry. They felt that with increasing literacy, the superstitious beliefs of the people would eventually decrease.

FORCES OF CHANGE DURING THE REFORMATION

By the year 1500 the population in Germany had risen to 20 million, but most still resided in villages with fewer than 1000 people. With poor agricultural methods and less land on which to raise livestock and crops, the increased population of peasants was unable to make a profit and became unable to pay taxes.[11]

Heavy taxation had traditionally been used to oppress the peasantry, and restrictions such as taxes when individuals of politically distinct territories married made the peasantry increasingly upset.[12] The educational developments of the Reformation are linked to the economic conditions in society at that time. Social reform was envisioned by Luther and others to correct the social inequalities they saw.

The educational developments of the Reformation in Europe are linked to the growth and development of towns, the rise of commerce, and the Crusades, as well as to the changing conception of the monarchy. More effective government was increasingly seen as the way to solve problems.

Modern historians point out that it is impossible to decide whether the Reformation occurred because of political, economic, social, or religious forces, as the sixteenth century was a period in which church and state were inseparable and even indistinguishable.[13]

Max Steinmetz, a Marxist historian, points out that Germany was the site of reform because it was the chief object of exploitation by the papal church, and at all levels of society the Lutheran aspirations grew into a national movement that touched all classes of the German people.[14] Most historians feel that an increasingly growing middle class, combined with an increasingly impoverished peasantry and laboring class, was a prime cause of the Reformation. This change in class system, combined with a deteriorating economic situation of overpopulation and an inefficient and outmoded system of food production, was responsible for the increased support of Lutheranism and the Peasant Rebellion of 1525.[15]

The importance of the Reformation is that it represented an attempt by the population to change conditions they felt were extremely inequitable and unfair.

The shift in emphasis from the clerical and theological to the secular in society is a key feature of the Reformation. Although the Church and religion remained powerful influences, their control was indeed lessened over time.[16]

LITERACY FOR THE MASSES: INVENTION OF THE PRINTING PRESS

An important catalyst in the change process that occurred during the Reformation was the invention of the printing press, which made it possible to disseminate information to the general population, especially since Luther's insistence on literacy had gained momentum and acceptance. The printers themselves played an important role in the Reformation, because they were often well educated, skilled, and versatile.[17] It is unlikely that the Reformation would have occurred without the printed copies of Luther's sermons, essays, and biblical translations that were circulated.[18]

The printing press was invented in Mainz, Germany, by **Johannes Gensfleisch zur Laden zum Gutenberg,** between 1448 and 1451. His first book off the press was a Latin Bible that was printed between 1452 and 1455. Ultimately, 200 copies of this volume were printed. In 1457, Furst and Schoffer, Gutenberg's business partners, produced a Latin psalter.

The use of the press spread rapidly: at the University of Cologne, the first book was printed in 1466; in 1479 the first Dutch Bible was printed in Cologne.[19]

The printing industry went through its early development from 1450 to 1500. During that period families began to read more routinely, and households contained such books as the Bible and volumes on conduct and domestic affairs. Calendars and flyers that advertised upcoming community and regional events, and popular herbal manuals, were increasingly found in peasant households. The Bible was published in the vernacular, not Latin, which made more individuals interested in reading it.[20]

The use of the printing press was key to spreading Luther's ideas as well as the new theology of Protestantism. His insistence on printing items in the vernacular enabled those who could not read Latin to be able to understand the pamphlets and other printed material that were circulating. His ideas on education and child-rearing and his criticism of the Church were published in a format that was easy to read and understand. A survey of pamphlets either by or about Luther in the City and University Library in Frankfurt am Main, Germany, revealed that 457 of these pamphlets were printed.[21]

THE EFFECTS OF THE PRINTING PRESS ON CHILD-REARING PRACTICES

During the Reformation the issue of child rearing became of concern to many when pamphlets on the subject as well as on child care, health care, domestic conduct, and household management were published and distributed. Previously only of concern to women, the issue of child-care practices became a concern of men. A major change in rearing young children was an understanding that young children, including infants, are sensitive to physical discomfort. It was previously thought that infants were insensitive to physical discomfort, and so they were wrapped tightly in swaddling bands, which restricted the movement of their limbs.[22]

With the publication of many ideas on child-rearing practices, the oral stories that were passed down from generation to generation became used less frequently. Traditionally, information about child-rearing practices, including wet-nursing, play, and health care, was passed down orally by women, who had a low level of literacy. When a story is passed down through generations it can become distorted, and the information can become incorrect. Parents and caregivers could now read the printed pamphlets for themselves and not have to depend on someone else's memory. The pamphlets also gave parents access to new ideas that were previously unmentioned or untaught.

One of these ideas concerning the raising of children was the concept of compulsory education. The Lutheran movement emphasized compulsory childhood education because it was believed that reform efforts for society depended on the proper training of children.[23] The reformed Christian social order could be obtained only if childhood and youth practices were reformed as well, and education was seen as the way in which to accomplish this. In 1530 Luther wrote the pamphlet *A Sermon on Keeping Children in School,* which called on all parents to send their children to school.[24] As you will learn in the following section, Luther wrote a great deal about the importance of literacy and keeping children in school, and was a strong advocate for academic learning.

MARTIN LUTHER: CATALYST FOR EDUCATIONAL CHANGE

Martin Luther was a prolific writer, and his writings had a great effect on educational reform. In addition to the pamphlet *A Sermon on Keeping Children in School,* Luther also wrote *An Admonition to the Councillors of all German Cities to Establish and Maintain Christian Schools,* in 1524.[25] According to Luther, both boys and girls had to be sent to school to learn to read and write. The major purpose of a general education was to identify the most talented students and help them progress to a university education and on to careers in the church and government.[26] Luther did acknowledge the necessity for vernacular schools, which taught those who were not of the upper classes, both in rural and urban areas.[27] Luther and his followers believed that reading, writing, and religion should be taught in these schools, because youth should be familiar with the Holy Gospel.[28] He published two catechisms in 1529, which were thought to be the safest and most reliable method of teaching the masses what they needed to know about religion. School ordinances issued by all the Lutheran states about 1530 were specific in their ideas about what was to be taught, and how and why. The catechisms were used widely for the purpose of religious instruction in the school population at large.[29] Catechisms were available in sizes and grades for all ages and developmental levels. Students usually memorized them and repeated them, a process that was supposed to ensure correct

Spotlight On

MARTIN LUTHER (1483–1546)

Martin Luther was born in Eisleben, a copper mining town near Germany's Harz Mountains. His father was a miner by trade, and they moved when Luther was eight, to Mansfield, where the Luthers were highly respected. Luther's father was a mine owner and was an official in the town council.

As a youngster Luther had a difficult relationship with his father, who was extremely harsh and used corporal punishment. This may have made Luther rethink some of his ideas on how children should be treated. He was concerned with the well-being of the whole child, including his or her emotional state. This concern for an individual's well-being was displayed later in his life, as a professor at Wittenberg. He contacted the Elector John Frederick to help the poorest students, who could not afford to attend, obtain some financial assistance. Throughout his life Luther advocated for his students, writing some 4,211 letters, which often concerned his students' physical and social welfare.

thought patterns.[30] The catechism was taught by drill and recitation because the population was still minimally literate.[31]

Luther also wrote on the value of play, the issue of corporal punishment, and parenting practices, which were partly a reflection of his own childhood experiences. He advocated a more judicious use of corporal punishment than he had received during his own childhood.[32] He also used his observations of religious education in various German communities from 1527 to 1528. He believed that certain principles were necessary for effective instruction, especially when the learners had no prior education. For instance, he stated that instruction had to be short and simple and that the subject matter had to be sequenced appropriately, from simple to more advanced. Luther believed that people would be unable to remember or recall most of what they had learned unless it was structured in the proper manner.[33] This is the same philosophy in use in teaching today, for teachers are concerned about proper sequencing of material as well as using developmentally appropriate materials.

As a professor at Wittenberg, where he taught for 30 years and was a highly respected member of the faculty, Luther advocated a complete reform of the curricula in the universities of Germany. He called for a revised curriculum that included the study of the Bible, theology, mathematics, history, and the study of Latin, Greek, and Hebrew.[34] Luther saw no use in the work of Aristotle and recommended that students not read his writings, calling Aristotle a "defunct pagan."[35] The universities had to be reformed, or, as Luther stated, they would become "places for the exercise for youth, and for the Greekish fashion."[36] Women were not included in the university population at that time. They learned to read and write and studied the Scriptures. Girls were supposed to be instructed in Latin or German, for an hour each day.[37]

Although Luther was concerned that reforms be made at the university level for moral reasons, he also had a highly practical streak. He was concerned that students choose a course of study that would lead to a career. While insisting that education have a connection to religion, because each person should know the scriptures, Luther recognized that education also had to be thought of in realistic terms. Students whose parents were of a low socioeconomic status went to the university to get an education to help them rise above their current social status. Many wanted to study law or medicine, but Luther advised some of them to switch to other fields for which he thought they were better suited, that would not take as long to prepare for, and that would lead to a career. Luther believed that an individual's personal preferences, health, income, and living conditions all had to be taken into account.[38] Currently, educators working in higher education must counsel students about career choices on a regular basis and have to deal with the same practical considerations, especially financial ones, that Luther was concerned with during the sixteenth century.

Keep in mind that Luther's philosophy of education reflected the cultural period in which he lived. The Reformation was a time in which the Church was criticized for wastefulness and corruption. It was also a time in which questions were asked about the type of life a person ought to live or what it meant to be a good, decent individual. For Luther, a decent individual was an educated one. Although Luther's idea of education involved religion, in keeping with the cultural values of the period, it addressed some of the same issues that we face today when considering what type of curricula students should have and how best to educate them.

EDUCATIONAL POLICY AND THE UNIVERSITIES IN THE REFORMATION

Although Luther had a formidable influence on education in the Reformation, the state itself had an interest in establishing schools at that time. Luther wanted the school to prepare professionals to serve in leadership positions in the church and the state, but he also recognized that there was a place for general education in the society.[39] This concern was echoed by the state; school ordinances, as you have already learned, specified the curricula and instructional methods for schools. The curricula focused mainly on the use of the catechism, and the instructional methods were largely recitative in nature.[40] The children of working parents were instructed in the catechism, and were taught to pray, write, read, and sing psalms.[41]

Sixteenth-century educational policy in the German state held that literacy was very important for individuals who wanted to maintain or elevate their social standing.[42] The idea that literacy was important in maintaining law also arose; it was believed that people who were literate would have a better knowledge of law and be better citizens.[43] During the reign of Philip the Magnanimous (1504–1567), the Hessian state school system was supposed to train an elite educated in the classical Latin tradition. The educational reforms required that the Latin school curriculum be used because it would train future church officials in the interpretation of scripture, and future state officials in Roman law and policy matters.[44] The state reorganized existing schools, established new ones, and reinstituted the Latin curriculum.[45] Sometimes there was local resistance to the reforms. In one case, the government had to allow a German school to operate in addition to the Latin school. The German school was believed to serve the interests of the burghers, or businessmen, because it would train youth to work in business, not just prepare them for university.[46] Children of the upper classes began formal education early and were taught in Latin. They studied ancient Greek and Latin literature, because the study of classical works was the best way to prepare them for positions of authority, in which they had to act intelligently.[47] The humanistic curriculum proposed by Vives during the Renaissance was thought to be the best way to educate students for such roles. The school system in the Reformation reproduced the class system, preparing those who were from the upper classes for authoritative roles in society and giving those who were from the lower socioeconomic classes a general education, to teach them to be good law-abiding citizens.[48]

Just as schools today sometimes find it hard to staff their schools with qualified teachers, the state could not find qualified schoolmasters for the Latin schools. In 1537 a school order remarked on the need for better salaries for schoolmasters to motivate them to do their work better.[49] Schoolmasters generally worked for only a short period of time and had to work additional jobs to make enough money to survive. This concern with money also applies to schoolteachers today, for some teachers work summer jobs and second jobs part-time during the school year to make enough money for retirement or to support themselves.[50]

The educational policy of the state also dealt with the question of how to support university students. Most poor students had previously earned money to attend university by begging in the streets, but this practice was outlawed. Students in both the Latin schools and the university were given stipends through common sources of funding.[51] The stipend system existed in the German towns of Wittenberg, Jena, and Tubingen, with each town providing two stipends for university study.[52] This program strengthened the state school system by standardizing the classical curriculum and by preparing schoolmasters for the Latin schools. Many of those who became schoolmasters had previously received stipends; for instance, a third of the schoolmasters who went to the University of Marburg were recipients of stipends.[53] Today, many graduate students receive either financial aid or stipends, in the form of graduate assistantships or fellowships, to complete their graduate study at the master's, doctoral, or postdoctoral level.[54]

Although the German state may have focused on using the schools to train leaders for both the church and the state, it nonetheless recognized the power of literacy and provided for literacy instruction for all. That the state had to become involved in the education of youth was described by Luther as a necessity. He pointed out that parents could not be relied upon to teach their children appropriately, stating, "The common man doesn't have the means for it, he doesn't want to do it, and he doesn't know how."[55] In 1526 Luther pointed out to the prince that he must hold citizens to the support of schools and act as "guardian-general of the young."[56]

Luther's colleague Melanchthon agreed with the assessment that most parents were incapable of educating their children by themselves and that government had to take charge of educating the young. Melanchthon even stated that government would be "a common father" to all.[57]

PHILIPP MELANCHTHON: COLLEAGUE OF LUTHER, HUMANIST, AND SCHOOL REFORMER

Like Luther, Melanchthon was a school reformer. In 1528 he wrote, in a school ordinance for Saxony, that schools should function to "raise up people who are skilled to teach in the church and govern in the world."[58]

As you read in his biographical sketch, Melanchthon was an instrumental reformer at the University of Wittenberg. Although he and Luther initially disagreed, the two soon became friends while on the faculty there. Melanchthon was a humanist by training and felt that Greek language and culture and other humanistic studies should be the basis for the university curriculum.[59]

Although he wrote about curriculum reform at the university level, Melanchthon believed in a reform of education from top to bottom. He insisted on quality teaching and curricula in secondary schools, known as *gymnasia*. As an advocate of school visitations and supervision as part of the reform process, Melanchthon wrote *Instructions to the Visitors* in 1528, which was supposed to be a guidebook for school examiners. To eventually overhaul existing schooling practices, Melanchthon recommended that school examiners accumulate data on schools, teachers, parents, communities, and children.[60] All children were to be legally placed under the direct supervision and control of the school. The procedures, functions, and teachers of the school had to be regularly evaluated during school visitations. Melanchthon's *Instructions* was adopted so quickly that by the 1560s all "reformed" pro-Lutheran territories throughout Germany had implemented territorial visitations.[61]

Spotlight On ◀━━

PHILIPP MELANCHTHON (1497–1560)

Philipp Melanchthon was about 14 years younger than Luther, but the two worked together at the University of Wittenberg. Melanchthon was born in the Rhone Valley in the town of Bretton. His father was a skilled armament craftsperson in the service of the Reich but suffered from ill health from the time Melanchthon was a small boy. Melanchthon's father and grandfather died in 1508, and his mother was forced to remarry or be penniless. Soon after his mother remarried, Philipp and his brother George went to live with his grandmother. The change of residence shaped Melanchthon's early education, for Philipp's grandfather brought in a Latin tutor, Johann Unger, to teach the boy Latin grammar and also to prepare him to study Greek. This tutoring led to Melanchthon's lifelong belief that a study of the humanities was essential to an education.

School visitations were performed because the civil authorities wanted to supervise school curricula to ensure that standardized knowledge was transmitted.[62] Compulsory attendance laws were implemented, and authorities also reorganized the curriculum, teacher training, instruction, and classification of students according to age-grade levels and examination results.[63] The practice of overseeing schools and making recommendations on curriculum, student achievement, and the like, is seen today. State education departments visit schools and make curriculum recommendations. They also have great influence over teacher training, and they administer state assessment tests to determine student achievement levels.

After Luther himself visited a school in November 1528, he began to rethink the type of education needed to properly educate church and state leaders. He asked Melanchthon to redesign the Latin school curriculum with this goal in mind. Luther himself attended to the reform of the vernacular school curriculum, for those who were not going to school to prepare for the priesthood or for a career in the state. He wrote the Short Catechism and the Long Catechism, which replaced the Bible in vernacular schools, where instruction was given in German, not Latin.[64]

Melanchthon believed that infants were unaware of sinful impulses, but since sin and evil were found everywhere, children could easily learn immoral ways if not provided with proper parental guidance early in life. For this reason, home and school discipline were believed to be necessary to combat innate sinful tendencies. People were supposed to be able to overcome the tendency of the inheritance of original sin if they had an understanding of scripture.[65]

Today, we recognize that children and adolescents have to be disciplined and given guidance in appropriate behavior. Melanchthon remarked on this in the sixteenth century, stating that youths left to their own devices were unruly, "for never were our youth so impatient of laws and of discipline, so determined to live after their own wills."[66] To Melanchthon, schooling would provide the guidance, support, and habits needed to successfully resist the impulses to destroy, and to be impatient and disdainful of civil or spiritual responsibility.[67]

Melanchthon joined with the Jesuits, the members of the religious order known as the Society of Jesus, to establish gymnasia, the secondary or preparatory schools students had to attend before they could be admitted to the university.[68] This increased preparation at the secondary level resulted in an emphasis on the study of language and other humanistic subjects, so that by the time students entered the university they were already well prepared in those areas.[69]

Like Melanchthon, **John Amos Comenius,** a Czech reformer, believed that students had great potential. We look at the contributions Comenius made to today's educational system next.

JOHN AMOS COMENIUS: EARLY CHILDHOOD EDUCATOR

John Amos Comenius, as you learned from his brief biographical sketch, was shaped by his experiences in school. His ideas about education were rooted in reflections about his own experiences, as were Luther's and Melanchthon's. Comenius remarked that places designed for education were known as colleges, gymnasia, and schools and were supposed to be places of ease or literary amusements; however, in his opinion, schools did not live up to this. Instead, he said they were "grinding houses of torment and torture, especially true when the teachers were incompetent men uninstructed in piety and the wisdom of God."[70]

After 3 years at the Unitas Fratrum School in Prerov, Comenius went to Germany to study higher education and theology, first at Herborn and then at Heidelberg for his last year. While he was in Herborn he composed a Czech-Latin dictionary and already displayed the tireless activism that characterized much of his life. He once told a student that "we are born to do, therefore an active life is truly life. Idleness is the sepulcher of a living man."[71]

Comenius believed that education represented salvation for mankind and that it would protect people against disaster. For him, education was complementary to religion; he felt that his true life's work lay in making mankind more responsive to God's truth and direction.[72]

Comenius wrote *The School of Infancy,* a treatise on children. He pointed out that although children may seem insignificant, God has many plans for them and that "children are actually the future inhabitants of the world and possessors of the earth."[73] In this respect, his ideas about education for children were similar to those of Melanchthon, who once addressed the pupils assembled in a school by saying, "Hail, reverend pastors, doctors, licentiates, superintendents!"[74] Comenius quoted this incident in his book to show that, like Melanchthon, he believed that children had great potential and could become anything. He was a great advocate for children and felt that early childhood education would give children a great advantage. He believed that children were given to us "as a mirror in which we may

Spotlight On ◄───────────────────────────────────

JOHN AMOS COMENIUS (1592–1670)

John Amos Comenius was born in Prague, now the capital of the Czech Republic, in 1592. He began the walk back to his homeland from Heidelberg, Germany, in the spring of 1614, at the age of 22. Despite a happy and carefree childhood, he lost his parents and two sisters in an epidemic and was sent to live with an aunt for 4 years. He recalled his school experiences at that time as "the terror of boys, the slaughterhouse of the mind."

At the age of 16 Comenius entered the Unitas Fratrum School at Prerov, Czechoslovakia, where he felt at home. His family had formerly belonged to the Unitas Fratrum, a church that began with followers of the Protestant martyr John Huss, who was burned at the stake in 1415. The church held that men should dedicate their lives to living as Jesus told his disciples to live. Comenius himself advised his students that their theories should be "inseparable with practice."

We are indebted to Comenius for his ideas on early childhood education.

behold humility, gentleness, benign goodness, harmony, and other Christian virtues."[75]

Comenius said that although parents might be willing to instruct their children, they might find it took too much of their time, because they would be preoccupied with "duties or family affairs."[76] He believed that parents might find education to be of "trifling importance" and stated that since "remote antiquity,"

> youth in every state have been properly handed over for instruction to righteous, wise, and good persons. These were called pedagogues (leaders, not drivers, of children), masters, teachers, and doctors.[77]

Comenius held that children should be trained in piety, sound learning, morals, and health. In the area of morals and virtues, he advocated training in how to be careful about one's eating and drinking habits and cleanliness, and how to behave in a decorous manner. Children were supposed to be respectful of their elders, show kindness, and learn not to dread work, for work, according to Comenius, was a very proper thing for children to learn to do. With regard to what he called "sound learning," Comenius stated that in the first 6 years of life children should learn the names of fire, air, water and earth, rain, lead, snow, iron, and tree and plant names. He also thought children should learn the differences among animals, and their names, as well as the names of the parts of their own bodies and the purposes of these parts.[78] Children were to be instructed in chronology, to be able to measure the day, week, month, or year and to know and understand the differences in and names of the seasons of the year. They were also to be instructed in politics, so that children would know who the chief rulers and legislators were and what their purposes were. Furthermore, they should be taught the principles of dialectics, or speech. Comenius said that a child should be able to know what a question is and what an answer is and should be able to respond accurately and correctly to a question. Although he considered all these areas the basis for a sound education of a child by the age of 6, Comenius pointed out that instruction should not be set for certain ages and times, since "it is impossible to observe the order in their homes that is obtained in public schools, where no external matters disturb the regular course of things."[79]

Today, educators in public and private schools teach some of the same subject matter recommended by Comenius. Early childhood education is considered instrumental in shaping a child's educational experiences.

BRIDGES FROM THE PAST TO THE PRESENT: VALUE AND USES OF CONTRIBUTIONS OF THE REFORMATION TO EDUCATION TODAY

Today's educational system has benefited from the period known as the German Reformation in four primary areas (see Table 5-1). The first area is that of professionalism. The recognition of the importance of proper credentials and training

Table 5-1 **Similarities Between Educational Ideas of the German Reformation and Those of Modern Education**

EDUCATIONAL IDEA	SIMILARITY
Higher education	Not everyone goes to college or university.
	General education is provided to train people for responsible citizenship.
	University students should receive a stipend.
	Financial and personal considerations should enter into career choice. (For example, is medical school too expensive?)
Professional behavior	Candidates for a job must have appropriate certification and training.
	Professionals should never use their power to exploit others or for personal gain.
	Candidates for a job should be selected based on qualifications and training *only*.
	Jobs should not be offered to relatives or friends.
Role of government	Literacy for everyone is highly important.
	Federal and state governments mandate curricula and standards.
Educational methods	Educational materials are mass-printed.
	The value of play is recognized, and there is an increased interest in child development.
	Lessons are sequenced for each developmental level.

arose in the Reformation; this meant that an individual had to be properly qualified to obtain a job and not just have influential connections. Professionalism also meant that individuals had to conduct themselves properly at all times and not use their office for personal gain. You learned that Martin Luther focused his attention on the corrupt practices of the Church, for example, keeping priests in their offices who were illiterate, and tolerating the breaking of vows of celibacy by priests who kept concubines. Today, we expect professionals, including teachers, to be well prepared and literate, and not to use the power of their positions for personal gain or to exploit others. (Especially heinous today is the sexual exploitation of children by someone in power, such as a teacher or the clergy.)

Professionalism also means that schools should be staffed with qualified teachers and that these professionals be paid a salary commensurate with their abilities and training. Today, it is still difficult for some teachers to make ends meet; they are forced to take second jobs, and some leave teaching because of financial considerations. Improving teacher salaries was a concern during the Reformation, and it continues to be an issue of great importance today.

The second area of contribution from the Reformation is the idea that literacy should be a goal for the population at large. Luther deplored ignorance and wanted everyone to be able to read, so he published the catechisms and pamphlets in German, the language that people spoke, rather than in the more esoteric Latin. Comenius wanted children to be taught very early so that they would learn to read and write. This exposure to early childhood education increased the literacy rate as well. Today we not only believe that literacy is vital to our country, but we also understand that early childhood education is the way to ensure that all children are ready for school and learn to read well.[80] Seventy-five percent of all young children participate in preschool programs such as Head Start, begun by the federal government in 1965.[81]

Literacy can be most widely perpetuated by compulsory public schooling. This was recommended during the German Reformation, and the princes during Luther's time made governmental rulings about the importance of sending children to school. This was a deliberate attempt at what we would today call federal control of education. Today, we recognize that at-risk children have fewer chances to develop literacy-related experiences, and they lack decoding skills.[82]

Literacy continues to be a problem in the United States. A recent report by the National Center for Education Statistics revealed that 21 to 23 percent of the 191 million adults in America demonstrated limited skills. Some had difficulty performing such routine tasks as identifying a specific piece of information in a newspaper article or locating the time or place of a meeting on a form.[83] The issue of limited literacy is highly important, because those who have limited literacy will be unable to meet their basic needs and hold down a job and may have difficulty making decisions about their lives and their futures.

The third area of contribution from the Reformation was an increased interest in child psychology and in how children develop and learn. Many changes evolved in the ideas about child development. For instance, the long-established idea that children should be wrapped in swaddling clothes gave way to new understandings about how children should be raised, even extending to how they should be dressed, what they should eat, and what they should be taught at various ages. Recall that Comenius had definite ideas about what young children should learn, including the names of various objects or concepts, the differences among animals, and the parts of their own bodies, as well as what these parts were for. Modern preschool and early childhood education programs attempt to nurture both children's academic skills as well as their social and emotional development.[84]

The fourth area of contribution from the German Reformation concerns the increased importance of higher education and the rise of the universities. You will recall that Luther and Melanchthon both taught at Wittenberg, where Luther had an avid interest in the academic progress of his students. He also maintained an interest in their social and economic well-being, even considering how difficult it would be for them to complete several years of school when they could not afford it and were running heavily into debt. Today, career counselors in both high school and college help students consider how their economic situation will affect their career choice. At-risk students, or those who are likely to drop out because of social, economic, or emotional factors, are targeted to help them stay in school.[85] Financial aid options are available for qualifying students, but students still need to take into account how long it will take them to finish a program under difficult financial situations, so the choice of student major is a real concern for those in higher education today. Student loans have greatly increased as Pell grants and Social Security education benefits have been eliminated.[86] This increased emphasis on using loans to pay for education means that some students who may not want to go into debt will choose academic programs that take less time and money to complete. Socioeconomic status affects job choice early; a study by Henderson, Hesketh, and Tuffin found that socioeconomic status became a factor about the age of 9, when boys and girls were in the process of exploring job choice.[87] Stipends for graduate students are used to help graduate students support themselves during graduate study. This practice originated during the German Reformation.[88]

SUMMARY

Clearly, the German Reformation, which was a time of a critical examination of socioeconomic injustices in society, was also a period of new advances in education. These advances extended to Reformation England, the subject of chapter 6.

QUESTIONS FOR DISCUSSION

1. Define what is meant by the Reformation in this historical time period. Why is it of importance to us in the study of educational history and philosophy?

2. The peasants' revolt of 1525 has been cited as a consequence of their long-standing oppression and poor economic conditions for years before the Reformation. How important do you think economic factors are in determining societal change? Can you think of an example today?

3. Discuss the literacy rate in Reformation society. Did the Reformation make a significant impact in improving literacy among the general population? Do you believe we have similar problems with the literacy rate in today's society? Provide at least one example to back up your answer.

4. Describe some of the popular superstitions of the people during the Reformation. Do you believe that people have similar superstitions today? Why or why not?

5. Society began to be secularized during the Reformation. Today, we have calls for a return to more religious values. Do you believe that more religious values will help our society? How will they affect education?

6. What would have been the effect on the population if Luther's pamphlets and books had been printed in Latin rather than in the vernacular, German? What does this tell you about the importance of a common language for communication purposes?

7. Comment on the German system of compulsory education that existed during the Reformation. How is it similar to and different from the compulsory education system today?

8. Luther was concerned with the well-being of the whole student, including his financial situation, in career planning. Do we utilize a similar approach today in career planning? Do you think Luther had the right approach?

9. Melanchthon described the importance of education in disciplining the young. He thought schooling would subdue destructive impulses. Does education in our society help subdue or eliminate violent or destructive behavior in youth? Why or why not? Provide evidence for your answer.

10. In your opinion, what are the most important similarities between the Reformation period and today?

SUGGESTED ACTIVITIES

1. Pretend you are a parent who does not agree with Luther's views on education. From the perspective of a Reformation-era parent (assume you are a middle-class individual), write a letter to Luther explaining what your views are and why you feel as you do.

2. Suppose that you are Martin Luther, and you must convince parents that they should send their children to school. The parents are reluctant to do so, because they do not understand your agenda. Write an essay of at least one page, from Luther's perspective, advocating education for all children and stressing the lifetime benefits of education for children.

3. From the perspective of Melanchthon, write a one-page letter to school authorities who are reluctant to adopt the humanistic curriculum, and convince them of the benefits of adopting such a curriculum.

4. Luther's ideas on education for all children can be compared to those of Horace Mann, the founder of the American public school. Research Mann's ideas, found in chapter 10 of this text, and compare/contrast them with Luther's ideas. Present your findings in a 15-minute PowerPoint presentation.

5. Comenius believed that homeschooling was a bad idea. Many parents today hold the same belief as Comenius, but others insist on homeschooling their children. In a 15- to 20-minute PowerPoint presentation, present Comenius's ideas, and then explain the modern viewpoint of homeschooling. Include statistics on how many parents homeschool their children today and the requirements for homeschooling children, from the state department of education's perspective.

6. Developments in society at any time period can transform education. The development of the printing press during the Reformation transformed society, and education, because it allowed printed books to be distributed more widely and to be used by more people. How has the use of computer technology since the 1990s transformed education? Present a 15- to 20-minute PowerPoint

presentation on this topic, *or* write a five-page paper on the uses of computer technology today and how it is transforming education. In your presentation highlight how *at least one* specific school district has utilized technology to enhance instruction.

Bibliography

Barnett, W. S., & Hustedt, J. T. (2003, April). Preschool: The most important grade. *Educational Leadership,* 54–57.

Brickman, W. (1983). The educational evangelist of Eisleben: Martin Luther (1483–1546). In L. W. Spitz (Ed.), *Educational roots and routes in Western Europe.* Cherry Hill, NJ: Emeritus.

Chadwick, O. (1964). *The Reformation.* Grand Rapids, MI: Wm. B. Erdmans.

Cole, R. G. (1984). Reformation printers: Unsung heroes. *Sixteenth Century Journal, 15*(3), 327–39.

Comenius, J. A. (1956). *The school of infancy.* (E. M. Eller, Ed. & Intro.) Chapel Hill: University of North Carolina Press.

Conley, D. T. (2002, April). Preparing students for life after high school. *Educational Leadership,* 60–63.

Fisher, G. P. (1883). *The Reformation.* New York: Charles Scribner.

Gawthrop, R., & Strauss, G. (1984, August). Protestantism and literacy in early modern Germany. *Past and Present,* no. 104, 31–55.

Green, L. C. (1972). The Bible in sixteenth-century humanist education. *Studies in the Renaissance, 19,* 112–34.

Green, L. C. (1973). Faith, righteousness, and justification: New light on their development under Luther and Melanchthon. *Sixteenth Century Journal, 4*(1), 65–86.

Green, L. C. (1979). The education of women in the Reformation. *History of Education Quarterly, 19*(1), Women's Influence on Education, 93–116.

Grossman, M. (1970, January). Wittenberg printing: Early sixteenth century. *Sixteenth Century Essays and Studies, 1,* 53–74.

Hibler, R. W. (1985). Martin Luther, the educator. *Educational Forum, 49*(3), 297–305.

Hyson, M. (2003, April). Putting early academics in their place. *Educational Leadership, 60, 7,* 20–23.

Klassen, P. J. (Ed.). (1980). *Problems in civilization; The Reformation: Change and stability.* St. Louis, MO: Forum Press.

Lawson, J. (1967). *Medieval education and the Reformation.* New York: Routledge and Kegan Paul.

Leslie, L., & Allen, L. (1999). Factors that predict success in an early literacy intervention project. *Reading Research Quarterly, 34*(4), 404–11.

Lortz, J. (1964). *How the Reformation came.* New York: Herder and Herder.

Luke, C. (1989). *Pedagogy, printing, and Protestantism: The discourse on childhood.* Albany: State University of New York Press.

Pettegree, A. (Ed.). (1992). *The early Reformation in Europe.* Cambridge: Cambridge University Press.

Schnabel, K. U., Alfeld, C., Eccles, J. S., Koller, O., & Baumert, J. (2002). Parental influences on students' educational choices in the United States and Germany: Different ramifications—same effect? *Journal of Vocational Behavior, 60,* 178–98.

Schweikert, E. G. (1996). *The Reformation: Vol. 2. The Reformation as a university movement.* Minneapolis, MN: Fortress Press.

Sowards, J. K. (1982). Erasmus and the education of women. *Sixteenth Century Journal, 13*(4), 77–89.

Spitz, L. W. (Ed.). (1997). The educational evangelist of Eisleben: Martin Luther (1483–1546). In *The Reformation: Education and history.* Brookfield, VT: Ashgate.

Spitz, L. W. (Ed.). (1997). The importance of the Reformation for the universities: Culture and confessions in the critical years. In *The Reformation: Education and history.* Brookfield, VT: Ashgate.

Spitz, L. W. (Ed.). (1997). Luther's social concern for students. In *The Reformation: Education and history.* Brookfield, VT: Ashgate.

Steinmetz, M. (1980). Class conflict and the Reformation. In *The Reformation: Change and stability* St. Louis, MO: Forum Press.

Strauss, G. (1988). The social function of schools in the Lutheran Reformation in Germany. *History of Education Quarterly, 28*(2), 191–206.

Wright, W. J. (1987). Evaluating the results of sixteenth century educational policy: Some Hessian data. *Sixteenth Century Journal, 18*(3), 411–26.

Suggestions for Further Reading

In addition to the works cited in the bibliography, the following are suggested for further reading.

Dixon, C. S. (Ed.). (1999). *The German Reformation: The essential readings.* Oxford: Blackwell.

Edwards, M. U. (1994). *Printing, propaganda, and Martin Luther.* Berkeley: University of California Press.

Manschreck, C. L. (1975). *Melanchthon: The quiet reformer.* Westport, CT: Greenwood Press.

Ozment, S. (1975). *The Reformation in the cities: The appeal of Protestantism in sixteenth-century Germany and Switzerland.* New Haven, CT: Yale University Press.

Pettegree, A. (Ed.). (1993). *The Reformation of the parishes: The ministry and the Reformation in town and country.* Manchester, UK: Manchester University Press.

Scribner, R. W. (1994). *For the sake of simple folk: Popular propaganda for the German Reformation.* Oxford: Clarendon Press.

Stupperich, R. (1965). *Melanchthon* (R. H. Fischer, Trans.) Philadelphia: Westminster Press.

Relevant Web Sites

The Reformation (Questia) *http://www.questia.com* Questia is the world's largest online library. Great online source with books on Luther and the Reformation that have been put online.

History Learning Site *http://www.historylearningsite.co.uk/Lu1.htm* Contains modern translation of Luther's *95 Theses.*

Eduseek *http://www.eduseek.com/static/navigate1630.html* Contains information on Germany during the Reformation, the Protestant Reformation, and the role of women during the Reformation.

Life and Times of St. Martin Luther *http://www.reformation.org/luther.html* Biographical information on Luther, photographs, church history.

Education Week *http://www.edweek.org* Good source for current events in education. Released weekly.

National Center for Education Statistics *http://www.nces.ed.gov* Federal and state data on education.

U.S. Department of Education *http://www.ed.gov* Home page of the U.S. Department of Education, for information on NCLB and other federal and state policies.

Endnotes

[1] Carmen Luke, *Pedagogy, Printing, and Protestantism: The Discourse on Childhood* (Albany: State University of New York Press, 1989), 4–5.

[2] W. Steven Barnett & Jason T. Hudstedt, "Preschool: The Most Important Grade," *Educational Leadership* (April 2003), 54–57.

[3] Ibid.

[4] Joseph Lortz, *How the Reformation Came* (New York: Herder and Herder, 1964), 45.

[5] Owen Chadwick, *The Reformation* (Grand Rapids, MI: Wm. B. Erdmans, 1964), 4.

[6] Luke, *Pedagogy, Printing, and Protestantism,* 74.

[7] Chadwick, *The Reformation,* 4.

[8] George P. Fisher, *The Reformation* (New York: Charles Scribner, 1883), 13.

[9] Ibid., 22.

[10] Robert Whiting, *The Blind Devotion of the People: Popular Religion and the English Reformation* (New York: Cambridge University Press, 1989), 1.

[11] Luke, *Pedagogy, Printing, and Protestantism,* 78.

[12] Ibid., 79.

[13] Peter J. Klassen, Ed. *Problems in Civilization: The Reformation, Change, and Stability* (St. Louis, MO: Forum Press, 1980). See p. 1 of the introduction.

[14] Max Steinmetz, "Class Conflict and the Reformation," in *Problems in Civilization; The Reformation: Change and Stability* (St. Louis, MO: Forum Press, 1980). See p. 16.

[15] Luke, *Pedagogy, Printing, and Protestantism,* 10.

[16] John Lawson, *Medieval Education and the Reformation* (New York: Routledge and Kegan Paul, 1967), 69.

[17] Richard G. Cole, "Reformation Printers: Unsung Heroes," *Sixteenth Century Journal, 15,* no. 3 (1984), 327.

[18] Ibid.

[19] Lawson, *Medieval Education,* 56–57.

[20] Andrew Pettegree, Ed. *The Early Reformation in Europe* (Cambridge: Cambridge University Press, 1992), 9.

[21] Cole, "Reformation Printers," 330.

[22] Pettegree, *Early Reformation*, 55.

[23] Lawson, *Medieval Education*, 44.

[24] Pettegree, *Early Reformation*, 55–56.

[25] Richard Gawthrop & Gerald Strauss, "Protestantism and Literacy in Early Modern Germany," *Past and Present*, no. 104 (August 1984), 32.

[26] Ibid., 33.

[27] Ibid.

[28] Ibid.

[29] Ibid., 35–36.

[30] Ibid., 37–38.

[31] Ibid., 38.

[32] Luke, *Pedagogy, Printing, and Protestantism*, 93.

[33] William Brickman, "The Educational Evangelist of Eisleben: Martin Luther (1483–1546)," in *Educational Roots and Routes in Western Europe* (Cherry Hill, NJ: Emeritus, 1983), 22.

[34] Ibid., 27.

[35] Lewis W. Spitz, *The Reformation: Education and History* (Brookfield, VT: Ashgate, 1997). See chapter 3, "The Importance of the Reformation for the Universities: Culture and Confessions in the Critical Years," 42.

[36] Ibid.

[37] Ibid.

[38] Spitz, "Luther's Social Concern for Students," in *The Reformation*, 265.

[39] Gawthorp & Strauss, "Protestantism and Literacy," 33.

[40] Ibid., 36.

[41] Ibid.

[42] Ibid, 38.

[43] Ibid., 39.

[44] William J. Wright, "Evaluating the Results of Sixteenth-Century Educational Policy: Some Hessian Data," *Sixteenth Century Journal, 18*, no. 3 (1987), 414–15.

[45] Ibid.

[46] Ibid., 415.

[47] Ibid., 198.

[48] Ibid., 199.

[49] Ibid.

[50] Ibid., 416. This information was also obtained through the author's interview with a fourth-grade teacher in the small town of Kersey, PA, at Fox Township Elementary School. She works part-time at the local Wal-Mart, in nearby St. Marys, Pennsylvania, where she is paid $9 an hour. She told the author that it will really help toward her retirement.

[51] Ibid., 418.

[52] Ibid.

[53] Ibid., 418–19.

[54] Ibid., 419. The numbers of students who currently receive assistance with doctoral studies are discussed in the "Bridges" section of this chapter.

[55] Gerald Strauss, "The Social Function of Schools in the Lutheran Reformation in Germany," *History of Education Quarterly, 28,* no. 2 (1988), 192.

[56] Ibid., 193.

[57] Ibid., 193.

[58] Ibid., 196.

[59] Spitz, *Reformation: Education and History,* 51.

[60] Luke, *Pedagogy, Printing, and Protestantism,* 84.

[61] Ibid.

[62] Ibid.

[63] Ibid.

[64] Ibid., 85–87.

[65] Ibid., 91.

[66] Ibid., 102.

[67] Ibid.

[68] Spitz, *Reformation: Education and History,* 58.

[69] Ibid.

[70] John Amos Comenius, *The School of Infancy,* ed. and intro. Ernest M. Eller (Chapel Hill: University of North Carolina Press, 1956), 59. This is a direct quote from Comenius.

[71] Ibid., 68.

[72] Ibid., 7.

[73] Ibid., 9.

[74] Ibid., 59.

[75] Ibid., 60. The full quote is, "Hail, reverend pastors, doctors, licentiates, superintendents! Hail, most noble, most prudent, most learned lords, consuls, praetors, judges, governors, chancellors, secretaries, magistrates, professors!"

[76] Ibid., 62.

[77] Ibid., 67.

[78] Ibid., 68.

[79] Ibid., 72–73.

[80] Ibid., 74.

[81] Barnett & Hudstedt, "Preschool: The Most Important Grade," 54–57.

[82] Ibid.

[83] Lauren Leslie & Linda Allen, "Factors that Predict Success in an Early Literacy Intervention Project," *Reading Research Quarterly, 34,* no. 4 (1999), 404–11.

84 See "Executive Summary of Adult Literacy in America: A First Look at the Results of the National Adult Literacy Survey," available on the Web site of the National Center for Education Statistics, http://www.nces.ed.gov

85 Marilou Hyson, "Putting Early Academics in Their Place," *Educational Leadership* (April 2003), 20–23.

86 David T. Conley, "Preparing Students for Life After High School," *Educational Leadership* (April 2002), 60–63.

87 Edward P. St. John, "The Influence of Debt on Choice of Major," *Journal of Student Financial Aid, 24,* no. 1 (1994), 5–12.

88 Jo-Ann S. Hannah & Sharon E. Kahn, "The Relationship of Socioeconomic Status and Gender to the Occupational Choices of Grade 12 Students," *Journal of Vocational Behavior, 34,* no. 2 (1989), 161–78.

Chapter 6

Reformation and Education in Tudor England (1534–1625)

Learning Objectives

1. Describe the factors that led to the English Reformation.
2. Understand the development and expansion of schools in the Tudor period.
3. Describe the qualifications for teaching and the teaching methods used during the English Reformation.
4. Compare and contrast the teaching philosophies and methods of Thomas Elyot and Richard Mulcaster.
5. Explain the growth and development of law schools and professional schools in Tudor England.
6. Compare and contrast education at all levels (elementary, secondary, university) with education today.
7. List and explain the contributions from Reformation England to today's educational system.

INTRODUCTION

In chapter 5 you learned how the events of the German Reformation shaped education. Educational policy was defined by a growing awareness of the need for literacy and education for all. The government even became involved, mandating compulsory education for young children in Reformation Germany. The concept of professional preparation and appropriate compensation for teachers also developed. Martin Luther, the German reformer and educator, wrote many pamphlets and books in the vernacular on education and on the corrupt practices of the Church, and these were widely disseminated.

Similar developments occurred in Reformation England; however, the situation was different there because of the volatile situation within its monarchy. King Henry VIII's fight with the pope and the Church of England over the issue of divorce from his first wife led to the king's eventual dissolution of the monasteries, which provided educational opportunities for certain groups, such as charity boys.[1]

The concept that education could be used to prepare for a better life, and to become a member of the upper classes, had taken root in England. English society underwent great changes during the Tudor age. The idea of having enough land to be

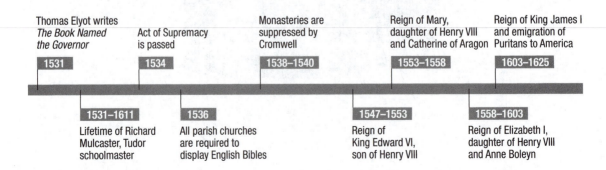

Thomas Elyot writes *The Book Named the Governor* — 1531

Act of Supremacy is passed — 1534

Monasteries are suppressed by Cromwell — 1538–1540

Reign of Mary, daughter of Henry VIII and Catherine of Aragon — 1553–1558

Reign of King James I and emigration of Puritans to America — 1603–1625

1531–1611 — Lifetime of Richard Mulcaster, Tudor schoolmaster

1536 — All parish churches are required to display English Bibles

1547–1553 — Reign of King Edward VI, son of Henry VIII

1558–1603 — Reign of Elizabeth I, daughter of Henry VIII and Anne Boleyn

considered wealthy was important, because landholding was a representation of wealth. Furthermore, a new social class had arisen: the gentry, or the upper classes, who wanted a humanistic education for their children to prepare them for higher positions in society.

During the English Reformation, schools grew in size and number. This was a major development of the sixteenth and seventeenth centuries that occurred as people realized that education would allow them to enter the expanding professions.[2]

Important humanistic writers and scholars in this period were Tudor schoolmaster **Richard Mulcaster** (1531–1611), who wrote about teaching methods and the problem of salaries in Tudor England, and **Sir Thomas Elyot,** who was concerned with education as an instrument of social policy. Whereas Mulcaster was concerned with education for all, Elyot focused his attention on education for the gentry, who he believed should be powerful in government, and the ruling class. Mulcaster and Elyot represent the two extremes in the development of educational policy.

This chapter ends with the year 1625 because that was when many **Puritans** were immigrating to America to escape persecution in England. The year 1625 is considered to be the point at which the Calvinist influence in the English Reformation reached its peak.[3]

Although this chapter begins with the decision of Henry VIII to dissolve the monasteries and the subsequent effect on education, the following English monarchs also were involved in establishing educational policy. King Edward VI, son of Henry VIII, reigned from 1547 to 1553. He was followed by Mary I, the daughter of Catherine of Aragon and Henry VIII. Mary reigned from 1553 to 1558. She was followed by Queen Elizabeth I, who reigned from 1558 to 1603. Elizabeth I was the daughter of Anne Boleyn. Elizabeth was followed by King James I in 1603. King James was monarch of England by 1625, the ending date for this chapter.

We begin our examination of education in **Tudor England** with a brief background look at the governmental and religious policies of **King Henry VIII,** who was king at the beginning of the English Reformation.

TUDOR ENGLAND: LIFE DURING THE REIGN OF HENRY VIII

The English Reformation was originally thought to have resulted from Henry VIII's decision to divorce **Catherine of Aragon** and marry Anne Boleyn, his long-time mistress; however, modern historians have debated this traditionally sixteenth-century point of view. They point to deeper causes of the English Reformation, such as an increasing interest in accumulating wealth and material possessions.[4] English society during the Tudor age had two expanding social classes: prosperous landowners and businessmen.[5] In the Tudor age, landholding was a representation of wealth. As Henry VIII dissolved the monasteries their lands were sold at prices below market value, which allowed purchasers to profit from the subsequent steep rise in land values.[6]

An important characteristic of the English Reformation was a focus on literacy for the masses, which demonstrated that English society considered education to be an important part of life. A growing movement in parochial education affected individuals of middle-income levels. This meant that artisans, merchants, and farmers supported parish scholars and schools.[7] In everyday life, education was becoming more widely accepted among all classes of society, since literacy began to be viewed as a necessary component of daily life.[8] This certainly should not be taken to mean that every citizen of Tudor England was literate, but the fact that townspeople were supporting schools was an important step in the recognition that literacy was desirable for all. Upper-class women and girls in Tudor England received only basic education. Women of the laboring classes in Tudor England were mostly illiterate; 89 percent of the women in East Anglia, a rural district, could not write their names.[9] Tradespeople and craftsmen generally had an illiteracy rate of 44 percent. The farmers and agricultural laborers had an illiteracy rate of 79 percent.[10]

While the change in social structure was occurring, with emphasis on landowning and obtaining material wealth, Henry VIII's personal problems affected the lives of the citizens of Tudor England. Married to Catherine of Aragon, a Spanish princess and daughter of Queen Isabella and King Ferdinand of Spain, Henry wanted a son as an heir to the throne. Catherine had given birth to six children, but five had died in infancy. Thus, they had only one living child: a daughter, Mary, whom Henry initially adored but later disowned owing to religious differences. To have a son, Henry VIII wanted to divorce Catherine and marry his long-time mistress, Anne Boleyn; however, the pope, as head of the church, would not grant Henry a divorce. Henry soon figured out a way around this dilemma, by passing the **Act of Supremacy** of 1534, making himself head of the Church of England.[11] Next, he undertook to dissolve the monasteries.

DISSOLUTION OF THE MONASTERIES

Henry VIII and his advisors noted that corruption existed in the religious houses and monasteries of the Church of England. For example, in certain monasteries, there were four or five servants for each inhabitant.[12] An estimate of the total revenue of the religious houses in the mid-1530s was found to be half the total revenue of the Church of England.[13] This meant that the religious houses cost too much to maintain. Although Henry VIII recognized that the monks and friars had played a role in education, he was convinced that their contributions were no longer as great as they had been and decided they were not necessary just to provide education. Henry cited other reasons for his decision, including the breaches of ecclesiastical discipline, such as sexual misconduct, nepotism, and pluralism, which were widespread. **Pluralism** meant that a clergyman could hold more than one office at a time in different locations. Some bishops, for instance, were in charge of more than one diocese. **Nepotism** involved granting an office to an individual because of close connections or as a personal favor.

At this time in Reformation England literacy was by no means widespread, and clergy, who had attained at least a basic level of literacy, were looked to for help with everyday matters by many people who were not well educated. People held the Church in high esteem, for it provided bequests to local churches and religious foundations. Although some historians, including John Foxe, believed that people hated and ridiculed the clergy of the Church of England, evidence suggests that this may not have been the case for all parishioners. Local traditions and customs, such as observance of saints' days, continued well into the 1500s, and books of traditional devotion went through many editions well into the 1530s.[14]

Dissolving the monasteries was not complicated. **Thomas Cromwell** dissolved the condemned monastic houses in a formal process. During the visit, an inventory of any movable wealth they possessed was made, and the monks were provided for.[15] Monks and religious did not resist the order to leave. Between 1538 and 1540, Cromwell's commissioners suppressed approximately 200 monasteries, 200 friaries, and 40 nunneries, and evicted some 8,000 religious.[16]

THE EFFECT OF THE DISSOLUTION ON EDUCATION: TYPES OF SCHOOLS

Although the historian A. F. Leach estimated that there were more than 300 monastic schools by the 1530s and declared that educational opportunities were devastated by the dissolution of the monasteries, the effect of the dissolution on education may not have been quite that drastic.

Other historians have reassessed the effect of the dissolution on education in the Tudor age. Another factor was that the Tudor government was beginning to take on the role that the church formerly played in the establishment of schools.[17]

Joan Simon, a more recent educational historian who analyzed the effect of the dissolution of monasteries on educational opportunity in Reformation England, explained that schools associated with monasteries were of four types: **almonry schools,** or schools responsible for educating poor children, a very valuable service in Tudor society, with its increasing concern over relief for the poor; **outside schools,** which had a private endowment;[18] **chantry schools;** and song schools.

After the larger monasteries were dissolved, in their place Henry VIII founded 11 cathedral **grammar schools,** which were for students from the ages of 7 or 8 to 14 or 15.[19] Chantry schools were endangered by Henry VIII as well. These were schools attached to **chantries,**[20] which were chapels where Masses were said for the souls of the dead. Chantry priests often had to teach school as part of their duties, which were predetermined by the founders or sponsors of the chantries.[21] It is presumed that chantry priests, according to the usual custom, taught a few children to assist at the Mass;[22] however, chantry schools could have been either song schools or grammar schools. In song schools, children were taught basic reading and writing and sometimes the rudiments of Latin grammar. Students also learned plainsong and how to assist at Mass.[23]

Grammar schools after the dissolution of the monasteries were of eight types: cathedral schools, collegiate schools, monastic schools, almonry schools, hospital schools, guild schools, chantry schools, and grammar schools held at universities (see Figure 6-1).

Figure 6-1   Schools Before and After the Dissolution of the Monasteries

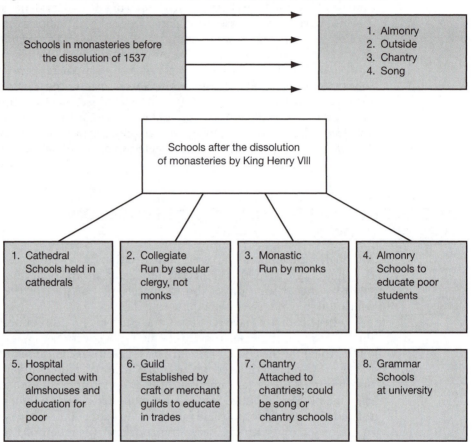

Grammar schools characterized as cathedral schools were established at cathedrals. **Collegiate schools** were run by secular clergy, not monks. Winchester and Eton are examples of such schools; these are still in existence today. Monastic and almonry school students studied with the choirmaster, who could also serve as the grammar master. Often, a grammar master was brought in to teach them.[24]

Hospital schools were connected with **almshouses,** or charity homes for the poor. **Guild schools** were established by craft or merchant guilds, which picked chaplains to run the schools. The first boys admitted to these guild schools were sons of guild members, but later, other boys were admitted as well. Grammar schools could also be held at universities, such as Magdalen College School in Oxford.[25]

Regardless of the type of grammar school students attended in Tudor England, they completed their grammar school education by the age of 14 or 15, at which time they went to a university, if they could afford it and if they wished to go.

In the next section we look at the curriculum of an elementary school student during the English Reformation.

SCHOOL CURRICULA DURING THE TUDOR AGE: ELEMENTARY SCHOOL

One direct effect of the dissolution of the monasteries was a modification of the curriculum at school and at the university.[26] In 1536, Thomas Cromwell specified that the English version of the Bible must be placed in every parish church. Then, a series of prescribed catechisms, primers, and grammars for the schools were put out.[27]

A direct outcome of the English Reformation was elementary teaching in the vernacular.[28] During the sixteenth century, pupils entered what was known as the **petty school** at the age of 4. Students were taught the catechism and primer so that they would be familiar with Anglican doctrine.[29] Students were given a *hornbook,* which later was also used by Puritans in America, to learn their alphabet. The hornbook was a wooden tablet with a handle on which was pasted a sheet of paper, or parchment, on which was printed the alphabet and the Lord's Prayer in English. This parchment was protected by a thin sheet of transparent horn.[30]

Children were taught to read by recitation. They were made to recite the letters of the alphabet, then phrases. Teaching methods focused on memorization and recitation. Those who wanted to enter grammar school at the age of 7 or 8 often had to recite the Lord's Prayer, Nicene Creed, and the Ten Commandments as a requirement for admission.[31]

There are some similarities between the age-grading practices of education in Tudor England and in today's educational system. The petty school of Tudor England, for 4-year-olds, would be analogous to our preschools. Students in preschool are also taught letters of the alphabet, colors, and how to write their names. The age at which students entered grammar school in Tudor England is similar to the ages at which students enter elementary school today. The age of 6 or 7 is traditional for first graders. Grammar schools in Tudor England stopped at the ages of 14 or 15, which is the age that students of today are in about eighth grade, or middle school.

A complete description of the teaching practices and subjects studied in the schools of Tudor England is difficult, because documents from this period about the exact ages and grade levels of students are rare.[32] In fact, historians of the English Reformation recognize that in Tudor times the elementary and grammar levels were not completely separate and distinct periods of education.[33]

LIFE OF A TUDOR SCHOOLBOY: THE GRAMMAR SCHOOL YEARS

Despite the difficulties in distinguishing the elementary and grammar levels of Tudor education, some facts about the education can nevertheless be determined. For instance, we know that Tudor schoolboys, beginning at the ages of 7 or 8, spent 8 to 10 hours a day, 6 days a week, in school.[34] They began school at 6:00 a.m. in summer and at 7:00 a.m. in winter.[35] They were given a break from 11:00 a.m. until about noon or 1:00 p.m., at which time school resumed and lasted until 5:00 or 6:00 p.m. At the famous grammar school Eton in 1530, students began work at 6:00 a.m. and did not eat breakfast until 9:00 a.m. Breakfast lasted only about 15 minutes.[36] Lunch was eaten at 11:00 a.m., and supper was held at 5:00 p.m. This schedule, in contrast to our present-day classroom schedule of beginning classes between the hours of 8:00 and 8:30 a.m. and leaving school at 2:30 or 3:00 p.m., seems overly long and rigid.

In addition to spending such long hours in school, grammar school pupils had to tolerate endless hours of drill and recitation to learn Latin, the focus of grammar school instruction in Tudor England. Daily instruction consisted of memorizing grammar, analyzing texts, and practicing composition. Students kept record books in which they wrote down idioms, quotations, or figures that would be useful in composition.[37] Other subjects, such as ancient history, and Greek, were taught as well, but the focus was on a linguistic curriculum to make students fluent in Latin. The reason for this was that knowledge of Latin was necessary to enter careers in the church, law, and medicine, and even to teach, although teaching was not viewed as a profession at that time. Teachers' salaries were low, and until about 1540, schoolmasters had the label "clerks."[38] Teachers had to obey Christian principles set forth by the Church, because the schools and universities of the English Reformation were controlled by ecclesiastical authority. Grammar teachers were licensed by the bishop.[39]

The grammar school student in Reformation England could expect to be disciplined if he did not study. Discipline in the grammar school in Reformation England has been characterized as severe. Although grammar school teachers were expected to be educated and have a good reputation, many of them resorted to severe methods of discipline when their students did not learn. Students at Eton were reported to have run away to escape being beaten. Although practices did vary, grammar schools in Tudor England used corporal punishment to enforce discipline. Students were hit with a birch rod or a ruler. Students who were slow in thinking up an answer were hit. Today, we consider this a completely improper practice, recognizing the individual differences in students and that some students take longer to process information than others. This sometimes occurs with students who have learning disabilities, which were unheard of in Tudor times, as were the concepts of processing information and individual differences.

Did all schoolmasters hold such ideas about discipline and use the same methods of teaching? One schoolmaster, Richard Mulcaster, advocated against corporal punishment, saying that better methods should be used. His ideas on teaching are found in the next section.

TEACHING METHODS: IDEAS OF RICHARD MULCASTER

Reading the ideas of Richard Mulcaster in his own words is the best way to understand his teaching philosophy and teaching methods. He begins his work *Positions* by describing appropriate preschool education for children. He did not believe in forcing young children to go to school, saying that they should attend only when they were physically and mentally ready. Mulcaster did not give a specific age when children should begin school, saying, "at what years I cannot say, because ripeness in children is not tied to one time."[40] With regard to the elementary curriculum,

RICHARD MULCASTER (1531–1611)

Richard Mulcaster was the headmaster at two of London's grammar schools: Merchant Taylors' (1561–1586) and St. Paul's (1596–1608). He was married in 1560 to Katherine Asheley, the daughter of a London grocer, and they had six children. Mulcaster added subjects such as instrumental and vocal music, physical education, and acting to the curriculum at Merchant Taylors' School, London's largest grammar school. He also taught Hebrew, the classics, mathematics, history, and poetry. Successful students included Samuel Foxe, diarist, and Nicholas Hill, philosopher.

he believed that the first subject to be taught should be reading, because it represented "the most fruitful principle in training the mind."[41] Unlike his contemporaries, Mulcaster thought that children should be taught to read in both English and Latin. In fact, he did not believe that instruction should be focused so heavily on Latin. He stated that children should "read English before Latin" and "write English before Latin, as a thing of more hardness and readier in use to answer all occasions."[42] Thus, Mulcaster was concerned that curriculum should be developed with practical considerations in mind. He also recognized the importance of having children read on a daily basis, reporting that "by daily spelling and continual reading, till partly by use and partly by argument, the child get the habit and cunning to read well."[43]

Mulcaster concluded his thoughts on elementary curriculum by describing the other subjects that students should study. In addition to reading and writing, he recommended instruction in drawing, music, and physical education. He thought drawing was important because it would "make a man able to judge what that is which he buyeth of artificers and craftsmen, for substance, form, and fashion."[44] In other words, by drawing objects, the pupil would have some idea of the quality they should be and what they should look like to give him a basis by which to judge things he would purchase from craftsmen. Music was included in the curriculum because it helped children develop their voices and lung capacity, and it also provided them with an emotional release "against our sorrows upon earth."[45] As for physical education, Mulcaster recognized its importance in developing the body and its role in preventing illness. He even recommended that children be allowed to play, because play would have the same effect.

Sir Thomas Elyot, a contemporary of Mulcaster's, also wrote about his ideas on educating youth; however, unlike Mulcaster, Elyot was more interested in the type of education that a young man of the **gentry,** or the wealthy, should receive (see "Shapers of Education" feature, p.122). Elyot does not seem to have focused at all on education for the poor. The biographical sketch of Elyot reveals that he appears to have learned that although he was the son of a wealthy landowner and well prepared academically, he was unprepared to deal with the political intrigue of Henry VIII's time, which affected his ability to make money.

CONTRIBUTIONS OF SIR THOMAS ELYOT

Sir Thomas Elyot, who worked with Thomas Cromwell during the reign of Henry VIII, provides us with information on the type of education a wealthy child was supposed to receive. In *The Book Named the Governor* Elyot explains how children of the gentry should be raised and educated, beginning with his ideas on infants. For example, he believed that the moral character of a **wet nurse,** or a woman hired to breast-feed newborn infants of the gentry, should be impeccable. He even said that another woman should be hired to help the nurse, to make certain that no words were spoken in the infant's presence that would corrupt the young mind. He stated this was necessary because such behavior would "corrupt the soft and tender buds."[46] Elyot understood that young children would "follow, not only the words but also the acts and gesture of them that be advanced in years."[47] This meant that if young children were to be educated to behave appropriately, in a manner befitting the gentry, they could not be exposed to people who would teach them improper language or behavior from an early age, because it would then be hard to eradicate later. Elyot stated "it shall be expedient that a nobleman's son in his infancy have with him continually only such as may accustom him by little and little to speak pure and elegant Latin."[48]

Spotlight On ◄───

SIR THOMAS ELYOT (1490–1546)

Sir Thomas Elyot was known as a Christian humanist. The son of a jurist and member of three parliaments, Elyot was educated at home until he entered the Middle Temple, one of the law schools of Tudor England, also known as the **Inns of Court.** Elyot recommended that young men complete a course of study in the humanities before taking up the study of law. He was never admitted to the bar and did not practice law but took government jobs.

Despite his education, Elyot had trouble making money. Named Clerk of the King's Council in 1523, Elyot held this job until 1530. He was never paid but was discharged with a knighthood as reward. He was reduced later to begging Cromwell for money, such as a pension, or asking him for a more lucrative position. It is thought that he wrote *The Book Named the Governor,* which he dedicated to Henry VIII, to get back into Henry VIII's favor. He was given the job of ambassador to the court of the Holy Roman Emperor after the book was published.

At the age of 7, the nobleman's child was to be taken away from women and assigned to a tutor, who should be "an ancient and worshipful man in whom is approved to be much gentleness mixed with gravity."[49] The tutor's first responsibility was to get to know the young boy and find out what his personality and work habits were like and what his strengths and weaknesses were.[50] The tutor's job was to develop a balanced schedule of work and play for the child of the nobleman, so that the tutor "suffer not the child to be fatigued with continual study or learning, wherewith the delicate and tender wit may be dulled or oppressed."[51] Music was to be studied to provide some respite from more serious studies. Elyot, who was a great admirer of the ancient Greeks and the Hebrews, mentioned that King David "during his life delighted in music."[52]

Like Mulcaster, Elyot believed in teaching art; however, he did not discuss drawing, as Mulcaster did, but recommended that children learn to paint. He gives an example of why this might be necessary: If a nobleman went into the armed forces, he could paint "the country of his adversary."[53] Thus, painting could serve a practical purpose as well as being used for recreation.

Elyot believed that learning should be made enjoyable for the nobleman's child. At the age of 7, a child should start studying **Aesop's fables** and then read the comedies of the Greek writer Aristophanes.[54] As a humanist scholar, Elyot recommended that Homer and Virgil be studied, and that poetry be read until the ages of 13 or 14.[55]

Elyot's ideas on the study of grammar and rhetoric show a modern-day understanding of a young child's developmental capacity to learn. Although Elyot recommended that children study grammar, logic, and rhetoric, he also understood that they could not study it for too long, and the study could not be too advanced or the student would grow to dislike the subject matter and thus avoid it in future. Today, we likewise recognize that difficult subjects must be carefully analyzed so that they are taught in small increments, to ensure that students are not bored or frustrated and thus do not develop a dislike for the subject matter.

Although the subjects that Elyot recommended for the course of study for a nobleman's son may seem impractical to us, they were practical for preparing someone to be able to speak effectively in public and deal with foreign visitors who might not understand the customs of Tudor England.[56] With this in mind, Elyot also recommended that after the age of about 15, the nobleman's son study oratory, or public speaking, geography, and cosmography, to learn more about the world, and to learn something of mathematics.[57] Elyot also believed that history was highly appropriate for the preparation of the modern statesman, because it would provide examples of how states and governments functioned in the past and how these examples might apply to Tudor-age politics.[58]

Elyot discussed whether young men past the age of 14 should continue their studies. He thought it unwise for them to continue their education to study only Latin. He made the point that if young men studied only Latin and did not have anything of substance to say, from having studied other subjects, they would make speeches in Latin that would sound very pompous and "make a sound without any purpose."[59] If young men were to attend the university to become orators,

SHAPERS OF EDUCATION	
Richard Mulcaster **(1531–1611)**	**Thomas Elyot** **(1490–1546)**
■ Described educational practices for all children, not just the children of the wealthy.	■ Focused on the appropriate type of education for a child of the gentry (wealthy).
■ Put children in school only when they are mentally and physically ready.	■ Begin moral education in infancy.
■ Teach reading first.	■ Do not use any vulgar expressions or obscenities around young children, because their minds are so impressionable.
■ Read in both Latin and English, but do not focus so much on Latin as earlier.	■ Teach appropriate behavior starting in infancy.
■ Develop curricula with practical considerations in mind.	■ Assign nobleman's son, at age 7, to a tutor.
■ Teach drawing, music, and physical education.	■ Develop a balanced schedule of work and play so the child does not suffer from overwork.
■ Eliminate corporal punishment; find other ways to motivate students to behave.	■ Make learning enjoyable for children.
	■ Start by reading *Aesop's fables*, followed by work of Aristophanes.
	■ Study music and painting—music for relaxation, and painting for practical purposes
	■ After age 15, nobleman's son should study public speaking (oratory), geography, cosmography, history, and mathematics.

which was Elyot's conception of the ideal role for a young nobleman, they had to know more than just how to make fancy speeches in Latin. Elyot stated that an orator "is required to be a heap of all manner of learning."[60]

HIGHER EDUCATIONAL OPPORTUNITY AND SOCIOECONOMIC STATUS IN TUDOR ENGLAND

If a young man did further his education by attending a university, he was either a son of a member of the gentry, or a son of a clergyman or tradesman. Most likely, however, he was the son of a member of the gentry. A pattern of socioeconomic discrepancy is found in the records of university colleges, showing that approximately the same percentages of gentleman's sons, and sons of clergymen, tradesmen, and peasants enrolled at Cambridge as attended the Free Grammar School at Colchester.[61] The concept of getting an advanced education to prepare for a profession had become accepted and established.

Most of the university students in Reformation England were of the gentry, who believed that a university education was necessary not only to obtain the professional preparation for a career but also to make contacts with those who would help them obtain a good position.[62] That the gentry were disproportionately represented in the universities can be verified by the finding that 33 percent of the students admitted to the four colleges of Cambridge University were sons of the gentry.[63] The other students were sons of clergy members and other professionals and represented 22 percent of the other undergraduates enrolled at Cambridge.[64] Tradesmen and merchants did send their sons to the university, but they did not do so in as great a number as the other socioeconomic groups described in this section. Only about 16 percent of the sons of tradesmen and merchants went to Cambridge, compared with 33 percent of the sons of gentry.[65] William Harrison, a resident of England during that time, commented on this situation in his book *The Description of England,* published in 1587. Harrison explained that some colleges were "erected by their founders at the first only for poor men's sons, whose parents were not able to bring them up unto learning."[66] He was quick to point out, however, that the wealthy had taken over these colleges, stating that the poor "have the least benefit of them, by reason the rich do so encroach upon them."[67]

Although the gentry may have sent their sons to the university to assure them of a successful career and a prosperous lifestyle, the sons did not always complete their education. It is interesting that only 30 percent of the gentlemen's sons at Caius College, one of the four colleges at Cambridge University, remained to graduate.[68]

The work was hard at the universities, and much was expected of the students. The curriculum, as you have learned, was humanistic in nature. Students began their studies at the age of 14 or 15 and usually graduated by age 18. The curriculum focused on the trivium (grammar, rhetoric, logic) and the quadrivium (arithmetic, music, geometry, astronomy). The teaching methods, formerly oral in nature, were being replaced by the tutorial method, which was private study with a professor. For example, those studying grammar might read the *Institutiones Grammaticae* of the sixth-century Latin author Priscian. Most students for the bachelor of arts degree read non-Christian authors, because the best teaching material was considered to come from the ancient world.[69]

Just as the upper classes recognized the value of university education to obtain a position with earning potential and prestige, so, too, did the lower classes understand that a university degree might transform their lives.[70] University students of poorer socioeconomic status also were more serious about their studies. William Harrison said that the upper classes who went to the university "study little other than histories (tales, romances), tables, dice, and trifles,"[71] meaning that they were gambling when they should have been studying. Harrison deplored the behavior of such young men at the university, stating that they would keep "riotous company, which draweth them from their books unto another trade."[72] Thus, the propensity of the wealthier students to spend their time gambling and socializing with friends was remarked on in Reformation England. Figures from this period reveal that degree completion was a matter of concern; 82 percent of the students from the "peasant" classes at Caius College of Cambridge University received their bachelor degree, compared with 50 percent in the whole university.[73] Despite the higher rate of degree completion for the lower classes, however, they represented only about 15 percent of the Cambridge University student population.[74] David Cressy, a noted historian of the English Reformation, believes that the lower socioeconomic classes in this period took their studies more seriously because they believed that the education was the way to a better life. In contrast, the upper classes believed that a university education was more for show, or to make a good impression. It was not really necessary because they already had money and did not have to make their own living.[75]

The same pattern, of unprecedented access to higher educational opportunity by the gentry, was reproduced in the professional law schools of Tudor England, known as the Inns of Court, in London. Keep in mind that their emphasis on professional preparation was consistent with the interest in material possessions and accumulation of wealth characteristic of the Tudor period.

EDUCATION FOR A PROFESSION: THE INNS OF COURT

As you have already learned, the Inns of Court in London were law schools, attended mainly by sons of the aristocracy and prosperous members of the middle class.[76] During the reign of Elizabeth I (1558–1603), law was a very profitable occupation, and someone educated in law might have the opportunity to be elected to Parliament.[77] Elizabeth herself was very supportive of higher education; she visited the universities often. In fact, her court consisted of very educated individuals, and she was fond of the classics. Because she believed that everyone should be educated in the humanistic tradition, it became fashionable not only to know the classics but also to have legal training.[78]

More than 80 percent of the students admitted to the Inns of Court came from the aristocracy, and many of the members of the original Long Parliament were educated at the Inns of Court.[79]

Students entering the Inns of Court to study law were accepted regardless of academic qualifications or interest in pursuing a career in law. Whereas law students today study the separate branches of criminal law, in the time of Elizabeth I no such divisions existed.[80] The study of law was so difficult that the student dropout rate was quite high.[81] Students who learned the law were forced to do a great deal of reading and commit many facts to memory. Most of the textbooks used to teach law either were too comprehensive, with so much detail that they could not be clearly organized, or else they omitted too many vital facts.[82] The three major methods of learning the law—private reading, court attendance, and participation in the recitation exercises—were widely used from 1560 to 1640 at the Inns of Court. Students also observed the courts in action, to learn how the process of conducting legal proceedings actually worked.[83]

Despite the difficulties of learning law, students from the gentry who attended the Inns of Court were able to learn if they applied themselves. Furthermore, the intellectual atmosphere of the Inns of Court encouraged young men of the gentry to attend plays, hear sermons, and be seen at court, or to learn to dance, fence, and play music. These extracurricular activities were helpful for those who wanted to go beyond a legal career.[84] Today, parents who want their children to attend highly selective liberal arts colleges or law school encourage their children from a young age to become involved in many extracurricular activities to broaden their skills and even to make contacts that can help them in their future careers or education.

The concept of preparing youth from the upper socioeconomic classes in society for professional careers and equipping them with the right social and academic skills has persisted from Reformation England to the present day.

BRIDGES FROM THE PAST TO THE PRESENT: VALUE AND USES OF CONTRIBUTIONS FROM REFORMATION ENGLAND TODAY

In this section we explore the major contributions from the Tudor educational period to today's educational system (see Table 6-1). There are many similarities between the Tudor educational system and the present system:

Table 6-1   **Educational Philosophy in Tudor England Versus Today's Philosophy**

TUDOR ENGLAND	TODAY
Literacy was important for the masses.	Federal policy, such as *NCLB* and *Goals 2000*, mandate literacy for all.
Education in the law was popular choice for upper-class students.	Many students enter law school each year, but not necessarily all from the upper classes; many get loans.
Only upper-class women were educated.	Education is for *all* girls and women.
Both English and Latin were studied.	Lessons are in English only. Latin is rarely studied.
Petty school was for children aged 4.	Preschool is for children aged 4.
Grammar school started at age 7.	Elementary school starts at age 6 (first grade).
Long school day	Shorter school day
Elementary school focused on reading.	There is an emphasis on reading, especially in the early grades.
Corporal punishment was used.	Corporal punishment is outlawed in most states.
Teacher salaries and qualifications were poor.	There are federal and state policies regarding teacher qualifications.
Male teachers predominate.	Female teachers predominate.
Hornbook was used for teaching.	Textbooks are used for teaching.
Universities were for students aged 14 or 15 to age 18.	High school students are aged 14–18.
Learning was by memorization.	Learning is by activity; cooperative learning is also used.

1. The concept of using schools to perpetuate a social class system by providing unequal educational opportunity for the wealthy versus the poor

2. A concern over teacher quality and salaries, teaching methods, and discipline procedures

3. Concerns over literacy and how best to teach reading

4. The type of curriculum for students in the early elementary grades, or preschool

5. The idea that reading should be taught first in the elementary school routine

6. The concept that students' strengths and weaknesses should be assessed in lesson planning and that teachers should make learning interesting and enjoyable for pupils.

Because each of these areas is very comprehensive, we have chosen two of them for discussion. First, we address the issue of using schools to perpetuate a social class system, because this is something you will experience as a teacher. You will find that students in your class who come from families that do not expose their children to books, read to them, or encourage them to do well in school are often less interested than students whose parents are highly involved in their education. Second, we discuss the concerns with teacher quality and salaries, teaching methods, and discipline procedures. As a future teacher reading this text, you need to be aware that teachers are often criticized for being poorly prepared, and the public perception of teachers is quite low, as is reflected in teacher salaries. Although teacher salaries are on the rise, as a teacher you will not earn as much as a physician or a lawyer. Discipline is a real issue of concern. New teachers also often have concerns about disciplinary issues in schools, and with teaching methods.

BRIDGE 1: SOCIAL CLASS AND HIGHER EDUCATIONAL OPPORTUNITIES

Many changes in society occurred in the period known as the English Reformation, during the reigns of Henry VIII, Edward VI, Mary, and Elizabeth I. One of the most notable changes was the concept that education could be used to further a person's social standing and economic status in society, in contrast to the Middle Age belief that the social status into which a person was born was the status that God had intended that person to occupy in society, and it was not supposed to change. For instance, the gentry utilized education to make sure that their sons would get ahead in society. A common way to do this was to send them to law school, or the Inns of Court, in London. Today, we see the same concept being applied in the choice of colleges that students of varying social classes make; parents in higher socioeconomic classes tend to send their children to more selective and expensive colleges. An article in the *Journal of Negro Education* states that college students who attend nonselective institutions are more poorly prepared academically and have little training in critical thinking because faculty members believe they are incapable of being taught such skills.[85] These students are also those who have less educational capital; they have not been exposed to enough books, have poorer reading skills, and have had fewer advantages than those students who come from higher income families, thus reproducing the social class system through higher educational opportunity.[86] Students from higher social classes receive such advantages as tutoring for the SAT. In fact, it has been reported in the *New York Times* that parents will pay $100 per hour for tutoring sessions for their high school–aged children, so that they can gain the skills and learn the test-taking strategies necessary to get high scores on the Scholastic Aptitude Test (SAT) used by college admissions offices.[87] Some tutors work independently tutoring wealthy students as their full-time job. An April 2004 *New York Times* report states that the wealthy students are taking over in higher education and edging out those from the middle class, causing friction among social classes.[88] It is reported that at the most selective private universities across the country, more fathers of freshmen are doctors than teachers or clergy members.[89] College admissions officers and administrators are awarding scholarships to students to remedy the discrepancy, instead of forcing them to take out loans to pay tuition. They are worried that the admissions policies are reproducing social class inequalities in society.[90]

BRIDGE 2: CONCERNS OVER TEACHER QUALITY AND SALARIES

It appears that it was rare that a member of the aristocracy in Tudor England would choose teaching as a career, because the salaries, as previously mentioned, were low. Another area of concern with regard to schoolteachers in Tudor England was the quality of schoolmasters. Tudor scholars and educators such as Charles Hoole, Richard Mulcaster, and Sir Thomas Elyot all described problems with the quality of schoolmasters. They mentioned that teachers were poorly prepared academically and ill prepared to teach because they did not know enough. They also had little understanding of how to discipline students. Elyot even remarked, "Lord God, how many good and clean wits of children be nowadays perished by ignorant schoolmasters?"[91] He also commented on the fact that people did not think highly of schoolteachers, and they were not paid enough, saying, "if the name of a schoolmaster were not so much had in contempt and if their labours with abundant salaries might be requited."[92] Charles Hoole wrote of the difficulties of getting parents to recognize that a schoolmaster had the right to correct a child's bad behavior, in his book *A New Discovery of the Old Art of Teaching School,* published in 1660. Hoole said, "we call to mind the too much indulgency of some parents, who neither love to blame their children's untowardness nor suffer the master to correct it."[93] Teachers today often are frustrated in their attempts to correct a child's misbehavior by the parents' or guardians' complaints that they are too harsh and that the child does not show that sort of behavior at home.

The quality of schoolteachers is an issue that has persisted from the period of Reformation England to the present day. The concept of having proper credentials to teach the elementary grades is an important contribution from the English Reformation. Today, states have requirements for teacher licensing, both at the elementary and secondary levels.

The issues of teacher quality and teacher pay continue to be worrisome concerns for educators and education policy makers. Unlike in the English Reformation, however, today's teaching force is largely women, whereas schoolteachers in the Tudor period were men. Women aged 25 to 34 make up about 75 percent of the teaching force. Women with higher test scores are no longer going into teaching as a career in such high numbers as they formerly did.[94] A study by the economist Sean P. Corcoran and colleagues William N. Evans and Robert M. Schwab analyzed test results and career choices of students in five high school classes from 1964 to 2000. These longitudinal studies matched the students' verbal and math scores with their eventual occupations. It was found that in 1964 the best female students (about 20 percent) chose teaching as a profession, whereas only 3.7 percent of the best female students in 1992 chose teaching.[95] Students with the higher scores do not choose teaching as a career because of salary. Corcoran et al. found that if women graduates from the top colleges were paid a top wage as teachers, they would choose to enter the teaching profession.[96] It is evident from this study, conducted by experienced economists, that the issue of salary, although not the only reason that teacher quality has declined, has a significant role in determining teacher quality. Attracting qualified teachers, both male and female, is a critical issue that will persist into the future.

SUMMARY

This chapter described the spread of the Reformation from Germany to England and the effect of governmental policies, particularly the dissolution of the monasteries in King Henry VIII's reign, on education. It also discussed how social class affected education, since many children of the gentry went into the higher paying professions, such as law.

Two major educators of the Tudor period in England were Richard Mulcaster, who described his educational policies for all children, and Thomas Elyot, who focused on education for children of the wealthy. The policies of these two educators further delineated the class consciousness of society in Tudor England.

The next chapter focuses on the Puritan migration to America and on education in the American colonies, specifically in Virginia and New England.

QUESTIONS FOR DISCUSSION

1. Social class and wealth were important in determining entrance to a university or profession in Tudor England. How important are those factors now? Is the situation different or similar in America with regard to the effects of social class and wealth in educational attainment and occupational status? Why or why not?

2. In Tudor England, education for girls was traditionally unpopular; girls received only a minimal education. How do those beliefs compare and contrast with today's beliefs about education for girls?

3. How were the divisions in age and curriculum in Tudor England similar to or different from age and curriculum divisions in our current educational system? Give at least one example to back up your answer.

4. In Reformation England, literacy and education for the masses was becoming an important issue. How does the literacy rate in Tudor England compare with the current U.S. literacy rate?

5. The policies of King Henry VIII, especially the dissolution of the monasteries, had a large impact on education. This could be considered governmental legislation and regulation of education. Can you think of any recent federal legislation that has had an impact on education?

6. The qualifications of Tudor schoolmasters were explored in this chapter. Compare and contrast them with the qualifications required of schoolteachers today.

SUGGESTED ACTIVITIES

1. Using the NCES (National Center for Education Statistics) Web site, research the factors involved in student dropout rates, such as parental support for education and financial support. Make a list of the 10 most important factors involved, in order of importance, with 1 being the most important, and present it to your class as a PowerPoint presentation. You may also use other Web resources, such as those listed below.

2. Research at least one of the most important pieces of federal legislation concerning education in the last 5 years. Describe (a) why it was developed (its rationale); (b) whom it was intended to serve; (c) the research behind the legislation; and (d) the effects of the legislation on education. Present your findings to the class as a PowerPoint presentation.

3. Interview a teacher who has consistently received high ratings for teaching excellence about what he/she thinks should be required for preparation to teach. Analyze how that individual's preparation in teaching compares and contrasts with the preparation you are receiving for teaching at your college or university. Write a three- to five-page paper explaining your findings and analysis.

4. Research the literacy rates for different races and/or socioeconomic groups in America. Present your findings on the role of socioeconomic status in learning to read and write to the class as an interactive presentation. This means that you will involve the class by letting them work together in small groups to brainstorm possible solutions to this problem.

5. Suppose you are running for president, and you are interested in improving teacher quality. Write a letter to a newspaper in which you inform the public

about how you plan to change funding to attract more qualified teachers to the profession. Present your letter to the class in the form of a mock campaign address.

Bibliography

Brigden, S. (1982, May). Youth and the English Reformation. *Past and Present,* no. 95, 37–67.

Britnell, R. (1997). *The closing of the Middle Ages: England, 1471–1529.* Oxford: Blackwell.

Brown, J. H. (1972). *Elizabethan schooldays: An account of the English grammar schools in the second half of the sixteenth century.* New York: Benjamin Blom (Originally published in Oxford, 1933).

Caspari, F. (1968). *Humanism and the social order in Tudor England.* New York: Teachers College Press.

Cressy, D. L. (2003). Describing the social order of Elizabethan and Stuart England. In *Society and culture in early modern England.* Burlington, VT: Ashgate Press.

Cressy, D. L. (2003). A drudgery of schoolmasters: The teaching profession in Elizabethan and Stuart England. In *Society and culture in early modern England.* Burlington, VT: Ashgate Press.

Cressy, D. L. (2003). Educational opportunity in Tudor and Stuart England. In *Society and culture in early modern England.* Burlington, VT: Ashgate Press.

Cressy, D. L. (2003). Levels of illiteracy in England, 1530–1730. In *Society and culture in early modern England.* Burlington, VT: Ashgate Press.

DeMolen, R. L. (1974). Richard Mulcaster and the profession of teaching in sixteenth-century England. *Journal of the History of Ideas, 35*(1).

Elyot, Sir T. (1969). *The book named the governor* (J. M. Major, Abr. & Ed.) New York: Teachers College Press.

Friedman, A. T. (1985). The influence of humanism on the education of girls and boys in Tudor England. *History of Education Quarterly, 25*(1/2).

Gross, J. (2003, October 23). Competition among the well-to-do is good business for tutors. *New York Times.*

Harrison, W. (1994). *The description of England: The classic contemporary account of Tudor social life.* Washington, DC: Folger Shakespeare Library.

Knowles, D. (1976). *Bare ruined choirs: The dissolution of the English monasteries.* Cambridge: Cambridge University Press.

Leonhardt, D. (2004, April 22). As wealthy fill top colleges, concerns grow over fairness. *New York Times.*

Logan, F. D. (1991). The first royal visitation of the English universities, 1535. *English Historical Review, 106*(421).

McMahon, C. M. (2004). A short history of Calvinism. Retrieved from http://www.apuritansmind.com

A very comprehensive Web site devoted to the study of Calvinism in England and its effects on English society and immigration to America.

Moran, J. H. (1985). *The growth of English schooling, 1340–1548.* Princeton, NJ: Princeton University Press.

Mulcaster, R. (1971). *Positions.* (R. L. DeMolen, Abr. & Ed.) New York: Teachers College Press.

Newcombe, D. G. (1995). *Henry VIII and the English Reformation*. New York: Routledge.

Postrel, V. (2004, March 25). Economic Scene: In their hiring of teachers, do the nation's public schools get what they pay for? *The New York Times*. See the Business/Financial Desk section.

Powell, K., & Cook, C. (1977). *English historical facts, 1485–1603*. Totowa, NJ: Rowman and Littlefield.

Prest, W. (1967, December). Legal education of the gentry at the Inns of Court, 1560–1640. *Past and Present*, no. 3, 20–39.

Rex, R. (1993). *Henry VIII and the English Reformation*. New York: St. Martin's Press.

Sheils, W. J. (1989). *The English Reformation, 1530–1570*. New York: Longman.

Simon, J. (1957, April). The Reformation and English education. *Past and Present*, no. 11, 48–65.

Simon, J. (1963, November). The social origins of Cambridge students, 1603–1640. *Past and Present*, no. 26, 58–67.

Simon, J. (1967). *Education and Society in Tudor England*. Cambridge: Cambridge University Press.

Thompson, C. (1973). *Schools in Tudor England*. Charlottesville: University Press of Virginia.

Thompson, C. (1979). *Universities in Tudor England*. Charlottesville: University Press of Virginia.

Trusty, J., Robinson, C. R., Plata, M., & Ng, K.-M. (2000). Effects of gender, postsecondary status, and early academic performance on postsecondary educational choice. *Journal of Counseling and Development*, *78*(4), 463–472.

Tsui, L. (2003). Reproducing social inequalities through higher education: Critical thinking as valued capital. *Journal of Negro Education*, *72*(3), 326.

Watson, F. (1900). The state and education during the Commonwealth. *English Historical Review*, *15*(57), 58–72.

Watson, F. (1908). *The English grammar schools to 1660*. Cambridge: Cambridge University Press.

Suggestions for Further Reading

In addition to the works cited in the bibliography, the following are suggested for further reading.

Smith, P. (1910). Luther and Henry VIII. *English Historical Review*, *125*(100).

Stone, L. (1969, February). Literacy and education in England, 1640–1900. *Past and Present*, no. 42.

Relevant Web Sites

Michigan State University *http://www.educ.msu.edu/homepages/laurence/reformation/English/English.htm* This site is a permanent site, which contains pages of information on the English Reformation.

History Learning Site *http://www.historylearningsite.co.uk/reformation.htm* Another good source of information on England and the Reformation.

BBC History: The English Reformation. By Professor Andrew Pettegree *http://www.bbc.co.uk/history/state/church_reformation/english_reformation_03.shtml* Good explanation of the political, social, and religious aspects of the English Reformation.

The English Reformation: Puritanism online *http://puritanism.online.fr/engref.html* Great site with many primary sources on Puritan theology and original writings from Puritan educators.

Questia online *http://www.questia.com* World's largest online library. Good for looking up anything pertaining to England, English history, and the Reformation.

Annenberg/CPB *http://www.learner.org* Provides lesson planning information for K-12 teachers on many topics.

Education Week *http://www.edweek.org* Weekly newspaper on current educational topics, including federal and state legislation.

National Center for Education Statistics *http://www.nces.ed.gov* Valuable for looking up past and previous statistics and other information on American education.

U.S. Department of Education *http://www.ed.gov* Good website for understanding the policies of the U.S. Department of Education.

Endnotes

[1] Craig R. Thompson, *Schools in Tudor England* (Charlottesville: University Press of Virginia, 1973), 3.

[2] Joan Simon, *Education and Society in Tudor England* (London: Cambridge University Press, 1966), 11.

[3] C. Matthew McMahon, "A Short History of Calvinism," available on the Web at *http://www.apuritansmind.com* This is a very comprehensive site devoted to the study of Calvinism in England and its effects on English society and emigration to America. Works cited in this short article include Lewis W. Spitz, *The Protestant Reformation* (New York: Harper and Row, 1984) and Earle E. Cairns, *Christianity Through the Centuries* (Grand Rapids, MI: Zondervan, 1981).

[4] David Knowles, *Bare Ruined Choirs: The Dissolution of the English Monasteries* (Cambridge: Cambridge University Press, 1976), 5.

[5] Ibid.

[6] Simon, *Education and Society,* 170.

[7] Jo-Ann Hoeppner Moran, *The Growth of English Schooling, 1340–1548* (Princeton, NJ: Princeton University Press, 1985), 164.

[8] Ibid.

[9] David Cressy, "Educational Opportunity in Tudor and Stuart England," in *Society and Culture in Early Modern England* (Burlington VT: Ashgate Press, 2003), 314.

[10] Ibid.

[11] W. J. Sheils, *The English Reformation, 1530–1570* (New York: Longman, 1989), 85.

[12] Ken Powell & Chris Cook, *English Historical Facts, 1485–1603* (Totowa, NJ: Rowman and Littlefield, 1977), 101.

[13] Ibid.

[14] D. G. Newcombe, *Henry VIII and the English Reformation* (New York: Routledge, 1995), 19.

[15] Simon, *Education and Society,* 59.

[16] Richard Rex, *Henry VIII and the English Reformation* (New York: St. Martin's Press, 1993), 66.

[17] Powell and Cook, *English Historical Facts,* 135.

[18] Simon, *Education and Society,* 179.

[19] Thompson, *Schools in Tudor England,* 15.

[20] Ibid., 8.

[21] Ibid., 5.

[22] Joan Simon, "The Reformation and English Education," *Past and Present,* no. 11 (April 1957), 52.

[23] Thompson, *Schools in Tudor England,* 2.

[24] Ibid., 3.

[25] Ibid., 4–5.

[26] Simon, "The Reformation and English Education," 55.

[27] Ibid., 56.

[28] Ibid.

[29] Thompson, *Schools in Tudor England,* 11.

[30] Ibid.

[31] Ibid., 12.

[32] Hoeppner Moran, *Growth of English Schooling,* 21–22.

[33] Ibid., 23.

[34] Thompson, *Schools in Tudor England,* 36.

[35] Ibid.

[36] Ibid.

[37] Ibid., 20.

[38] Ibid., 16–18.

[39] Ibid.

[40] Richard Mulcaster, *Positions,* abr. & ed. Richard L. DeMolen (New York: Teachers College Press, 1971), 47.

[41] Ibid., 60.

[42] Ibid., 66.

[43] Ibid., 60.

[44] Ibid., 68.

[45] Ibid., 69.

[46] Sir Thomas Elyot, *The Book Named the Governor,* ed. & abr. John M. Major (New York: Teachers College Press, 1969), 64. In this edition, pp. 62–65 are chapter 4, "The Education or Form of Bringing Up of the Child of a Gentleman Which Is to Have Authority in a Public Weal."

[47] Ibid.

[48] Ibid., 68.

[49] Ibid., 69.

[50] Ibid., 70.

[51] Ibid., 72.

[52] Ibid.

[53] Ibid., 76.

[54] Ibid., 19. This is in the introduction to this edition.

[55] Ibid.

[56] Ibid., 21.

[57] Ibid., 24.

[58] Ibid., 22.

[59] Ibid., 110.

[60] Ibid., 112.

[61] David Cressy, "Educational Opportunity in Tudor and Stuart England," in *Society and Culture in Modern England* (Burlington, VT: Ashgate Press, 2003), 311.

[62] Ibid., 312.

[63] Ibid.

[64] Ibid.

[65] Ibid.

[66] William Harrison, *The Description of England: The Classic Contemporary Account of Tudor Social Life*, ed. Georges Edelen (Washington, DC: Folger Shakespeare Library, 1994). See p. 70. This version was originally published in 1587. This edition is based on one of the four reprints of the 1587 edition. See the Preface, pp. vii–ix, for details.

[67] Ibid., 71.

[68] Cressy, *Educational Opportunity,* 312.

[69] Richard Britnell, *The Closing of the Middle Ages: England, 1471–1529* (Oxford: Blackwell, 1997), 160–62.

[70] Cressy, *Educational Opportunity,* 313.

[71] Harrison, *Description of England,* 71.

[72] Ibid.

[73] Cressy, *Educational Opportunity,* 313.

[74] Ibid.

[75] Ibid.

[76] Fritz Caspari, *Humanism and the Social Order in Tudor England* (New York: Teachers College Press, 1968), 266.

[77] Ibid., 269.

[78] Ibid., 270.

[79] Wilfrid Priest, "Legal Education of the Gentry at the Inns of Court, 1560–1640," *Past and Present,* no. 38 (December 1967), 20.

[80] Ibid., 30.

81　Ibid., 31.

82　Ibid., 32.

83　Ibid., 25.

84　Ibid., 38.

85　Lisa Tsui, "Reproducing Social Inequalities Through Higher Education: Critical Thinking as Valued Capital," *Journal of Negro Education, 72,* no. 3 (2003), 326.

86　Ibid.

87　Jane Gross, "Competition Among the Well-to-Do Is Good Business for Tutors," *New York Times,* October 23, 2003.

88　David Leonhardt, "As Wealthy Fill Top Colleges, Concerns Grow Over Fairness," *New York Times,* April 22, 2004.

89　Ibid.

90　Ibid.

91　David Cressy, *Education in Tudor and Stuart England* (New York: St. Martin's Press, 1975), 60–61.

92　Ibid. The spelling is the original from Elyot's book *The Book Named the Governor* (1531).

93　Cressy, 63.

94　Virginia Postrel, "Economic Scene: In Their Hiring of Teachers, Do the Nation's Public Schools Get What They Pay For?" *New York Times,* March 25, 2004. See the Business/ Financial Desk section.

95　Ibid.

96　Ibid. The findings of this study will be published in the summer of 2004, in the *American Economic Review* as part of the Papers and Proceedings of the American Economic Association's 2004 meetings. The paper is online at *http://www.csus.edu/indiv/c/corcorans/research.htm*

PART 3

Formation of the American Education System

Chapter 7

Puritan Life: Education in the New England and Virginia Colonies

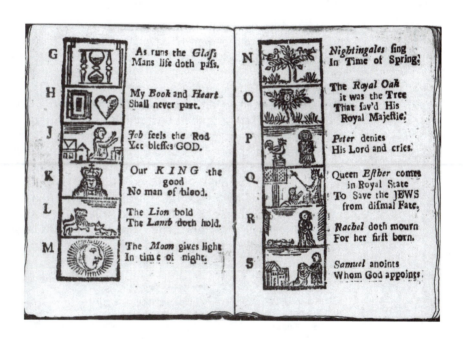

Learning Objectives

1. Give the reasons for Puritan migration to America.
2. Explain the lifestyle of the Puritans.
3. Connect the Puritan lifestyle to the development of the Puritans' educational system in both the New England and Virginia colonies.
4. List significant dates in the development of literacy laws for states.
5. Understand the timeline of the development of higher educational institutions in America circa 1625–1820.

INTRODUCTION

In chapter 6 you learned about how the German Reformation spread to England and how the rise of the English upper classes led to an increased emphasis on using education to improve one's socioeconomic status. The chapter covered the years from 1534, when Henry VIII passed the Act of Supremacy to 1625, the height of Puritan persecution in English society.

Like the Lutherans in the German Reformation, the Puritans broke with the established Church to form their own religion. The Puritans and Lutherans shared a dislike of the emphasis on ritual and of the corruption in the Church; in England, the Puritans joined with Luther to protest the extravagances of the Church. They found it intolerable that priests broke the vow of celibacy, held multiple offices, and were ill prepared to hold the priesthood.

The Puritans were persecuted for their beliefs as English society did not take kindly to their disdain of the established rituals of the Anglican Church and their desire to break with tradition. Therefore, the Puritans began to immigrate to the American colonies in increasing numbers, starting in 1620.

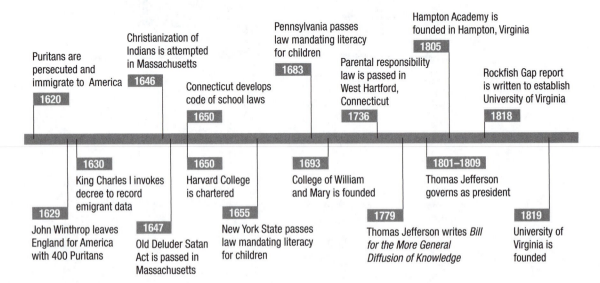

The Puritans settled in the Mid-Atlantic and New England regions. Their educational system was religious in scope, in keeping with their belief that life should be centered around worship. For instance, children did not read anything that was not religious based.

This chapter focuses on education in the Puritan colonies of New England and Virginia because these geographical areas represent two extremes in the use of socioeconomic status and religious beliefs to establish an educational system in a newly developed area. The Virginia colonies, including Jamestown and Williamsburg, were economically dependent on growing tobacco, which necessitated a slave economy. The gentry in Virginia, who were sons of plantation owners, went to college, such as the College of William and Mary in Williamsburg, founded in 1693. Later, they attended the University of Virginia, founded by **Thomas Jefferson** in 1819. Education was mainly for the wealthy, and slaves rarely received any education. Women and girls in the Virginia colonies were educated mainly at home, with the focus of their education on domestic skills.

In the New England colonies, by contrast, the ideas of **Cotton Mather** and **John Winthrop,** both strict Puritan leaders, led to more homogeneous goals for education of the young in small villages. The Puritans of New England lived and worked on small farms; their economy did not depend on growing tobacco. The Puritan New England colonies were more successful, with better living conditions, than the colonies in Virginia. This meant that it took less time to establish schools in the New England colonies than the Virginia colonies. Owing to terrible living conditions at Jamestown, Virginia, repeated attempts at settlement were required, which delayed the development of education in the Virginia colonies.

Spotlight On ←———————————————————————————

REASONS FOR PURITAN MIGRATION

Religious persecution and economic problems were both responsible for the Puritan migration to the American colonies. England's population had risen by 40 percent between 1580 and 1640 while at the same time the English textile industry had begun to fail, leaving many unemployed.

Individuals left for the colonies in search of apprenticeships or to work as domestic servants, since such jobs were scarce in England.

The English monarchy took legal action against the migration. In May 1630 King Charles I invoked his father James I's earlier decree, which required that commissioners of the English ports record biographical data of those leaving, including name, place of birth, and vocation or trade. Passengers often disguised themselves as servants to avoid attracting undue attention when boarding ships so they would not be identified and held as nonconformists.

This chapter details the educational philosophies of John Winthrop in New England and Thomas Jefferson, of Virginia. John Winthrop, the New England Puritan leader, was institutional in developing the educational system in Massachusetts.

The Puritans of both the New England and the Virginia colonies may have had different types of educational systems and lifestyles, but they migrated to America for similar reasons. This chapter begins by describing the migration and educational system of the Puritans and ends with the establishment of the University of Virginia in 1819, the first state university. By 1820, most of the state universities of the original thirteen colonies had been established.

THE VISION OF JOHN WINTHROP, GOVERNOR OF THE MASSACHUSETTS BAY COMPANY

The city lawyer and Puritan activist John Winthrop detested the policies of King Charles I and by the late 1620s had decided to leave England. In March 1629 Winthrop sold his large country estate and moved to America along with 400 other Puritans. He joined the Massachusetts Bay Company and was elected governor of the company by a general court in 1629. By the winter of 1629/30, Winthrop and his family had moved with about 1000 others to Massachusetts.[1] This was the beginning of the Puritan migration to New England. As the new governor of the Massachusetts Bay Company, which had received a royal charter that granted powers of self-government, Winthrop had a great deal of responsibility. He kept a diary in which he recorded the difficulties of migration to Massachusetts. Mortality rates were high on board ship, and the settlers were not prepared for the cold winters or the problems of life in the New England area. Winthrop reported that people had frostbite and that the settlers endured fire, because the roofs were thatched and the chimneys poorly constructed. There were epidemics of smallpox, and diphtheria, whooping cough, and scarlet fever, caused by untreated strep throat, were common causes of death among children.

Despite the difficulties, the Puritans who settled in New England persevered, to find a place "of Cohabitation and Consorteshipp under a due forme of Government both civill and ecclesiasticall."[2] Winthrop envisioned that New England would become a model of Christian charity, a place that others would look up to because it was a model of godly discipline.[3] The early days of the colonies were marked by attempts to educate the Indians. John Eliot, a great favorite of Cotton Mather's and a graduate of Cambridge, tried to preach to the Native Americans in 1646, with little success. A second attempt was more successful. Eliot had studied the Native Americans' language and preached to them in their own language for an hour and a half. This could be considered the first attempt at adult education.[4] The government of Massachusetts was concerned that the Native Americans obey and understand the laws of the new colony. Fines collected from the Native Americans were used to build meetinghouses and to educate their children. Native American scholars even attended Harvard College in later years.[5]

From the outset the founders of the New England colonies had definite ideas about the type of settlement they wanted to establish, including the type of education their children would receive and the lifestyle they would follow.

THE NEW ENGLAND COLONIES: RELIGION IS THE FOCUS

The lifestyle of the Puritans in the New England colonies was extremely rigid. It is necessary to understand the Puritan lifestyle to place the development of their educational system in context. Religion was interwoven throughout the activities of daily life, including education; it was the glue that cemented families together in the towns and villages of colonial New England and was the major force in shaping their lives and educational systems.

The focal point of Puritan towns and villages was the meetinghouse. A law enacted in 1675 mandated a meetinghouse for every town in the colony, and colonists' homes had to be built within half a mile of the meetinghouse.[6] In fact, the colonists were forced by law to participate in raising the meetinghouse.[7] Children attended church with their parents.

Although the education of Puritan children was primarily religious in scope, it also had a vocational component. By participating in the daily farm chores necessary for survival, Puritan children learned important skills such as spinning flax or wool to make clothing, making candles, weaving, and harvesting the agricultural crops such as corn, hay, wheat, and rye. Colonial families had to make or grow everything and all family members, including the children, helped with whatever had to be done.

Daily life included some form of daily household reading of the Bible. Some families also used the text *The English Scholemaister,* published in 1596, which systematically taught letters, syllables, words, sentences, and paragraphs. All instruction in reading was based on some sort of religious text.

Although the New England Puritans did some reading at home, they understood the concept of sending young children to school to learn to read. Early schooling included sending children to the *dame school,* a school taught by a housewife who taught neighborhood children in exchange for a small fee. Her major responsibility included preparing them to receive the Word of God.[8] The dame school was the equivalent of a present-day nursery school or preschool.

The Commonwealth of Massachusetts, with the institution of the **Old Deluder Satan Act** of 1647, mandated the establishment of a school where children were taught to read and write in each town with 50 or so families. Every town of 100 householders was required to establish a grammar school. The same laws applied in the Connecticut Code of Laws of 1650. Such schools were public, but not free, as the parents had to support them.[9] In 1644 in Salem, Massachusetts, lists of children who should be attending school were compiled, and if their parents were wealthy, they had to pay tuition regardless of whether the children attended school.[10] The idea that education was necessary to prevent corruption of youth had taken firm hold. Laws requiring that children learn to read were passed by Connecticut in 1650, New York in 1655, and Pennsylvania in 1683.[11]

PARENTING PRACTICES IN PURITAN NEW ENGLAND

Puritan children received a strict upbringing, starting in infancy. Church members had to bring newborns to the meetinghouse within 2 weeks of the child's birth to be baptized, which involved pouring water over the child's head. This ritual was observed even in the bitter New England winters, in the unheated meetinghouses, because it was believed that the souls of unbaptized children might end up in hell if they died. It was less of a risk to miss the baptism than it was to incur the high odds of natural death to get the child baptized.[12] Infants were supposed to be taught the message of Christ according to Puritan beliefs. The teacher of the First Church in Boston, Reverend Benjamin Wadsworth, said, "While you lay them in your bosomes, and dandle them on your knees, try by little and little to infuse good things, holy truths into them."[13]

Children went to meeting with their families on Sunday and were expected to sit still and listen attentively to the sermon, which usually lasted about 2 hours. During the winters the building was so cold that the communion bread froze on the plates.[14] If the children fell asleep, they were rapped on the head with a stick by the tithingman, who was a type of enforcer in Puritan New England. He also served as tax collector, disciplinarian, and teacher.[15]

The children's clothing reflected the colonists' belief that children should conform to adult expectations and behavior from the age of 7, so children were dressed like adults. Children were fined if they did not observe the Sabbath by the age of 14. At age 16 they were supposed to be mature enough to understand the consequences of bad behavior. One of the most important and serious rites of passage into adulthood was choosing a career, a serious matter for a young Puritan, for it had religious significance. The young Puritan had to decide for himself which vocation he was called to by God and had to try to enter that occupation.[16] Only boys and young men were able to choose a vocation or career. Girls and women stayed at home. They did learn to read and write, but their careers were centered on their farms and homes.

Parental responsibility for education was taken seriously. Children whose parents failed to provide the required amount of wood to heat the schoolhouse were often made to sit in the coldest corner of the classroom.[17] By 1736 the town of West Hartford, Connecticut, had passed an order that children whose parents had not contributed the required amount of wood could not attend school.[18] This insistence on parental involvement in education is a direct contribution to the present-day educational system.

Puritan parents insisted on good behavior at school, in keeping with the Puritan emphasis on individual responsibility and strength of character. Despite the physical discomforts of the New England winters, the monotonous teaching methods, and the lack of resources in the schoolhouses, pupils were successful at learning to read and write in the New England schools. The next section focuses on the curriculum of this period and the instructional methods used. Table 7-1 summarizes the characteristics of education in the New England colonies.

PURITAN NEW ENGLAND CURRICULUM AND TEACHING METHODS

Books used in Puritan New England schools were entirely religious or moral in scope. The hornbook was used first in teaching students to read. It was used to teach the alphabet, and students learned how syllables formed words by studying the Lord's Prayer at the bottom of the hornbook.

Table 7-1 **Characteristics of New England Education**

- School was mandatory, and it was free. This was the beginning of public education in America.
- Schoolhouses lacked comfort. Students sat on hard benches, and basic supplies, including paper and globes to teach geography, were unavailable.
- Only religious texts, such as the *New England Primer* and the Bible, were used for learning. No secular books or materials were permitted.
- Students had to study the catechism, and their families were visited by deacons and ministers to ensure that this was enforced
- Parents had to cooperate and provide supplies, such as fuel to heat the schoolhouses in winter
- Dame schools, or preschools, taught reading and writing to young children
- There was an emphasis on penmanship in teaching writing. Students learned to master the individual letters and then later would copy, five or six times, moral sentences assigned by the teacher.
- Teaching involved one method: memorization and recitation.
- Women did not go to universities or into the ministry.
- Boys were taught grammar if they planned to attend the university or enter the ministry.
- Corporal punishment was used in the schools.
- Upperclassmen in universities or colleges, such as Harvard College, taught school, to pay for their education.
- Teaching was not seen as a permanent, lifelong profession.
- There was a lack of independent thought, the emphasis was on following directions.

The *New England Primer,* known as the "Little Bible of New England" because of the highly religious nature of its teachings, succeeded the hornbook.[19] The *Primer* contained prayers to be said morning and evening by children and a grace that was to be said before meals. Each letter of the alphabet was illustrated with a small picture, followed by a verse. Two thirds of these verses represented Biblical incidents. For instance, the letter *A* was taught by the verse "In Adam's Fall, we sinned all." The Lord's Prayer and the Apostles' Creed were also found in the *Primer.* After 1737, the Shorter Catechism, a great favorite of Cotton Mather's, was found in the *Primer* as well. Students were supposed to master the Old and New Testaments of the Bible in the final stages of the reading curriculum. Imported English Bibles were used for this task, because it was illegal to print Bibles on American presses until after the Revolution.[20]

Writing was also an important part of the elementary curriculum in Puritan New England. Writing masters, who focused on penmanship, chose sentences from Mather's *Catechism* for their students to copy. Today, penmanship is still taught, particularly in the early elementary grades.

Teaching methods consisted mostly of recitation; students would arise in a group and recite out loud whatever the teacher requested. Students who made a mistake in recitation were singled out by the teacher. Spelling, reading, and arithmetic were studied. Spelling was a problem, though, because until Noah Webster published his spelling book and dictionary, words were spelled as they sounded; there was no uniformity in spelling.[21]

Books for teaching arithmetic were unknown; teachers used "sum books" in which they gave rules and problems in arithmetic to their pupils. Students copied these sums down, but the schoolmaster did not explain the process by which they were solved. Students could struggle to solve problems without any explanation from their teacher for quite some time.[22] Today, specific methods exist for teaching mathematics, to make certain that students understand the process of solving arithmetic equations.

Keep in mind that teachers in Puritan New England were not trained as teachers are today. No teacher training schools or courses existed until Horace Mann developed his institution in the 1830s, in Massachusetts. Teachers in Puritan New England taught merely to make some money to pursue another vocation, such as the priesthood, or another profession and taught only for a short time. Teachers occupied a low status in society.

Besides teaching methods, another important difference between the elementary classes in Puritan New England and elementary classrooms of today was the gender difference in studies. Most Puritan children did not progress beyond an elementary education unless they were preparing to enter the ministry or other professions, in which case they went on to study grammar in preparation for going to university. Only boys were expected to use *Lilly's Grammar,* a comprehensive text that named 25 different kinds of nouns, which boys were expected to learn.[23]

HIGHER EDUCATION IN NEW ENGLAND: HARVARD COLLEGE

The establishment of a system of higher education was a milestone in the colony's development, indicating a serious acceptance of education. In New England, Harvard College, chartered in 1650, was established by Puritans who wanted to replicate the quality of learning at home in England but without the moral problems they thought were prevalent in the English universities.[24] Winthrop wrote in 1629 of the corrupt practices of the English colleges and universities:

> Most children (even the best witts and of faierest hopes) are perverted, corrupted and utterlie overthrowne by the multitude of evill examples and the licentious government of those Seminaries.[25]

The Harvard College charter states that it was founded to advance literature, arts, and sciences and to educate both English and Indian youth in knowledge and godliness.[26] The charter created a corporation comprising the president, treasurer, and five fellows who were to govern the college and manage its resources.[27] To declare its independence from England and the king, Harvard granted degrees to students with no explicit authority from the king or Parliament.[28]

Most boys were admitted to Harvard at age 15. Unruly behavior was not tolerated. Young pupils who did not conform to expected norms of behavior could be disciplined by corporal punishment; the older students were subjected to fines. They could also be publicly humiliated for their behavior.

Between 1650 and 1660 most of the students at Harvard came from wealthy families and were usually the sons of physicians, merchants, ministers, magistrates, and prosperous farmers, many of whom were alumni of Harvard. Although they did not receive any kind of financial aid, many students earned money to finance their education by teaching school. For instance, Josiah Cotton, who graduated from Harvard, taught school for three winter sessions, despite being only 16 years old.[29]

The curriculum at Harvard was strictly classical in nature. The formal curriculum lasted for 3 years and required an understanding of Cicero, fluency in Latin, and at least an elementary knowledge of Greek grammar. Students were usually taught using the disputation method, and the themes for debate were organized according to the course of study, which could be either the trivium (grammar, logic, rhetoric) or the three branches of philosophy (physics, ethics, metaphysics.)[30] The goal of the instructional methods was to force students to process and systematize information and to dispute expertly. Because Puritan culture emphasized following authority and the rules, and developing a highly moral character, the curriculum did not focus on independent thought or cooperative learning, both of which are popular today. Although educational historians have characterized the curriculum at Harvard as extremely formal and even dull, the methods of instruction made sense given the character of Puritan life during that time.

Although the curriculum at Harvard College has changed since Puritan times, the socioeconomic factor related to educational opportunity has not. Poorer students had difficulty obtaining an education at Harvard, whereas wealthy students did not. This discrepancy persists to the present.

THE VIRGINIA COLONIES: EARLY ATTEMPTS AT EDUCATION

As you have seen, education in the Puritan colonies developed in a religious context, and religious obedience was the most important component of that development. Education in the colonies of Jamestown and Williamsburg, Virginia, developed in quite a different way.

The earliest attempts at education in the Virginia colonies were constrained by the difficulties of settlement. Initial attempts at settlement began about 1607 with the London Company of Virginia, also called the Virginia Company. Despite the successful growth of tobacco on plantations along the eastern rivers of Virginia and the Chesapeake Bay, the Virginia colonies experienced fires, Indian massacres, and other problems that hindered the development of formal education. There were very few schoolhouses available for children to attend for more than a century. Establishing schoolhouses to promote learning, as in the New England colonies, did not appear to be of interest to those in the Virginia colonies. There were no laws, as in Massachusetts, to force parents to send their children to school. Governor Berkeley, one of the governors of the Virginia colony, wrote home to

England in 1670 that he was glad there were no free schools in Virginia, because "learning hath brought disobedience and heresy into the world."[31]

COLONIAL VIRGINIA: THE ESTABLISHMENT OF FREE SCHOOLS

Fortunately, others did not agree with Berkeley's dire prophecies about education. Robert Beverley, writing in 1705, described the free schools established in Virginia, stating that the schools "have been founded by the legacies of well-inclined gentlemen, and the management of them hath commonly been left to the direction of the county court or the vestry of their respective parishes."[32] Free schools were begun when a wealthy planter bequeathed land or money to start a school in his will.

Because the success of the Virginia colonies reflected on England, the English wanted education in Virginia to be successful. In 1621 the Virginia Company used the 70 pounds donated by a ship's chaplain, the Reverend Mr. Copeland, to build a "publique free schole in Virginia."[33] Named the East India School, it was to be set on 1,000 acres of land in Charles City, Virginia; however, before it was built, an Indian massacre nearly destroyed the entire colony, delaying plans for the formal establishment of schools in Virginia. In 1642 Benjamin Syms bequeathed land and cattle to found a free school in Elizabeth City County. The profits from the sale of the milk and the first newborn cattle were to be used to build a schoolhouse, and later profits were to be used to carry on the school.[34] Another wealthy planter, Thomas Eaton, left 500 acres of land, including slaves, his house and its contents, and the orchards and farm animals, to build a second free school for children in Elizabeth City County. Poor children attended both schools; however, many children whose parents could afford to pay for their education attended the Eaton School. By 1805 the Eaton and Syms schools combined to form Hampton Academy, which eventually became part of the public school system of the town of Hampton, Virginia.[35]

By 1648 there were 20 parishes in the colony, and each had a minister. The ministers held schools as part of their mission to educate youth of the parishes.[36] Beverley wrote that little schools were formed to educate children. In 1722 the Reverend Hugh Jones wrote that most parishes had "schools, little houses, being built on purpose where are taught English and writing, &c."[37]

Children of the wealthy had access to private schools and private tutors, who taught them such subjects as Latin and Greek. Other subjects were reading, writing, and arithmetic.[38] Tutors might be indentured servants. Often, young ministers came over as tutors.[39]

The idea of advertising for qualified tutors caught on in the Virginia colonies. Advertisements in the *Virginia Gazette* asked for such qualifications as "capable of teaching children to read and write," or "a tutor for a private family, who among other things thoroughly understands mathematics."[40]

Although most students from the wealthy families were boys, education for girls was evidently not unheard of; a boarding school for girls was seen in Williamsburg about 1760.[41]

Table 7-2 summarizes the characteristics of education in the Virginia colonies.

Table 7-2 **Characteristics of Education in the Virginia Colonies**

- Education in the Virginia colonies began as highly religious, rather than secular.
- It was difficult to establish schools owing to the geography of Virginia. There were no small towns or villages as in New England; plantations were scattered.
- There was no agreed-on or universal vision as to the purposes of education in colonial Virginia, unlike in New England.
- Education did not exist for slaves.
- Women were educated only at home.
- Few schoolhouses existed.
- Government did not mandate education, as in New England.
- The first school was established in 1621 by the Virginia Company.
- The poor were taught to read and write by government mandate in 1705.
- Free schools were begun by wealthy individuals.
- Schools were started by ministers.
- Boarding school for girls started in 1760.
- Education was mainly for wealthy people, who had private tutors and went to private schools or to Europe for their education.

EDUCATION OF POOR AND ORPHANED CHILDREN IN THE VIRGINIA COLONIES

Members of the parish vestry served as guardians of poor children, and their education was taken seriously. Although poor children usually served as apprentices, they did receive some education. An act of 1705 stated: "And the master of every such orphan (bound apprentice) shall be obliged to teach him to read and write."[42] To make sure that guardians fulfilled their obligations, an **Orphan Court** met each year to inquire into their conduct.[43] If the justices of the court found that guardians were delinquent in carrying out their duties, they could be removed as guardians.

The welfare of children was evidently very important in the Virginia colonies. Records show that parents who were considered to be of immoral character were not allowed to take care of their own children. A record from 1737 states that a couple who did not take "sufficient care in bringing up their children to an honest way of Living as well as in ye fear of God" must appear in court.[44]

HIGHER EDUCATION IN VIRGINIA: EARLY EFFORTS

Higher education in colonial Virginia could be obtained by attending a college or university in Virginia, or through private tutoring. Students also attended English and Scottish schools and universities.[45] In addition to the College of William and Mary in Williamsburg, students could go to the College of New Jersey at Princeton, and the schools of Pennsylvania.[46] However, until the College of William and Mary was established, the wealthier classes sent their sons to England or Scotland, or else employed private tutors for them.[47] Sons of wealthy families who were to attend school in England or Scotland went overseas at an early age, even as early as 15.[48] Having an institution of higher education at home in the Virginia colonies, however, was considered very important, because it was very expensive for planters to send their sons to England for an education.[49]

HIGHER EDUCATION IN VIRGINIA: THE COLLEGE OF WILLIAM AND MARY

The College of William and Mary was originally established to train Anglican ministers. In 1660 Virginians became interested in formally establishing higher education within the colony, and the General Assembly wanted to establish a liberal arts institution. By 1689 Dr. James Blair, the Commissary of the Bishop of London, and Francis Nicholson, Governor of Virginia, had developed a plan for a free school and college whose objectives were to educate colonists' sons, to train ministers to fill parish churches, and to educate and convert the Indians.[50]

The College of William and Mary was initially patterned after the Scottish model of education, advocated by Dr. James Blair, a Scot himself. The college began with the establishment of a grammar school about 1693, which operated until 1712. The college was to include a grammar school, a philosophy school, and a divinity school. Grammar school classes were to be taught by grammar school masters; the philosophy school was to be run by two professors qualified to teach logic, natural philosophy, and mathematics; and the divinity school was to be staffed by a professor of Oriental languages and a clergyman.[51] Classes were taught by highly educated scholars skilled in teaching the classics. By 1712 a chair of natural philosophy and mathematics was added. By this time also, 20 Native American boys were attending, leading Nicholson and Blair to hope that their long-standing dream of converting and educating the Native Americans would succeed.[52] Most Indian youth, however, returned to their native populations, which was a disappointment to Blair and Nicholson, for they expected them to renounce their native culture and join the white population.

By 1729 a president and six professors were installed. Boys first entered the grammar school, where they learned Latin and Greek, studying the same books that were used in England for this purpose. All lessons had to be carefully taught so as not to go against good religion and moral values.[53]

In the early years of William and Mary no instructor in the philosophy school was in office for more than a few months. This situation changed when Dr. Hugh Jones became professor of mathematics in 1717.[54]

In its formative years the college required 2 years to finish the bachelor's degree and 4 years to finish the master's degree. Students could live away from the campus if they chose, the same system used at the University of Edinburgh in Scotland.

Students at the College of William and Mary usually attended for a year, either before or after they studied with a private tutor, or in England.[55]

The curriculum at the college was classical in nature and grew to include the study of law when George Wythe was appointed professor of law and police.

Spotlight On ←————————————————————————————————————

THOMAS JEFFERSON (1743–1826)

Understanding the educational philosophy of Thomas Jefferson requires an understanding of his background. Jefferson, president of the United States from 1801 to 1809, was a member of the Virginia plantation society. A slave owner, Jefferson was always passionate about education. Born in 1743 to a Virginia planter, Jefferson was tutored until age 14 by a private tutor, the Reverend William Douglas. At age 14 he attended a one-room schoolhouse, taught by the Reverend James Maury, who introduced Jefferson to the classics.

By the age of 16 Jefferson was at the College of William and Mary, studying mathematics. He also studied law under George Wythe. Jefferson was admitted to the Virginia bar in 1767 and served as governor of Virginia from 1779 to 1781.

Jefferson believed education was the way to progress. Advances in medicine, science, and agriculture caused him to believe that social progress was definitely a possibility. He was an Enlightenment thinker.

Thomas Jefferson, the famous Virginia planter, inventor, and educator, attended William and Mary, where he studied philosophy and law under Wythe. He credited the school with shaping his subsequent philosophy of education.[56]

THOMAS JEFFERSON; EDUCATIONAL PHILOSOPHY: THE BILL FOR THE MORE GENERAL DIFFUSION OF KNOWLEDGE

Jefferson, a planter's son, grew up thinking that slavery was a normal and accepted part of life. It may seem ironic that Jefferson believed in the power of education while a slave owner, but at the time everyone in Virginia had slaves. Virginia's economic system required that they be available to work the land; otherwise, the plantation system could not have survived.

Jefferson did propose a denunciation of the African slave trade in the Declaration of Independence and wanted it to be prohibited in Virginia.[57] He recognized that people of different socioeconomic backgrounds did not have the same opportunities, and this seemed unfair to him. This recognition led him to use education as a tool to equalize opportunity for everyone. He envisioned the state of Virginia, during his lifetime, as a model republic, socially and politically different from any society in the past. This vision led to the development of the *Bill for the More General Diffusion of Knowledge,* in 1779. Unfortunately, the bill was rejected. It is noteworthy that the bill would have been an attempt by the state to control education and dictate educational policy.

The bill proposed free elementary education for all future citizens of Virginia. Jefferson wanted the Commonwealth of Virginia to be divided into *hundreds,* or districts, each of which was supposed to have a school in which reading, writing, common arithmetic, and history were taught. All free children of the hundreds were to attend school without cost for 3 years; thereafter, their parents would be required to pay for their attendance.[58] The purpose of this bill was simple. Jefferson wanted all citizens of Virginia to be able to read, for if they could read, they would learn history and find out that governments throughout history had been corrupt and that all men had to participate in governmental affairs because "the people themselves are its only safe depositories."[59] The Bill for the More General Diffusion of Knowledge called for the teacher to "weed out" the best scholars from elementary school and send them to a grammar school, where they would learn Latin, Greek, English grammar, and more advanced arithmetic. Boys would remain at the grammar school for 1 to 2 years. Those who did not perform well at the grammar school level would be dismissed, whereas those who succeeded would remain for 6 years.[60] At the end of 6 years, boys at the grammar school who had excelled would go on to college for 3 years to study "such sciences as they shall choose," at William and Mary, at public expense.[61]

Jefferson pointed out that half of the grammar school pupils would be dismissed after 6 years of instruction and would go on to teach grammar school themselves.[62] Thus, his views on the abilities of teachers do not appear to be very favorable.

Academic success determined a student's future educational opportunities from the time a student entered school: Only those who succeeded went on to higher study. Jefferson himself referred to the process of choosing the best students as "raking from the rubbish annually,"[63] which shows that he believed that certain individuals have greater talents than others. Those with lesser talents might be seen as inferior.

This viewpoint carries over to the present day. Students with learning disabilities, who may have trouble with reading comprehension, or other learning problems, may be seen by their teachers as less capable and subsequently may be treated that way. Often, teachers unconsciously behave this way. Also, wealthier students generally are more successful in school than poorer students, a common occurrence in Jefferson's time in the Virginia colonies as well.

A state university in which everyone, regardless of income level, race, color, or religion, could obtain an education was Jefferson's lifelong dream (see the "Shaper of Education" feature). One of his biggest contributions to education was the establishment of the University of Virginia.

ESTABLISHMENT OF THE UNIVERSITY OF VIRGINIA

The University of Virginia, established on February 21, 1818, when the Virginia legislature passed a bill authorizing it, is considered the first state university. Jefferson was convinced that higher education was very important for the public good and had been involved in higher educational reform since 1779, when he tried to put forth proposals to reform the College of William and Mary. He had proposed

SHAPER OF EDUCATION

Thomas Jefferson
(1743–1826)

- Developed his educational philosophy within the context of Virginian society, in which slavery was accepted as part of everyday life
- Proposed a denunciation of the African slave trade in the Declaration of Independence and wanted to prohibit slavery in Virginia
- Developed the Bill for the More General Diffusion of Knowledge in 1779, which proposed free elementary education for all future citizens of Virginia
- Each district (called a *hundred*) was to have a school, and all free children of each district were to attend school without cost for 3 years
- Major focus of Jefferson's bill was on literacy, for if people could learn to read, they could participate in governmental affairs
- Envisioned the state of Virginia as a model republic, different from any society in the past
- Planned for the opening of a state university in Virginia, now the University of Virginia, which opened for classes in 1825.

a national university in 1806, but nothing happened. For Jefferson, the university was part of a total plan for establishing a system of public education.

In 1814 a study and report were commissioned to establish the location of the University of Virginia. This report, known as the *Rockfish Gap Report,* written by Jefferson as chairman, was instrumental in establishing the University of Virginia.[64] Jefferson had help from a friend, Joseph C. Cabell, a member of the Virginia state legislature, who tried to influence the other members of the legislature to accept Jefferson's ideas.

Despite Jefferson's intention that the state university serve to equalize higher educational opportunity, it did not. Students were overwhelmingly from the upper and middle classes; most came from the slave-owning classes.[65] Today, we find similar discrepancies regarding socioeconomic status and access to higher education.

In an article describing student life at the University of Virginia during its early years, Jennings Wagoner, an educational historian at the University of Virginia, remarks on student disobedience. Jefferson had intended students to be self-governing, or to learn to monitor their own behavior away from parental influence.[66] This did not happen. Over the years, students' misbehavior continued to increase, with the result that the university had a corresponding increase in rules. Alcohol appears to have been a significant problem. It led to such behavior as "noisemaking," when students would ring the college bell and blow on tin horns until late at night, and even early in the morning. This kept faculty members and their families awake. Students even used firecrackers and homemade bombs, which they left on the windowsills or stoops of faculty houses.[67]

Before Jefferson died in 1826 his view that students would monitor their own behavior and behave properly must have been shaken when he saw a student rebellion. Students threw a bottle of urine at a professor's window and were seized by two professors who were then promptly named the next day as having caused the riot in a resolution signed by 65 students![68] Two professors, who had studied in Europe, resigned because they were so unhappy with what had occurred, and they were backed up by other faculty, who threatened to resign if order was not restored.[69] Finally, Jefferson and other members of the board of visitors met to discuss what to do about the student rebellion. The offenders were expelled from the university.

Today, university and college students who disobey the rules of the institution can be expelled. Drinking alcohol on college and university campuses is a significant problem that administrators address every year. Criminal activities such as date rape and other forms of assault often arise from the excessive use of alcohol. Fraternity hazing parties, in which large amounts of alcohol are usually consumed, have been banned at many universities and the offending fraternity shut down. Administrators continue to struggle with ways to ensure that students who attend their institutions follow the rules so that they graduate safely. The dropout rate among college and university students, however, is high; only 63 percent of full-time students graduate from 4-year liberal arts colleges.[70] The dropout rate at the University of Virginia in Jefferson's time was also high.

The similarities and differences between educational philosophy today and in colonial New England and Virginia are found in Table 7-3.

BRIDGES FROM THE PAST TO THE PRESENT: VALUE AND USES OF CONTRIBUTIONS FROM PURITAN NEW ENGLAND AND THE VIRGINIA COLONIES

The connections between education in the New England and Virginia colonies in the period 1625–1820 and today's educational system are listed. Two are discussed in detail: parental involvement in education, and the problem of student misbehavior and alcohol abuse in colleges and universities.

Table 7-3 **Education in the Colonial Era Versus Education Today**

COLONIAL-ERA EDUCATION	MODERN EDUCATION
The emphasis was on reading, writing, and math.	Tests point to need to spend more time teaching reading, writing, and math.
There was an emphasis on penmanship, memorization, and recitation.	Students no longer recite. Teachers use activities, including cooperative learning, to get students involved. Penmanship is no longer so important.
Dame schools	Preschools
Virginia had fewer schools owing to survival issues (Jamestown).	Impoverished areas with fewer resources, such as housing and medical care, have poorer schools.
Wealthy individuals sent children to college. There was no education for slaves or Native Americans.	Disproportionately low numbers of African Americans, Hispanic Americans, and Native Americans receive higher education.
College students set fires, hounded professors over grades, and were disciplined for drinking.	College or university students can become unruly, set fires in dorms, be disciplined for drinking.

CONNECTIONS BETWEEN COLONIAL NEW ENGLAND AND VIRGINIA AND TODAY

1. The elementary curriculum in the New England colonies was similar to the present-day curriculum, with its emphasis on teaching reading; writing, which includes penmanship; and arithmetic.
2. Dame schools in New England were precursors to preschool or early childhood education programs today.
3. Parental involvement in education is crucial to assure students' success in school.
4. The economics of the area in which a school is established have a great influence on whether the school is successful. Areas that are impoverished, such as East Saint Louis, Illinois, and Camden, New Jersey have schools that are failing, with low student graduation rates.
5. Wealthy children have more advantages in education. Some have private tutors or get private tutoring for the SATs.
6. Socioeconomic status is tied to the ability to attend college or university.
7. Females still do not have the same opportunity as males to obtain an education.
8. Jefferson's Bill for the More General Diffusion of Knowledge was a step by the government toward providing free public education for all. Today, other governmental legislation, such as the NCLB Act of 2001, affects students.

9. College and university students often get into trouble by drinking too much, which sometimes leads to rioting. Administrators have implemented policies to deal with such behavior, including expulsion.

BRIDGE 1: PARENTAL INVOLVEMENT IN EDUCATION

As any future or present teacher knows, parental involvement is crucial for a child's success in school, whether at the elementary, middle school, or high school level. Parents can help students by making them feel more secure in school and can give their child support with homework or school projects.[71] Parents can also provide resources. In the New England colonies, you will recall that parents had to provide firewood to heat the schoolhouse. If they did not follow through with their obligations, the children had to suffer the consequences and sit in the coldest corner of the room.

Children with special health needs or learning disabilities benefit by having parents or guardians who inform the teacher of their special needs. The idea is to have a partnership between parents or guardians and teachers. Teachers can be frustrated because parents or guardians do not get involved in their child's education by attending parent-teacher conferences, helping out in the classroom, or volunteering at school events. According to research, parents do not become involved in their children's education because of cultural differences, fear of authority-based institutions, parent illiteracy, family problems, negative experiences with education, lack of child care, health problems, economic issues, and job-related problems.[72]

Teachers and administrators need to take a more active role in encouraging parents to become involved in their children's education. One way to increase such involvement would be to distribute a written policy jointly developed by parents and teachers. School districts that already have successful parental involvement could be recruited to help in this process as well.[73] Research has shown that communication among parents, teachers, and administrators needs to be improved if parental involvement in education is to increase.[74]

Teachers benefit from involvement by parents or guardians as much as the students do. Teachers have higher expectations for students whose parents or guardians are involved in their education. Students at the junior high school and high school levels whose parents continue to be involved in their education adjust better to their new environment and make realistic plans for their futures.[75]

Teachers communicating with parents or guardians must be sensitive to any language issues, especially if English is a second language. Parents or guardians do not want to hear any educational jargon; they want to know how their children are doing in plain language. It is important to keep these issues in mind when planning for any communication with parents or guardians, whether through an individual teacher or as a schoolwide effort.[76] Ideally, parents should be involved in a school's decision-making process.[77] Above all, teachers need to be aware of the so-called three Rs of working with parents or guardians: reassurance, recognition, and respect.[78]

BRIDGE 2: HIGHER EDUCATION POLICY MAKING: STUDENT RIOTS AND DRINKING

Student riots and problems with alcohol abuse such as occurred at the University of Virginia in its early days have continued to be of concern to students, faculty, and administrators alike. New policies have had to be instituted to discipline students for such infractions, just as they were at the University of Virginia in the 1820s.

Over the years, numerous reports of student riots, fueled by alcohol, have surfaced. An incident at Michigan State University in 1998 involved 2000 students who protested the ban on alcohol at the school's football games.[79] After police were called in to disperse the crowds of students with tear gas, the president of Michigan State decided to increase efforts to stop alcohol abuse.[80] A no-alcohol-allowed dormitory was to be built, and students and administrators were to form a committee to discuss alcohol abuse and to hold public forums.[81] Since the deaths from alcohol poisoning and drunken riots in 1999, police and university officials and law enforcement have limited the availability of alcohol, and increased enforcement of laws and policies.

College and university administrators have had to think more often about ways to deal with student drinking, as the incidence of drinking has sharply risen. In 2002, 81 percent of college administrators characterized student drinking as a "problem" or "major problem" on their campus, whereas in 1999 only 68 percent of administrators agreed with that statement.[82] The National Institute on Alcohol Abuse and Alcoholism (NIAAA) has released a report that 1,400 students die each year from alcohol-related unintentional injuries.[83] These findings were reported in the Harvard School of Public Health College Alcohol Study, completed in 2002. Highly selective colleges and those with enrollments of more than 10,000 undergraduates were more likely to have alcohol problems. According to the study, college administrators came up with policies to curb alcohol abuse, including prohibiting drinking in all dormitories (43 percent); establishing alcohol-free residence floors or halls (81 percent); providing alcohol education for freshmen (84 percent), and restricting alcohol at campus events.[84] Fifty percent of small colleges restricted alcohol at campus events, but only 20 percent of large colleges did so.[85]

Students themselves are becoming involved in policy making. At the University of Virginia in 1999, more than 300 students protested that a student who attacked a freshman was allowed to remain on campus.[86] Colleges and universities are beginning to take steps to police students' behavior off campus as well, holding them responsible for criminal behavior that occurs off campus premises.[87]

SUMMARY

This chapter described the conditions that led to the Puritans' migration to America and the type of education they established in both the New England and Virginia colonies. Education in these geographic regions was influenced by both location and religion, with the Puritan influence being strongest in the New England colonies. This chapter also explored the establishment of higher educational institutions in the colonies of both New England and Virginia, with an emphasis on the role that Thomas Jefferson played in founding the University of Virginia.

In chapter 8, which describes education during the Enlightenment and early national periods, you will learn more about how higher education policy changed as the Enlightenment movement advanced.

QUESTIONS FOR DISCUSSION

1. Compare and contrast the New England Puritan style of parenting with the styles of parenting commonly seen today. How does parenting style affect a child's success in school?

2. Describe the teaching methods used by the New England Puritans to teach children to read, write, and do arithmetic. How were the teaching methods and curriculum similar to and different from those used today to teach the same subjects?

3. The Puritans of New England had common goals for their children's education, all tied to religion. How do we determine common goals for education for children today? Give at least one example to back up your answer.

4. Discuss the differences between educational policies in the New England colonies versus those in the Virginia colonies. Which do you feel were more advanced, and why? Give evidence to back up your answer.

5. Jefferson's philosophy of annually selecting the best students, then sending them on to grammar school or college, was referred to as "annually raking the rubbish." This does not say much about his opinion of those who did not succeed. Do you think teachers and education policy makers today believe that those who do not succeed in school are inferior? Explain your answer.

6. In your opinion, what was Jefferson's greatest achievement? Why?

7. In your opinion, what could or should be done by the government to equalize access to higher education for all students? Explain your answer.

SUGGESTED ACTIVITIES

1. Penmanship was an important subject taught in both the Puritan New England and Virginia colonies. What is the status of teaching penmanship today in the elementary curriculum? How important, in your opinion, is having good handwriting? Present your findings in a 15- to 20-minute presentation.

2. Education for poor or orphaned children was discussed in this chapter. What educational opportunities are provided for children in foster care or those who

live in shelters? Write a five-page report on your findings, or make a PowerPoint presentation to the class, of approximately 20 minutes.

3. Research the early efforts to establish public schools in your home state in the period 1625–1820, the dates covered in this chapter. What are the similarities and differences between education in your home state and that in the New England and Virginia colonies discussed in this chapter? Present your findings in a class presentation of approximately 20–25 minutes.

4. The concept of common goals for education for children was discussed in this chapter. Survey a group of teachers on what they believe are common goals for education for children. Present your findings in a PowerPoint presentation of approximately 25 minutes.

5. Research the tuition rates of 2 (two) private colleges, such as the College of William and Mary, and those of two public state universities, such as the University of Virginia. Compare the tuition rates between public and private institutions, and determine how many students at each institution receive financial aid. Present your findings in chart form.

6. Interview a college dean or faculty member about the dropout rate at your institution. What policies are being taken to stop this trend? Present the results of the interview in a short presentation of about 15 to 20 minutes.

Bibliography

Adams, S. (2001). *The best and worst country in the world: Perspectives on the early Virginia landscape.* Charlottesville: University Press of Virginia.

Aronson, K. W. (2004, May 27). Study faults colleges on graduation rates. *New York Times,* p. A23.

Axtell, J. (1974). *The school upon a hill: Education and society in colonial New England.* New Haven: Yale University Press.

Cremin, L. A. (1970). *American education: The colonial experience 1607–1783.* New York: Harper and Row.

Cressy, D. (1987). *Coming over: Migration and communication between England and New England in the seventeenth century.* Cambridge: Cambridge University Press.

Earle, A. M. (1974). *The Sabbath in Puritan New England.* Williamstown, MA: Corner House. (Originally published 1898)

Earle, A. M. (1975). *Child life in colonial days.* Williamstown, MA: Corner House. (Originally published 1897).

Gose, B. (1998, October 9). Some colleges extend their codes of conduct to off-campus behavior. *Chronicle of Higher Education, 45,* A51.

Hoover, E. (2004, March 26). College officials cope differently with student drinking, study finds. *Chronicle of Higher Education, 50,* A35.

Jefferson, T. (2002). *Notes on the state of Virginia* (D. Waldstreicher, Ed.). New York: St. Martin's Press.

Lively, K. (1998, May 15). At Michigan State, a protest escalated into a night of fires, tear gas, and arrests. *Chronicle of Higher Education 44,* A46.

Monaghan, E. J. (1988). Literacy instruction and gender in colonial New England. *American Quarterly, 40*(1).

Pepe, B. (1999). Involving parents lets students and teachers win. *Education Digest, 64*(6), 48.

Plevyak, L. H. (2003). Parent involvement in education: Who decides? *Education Digest, 69*(2), 35.

Postman, N. (1999). *Building a bridge to the eighteenth century: How the past can improve our future.* New York: Knopf.

Stanard, M. N. (1917). *Colonial Virginia: Its people and customs.* Philadelphia: J. B. Lippincott.

Tanis, N. E. (1970). Education in John Eliot's Indian utopias, 1646–1675. *History of Education Quarterly, 10*(3), 310–11.

Tyler, L. G. (1897). Education in colonial Virginia: Part 1. Poor children and orphans. *William and Mary College Historical Quarterly Magazine, 5* (4).

Tyler, L. G. (1897). Education in colonial Virginia: Part 2. Private schools and tutors. *William and Mary College Historical Quarterly Magazine, 6*(1).

Tyler, L. G. (1897). Education in colonial Virginia: Part 3. Free schools. *William and Mary College Quarterly Historical Magazine, 6*(2).

Tyler, L. G. (1898). Education in colonial Virginia: Part 4. The higher education. *William and Mary College Quarterly, 6*(3).

Wagoner, J., Jr. (1986). Honor and dishonor at Mr. Jefferson's university: The antebellum years. *History of Education Quarterly, 26*(2).

Wilson, L. (1999). *Ye heart of a man: The domestic life of men in colonial New England.* New Haven: Yale University Press.

Winthrop, J. (1996). *The journal of John Winthrop, 1630–1649* (R. S. Dunn, J. Savage, & L. Yeandle, Eds.). Cambridge, MA: The Belknap Press of Harvard University Press.

Suggestions for Further Reading

In addition to the works cited in the bibliography, the following are recommended for further reading.

Dunn, R. S. (1984). John Winthrop writes his journal. *William and Mary Quarterly,* 3rd series, *41*(2), 185–212.

Kaplan, S. (1948). The reduction of teachers' salaries in post-revolutionary Boston. *New England Quarterly, 21*(3), 373–79.

Stone, L. (1969). Literacy and education in England, 1640–1900. *Past and Present,* no. *42*(1), 69–139.

Teaford, J. (1970). The transformation of Massachusetts education, 1670–1780. *History of Education Quarterly, 10*(3), 287–307.

Relevant Web Sites

Leslie Brock Center for the Study of Cultural Currency at the University of Virginia *http://www.people.virginia.edu* Information on economic conditions in New England and Virginia, and primary sources, such as Hutchison and Franklin, online.

The New England Primer *http://www.bartleby.com* Illustrations and information on the *New England Primer.*

Archiving Early America *http://earlyamerica.com/index.html* Primary source documents from the seventeenth and eighteenth centuries.

Education World: Lesson planning skills *http://www.education-world.com* Contains lesson planning ideas for all levels.

The 13 American colonies: Virginia *http://www.socialstudiesforkids.com* Contains links to lessons and information on the American colonies, geographic information on Jamestown, and colonial life and history.

http://www.edc.org/hec The U.S. Department of Education Higher Education Center for Alcohol and Other Drug Abuse and Violence Prevention. (This site provides statistics on college and binge drinking and drug use, and information on prevention initiatives.)

National Park Service: Virginia *http://www.nps.gov/colo/* The official site for the historical park at Jamestown, Virginia.

The English Reformation: Puritanism online *http://puritanism.online.fr/engref.html* Contains links to other sites, including Puritanism. Great resource for researching all aspects of the English Reformation and Puritan life in the American colonies.

Questia online *http://www.questia.com* World's largest online library. Look up anything pertaining to colonial education. Books and pamphlets, including primary sources, are online.

Education Week *http://www.edweek.org* Pertinent information on education, released weekly.

National Center for Education Statistics *http://www.nces.ed.gov* Federal and state statistics on any topic in education.

U.S. Department of Education *http://www.ed.gov* Home page of the U.S. Department of Education.

Endnotes

[1] John Winthrop, *The Journal of John Winthrop, 1630–1649,* ed. Richard S. Dunn, James Savage, & Laetitia Yeandle (Cambridge, MA: The Belknap Press of Harvard University Press, 1996). See Introduction p. xvii.

[2] James Axtell, *The School Upon a Hill: Education and Society in Colonial New England* (New Haven: Yale University Press, 1974), 3. Note the original spelling.

[3] David Cressy, *Coming Over: Migration and Communication Between England and New England in the Seventeenth Century* (Cambridge: Cambridge University Press, 1987), 20.

[4] Normal Earl Tanis, "Education in John Eliot's Indian Utopias, 1646–1675," *History of Education Quarterly, 10,* no. 3 (1970), 310–11.

[5] Ibid., 318.

[6] Alice Morse Earle, *The Sabbath in Puritan New England* (Williamstown, MA: Corner House, 1974; orig. pub. 1898), 2.

[7] Ibid., 7.

[8] Axtell, *School Upon a Hill,* 175.

[9] Alice Morse Earle, *Child Life in Colonial Days* (Williamstown, MA: Corner House, 1975; orig. pub. 1899), 68.

[10] Ibid.

11 E. Jennifer Monaghan, "Literacy Instruction and Gender in Colonial New England," *American Quarterly, 40,* no. 1 (1988), 26–27.

12 Ibid, 6.

13 Ibid., 10.

14 Ibid., 85.

15 Ibid., 76.

16 Ibid., 99, 101.

17 Earle, *Child Life in Colonial Days,* 69.

18 Ibid., 70.

19 Ibid., 128.

20 Monaghan, "Literacy Instruction and Gender," 21.

21 Axtell, *School Upon a Hill,* 136.

22 Ibid., 138.

23 Axtell, *School Upon a Hill,* 133.

24 Ibid., 203.

25 Ibid.

26 Lawrence A. Cremin, *American Education: The Colonial Experience, 1607–1783* (New York: Harper and Row, 1970), 352.

27 Ibid., 220.

28 Ibid., 221.

29 Lisa Wilson, *Ye Heart of a Man: The Domestic Life of Men in Colonial New England* (New Haven: Yale University Press, 1999), 14.

30 Cremin, *American Education,* 215.

31 Stephen Adams, *The Best and Worst Country in the World: Perspectives on the Early Virginia Landscape* (Charlottesville: University Press of Virginia, 2001), 71–72.

32 Lyon G. Tyler, "Education in Colonial Virginia: Part 3. Free Schools," *William and Mary College Quarterly Historical Magazine, 6,* no. 2 (1897), 71.

33 Mary Newton Stanard, *Colonial Virginia: Its People and Customs* (Philadelphia: J. B. Lippincott, 1917), 266.

34 Ibid.

35 Ibid., 267.

36 Lyon G. Tyler, "Education in Colonial Virginia: Part 2. Private Schools and Tutors," *William and Mary College Historical Quarterly Magazine, 6,* no. 1 (1897), 1.

37 Ibid. &c means "and so forth" or "etc."

38 Ibid., 4.

39 Ibid., 5.

40 Ibid., 5. These advertisements are reprinted in this article from the *Virginia Gazette.*

41 Ibid.

[42] Lyon G. Tyler, "Education in Colonial Virginia: Part 1. Poor Children and Orphans," *William and Mary College Historical Quarterly Magazine, 5,* no. 4 (1897), 220.

[43] Ibid., 221.

[44] Ibid., 223.

[45] Lyon G. Tyler, "Education in Colonial Virginia: Part 4. The Higher Education," *William and Mary College Quarterly, 6,* no. 3 (1898), 171.

[46] Ibid.

[47] Ibid., 172.

[48] Ibid., 174. This comes from a list of individuals who were sent to English schools. The youngest age recorded in this list is 15.

[49] Ibid., 173.

[50] Stanard, *Colonial Virginia,* 283.

[51] Cremin, *American Education,* 335.

[52] In the literature of the times, the Native Americans were referred to as "Indians." The term *Native Americans* is used today.

[53] Tyler, "Education in Colonial Virginia: Part 4," 177.

[54] Cremin, *American Education,* 337.

[55] Ibid.

[56] Adams, *Best and Worst Country,* 438.

[57] Neil Postman, *Building a Bridge to the Eighteenth Century: How the Past Can Improve Our Future* (New York: Knopf, 1999), 19–21.

[58] Cremin, *American Education,* 440. See also Thomas Jefferson, *Notes on the State of Virginia,* ed. David Waldstreicher (New York: St. Martin's Press, 2002), 182.

[59] Ibid., 184.

[60] Ibid.

[61] Ibid.

[62] Ibid.

[63] Ibid., 182.

[64] Ibid.

[65] Jennings Wagoner, Jr., "Honor and Dishonor at Mr. Jefferson's University: The Antebellum Years," *History of Education Quarterly, 26,* no. 2 (1986), 167–168.

[66] Jennings Wagoner, Jr., "Honor and Dishonor," 171.

[67] Ibid., 173.

[68] Ibid., 176.

[69] Ibid.

[70] Karen W. Aronson, "Study Faults Colleges on Graduation Rates," *New York Times,* May 27, 2004. p. 23.

[71] Linda H. Plevyak, "Parent Involvement in Education: Who Decides?" *Education Digest, 69,* no. 2 (2003), 35.

[72] Ibid., 32.

[73] Ibid., 33.

[74] Ibid., 36.

[75] Barbara Pepe, "Involving Parents Lets Students and Teachers Win," *Education Digest, 64,* no. 6 (1999), 48.

[76] Ibid.

[77] Ibid., 50.

[78] Ibid.

[79] Kit Lively, "At Michigan State, a Protest Escalated Into a Night of Fires, Tear Gas, and Arrests," *Chronicle of Higher Education,* May 15, 1998, p. A46.

[80] Ibid.

[81] Ibid.

[82] Eric Hoover, "College Officials Cope Differently With Student Drinking, Study Finds," *Chronicle of Higher Education,* March 26, 2004, p. A35.

[83] Higher Education Center: NIAAA College Drinking Report A Call to Action: Changing the Culture of Drinking at U.S. Colleges *http://www.edc.org/neu/niaaa.report.html*

[84] Ibid.

[85] Ibid.

[86] "UVA Students Demand Classmates' Expulsion," *Chronicle of Higher Education,* May 14, 1999, p. A10.

[87] Ben Gose, "Some Colleges Extend Their Codes of Conduct to Off-Campus Behavior," *Chronicle of Higher Education,* October 9, 1998, p. A51.

Chapter 8

The Enlightenment and Early National Periods: Advances in Thought and Education (1820–1890)

Learning Objectives

1. Define the term Enlightenment and state its importance.
2. Define the early national period in American education and discuss the major educational leaders during this period.
3. Describe the development of the monitorial school in England, and discuss how this school was significant to education in the United States.
4. Discuss the development of early teacher training programs and the work of Horace Mann and Henry Barnard.

INTRODUCTION

The previous chapter focused on the settlement of the New England and Virginia colonies and the development of each colony's educational system within the context of its geographic, economic, and social characteristics. During the same period, the ideas of the Enlightenment were spreading across Europe, where they originated, and into America, where they spread slowly and sporadically.

The term *Enlightenment* describes the gradual eradication of superstitious beliefs in society as a new emphasis on education and an increased interest in literature, mathematics, science, art, and advances in medicine occurred. A key concept of the Enlightenment was that because humankind could use its ability to reason, it did not need God to make all its decisions.[1] The idea was that people could use their own powers to work and improve their lives on earth and make things better for future generations, especially through advances in science.[2]

There is debate over when the American Enlightenment began and ended. Some overlap necessarily exists, since developments or movements in education do not have *specific* beginning and ending dates. Therefore, keep in mind that Enlightenment ideas were spreading slowly *at the same time* the American colonies were being developed.

The early national period is vitally important because it is the time during which the idea of education for *all* people, or the nation, to promote an intelligent and informed citizenry who could make decisions for the common good, arose.[3] During this period, the monitorial schools and Sunday schools were

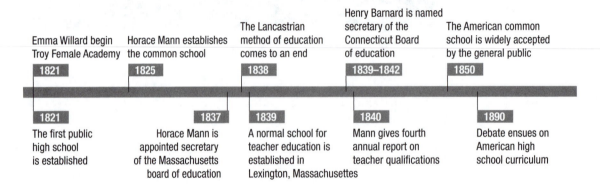

Emma Willard begin Troy Female Academy	Horace Mann establishes the common school	The Lancastrian method of education comes to an end	Henry Barnard is named secretary of the Connecticut Board of education	The American common school is widely accepted by the general public
1821	**1825**	**1838**	**1839–1842**	**1850**

1821	**1837**	**1839**	**1840**	**1890**
The first public high school is established	Horace Mann is appointed secretary of the Massachusetts board of education	A normal school for teacher education is established in Lexington, Massachusettes	Mann gives fourth annual report on teacher qualifications	Debate ensues on American high school curriculum

commonly used to educate children of the working class. The academies were secular and were precursors to public education.

Furthermore, the Early National Period saw the beginnings of early teacher training programs. You will learn about the beginnings of teacher training institutions, or "normal schools."

Chapter 8 ends at the date 1890, at which time the work of Horace Mann, who was instrumental in the establishment of the American common school beginning about 1825, was becoming influential.

EARLY YEARS OF THE ENLIGHTENMENT: 1750–1820

The early years of the Enlightenment include the time period of the previous chapter. During the period from 1750 to 1825, the colonial liberal-arts colleges, including the College of William and Mary in Virginia, were undergoing many changes and expanding. This rapid expansion of colleges led to battles over how the college curriculum should be defined.[4]

In 1750, Benjamin Franklin established the Academy in Philadelphia, which would become the University of Pennsylvania. Note that this event predates the establishment of the University of Virginia by Thomas Jefferson.

BENJAMIN FRANKLIN: PHILOSOPHY OF EDUCATION AND ENLIGHTENMENT THOUGHT

Franklin's philosophy of education reflected his practical side in that he was concerned with expense. As early as 1743 he had drafted a proposal for an academy, and by 1749 he had announced the plan to educate Pennsylvania youth so they did not have to "suffer the extraordinary expense and hazard in sending them abroad for that purpose."[5] Franklin believed that the existing educational system was

Spotlight On ◄───

BENJAMIN FRANKLIN (1705–1790)

Benjamin Franklin, born January 6, 1705, was one of 10 children. Because he learned to read early, he started at the Boston Latin School at age 8. At age 10, his father put him to work in his chandler trade, learning to make soap and candles, waiting on customers, and running errands. Because the young Franklin disliked this line of work, his father took him to other shops to explore other vocations. He went to work helping his older brother James, a printer, with the publication of the *New England Courant,* which he continued to publish after his brother went into hiding to escape a prison sentence for denouncing the Puritan minister Cotton Mather. By 1723, Franklin was working as a printer in Philadelphia. An avid observer, Franklin recorded natural phenomena, such as the eclipses of the sun and moon in his diary. He also debated moral questions in the Junto Club.

inadequate, and should be improved so that future generations could solve problems in a productive, efficient manner for the common good.

THE ESTABLISHMENT OF THE ACADEMY IN PHILADELPHIA AND ITS CURRICULUM

The Academy was to be taught by a rector or clergyman who had to be "of good understanding, good morals, diligent and patient."[6] The curriculum would consist of instruction in arithmetic, geometry, astronomy, rhetoric, grammar, literature, history, natural history, drawing, handwriting, accounting, geography, morality, and logic. Mechanics, gardening, and physical education would also be taught.

Franklin's book, *Poor Richard's Almanac,* which contained astronomical tables, weather predictions, articles, and poetry, was no doubt also used at the Academy. It was read widely and provided reading material and a type of informal instruction. Franklin sold 10,000 copies each year for about 25 years.[7]

The Academy was supposed to be independent of any religious affiliation. An early administrator, Provost William Smith, an Anglican clergyman, did not agree with this viewpoint and insisted that Anglican philosophy and theology be a part of the curriculum and daily operations of the school.[8]

Franklin's Academy was supposed to stress not only classical but also vocational education. In his proposal for the Academy, Franklin described a plan of education which included utilitarian subjects to help young men be successful. When the Academy opened in 1751, the curriculum included more of the classical subjects than Franklin had originally intended because others thought they should be included.[9] These same curriculum battles, over classical (liberal-arts) subject matter, versus practical (vocational) training, are being fought today. This topic will be covered in more detail in chapter 9.

BENJAMIN RUSH: THE REPUBLIC AND SCHOOLS FOR ALL

Benjamin Rush, trained as a physician in Edinburgh, was another Enlightenment leader in Philadelphia, and a colleague of Franklin's. Rush said that tax money should be spent on a system of educational institutions in Pennsylvania because to invest in education was ultimately to invest in human potential. This meant that society would improve, for there would be better government, improved methods of manufacturing, and more efficient uses of land and improved methods of agriculture. Rush even linked crime with ignorance, stating that "fewer pillories and whipping posts and smaller jails, with their usual expense and taxes, will be necessary when our youth are properly educated than at present."[10] He thought that people became criminals because of "the fatal consequences of the want of a proper education in early life."[11] Rush's statement has implications for the present; a review of prison statistics shows that the prison population is largely illiterate.

Rush was also very interested in moral education. He believed that in a world of constant change, education in moral values and an understanding of basic virtues were necessary to maintain order.[12] Rush established the Presbyterian-supported Dickinson College in Carlisle, Pennsylvania, which was organized in 1784.[13] He also established Franklin College at Lancaster in 1787, which is now Franklin and

Marshall College.[14] The years 1785 and 1787 were notable also because Congress passed the *Northwest Ordinance,* a bill that called for the establishment of schools in townships across the western part of the United States.[15] Benjamin Rush was an advocate for a republican society. A republic, unlike a monarchy, would create a balanced and ordered relationship between people and government and among the various social classes.[16] The main occupation was to be agriculture, combined with commerce and manufacturing, which would provide a balanced system.

Benjamin Rush said that "schoolmasters of every description" should be "supported in part by the public."[17] Rush also called for all the states to have colleges, and for a federal university sponsored by Congress that students would attend after they had "acquired the first principles of knowledge in the colleges of their respective states."[18]

Recognizing that a higher education was out of reach for the poor, Rush wanted to improve educational opportunity for the majority of citizens who did not have money to send their children to academies or colleges.[19] He called for free schools to be established, with at least one in each township or school district of 100 families. Free schools would be funded by public funds as well as through private contributions.[20]

Above all, Benjamin Rush believed that education had to be an integral part of society, and it would be difficult to have education work well in a society whose values conflicted with what was taught in the schools.[21] Today, teachers and educational policy makers struggle with the same issues. Our society favors celebrities and those who make money without working too hard or studying too much, yet students are told that they should work hard and they will succeed in life if they only study.

The ideas of both Franklin and Rush are summarized in Table 8-1.

Table 8-1 **Enlightenment Educators of Philadelphia**

BENJAMIN FRANKLIN	BENJAMIN RUSH
Occupation: printer	Occupation: physician
Drafted proposal for Academy in 1743, which opened in 1751; Academy is now the University of Pennsylvania	Established Dickinson College in Carlisle, Pennsylvania, in 1784 and Franklin and Marshall College in 1787
Academy was to be independent of any religious affiliation	Linked ignorance to crime and said education would keep people out of jail
Academy curriculum: arithmetic, geometry, rhetoric, grammar, literature, history, drawing, handwriting, accounting, geography, morality, and logic	Was interested in moral education, and believed in teaching common moral virtues such as honesty, truth, temperance, and gratitude
Wanted to include practical subjects such as mechanics, gardening, and physical education	Felt limits should be placed on the amusements available to youth (drinking, horseracing); amusements should prepare them for a future profession
Thought an important part of education was learning to write; had students read something, put it in their own words, then compare with the original to see if they expressed the same ideas	Believed children learned through sensory experience with objects used in daily life; propounded that models and samples be used when teaching new subjects

THE EARLY NATIONAL PERIOD: THE ACADEMY MOVEMENT (1820–1830)

The academy movement was an important component of education in the early national period. A key factor in this period was the insistence upon formal education for youth.

The establishment of academies made a secular school system possible. A new recognition that learning and education can improve the conditions in society was occurring. The American academy, while tied to the academy movement in England, reflected the conditions in the colonies. The academy was an alternative to the classical education of the grammar schools and colleges of the seventeenth and eighteenth centuries and served as an early model for the development of the American high school.[22] The first public high school was begun in 1821 by Boston's civic leaders.[23] The utilitarian nature of education in the academies provided social mobility to the average citizen in America during the eighteenth and nineteenth centuries. Academies were financed by both private and public funds, and the curricula were adaptable to students' needs. For instance, the Phillips Exeter Academy in New England, founded in 1778, emphasized that students were to be taught "the great end and real business of living," in addition to the traditional subjects of Latin, English grammar, writing, and arithmetic.[24]

Girls also attended academies because educational reformers argued that an education would help a woman be the "helpmate" of her husband as well as to teach children; women were seen as the best teachers of primary grade children.[25] The curriculum in female seminaries and academies between 1742 and 1871 has been studied and it was found that girls studied natural philosophy, astronomy, chemistry, and botany.[26] Science was thought to be an important subject for study because it would train women's minds to critically observe and to think logically.[27] Botany was thought to be particularly useful because it would encourage women and girls to get outdoor exercise and activity.[28] In the Troy Female Academy, begun in 1821 by Emma Willard, girls studied mathematics, science, modern languages, history, philosophy, literature, and geography.[29]

Girls who studied the sciences were generally from the upper or middle classes, but efforts were made to teach science to other groups as well. Some Catholic schools and academies which taught Native Americans also taught science. For example, the curriculum at Cherokee Female Seminary in Arkansas in 1843 included a study of the natural sciences.[30] This practice did not extend to African Americans, who had very few opportunities to study the sciences and who were generally restricted in their access to education.[31]

In general, the curriculum at the academy level was classical in nature. Most academy students did not go on to college but instead managed their fathers' plantations, especially in the South, or went on to a career in business.[32] Because so few career opportunities in physics, astronomy, geology, or botany existed at this time, there was not much reason to train young men at the academy level in these areas of study. Future physicians studied the sciences at the college level, after first getting classical training at the academy level.[33]

Girls studied science more often than boys at the academy level because the female academies and seminaries had more freedom with the curriculum than male academies, since the latter were concerned with preparing boys for college entrance requirements. Female schools did not have this concern, since girls were generally not admitted to college until 1850.[34]

THE EARLY NATIONAL PERIOD: THE MONITORIAL SCHOOL AND EDUCATION FOR THE MASSES

In contrast to the more esoteric curriculum of science and classical studies offered at the academies, the monitorial schools of the early national period offered an inexpensive form of education to large numbers of students.

This method of schooling, named for the monitors, or assistants, who ran the schools, was begun in England and adopted in the United States by educators Joseph Lancaster and Andrew Bell.

The monitorial school was a cost-effective method of providing education for large numbers of students using only a single schoolmaster or headmaster. Lancaster used monitors to maintain order. Lancaster chose students to serve as assistants because they had learned quickly and could teach the other students. Students were all poor children who required a rudimentary education in reading, writing, and arithmetic.

A child attending a monitorial school was assigned a place in class by one of the monitors, who checked on student absences or promoted students if they made progress. Monitors oversaw many of the details that a single headmaster could not manage alone, such as distributing paper, making or mending pens, and distributing books and slates. Lancaster believed that the schoolmaster's role should be that of a "silent bystander and inspector."[35]

Time-saving devices were used. For example, the class was lined up into position, and students took their places under their number painted on the wall. A quick glance at the wall showed who was absent, thus saving the time involved in calling names for attendance.[36]

The psychological effects of Lancaster's teaching methods must have had a negative impact on some students, especially those who were punished. Rewards were given out to students who behaved well and who performed adequately. Lancaster spoke of buying gifts for the 217 pupils on the rolls in his school in 1803, stating, "it is not an unusual thing with me to deliver one or two hundred prizes at the same time."[37]

Punishments often were peculiar; one practice involved putting boys who misbehaved into a sack or basket that was then hoisted to the roof of the school in sight of the rest of the students, who smiled at the sight of the "birds in the cage."[38] Students who repeatedly came to school with dirty faces or hands had their faces and hands washed by a member of the opposite sex, in sight of the whole school.

The curriculum and methods of teaching in the monitorial schools were based on cost effectiveness. To save money, Lancaster used reading sheets, thus saving on the cost of buying books. He also used slates so that he did not have to pay for the costly copy books into which children copied their arithmetic sums. Monitors were given books of arithmetic problems and a key showing the step-by-step instructions for obtaining the answer. The monitor read the arithmetic problems from the key, and the students copied them down. Many monitors probably did not understand how the answer was obtained in the first place, and there was no established research and theory on which to base these methods of teaching. It is easy to picture large numbers of students sitting quietly and following the monitor's directions in learning arithmetic, without understanding why they obtained a certain answer. Students who were slower to learn probably had a very difficult time, for the concept of learning disabilities was unknown at that time.

Although Lancaster did succeed in establishing eight schools, which served 1500 children, his spending habits affected the future of his schools. It is partly because of Lancaster's financial difficulties that the Lancastrian method of education died with him in 1838.

Lancaster's method of teaching made sense in the economic and social context of the time, because it trained large numbers of students in how to follow directions and prepared them for the factory, where many would be working. Lancaster took the requirements of the factory setting in a new technological age and applied them to the problem of mass education.[39]

By 1838, the year that Lancaster died, the common school movement, headed by Horace Mann, Secretary of the Massachusetts Board of Education, was being established. Communities were making a commitment to free public education for all children. The ideas of both Lancaster and Mann are summarized in the "Shapers of Education" feature on page 174.

HORACE MANN: BEGINNINGS OF THE AMERICAN COMMON SCHOOL (PUBLIC SCHOOL) SYSTEM

During the early national period, by the 1830s, states had begun to take responsibility for supervising and organizing schools.[40] Horace Mann, appointed secretary of the Massachusetts Board of Education in 1837, and trained as a lawyer, wanted to develop a system of education to reach all children, regardless of social class or economic status. He also began a teacher training institution, known as a **normal school,** in Lexington, Massachusetts, in 1839. Henry Barnard, secretary of the Connecticut Board of Education from 1839 to 1842, also helped with the development of the American common school system. William Torrey Harris, whose work is covered in chapter 9, was superintendent of the Saint Louis, Missouri, school system and helped develop the curriculum of the American public high school in the 1890s.

By 1850, the American common school, so named because it was controlled by the community and because all children would be educated regardless of socioeconomic status, had become an institution. Also, the teaching force had become overwhelmingly female, because common school reformers viewed women as a stable, inexpensive, and moral teaching force.[41]

Horace Mann's philosophy of education stemmed partly from experiences in his youth.

Mann saw the common school to be a way to reform society and to transmit culture and national unity.[42] Thus, citizenship training had become an important duty for the American common school teacher.

Spotlight On ←————————————————————————————————

HORACE MANN (1796–1859)

Horace Mann lost his older brother to a drowning accident at age 17. At the funeral, the 14-year-old Horace heard the minister say that since his brother had not converted to Calvinism before he died, his fate in eternity was doubtful. Mann became very bitter about Calvinism after this experience and determined not to infuse any religious elements into the common school.

Mann did not want children to be subjected to the same strict and rigid upbringing he had endured in his own youth. He disliked the teaching methods of his youth, saying that the methods were monotonous and did not challenge students' other abilities, since the only method used was memorization.

Although working-class voters rejected school tax proposals because they believed that the schools would help mostly middle-class and upper-class students, Mann's ideas were largely accepted. As secretary of the Massachusetts Board of Education from 1837 to 1848, he gave annual addresses at the conferences on the state of education in the Commonwealth of Massachusetts, delivering the first of these reports in 1838. Each year, Mann gave an address on a different subject involving education that he considered to be highly important. In the address of 1840, he described the poor salaries of schoolteachers and how they were regarded by society. He compared the salaries "given to engineers, to superintendents of railroad, to agents and overseers of manufacturing establishments, to cashiers of banks and so forth, with the customary rates of renumeration given to teachers."[43]

In his *Eleventh Annual Report* of 1847, "Expenses of Education, and Other Expenses," Mann concentrated on the personal and moral qualities necessary to become an effective teacher and on the wages paid to teachers. He was ahead of his time in recognizing the economic inequities of male and female teachers, stating in his report that "in Maine, the average rate of wages paid to teachers is $15.40 per month to males, and $4.80 to females."[44] Mann was particularly upset about this because he recognized that individuals who would otherwise be well qualified for teaching would not consider going into the profession strictly for financial reasons.

Mann was also ahead of his time in recognizing that education can play a role in ending poverty. In his *Twelfth Annual Report* of 1848, he stated that poverty was "a public as well as a private evil."[45] He wrote about the children of the working poor, declaring that "the children of the workpeople are abandoned to their fate; no power in the realm has yet been able to secure them an education."[46] He recognized the paradox that a poor child who had to work to support his or her family had no chance to attend school. He worried about what would happen to those children when they became adults, because "when the adult laborer is prostrated by sickness, or eventually worn out by toil and age, the poor-house, which has all along been his destination, becomes his destiny."[47] Mann stated that "our country in general and the state of Massachusetts in particular, owes a vast economic debt to that class of people, whose labor has been mainly instrumental in rearing the great material structures of which we so often boast."[48]

Another concern of Horace Mann's was the plight of children who came from immigrant families. At a time when immigration to the United States was increasing, Mann was alert to the condition of the many Irish children who were working in factories in Massachusetts. He disliked the way Irish children were treated by the other students in school, reporting that they were treated with "indignity and contempt" and that their treatment was "unmanly and unjust."[49] He said that it was the teacher's job to make the other students understand and appreciate the plight of those less fortunate. Mann's ideas on encouraging students to have empathy for others in their classes, and in preventing poverty are still applicable, with bullying on the rise in schools.

Mann also gave recommendations on the management of difficult students, reporting in the *Common School Journal* that the "management of disobedient children is one of the most difficult of duties."[50] He said that the difficulties students

SHAPERS OF EDUCATION

Joseph Lancaster	Horace Mann
■ He developed an inexpensive, cost effective system of education by using older students, called monitors, to oversee and teach younger children.	■ Mann promoted a system of education to reach all children, regardless of social class or economic status. Trained as a lawyer, he espoused egalitarian education.
■ Monitorial schools started in England and were adopted in America.	■ Mann declared that education should not have religious elements.
■ Large numbers of students were taught in monitorial schools.	■ Citizenship training was important as a way to reform society.
■ A harsh system of punishment was used, involving humiliation.	■ Mann was secretary of the Massachusetts Board of Education and gave annual reports on the status of education in Massachusetts.
■ There was strict order and discipline, to prepare students for the factories where they would eventually work.	■ Mann's report of 1840 stated that schoolteachers' salaries were below those paid to bank cashiers, engineers, or railroad superintendents.
■ No textbooks were purchased, reading sheets were used, and slates were used in place of expensive copy paper.	■ Mann's goal was to give the children of the working poor the chance for an education and a better life.
■ Monitors had no training in how to teach students. Their goal was to have them follow directions.	

had in their home lives would affect school behavior and performance, and that teachers, regardless of a child's behavior, should "treat the less amiable children with great kindness and regard."[51]

Horace Mann was a visionary educational reformer who influenced today's system of education. His contributions are summarized in the feature "Shapers of Education."

Mann was not the only educator concerned about the education of those less fortunate. Robert Dale Owen developed the infant schools for children in England and transported the idea to America.

EARLY NATIONAL PERIOD: ROBERT DALE OWEN AND THE INFANT SCHOOLS

Robert Owen, the son of an English socialist, was interested in the best way to educate poor children from the ages of four to eight. The infant school movement formed the lower level of the American public school system.[52] Believing that the purpose of public education was national reform, Owen stated that the system should be "open and equal to all," and that the funds would come from "a tax for each child throughout the state from the age of 2 or 3, to the age of 13 or 14."[53] Each child was taxed, whether or not the parents chose to send the child to the state schools or not. Owen also called for an appropriation from the state treasury, if the parents' tax payments were insufficient. Owen stressed that the "tax of ignorance is a much heavier tax than any tax for education."[54] As an early leader of the labor movement, Owen called for state schools to "receive the children, not for 6 hours a day, but altogether."[55] Owen believed that schools should "clothe them, lodge them, direct not their studies only, but their occupations and amusements."[56] This philosophy of education coincided with the rising numbers of poor children, due to increasing immigration into the United States. The socialist philosophy was that the state had to be responsible for such children's upbringing. Owen had been very successful in establishing a school with this philosophy in New Lanark, England, and he used the same principles in establishing a school in New Harmony, Indiana.[57]

One of Owen's major contributions to American education was the philosophy that corporal punishment, used so frequently (even in the Lancasterian schools), should not be allowed. Owen added physical education to the curriculum to complement the intellectual component. Pupils ranged from 18 months to 12 years of age, and they attended the day school from 7:00 to 9:00 a.m., and then from 10:00 a.m., until noon, and then had a break until 3:00 p.m., when they returned to school and finished at 5:00 p.m. During the winter months, children did not begin school until 10:00 a.m., had a half hour recess, and then continued until 2:00 p.m., when they were dismissed for the day. Owen recommended that the children remain in school until age 12, because "the general adoption of such a measure would be productive of the most important advantages to the parents themselves, to the children, and to the society at large."[58]

Today's teachers, like Robert Dale Owen, attempt to tailor their lessons around the students' needs. Owen wrote that any learning "should be conveyed to them

Table 8-2 **Education for Poor Children: Infant Schools Versus Today's Schools**

INFANT SCHOOLS	TODAY'S SCHOOLS
Were concerned with educating poor children ages 4 to 8.	Ages 4 to 8 are in lower elementary grades.
State tax funded education for each child from age 2 to 3, to age 14.	Property taxes are highly important in school funding.
Schools should provide clothing and shelter, and supervise free time.	Teachers and schools are increasingly taking on a custodial role.
Philosophy of schooling coincided with increased numbers of poor children, caused partly by immigration.	Increased immigration and poverty are concerns of all educators today.
State was responsible for each child's upbringing.	Increased resources are needed for the education of poor children.
Used developmentally appropriate materials for children.	Use developmentally appropriate materials for children.

in as pleasant and agreeable a manner as can be devised."[59] He recommended that teachers must keep in mind the students' attention levels when planning lessons, stating: "If the interest or attention is observed to flag, the teacher looks to the lecture itself, and his manner of delivering it, rather than to the children, to discover the cause."[60]

Although Robert Dale Owen concentrated on providing educational opportunities for the children of the poor, his philosophy of education, and the subjects emphasized in the infant school curriculum, shaped education today. Just as teachers today have trouble finding developmentally suitable materials for their students, so did Robert Dale Owen. He even remarked that the books "at present in use, are in many respects defective: they are ill adapted to the capacities of children so young, and are consequently not calculated to interest them sufficiently."[61] He left us with a warning about choosing developmentally suitable materials that is still used today: "Children should never be directed to read what they cannot understand."[62] The similarities between Owen's infant schools for poor children and schools today are summarized in Table 8-2.

Sunday schools were another form of education for poor children.

EARLY NATIONAL PERIOD: SUNDAY SCHOOLS FOR WORKING CHILDREN

Another method of providing education for poor children, particularly those who had to work, focused on using the one free day they had in the week: Sunday, thus the term **Sunday school** movement. Begun about 1791 in Philadelphia by the First Day Society, which included such leaders as Benjamin Rush and the publisher Matthew Carey, the Sunday school movement provided free education to needy children.

Two Philadelphia schoolteachers, John Ely and John Poor, head of the Young Ladies' Academy in Philadelphia, were recruited to teach anyone, regardless of gender or age, to read and write. Students read from the Old and New Testaments and learned to write from them as well. Teachers also made sure that children behaved properly. This included no swearing, lying, or talking in an indecent manner.[63]

The Sunday school movement began because it was reasoned that education of the poor was necessary for the public good. Education would also help the poor learn certain habits deemed necessary for success, habits of "order and industry" to become good servants and apprentices in industry. School thus took on a custodial role, because it took over the role of parents in teaching certain habits, including respect for authority and proper moral behavior. To the founding members of the First Day Society, children could become productive, useful citizens who could participate fully in the republic if they were given the appropriate form of education.[64]

The Sunday school founders, whether Protestant or Evangelical, believed that both moral and intellectual ignorance among children was deplorable.[65]

Although the Sunday school movement and the common school movement occurred at the same time and overlapped, the Sunday school filled an important niche: it provided education for those who were excluded from public or tax-supported schools in the early nineteenth century.[66] Black adults and children often attended the Sunday schools because they wanted to learn, but were excluded from public education. Some Sunday schools that taught black students in the South, in cities such as Charleston, Nashville, and Saint Louis, held classes separately, and at different hours, from those for white students.[67] After 1831, classes for blacks were offered only orally. The reason for this was fear: If blacks became literate, they could acquire enough knowledge to revolt and might disrupt the entire economic system of the Southern states, which was dependent on slavery.

The method of instruction in both the Sunday schools, as well as the common schools was memorization. Sunday school teachers required their students to recite large quantities of Bible verses, catechism answers, and hymn verses.[68] Memorization was used as a teaching method because it was believed that it would discipline a child's mind; the prevailing view of this period was that a child's mind was an empty receptacle that had to be filled. Memorization was to provide the mind with sources for reflection in later years. Children whose minds were "stored" with Bible verses would have something to reflect upon during idle moments. To encourage students to memorize, teachers distributed rewards such as tickets that could be collected and exchanged for a prize, usually a book.[69] Today, teachers use the same method of tokens in developing a reward system to encourage students to behave well.

Attendance and punctuality were very important in Sunday school education. Teachers stressed that students come to school dressed neatly and that they be clean. Some Sunday schools, such as the one at the First Presbyterian Church in Elizabeth, New Jersey, maintained a "fragment society" that provided poor children with clothing.[70]

Corporal punishment was also prohibited in the Sunday schools. Teachers treated their students kindly and used persuasion to discipline students. By the year 1825, Sunday schools, although still in operation, were increasingly being taken over by public schools. State legislation for education played a major role in this development. As the states began to play larger roles in educational policy making, and the American common school continued to develop and evolve, free public education for all, whether rich or poor, became the responsibility of the state and the public schools.

EARLY NATIONAL PERIOD: TEACHER TRAINING PROGRAMS

During the 1830s, when Horace Mann was secretary of education in Massachusetts, he remarked on the poor quality of schoolteachers, saying that "any farmer's apprentice was competent to keep school."[71]

Teachers lacked subject matter knowledge as well as an understanding of pupils' developmental stages and how to adapt the subject matter to their students so that it could be understood by various age groups.[72] Schoolteachers lacked classroom management skills and often lost their tempers with unruly students. Lucy Larcom, who wrote *A New England Girlhood,* published in 1889, described an incident in which the schoolmaster had "a fearful leather strap, which was sometimes used even upon the shrinking palm of a little girl."[73] Larcom, who worked in the mills in Lowell, Massachusetts, in the 1880s, related another incident in which a boy, apparently not in good health, was made to kneel over a desk and given 90 blows with a sharp instrument, over a period of 3 hours. He was temporarily unable to walk after the punishment was over. This incident attracted attention and was reported in an editorial in The Boston Transcript of 1837.[74]

The normal schools, advocated by both Horace Mann and Henry Barnard, were supposed to end this type of inappropriate teacher behavior by preparing teachers to manage classrooms in a more productive way, without the use of such physical violence. The term *normal* comes from *norm* or *norma,* meaning "rule, pattern, or standard." The normal schools were intended to set standards, or rules, for teacher training and to teach the principles and rules of teaching.[75] The normal school concept of teacher training used in the United States came from Germany and was introduced to American teachers after 1834.[76] By 1838 the normal school concept was accepted in the Commonwealth of Massachusetts, and $10,000 was donated by a lawyer to promote teacher preparation for the common schools, with the stipulation that the legislature must match this contribution.[77] The state legislature agreed to this, and the resolution was signed by Governor Everett on April 19, 1838. Three normal schools were then set up as experimental schools for a period of 3 years. One was established in the northeastern part of Massachusetts, one in the western part, and one in the southeastern part of the state.[78]

Horace Mann believed that women, rather than men, should be employed as schoolteachers, especially in the primary grades. He thought that women were freer from political ambitions than men and would not become sidetracked by these ambitions.[79] He also recommended that women be used for a teaching force because they were gentler in nature and had stronger parental impulses than men and were also less likely to want jobs of a higher nature. The outcome of this emphasis on hiring female schoolteachers was that teaching became an important career for women, and the normal school became the method for training women for teaching and also providing them with an education.[80] There were economic advantages to hiring women to teach, because they could be paid less, a consideration in an age when school districts did not want to pay much for teachers for the common district schools in the first place.

Some individuals opposed normal schools, believing such training for teachers to be unnecessary. Objections included the lack of religious instruction and the Unitarian influence. It was felt that if the normal schools of Massachusetts, were to be successful in the long run, they had to be adopted by the state as part of its system of public instruction.

After the initial 3-year trial period, during which time teachers, such as the Reverend Cyrus Pierce for the school in Lexington, Massachusetts, were carefully chosen for the normal schools, the idea of special schools for training teachers was gradually accepted. Keep in mind that any pioneering efforts in education, or in any other field, are subject to criticism, but in the case of normal school education for teachers, those involved, such as Henry Barnard and Horace Mann, insisted on the necessity for these schools. In 1840 the Massachusetts Committee on Education of the House of Representatives declared that they did not like the way the Board of Education was training teachers because it emulated the German system of education. They also felt that the academies and high schools, which cost the Commonwealth of Massachusetts nothing, were just as good at training teachers as the normal schools. They argued that because schools were operated according to the agrarian calendar, and classes were not held when students were working in the fields, it was foolish to spend money to train teachers as professionals. The argument was that teachers could never be considered professionals because schools did not operate year round.[81] Fortunately, Henry Barnard, who had always been of invaluable assistance to Horace Mann, worked with him and Governor Everett to persuade the state legislature not to abandon normal school training, and it was allowed to continue. Barnard, writing in the *American Journal of Education* in 1858, stated that if normal school education were disbanded, the entire condition of public education in this country would be changed forever.[82]

The curriculum, which was another area of concern, was supposed to incorporate the "branches of knowledge to be taught in our common schools," according to Governor Everett. Subject matter competence was the first part of instruction, to be supplemented by instruction in the methods of teaching. The future teacher was also to have a moral influence on students by reading a portion of scripture each day.[83]

By 1848, when Mann had retired from his position as secretary to the Board of Education in Massachusetts, the expenditure for common schools in Massachusetts was $749,943, and it increased to $11,829,191 by 1896. The number of teachers increased from 2,424 men and 5,510 women in 1848, to 1,078 men and 11,197 women by 1896. By 1896 the idea of normal schools had gained such acceptance that 10 normal schools were in operation.[84] Today, normal schools, although they offer other majors, still offer teacher education programs to large numbers of students who want to enter the field of education as elementary or secondary school teachers.

EARLY NATIONAL PERIOD: CURRICULUM BATTLES AT THE UNIVERSITY

The concept of providing higher education to train good republican citizens, in the name of nationalism, arose during the early national period. The traditional liberal arts curriculum, designed for the aristocracy, had to be adapted to reflect the new Enlightenment thought. Higher education had to be reformed to serve public purposes; it was no longer sufficient to have a curriculum designed to train ministers and the gentlemen leaders of society.[85] State universities were analyzing their curricula and debating how best to educate students in light of changing needs. Institutions continue to adapt today. We will look more closely at curriculum issues in chapter 9.

BRIDGES FROM THE PAST TO THE PRESENT: CONTRIBUTIONS FROM THE ENLIGHTENMENT AND EARLY NATIONAL PERIOD TO THE PRESENT

The contributions from the Enlightenment and the early national periods to today's educational system came from the ideas of Benjamin Franklin, Benjamin Rush, Horace Mann, and his assistant Henry Barnard. From Benjamin Franklin came the emphasis on writing. Franklin had students to read something and paraphrase it. Students today use the same activity to improve their writing, beginning in elementary school. Franklin also started the Academy in Philadelphia, launching the academy movement in the early national period. Academies were the precursor to the secular high school in this country.

From Benjamin Rush came the concept that crime may result from a lack of education. The link between crime and ignorance is well documented from a statistical study of the educational level of prisoners in this country. The idea that society must support education, as Rush propounded, is still problematic in this country. More prisons have been built than schools, and the lack of respect and recognition given to schoolteachers, even today, is still an issue. Some students see celebrities and others getting rich quickly without much education and therefore are more interested in finding a get-rich-quick scheme than in obtaining an education.

To Benjamin Rush we also owe the idea that our youth have to be protected. You will recall that he spoke of limiting amusements for youth. Today, we restrict access to the Internet, and monitor the television programs children watch, or forbid them to play violent video games. The rating system for movies was developed because of this concept.

Finally, Rush's contribution to the methods of teaching was the use of audiovisual aids, especially for preschoolers.

Horace Mann, the secretary of the Massachusetts Board of Education, devoted his life to issues of education and teacher quality. The training you are receiving to become a future teacher has roots back in his time. Teacher quality continues to be an issue today, for the grade point average required for candidates in teacher education programs has been debated and has been raised in many states. Teacher salary remains a concern, for teachers earn less than many other professionals, raising the debate of whether teaching constitutes a profession.

Mann's discussion of the influence of family life on a child's performance and ability in school is relevant today. As a future teacher you will find that a child who comes to school without breakfast or who lives in an abusive or broken home may be unable to concentrate. A more recent educational critic, Jonathan Kozol, has studied this same phenomenon and detailed his findings in *Ordinary Resurrections* and *Savage Inequalities*.

Mann also discussed the necessity of increasing sensitivity toward their peers who may be different. Teachers today attempt to increase empathy among students, especially to prevent bullying, which can be a problem for some students today.

From Robert Owen, the English socialist who began the infant schools for children, came the concept of special teaching methods for those in the primary grades, including a reward system such as coupons that can be turned in for a prize. We recognize that teaching reading at a young age, from the ages of 2 through 5, is very important, because older children who cannot read often never catch up and drop out of school. The concept of tailoring lessons around a student's needs also has applications today, for there are many special needs students, including those with physical handicaps as well as learning disabilities, for whom lessons may need to be adapted.

Of the many connections between education in the American Enlightenment and early national periods, we shall discuss two of them in more details. Suggestions for further reading at the end of this chapter will allow you to pursue research in the other areas.

BRIDGE 1: THE CONNECTION BETWEEN EDUCATION AND CRIME: BUILD SCHOOLS NOT PRISONS!

The need to prevent youth from entering the criminal justice system by focusing on improving education is not a new idea. It has existed since Benjamin Rush's time, and more recently, state governors have been paying attention to this idea. An article in *Black Issues in Higher Education* noted that Governor Evan Bayh of Indiana, in 1988, assessed the Indiana Department of Corrections. His administration was told that to calculate how much money would be needed to expand prisons in the future, they should look at the at-risk juvenile population in the second grade. The reason for this was that most second graders are about 7 years old, and in 10 years, they will be old enough to enter the adult prison system. Bayh and his administration were told that such planning was necessary because of the correlation between children living in at-risk environments and those who enter prison. Such children are more likely to go to jail than to college, when they are of college age.[86] Ultimately, Governor Bayh transferred funds from correctional institutions to education, and saved Indiana $40 million.[87]

Legislators in other states have also noted the connection between increased spending for correctional institutions and the lack of spending for education. Since 1988 the state of New York has increased its prison funding and cut the support of public higher education in a one-to-one ratio, according to the report *New York State of Mind? Higher Education Funding vs. Prison Funding in the Empire State, 1988 to 1998*.[88] The report explains that in the years from 1977 to 1995, the states, on average, spent twice as much on funding for prisons as they have for funding public colleges. In Texas, funding for colleges has grown by 391 percent, while prison funding has increased by 2,232 percent.[89] Since 1988, the State University of New York (SUNY) and City University of New York (CUNY) systems have had a decrease of $615 million in funding, while prisons have received an increase in funding of $761 million.[90]

Public higher education is supposed to provide greater economic opportunities to people on the lower end of the socioeconomic scale, but the lack of funding, which means higher tuition, puts a college education out of reach for such individuals. These people are then forced to rely on the public high schools for training, but they are also underfunded, so they cannot provide appropriate training either.[91] U.S. Census Bureau data of state funding trends from 1977 to 1995, of the growth in prison funding to growth in education funding ratio, reveals that every state spent more on building and funding prisons than it did on funding education.[92] According to the U.S. Department of Justice Statistics, there has been a 452 percent increase in state expenditures for incarcerating prisoners between 1982 and 2001. The prison population continues to increase, with drug offenses listed as the most common offense.[93]

A report by the Educational Testing Service (ETS), *Captive Students: Education and Training in America's Prisons*, described the poor literacy skills of prisoners in America. This study found that one third of prisoners were unable to fill out an application, calculate the cost of a purchase, or read a mileage chart to determine miles per gallon.[94] This is of particular concern because 66 percent of those who will be paroled will not have the literacy skills needed to function in society.[95]

In addition to improving the quality of education for at-risk children and youth, who may be more likely to be incarcerated, we have to improve the quality of teaching. Often, poor-quality teachers are found in inner city schools and rural areas, which find it harder to attract teachers owing to crime, economically depressed areas, and higher costs of living.

BRIDGE 2: IMPROVING TEACHER QUALITY

Concern over the quality of teachers has existed since the time of the American Enlightenment and the early national period and is an issue with deep economic, social, and political implications. Presidential candidates use the improvement of education, which includes the improvement of teacher training, in their campaign platforms. Students who do not succeed in school because their schools are staffed by poorly qualified teachers may drop out, which has economic and social implications, because dropouts are more likely to end up becoming involved in crime and have poor literacy skills.[96] A report by the Education Trust, *In Need of Improvement: Ten Ways the U.S. Department of Education Has Failed to Live Up to its Teacher Quality Commitments,* concluded that improving teacher quality is the most effective way to help minority and poor children bridge the achievement gap.[97] Data have shown that minority and poor children attend school districts with a disproportionately high number of poorly qualified teachers, but the U.S. Department of Education has not done enough to correct this situation, although the NCLB act requires districts to do so.[98]

The improvement of teacher training (teacher education) programs in colleges and universities has been debated by such leading educators as John Goodlad, Diane Ravitch, Linda Darling-Hammond, and many others. One key problem is that the 2001 federal *NCLB Act,* requires that all teachers of core academic subjects be highly qualified.[99] Furthermore, Title II of the Higher Education Act mandates that the secretary of education issue an annual report on teacher quality based on data provided by the states.[100] The report *Meeting the Highly Qualified Teachers Challenge: The Secretary's Annual Report on Teacher Quality,* published by the Office of Postsecondary Education of the U.S. Department of Education in 2002, debates how to train teachers. The normal schools of Horace Mann's time have been criticized for not preparing teachers adequately to meet the demands of NCLB. One major criticism is that teachers come from education programs that have poorly prepared them in subject-matter content, and that they lack the language and grammar skills needed to teach to high standards.[101]

This is a very serious criticism and should be taken to heart by those wishing to reform teacher education programs so that they can train teachers who are qualified not only as subject-matter experts but also as good classroom managers. The secretary's report deplores what he calls the "low standards and high barriers" that keep many talented individuals who want to teach from entering the education profession while allowing those who are poorly prepared to teach.[102]

One suggestion, offered by the Carnegie Corporation of New York, is to give teacher education a major overhaul. This idea is not new; what is new about this suggestion is the addition of a "residency" program, to give teaching one of the requirements of a "true" profession, like medicine.[103] The residency program will last for two years, and the colleges of education have to provide academic content mentors and coaches to their graduates in their first two years of teaching.[104]

The Carnegie Corporation in its report "Teaching as a Clinical Profession: A New Challenge for Education" recommends that colleges track graduates' progress, create long term relationships with the graduates, and integrate the theory and practice of teaching.[105] The Carnegie Corporation pledged $40 million over 3 fiscal years to help six institutions restructure their schools of education. These schools include Bank Street College, California State University at Northridge, Michigan State University, and the University of Virginia. Each of these institutions will receive $5 million, and each has pledged to match the funds and put the money towards the restructuring of its school of education.[106]

John Goodlad, professor of education and director of the Center for Educational Renewal at the College of Education at the University of Washington in Seattle, Washington, has spoken and written at length about implementing changes in

Table 8-3 **Improving Teacher Education: Summary of Solutions**

PROBLEM	SOLUTION
Too many unqualified teachers are on staff at schools enrolling minority and poor children. Children in such schools often drop out, or graduate unprepared.	Incentives should be provided for qualified teachers to teach in these schools. Improving teacher quality will help bridge the achievement gap.
Normal school programs do not prepare teachers adequately for the demands of NCLB.	Education programs have to prepare future teachers in subject matter content as well as classroom management skills.
Teachers are poorly prepared and the training period is too short.	Carnegie Corporation recommends a 2-year "residency" program so that teaching has the same requirements as other professions, such as medicine.
Schools and colleges of education do not follow up on teacher education graduates.	Carnegie Corporation recommends that colleges track graduates' progress, and create long term relationships with graduates.

teacher training programs. He states, "Our research shows that teachers are not prepared to know where they are going or where they should go."[107] Goodlad also believes there is a lack of leadership; he states that "teachers are being pushed this way and that way—to phonics one day, to standards the next—and I think this destroys the profession."[108] He believes that a strong Commissioner of Education, such as Secretary Richard Riley or Terrel Bell, could do much to change the perception of teacher as a mechanic who is just called on to implement whatever changes are recommended. Instead, teachers should be seen as professionals, individuals who have the training and the autonomy to make professional decisions about the best practices necessary to educate their students. With high standards and high expectations, teachers can be seen as real professionals, and the perception of teachers will eventually change.[109]

Many solutions have been proposed to improve teacher training (teacher education) programs in colleges and universities (these are summarized in Table 8-3).

SUMMARY

This chapter described the effects of the spread of Enlightenment thought on America, beginning in 1820, when the University of Virginia was being established by Thomas Jefferson. Early educators such as Benjamin Franklin, a printer, and Benjamin Rush, a physician, were instrumental in establishing schools in which the curriculum was influenced by the Enlightenment school of thought. The monitorial schools, Sunday schools, and infant schools were important developments in education during this time.

This chapter also described the work of Horace Mann, secretary of the Massachusetts Board of Education, Henry Barnard, secretary of the Connecticut Board of Education, and others whose dedication to providing an education for all children led to the advancement of the common school. Also discussed were the contributions of Enlightenment thought to education, including ideas on educating teachers.

QUESTIONS FOR DISCUSSION

1. The idea of using education to eliminate poverty is not new, as noted in this chapter. In your opinion, is education effective in eliminating poverty? Why or why not? Give at least one reason to back up your answer.

2. The treatment of students was an important topic in this chapter. Think about Mann's ideas on teacher expectations for students. Teacher expectations for students may well determine whether students will be successful. In your opinion, what expectations should teachers have for students?

3. How does the teacher training during Mann's era compare with the training you are receiving at your college or university? Give at least three examples.

4. The issue of respect for teachers is one that has implications in the present day. Describe how your parents/guardians/friends/relatives responded when you told them you planned to become a teacher.

5. In your opinion, is the type of training you are receiving to become a teacher *adequate* to prepare you to work in a school with children or youth of the age group you want to teach? Do you feel comfortable with teaching? How could your training be improved? Write an opinion paper on this subject and present it to the class in a 10-minute presentation.

6. Think of your own school days, in either elementary school or high school. Do you recall any teacher who was unprofessional, unqualified, or poorly prepared? Describe this individual and the behaviors, attitudes, and characteristics that made you draw these conclusions about him or her. If you were a teacher educator preparing such an individual to teach in the public schools, would you recommend him or her? Why or why not?

SUGGESTED ACTIVITIES

1. Horace Mann's views on education were shaped by his own personal experiences, particularly his strict Calvinist upbringing. Do you believe he would have had less strict views on the separation of church and state in education if he

had been raised in a different, more liberal, environment? Present your argument in a one- to three-page paper.

2. Research teacher salaries in your community. If Horace Mann were alive today, how do you think he would deal with this problem? What recommendations would he make, based on his findings in the past with regard to teacher salaries and the respect accorded to teachers? Present your findings to your class in a 10- to 15-minute PowerPoint presentation.

3. Describe at least three ways that you, as a future teacher, would help encourage children in your class who you know came from limited financial resources to be successful. Present your viewpoint to your class using a handout for future reference.

4. Interview a teacher who went through a teacher education program within the last 20 years. Find out which courses he or she took and how well these courses prepared him or her to teach. Compare the classes that your interview subject took with the classes you are currently taking, and prepare a presentation of about 15 to 20 minutes on the differences and similarities between your training and that of the teacher you interviewed. Include a handout to the class with your recommendations on how teacher training might be improved.

5. Interview two parents or guardians, one male, one female, of school-age children. Ask them to describe their encounters with their children's teachers since their children began school, and their opinions on whether their children's teachers were well qualified, what the problems were, and so on. Find out the parents'/guardians' opinions on the professionalism of these teachers. Present your findings to the class in an interactive presentation with a handout for future reference.

6. Compare the education provided for the poor in the monitorial schools, Sunday schools, and infant schools with the education provided for the wealthier students in the academies. Summarize the similarities and differences in a chart.

Bibliography

Bartlett, I. H. (1982). *The American mind in the mid-nineteenth century* (2nd ed.). Arlington Heights, IL: Harlan Davidson.

Bayles, E. E. (1961). Sketch for a study of the growth of American educational thought and practice. *History of Education Quarterly, 1*(3), 43–49.

Boylan, A. M. (1988). *Sunday school: The formation of an American institution, 1790–1880.* New Haven, CT: Yale University Press.

Bynack, V. P. (1993). Noah Webster's linguistic thought and the idea of an American national culture. In F. Shuffleton (Ed.), *The American Enlightenment.* Rochester, NY: University of Rochester Press.

Cassara, E. (1976). *The Enlightenment in America.* Boston: Twayne.

Choe, S. (1999, January 7). The fund-a-mentality difference between prisons and schools. *Black Issues in Higher Education, 15,* 12–14.

Cordasco, F. (1963). *A brief history of education: A handbook of information on Greek, Roman, medieval, Renaissance, and modern educational practice.* Paterson, NJ: Littlefield, Adams.

Ferguson, R. A. (1997). *The American Enlightenment, 1750–1820.* Cambridge, MA: Harvard University Press.

Filler, L. (Ed.). (1965). *Horace Mann on the crisis in education.* Yellow Springs, OH: Antioch Press.

Fogg, P. (2002, October 4). Carnegie Corporation suggests residencies in teacher education. *Chronicle of Higher Education, 49,* A16.

Fraser, J. W. (2001). *The school in the United States: A documentary history.* Boston: McGraw-Hill.

Hardy, L. (2003, April). Overburdened and overwhelmed. *American School Board Journal, 190,* 41.

Hathaway, W. E. (1980, December). Testing teachers. *American School Board Journal, 381 (3),* 210–216.

Hebel, U. J. (Ed.). (1999). *The construction and contestation of American cultures and identities in the early national period.* Heidelberg: Universitatsverlag C. Winter Heidelberg GmbH.

Hinsdale, B. A. (1900). *Horace Mann and the common school revival in the United States.* New York: Charles Scribner.

Johnson, O. C. (1970). *Robert Owen in the United States* (Foreword by A. L. Morton). New York: Humanities Press.

Kaestle, C. (1973). *Joseph Lancaster and the monitorial school movement: A documentary history.* New York: Teachers College Press.

Kuritz, H. (1967). Benjamin Rush: His theory of republican education. *History of Education Quarterly, 7*(4), 432–51.

Larcom, L. (1920). *A New England girlhood.* Boston: Houghton Mifflin. (Originally published 1889)

Mann, M. P. (1865). *The life of Horace Mann, by his wife* (2nd ed.). Boston: Walker, Fuller.

May, H. F. (1976). *The Enlightenment in America.* New York: Oxford.

Meyer, D. H. (1976). The uniqueness of the American Enlightenment. [Special issue: An American Enlightenment]. *American Quarterly, 28*(2), 165–86.

Modisett, J. (2004, March 25). Shifting the emphasis from prison to education: How Indiana saved over $40 million. *Black Issues in Higher Education, 21,* 40–41.

Ostrander, G. M. (1999). *Republic of letters: The American intellectual community, 1776–1865.* Madison, WI: Madison House.

Owen, R. D. (1824). *An outline of the system of education at New Lanark* (K. E. Carpenter, Ed.). Glasgow, Scotland: University Press. (Reprinted 1971, New York: Arno Press)

Perkins-Gough, D. (2002). Teacher quality. *Educational Leadership, 60*(1), 85–86.

Prison population growing, but not educationally. (1997). *Journal of Adolescent & Adult Literacy, 40*(6), 477.

Rush, B. (1786). *Letters I. In A plan for the establishment of public schools and the diffusion of knowledge in Pennsylvania to which are added thoughts upon the mode of education, proper in a republic. Addressed to the Legislature and citizens of the State.* Philadelphia: Thomas Dobson.

Salmon, D. (1904). *Joseph Lancaster.* New York: Longmans, Green.

Sears, D. (2002). Yes, but—Remaking the making of teachers. *Journal of Education, 183*(2).

Spring, J. (1986). *The American school, 1642–1985.* New York: Longman.

Tell, C. (1999). Renewing the profession of teaching: A conversation with John Goodlad. *Educational Leadership, 56*(8), 15–19.

Tolley, K. (1996). Science for ladies, classics for gentlemen: A comparative analysis of scientific subjects in the curricula of boys' and girls' secondary schools in the United States, 1794–1850. *History of Education Quarterly, 36*(2), 129–53.

Welter, R. (1975). *The mind of America, 1820–1860.* New York: Columbia University Press.

Williams, E. I. F. (1937). *Horace Mann: Educational statesman.* New York: Macmillan.

Suggestions for Further Reading

In addition to the works cited in the bibliography, the following are suggested for further reading.

Finn, C. E., Jr. (2003). High hurdles. *Education Next, 3*(2), 62–67.

Lasley, T. J., Bainbridge, W. L., & Berry, B. (2002). Improving teacher quality: Ideological perspectives and policy prescriptions. *Educational Forum, 67*(1), 14–25.

Lawton, M. (1997, August 6). AFT, foundation find good and bad in state's standards. *Education Week 16,* 13–16.

National Center for Education Statistics. Condition of education report. Retrieved 2005 from http://www.nces.ed.gov

National Commission on Teaching and America's Future. (1996, September). *What matters most: Teaching for America's future.* Washington, DC.

Neilsen, L. (1991). The reading professional: Sticks and stones. *Reading Teacher, 44*(6).

This article describes the struggle between the public's expectations of what teachers should do, and the teachers' struggle with education policies which keep them from being professionals.

Wong, H. K. (2004, March). Induction programs that keep new teachers teaching and improving. *NASSP Bulletin, 88,* 41–58.

Relevant Web Sites

Antioch University: Horace Mann *http://www.phd.antioch.edu/Pages/horacemann* Mann was the founder of Antioch College (now Antioch University) in Yellow Springs, Ohio. This site profiles Mann's life and career and contributions to education.

Bartleby: Great Books Online *http://www.bartleby.com/65/en/Enlighte.html* Background on the European roots of the Enlightenment, with links to other resources and important individuals in the Enlightenment.

Manuscripts of Early National and Antebellum America: University of Notre Dame *http://www.library.nd.edu/rarebooks/collections/manuscripts/american/early_national.shtml* Research rare manuscripts and books from the early national period online.

Wikipedia: the free encyclopedia *http://en.wikipedia.org/wiki/American_Enlightenment* Great site with good explanations of the Enlightenment and links to further resources.

Horace Mann: article from Wikipedia, the free encyclopedia *http://en.wikipedia.org/wiki/Horace_Mann* Site with brief article on Horace Mann and links to other sites with information on his career and life.

Education Week *http://www.edweek.org* Good current information, updated weekly, on education at all levels.

National Center for Education Statistics *http://www.nces.ed.gov* Federal and state data about all topics on education.

Questia online *http://www.questia.com*

U.S. Department of Education *http://www.ed.gov*

Endnotes

[1] Ernest Cassara, *The Enlightenment in America* (Boston: Twayne, 1976) 17–18.

[2] Ibid.

[3] Lawrence A. Cremin, *The American Common School: A Historic Conception* (New York: Teachers College Press, 1951), 33.

[4] Joel Spring, *The American School, 1642–1985* (New York: Longman, 1986), 61.

[5] Ibid., 194–95.

[6] Ibid.

[7] Ibid., 151.

[8] Ibid., 153.

[9] Ibid., 152.

[10] Cassara, *Enlightenment in America,* 157.

[11] Ibid.

[12] Hyman Kuritz, "Benjamin Rush: His Theory of Republican Education," *History of Education Quarterly, 7,* no. 4 (1967), 434–36.

[13] Ibid., 437.

[14] Ibid.

[15] Martin Bruckner, "Contested Sources of the Self: Native American Geographies and the Journals of Lewis and Clark," in *The Construction and Contestation of American Cultures and Identities in the Early National Period,* vol. 78, ed. Udo J. Hebel (Heidelberg: Universitatsverlag C. Winter Heidelberg GmbH, 1999), 32–33.

[16] Ibid., 437.

[17] Benjamin Rush, Letters I, in *A Plan for the Establishment of Public Schools and the Diffusion of Knowledge in Pennsylvania: to Which Are Added Thoughts Upon the Mode of Education, Proper in a Republic. Addressed to the Legislature and Citizens of the State* (Philadelphia: Thomas Dobson, 1786). See Letters I, pp. 388–89.

[18] Ibid. See also Kuritz, "Benjamin Rush" 440.

[19] Kuritz, "Benjamin Rush," 440.

[20] Ibid.

[21] Ibid., 446.

[22] Spring, *American School,* 14.

[23] Ernest E. Bayles, "Sketch for a Study of the Growth of American Educational Thought and Practice," *History of Education Quarterly, 1,* no. 3 (1961), 46.

[24] Spring, *American School,* 21.

25 Ibid., 131.

26 Kim Tolley, "Science for Ladies, Classics for Gentlemen: A Comparative Analysis of Scientific Subjects in the Curricula of Boys' and Girls' Secondary Schools in the United States, 1794–1850," *History of Education Quarterly, 36,* no. 2 (1996), 130.

27 Ibid.

28 Ibid., 131–32.

29 Ibid., 133.

30 Ibid., 140.

31 Ibid., 141.

32 Ibid., 149.

33 Ibid., 150.

34 Ibid., 150–51.

35 David Salmon, *Joseph Lancaster* (New York: Longmans, Green, 1904), 7.

36 Ibid., 9.

37 Ibid., 11.

38 Ibid.

39 Carl Kaestle, *Joseph Lancaster and the Monitorial School Movement: A Documentary History* (New York: Teachers College Press, 1973), 48–49.

40 Spring, *American School,* 72.

41 Ibid., 115.

42 James W. Fraser, *The School in the United States: A Documentary History* (Boston: McGraw-Hill, 2001), 49.

43 Louis Filler, Ed. *Horace Mann on the Crisis in Education* (Yellow Springs, OH: Antioch Press, 1965), 37. These are direct quotes from Mann.

44 Ibid.

45 Ibid., 119. Reprinted in Mann's own words from the *Twelfth Annual Report.* Owing to difficulties in reading the original on microfilm, which was almost indecipherable, I had to read the reprinted version.

46 Ibid., 123.

47 Ibid.

48 Ibid., 147. These are excerpts from the *Common School Journal.* See also Mary Peabody Mann, *The Life of Horace Mann, by His Wife,* 2nd ed. (Boston: Walker, Fuller, 1865).

49 Ibid., 148.

50 Ibid.

51 Ibid., 150.

52 Francesco Cordasco, *A Brief History of Education: A Handbook of Information on Greek, Roman, Medieval, Renaissance, and Modern Educational Practice* (Paterson, NJ: Littlefield, Adams, 1963), 118. Although Cordasco's book is not the ultimate reference on dates, it is used here to give a sense of the timeline of the Enlightenment, the dates of which have been debated.

53 Cremin, *American Common School,* 38.

54 Ibid.

55 Ibid., 39.

56 Ibid.

57 Oakley C. Johnson, *Robert Owen in the United States,* with foreword by A. L. Morton (New York: Humanities Press, 1970), 3.

58 Robert Dale Owen, *An Outline of the System of Education at New Lanark,* ed. Kenneth E. Carpenter (Glasgow, Scotland: University Press, 1824; repr., New York: Arno Press, 1971), 32.

59 Ibid., 25.

60 Ibid.

61 Ibid.

62 Ibid., 36.

63 Anne M. Boylan, *Sunday School: The Formation of an American Institution, 1790–1880* (New Haven, CT: Yale University Press, 1988), 7.

64 Ibid., 8.

65 Ibid., 10.

66 Ibid., 22.

67 Ibid., 23.

68 In 1821 the 40 students in the McKendrean Sabbath School Society of Baltimore, Maryland, recited 18,038 verses, answers, and hymn stanzas, according to school records. See Boylan, *Sunday School,* pp. 40 and 44.

69 Ibid.

70 Ibid., 46.

71 E. I. F. Williams, *Horace Mann: Educational Statesman* (New York: Macmillan, 1937), 189. This is an excellent source for valuable information on the development of normal schools and Mann's beliefs on the necessity for teacher training and improving schoolhouses and schools in general. Chapter X, "Educating the Teachers," is cited here.

72 Ibid.

73 Lucy Larcom, *A New England Girlhood* (Boston: Houghton Mifflin, 1920; orig. pub. 1889), 151.

74 Williams, *Horace Mann,* 190.

75 B. A. Hinsdale, *Horace Mann and the Common School Revival in the United States* (New York: Charles Scribner, 1900), 145. Chapter VI, "The Massachusetts Normal Schools," is an excellent primary source devoted to the history of teacher training institutions.

76 Ibid., 146–47.

77 Ibid.

78 Ibid., 149.

79 Williams, *Horace Mann,* 202.

80 Ibid., 204.

81 Ibid., 216. These arguments resonate even today. In Pennsylvania, then-governor Tom Ridge wanted to disband the state department of education, believing it was not necessary.

82 Ibid., 218.

83 Ibid., 158.

84 Cremin, *American Common School,* 15.

85 Spring, *American School,* 61.

86 Jeff Modisett, "Shifting the Emphasis from Prison to Education: How Indiana Saved Over $40 Million," *Black Issues in Higher Education,* March 25, 2004, 40–41.

87 Ibid.

88 Ibid.

89 Ibid.

90 Ibid.

91 Ibid.

92 Ibid. See also U.S. Census Bureau reports.

93 This can be found on the U.S. Department of Justice website, at: *http://www.ojp.usdoj.gov/ bjs/glance/expgov.htm*

94 "Prison Population Growing, but Not Educationally," *Journal of Adolescent & Adult Literacy, 40,* no. 6 (1997), 477.

95 Ibid.

96 Ibid. See also Stan Choe, "The Fund-a-mentality Difference Between Prisons and Schools," *Black Issues in Higher Education,* January 1999, 12–14.

97 Lawrence Hardy, "No Child Left Behind: ED—In Need of Improvement?" *American School Board Journal,* November 2003, 7–8.

98 Ibid.

99 Deborah Perkins-Gough, "Teacher Quality," *Educational Leadership, 60,* no. 1 (2002), 85–86.

100 Douglas Sears, "Yes, But—Remaking the Making of Teachers," *Journal of Education, 183,* no. 2 (2002), 63.

101 Ibid.

102 Ibid., 64.

103 Piper Fogg, "Carnegie Corporation Suggests Residencies in Teacher Education," *Chronicle of Higher Education,* October 4, 2002, p. A16.

104 Ibid.

105 Ibid.

106 Ibid.

107 Carol Tell, "Renewing the Profession of Teaching: A Conversation with John Goodlad," *Educational Leadership, 56,* no. 8 (1999), 15–19.

108 Ibid.

109 Ibid.

Chapter 9

Urbanization and Expansion of the Public Schools (1890–1930)

Learning Objectives

1. Understand how social and economic forces such as immigration and the Great Depression shaped educational policy and changed the role of teachers.
2. Discuss the work of the Committee of Ten and the similarities and differences between the high school curricula of 1890 versus today.
3. Describe the educational philosophies of John Dewey and Edward L. Thorndike and the advantages and disadvantages.
4. Describe the development of kindergarten education at the turn of the century, and discuss the curricula in the kindergarten at that time, compared with those today.
5. Describe the development of teacher unions and their influence on education and teaching today.
6. Debate the type of training that future teachers should receive to be successful in teaching today.

INTRODUCTION

Many changes occurred in American society during the period from 1890 to 1930. The common school of the small towns and villages of agrarian America was evolving in response to increased immigration. Lawrence Cremin, the educational historian, remarked that the cities, with their diversified immigrant population, and the continual demands of commerce and industry were destined to test the claims of the common school.[1] Teachers were unfamiliar with the languages and culture of large classes of immigrant students in the schools, and struggled to meet the needs of these non-English-speaking students.

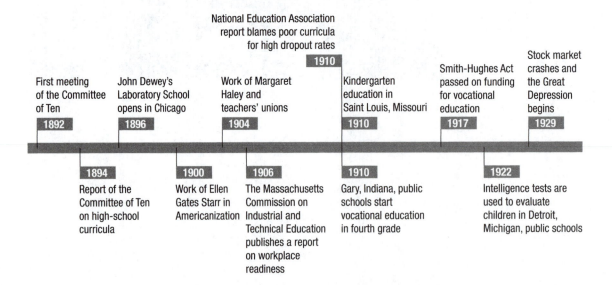

At this time, during the post–Civil War period, educational opportunities for African Americans also became an issue, because schools were segregated. Although more than 100 high schools had been established in Massachusetts by the end of the Civil War, African Americans did not have the same educational opportunities as whites, particularly in the Southern states. Thus, equality of educational opportunity became even more of a concern.[2]

By the year 1850, the idea of the common school (the elementary school) had generally been accepted in American society. It was understood that the common school had to receive public financial support; less acceptable was the idea that high schools also had to be publicly funded. In 1874, the State Supreme Court of Michigan heard a case brought by citizens in Kalamazoo, Michigan, challenging the legal authority of one of their districts, School District 1, to tax citizens to support the public high schools. The decision was that the state must publicly support a high school if it also supported a common school and a university, to provide a hierarchical system of public education.[3]

This chapter traces the evolution of the American public high school and the debate over its curricula. It also discusses the important work of educators John Dewey and Edward L. Thorndike, proponents of progressive education and scientific education, respectively. The debate over the type of programs that are best suited for high-school students continues to the present day.[4]

Chapter 9 also covers the expansion of the kindergarten program, largely due to the work of William Torrey Harris and Susan Blow, an early childhood educator, who wrote in 1910 about the value of kindergarten education.

The chapter concludes with a discussion of the formation of teacher unions in response to concerns about teacher welfare and a brief introduction to the Depression and its effect on schools and education.

ORIGIN OF THE HIGH SCHOOLS

In the post–Civil War period, about 1880, the public became more aware of the importance of obtaining an education. Although not all parents sent their children to school, the public recognized that an education had value for youth and were thus apt to demand more education.[5] Education past the elementary grades was considered necessary to improve the quality of the work force. The country was growing; railroads and cotton mills, for instance, had contributed to a population of 75,000 workers in the cotton factories of New England.[6]

During the nineteenth century only a small percentage of students attended high schools, which offered a primarily classical academic program.[7] The term *secondary education* referred to both private and public schools. Students who attended high school were enrolled in an academic program of study, although their education was supposed to prepare them for work.

Academies were transformed into public high schools, such as the Boston English Classical School, founded in 1821. This school is considered to be the first American high school. The school changed its name to English High School in 1824, and students took courses in English, mathematics, social science, and science.

They also studied bookkeeping, navigation, and moral and political philosophy. The program of study was 3 years long and had to be completed between the ages of 12 and 15.[8] Teachers were university graduates and the school was organized by grades, much as schools are today.

States took measures to make sure that high schools were established; in 1827 the Massachusetts legislature required every town of more than 500 households to hire a master to teach American history, bookkeeping, geometry, surveying, and algebra. The law further stipulated that towns with populations over 4,000 must have a master to teach Latin, Greek, history, rhetoric, and logic. In 1824 a high school for girls was established in Worcester, Massachusetts. The city of Lowell, Massachusetts, where many girls worked in the huge cotton mills for long hours each day, founded a coeducational high school in 1831, which offered both an English and a classical course of study.[9] By 1840, 26 schools had been established in this manner.

By the end of the Civil War, more than 100 high schools had been established in the state of Massachusetts.[10]

By the turn of the century, private academies and public high schools were developing rapidly. The programs, courses, and standards varied from school to school, and this lack of consistency caused problems. Although many students did not go on to college, the ones who decided to attend might find that the subjects they needed to have taken in high school had not been offered. Some colleges and universities were forced to establish preparatory schools with the curriculum the students would need in college. State universities began to demand that public officials establish more high schools to remedy this problem of unequal standards.

STANDARDIZING THE HIGH SCHOOL CURRICULUM: THE WORK AND REPORT OF THE COMMITTEE OF TEN

By 1892, it was evident that with the changing nature of the country, and more students attending high schools, that the curriculum of high schools would have to be evaluated. The nature of the Common School was changing; large numbers of immigrants were coming to America and settling in urban areas. The newly formed National Education Association (NEA) formed the Committee of Ten to establish a system of uniform high school curricula that would apply to every high school. The curriculum that high school students study today, while it has been modified over the years, has its roots in the work of the Committee of Ten, so named because it was comprised of ten individuals. A notable member was William Torrey Harris, the U.S. Commissioner of Education, who was also influential in expanding kindergarten education.

The Committee of Ten evaluated the curricula of the high schools to determine methods by which it could be improved. The group consisted of Charles Eliot, president of Harvard University, and William Torrey Harris, commissioner of education and former superintendent of the St. Louis, Missouri, school district. It also included five college presidents, one college professor, and three secondary school principals.

The committee, first met in 1892 and issued a report in 1894, which recommended that the curricula include four courses of study. Students studied the classics, including Latin, modern languages, science, and English.

It would appear that such curricula would prepare students to go on to college, although most students did not. The Committee of Ten said that no distinctions in course content or method should be made between students who were going directly into the workforce, and those who would attend college.[11] The quality of education was to remain the same regardless of the student's future postsecondary goals.

The classicists, who wanted to keep the study of Latin and Greek in the secondary schools, would eventually lose the battle, for society was moving toward a more general type of education instead of the study of esoteric subjects only.[12] In fact, 60 years later, by the year 1960, only 7.6 percent of high school students in grades 9 through 12 were taking Latin.[13]

The report of the Committee of Ten was the result of eight conferences, each on a different subject: Latin; Greek; English, other modern languages; mathematics; physics, astronomy, and chemistry; natural history, which included biology, botany, zoology, and physiology; history, civil government, and political economy; and geography, which included physical geography, geology, and meteorology.[14] Ten individuals participated in each conference.[15]

The NEA reported that "forty-seven were in the service of colleges or universities, forty-two in the service of schools, and one was a government official formerly in the service of a university."[16] Perhaps to avoid criticism that the committee's recommendations were made by those who had little experience at the secondary level, the NEA report added that "a considerable number of the college men had also had experience in schools."[17]

The NEA report stated that the most difficult conferences were those on physics, astronomy, and chemistry; natural history; history, civil government, political economy; and geography.[18] The NEA stated that these subjects were "more imperfectly dealt with in primary and secondary schools" because of the complexity of the conferences on those subjects, and the longer and more elaborate reports that were made on these subjects.[19] The difficulty was that these subjects should be given as much time in the curriculum as Latin, Greek, and mathematics, but the Committee recognized that "educational tradition was adverse to this desire."[20]

The reports of the Committee of Ten are very detailed; for example, in the "Study of English in the High School," it was states that English should be studied for "three hours a week for four years, or 480 hours in the total, to the study of literature."[21] Charles Eliot, head of the committee, compiled a chart showing the curricula for each of the 4 years of secondary school, including the number of periods per week that each subject should be offered.[22] This chart summarized the findings of the Committee as an aid to secondary teachers and principals. Over time, the amount of study devoted to various subjects in each course changed. For instance, the study of Greek occupied five periods per week initially, but decreased over time, whereas the amount of time students spent per week studying history, French, German, and the natural sciences increased.[23]

The problem with the Committee of Ten's report was that it addressed only those students who went on to higher education. The report recommended that a separate program be developed for the many students who would *not* go to college.[24] The industrial education movement, which began in the late 1870s and continued to gain momentum in the 1880s and 1890s, was becoming increasingly popular.[25]

THE ISSUE OF VOCATIONAL EDUCATION

Today, high school guidance counselors advise students on which course of study to pursue in high school: one that will give them an education in the skills they need to go right into the workforce, or one that will prepare them for college. This debate over the appropriate education for students has been debated since the turn of the century. At that time, vocational (industrial) education became "the movement" in American public education. In 1906, the Massachusetts Commission on Industrial and Technical Education published a report stating the importance of having a curriculum that would train students to enter the workforce. The problem was that progressive educators thought that students should stay in school as long as possible, rather than dropping out to enter the factories and work to support the family. However, this was not happening; only 40 to 50 percent of children completed eighth grade.[26] The figures for high school attendance were even worse, for only 8 to 10 percent of students finished the high school course.[27] The Massachusetts Report highlighted that students from the ages of 14 to 16 essentially had "two wasted years," for they had dropped out of school and were employed in low-paying, dead-end jobs.[28] They had left school because school did not provide them with a useful curriculum. The NEA Report of 1910 did not feel that inadequate teaching, ineffective compulsory education laws, which did not affect children over 14 even in the year 1918, or poverty were to blame for the dropout rate. Instead, they discussed the lack of suitable curriculum for such children. A 1913 article in the *Manual Training Magazine* stated that children left school because they found the work "distasteful" and because it "offers them little or nothing that they conceive to be of value in their lives."[29]

If meaningful educational reform was ever to be undertaken, then the system of public education had to readjusted to meet the needs of the masses, who needed industrial education. It was also argued that vocational training was the type of education students could best understand and appreciate because it was better suited to their intellectual abilities than the classical education.[30] John Dewey remarked on this when he stated that "in the great majority of human beings the distinctively intellectual interest is not dominant. They have the practical impulse and disposition."[31]

The vocational education movement required that school curricula as well as the daily school operations be revised so that students could read, follow directions, and conform to the requirements of industrial organizations, which had a large-scale factory routine.[32] Eventually, the curriculum to train youngsters for a factory life found its way down to the elementary grades; in 1910, the public schools in Gary, Indiana, began a system of vocational training starting in the fourth grade, a system that John Dewey and other progressives praised.[33] In 1915, Elwood P. Cubberley described the problems of teaching immigrants in the schools at this period, and approved the idea of matching the course of study (vocational or academic) to the socioeconomic status of a neighborhood.[34]

Like many other movements in education, the vocational or industrial education movement lost its advocates about 1917, with the passage of the Smith-Hughes Act, which restricted federal aid to schools that offered vocational training to students over age 14.[35] Today, many educators feel the same about early vocational training as Superintendent William H. Maxwell of New York City, who said that pushing students of 12 or 13 into vocational education was unwise, because they were too young to choose their future course of instruction and what they planned to do for a living.[36]

Vocational training is still very much a part of secondary school education today, but it varies from district to district. Wealthier districts are more likely to emphasize college preparatory curricula, because families intend for their children to attend college. In poorer districts, vocational or industrial education occupies a larger part of the curriculum.

JOHN DEWEY: PROGRESSIVE EDUCATOR

The period from 1890 to 1930 also saw the debate over the progressive education movement, epitomized by the work of John Dewey, versus the scientific education movement, propounded by Edward L. Thorndike, which involved testing. Table 9-1 summarizes the views of Dewey and Thorndike.

The changing view of society and children during this time was responsible for this debate. The school was taking on an increasingly custodial role, as the role

Table 9-1   **Dewey Versus Thorndike: Progressive Versus Scientific**

JOHN DEWEY	EDWARD L. THORNDIKE
Social environment must be adapted to enhance the child's best traits and abilities.	Children's abilities have to be quantified to evaluate their progress and help them learn more efficiently.
Educators should pay attention to children's living conditions.	Outside factors are not considered: only the classroom environment is studied.
Subjects have to be studied in relationship to one another, so students can see the interrelationships.	Success is defined and measured exactly with timed learning and testing periods.
Inquiry must be active (students made their own pencil boxes in the Laboratory School).	Grading scales, such as for handwriting, are used to judge students' performance.
Children of certain ages lack the developmental skills to study certain subjects.	Standardized criteria are used to evaluate students' work by age and grade level.

of the family declined and as the industrial system became too complex to train children and youth.[37] Mental discipline was believed to be very necessary. Psychologists questioned a student's mental ability to transfer the skills learned in one discipline to another; that is, how did the skills learned in understanding Latin grammar translate to balancing a checkbook?[38] This question, and others, were studied by men who were said to be "professional" educators, such as Edward L. Thorndike and John Dewey.[39]

Recall that in this period, large numbers of immigrant children were enrolling in the schools, where the major tasks for educators were to determine which teaching methods were best for students and how to "sort" large numbers of students into the best type of education for their particular ability. The idea of IQ (Intelligence) testing came into vogue at this time, led by the psychologist Edward L. Thorndike, who developed stimulus-response (S $\rightarrow$ R) psychology and applied it to learning. John Dewey, the leader of the progressive movement, argued that education had to be developed around a child's needs instead of fitting that child into an educational mold. Dewey's ideas were approved by the social workers in large cities, such as Ellen Gates Starr and Jane Addams, and were successfully adapted for use with immigrants in the settlement houses. For example, at the "American breakfasts" at Hull House in Chicago, Italian mothers learned to feed their children more nutritious breakfasts in the model apartment kitchens established in the tenement houses. Instead of feeding their children their usual breakfast of bread soaked in wine or tea, the mothers served oatmeal and cod liver oil, which would provide the calcium and vitamin D necessary to prevent rickets.[40] This was one way in which Dewey's philosophy of "learning by doing" was incorporated into immigrant education programs at the settlement houses.[41]

During the 1920s teachers were asked to change their teaching methods to adjust to the needs of non-English-speaking students. They were also asked to think

Spotlight On

JOHN DEWEY (1859–1954)

Born in Burlington, Vermont, John Dewey dedicated his life to narrowing the gap between real life and school. While working in his father's grocery business, he could not understand why the education he received working for his father, while informal, was so rich in content, while the formal instruction at school was so much less interesting.

Dewey studied at Johns Hopkins and taught at the University of Chicago from 1894 to 1904, then at Teachers' College, Columbia University, from 1904 to 1930. He was head of the Department of Philosophy, Psychology and Pedagogy at Chicago and developed the philosophy of instrumentalism. Dewey believed that children are shaped by the environment in which they are reared, meaning that the social environment must be adapted so as to enhance a child's most valued traits.

in terms of shaping the curriculum around the child's individual needs, which proved to be highly difficult during the Great Depression. Teachers used the method of Americanization, which forced these students to be taught in English. Bilingual education classes were unknown, so students had to be immersed in classes in which English was spoken. Robert A. Carlson refers to the Americanization trend of the 1900s in the cities as a "purification" of the immigrants.[42]

THE LABORATORY SCHOOL

Because Dewey's life and experiences are so rich and varied, it would be impossible to cover them all in one chapter. Thus, we focus on Dewey's work in the Laboratory School at the University of Chicago to explain his ideas on child-centered education, and their application to the classroom.

Dewey's Laboratory School earned its name at the suggestion of Ella Flagg Young, district superintendent of the Chicago Public Schools, who later became a teacher in the school. The term "implied a place for activity, for work, for the consecutive carrying on of an occupation."[43] It opened in January 1896 with 16 students and 2 teachers on a trial-and-error basis, and by December of 1897 it had grown to 60 students and 16 teachers. The science department had two laboratories, one for biology and the other for physics and chemistry.[44]

Dewey disliked what he called the "compartmentalization" of education of young children. He said that "the young child's day is compartmented into tiny cubicles of time without sufficient care for either social or intellectual relations."[45] For Dewey the question was how to develop interrelationships among the subjects, so that the child could see how one subject related to the others. To accomplish this he carefully chose the materials used for instruction to reflect the child's own environment and experience. Dewey believed that children did not realize they were learning as they investigated how things worked. For instance, as a child "boiled down his cane or maple syrup, watched the crystallization process, the effects of heat on water," the child was actually learning physics.[46]

Scientific investigation was especially encouraged in the Laboratory School. Dewey tells of children planting corn seeds in cotton and in soil and investigating whether these seeds would grow best in light or dark conditions. The kitchen was referred to as a laboratory, where students could take the corn they grew, husk it, pound it, grind it, and soak and cook the corn. Students also weighed and measured the corn on scales or with measuring cups, thus learning mathematics in the process of doing the activity but without being aware that they were doing so.[47]

Dewey wrote about the immaturity of children of certain ages and decided that based on their inability to grasp certain areas of subject matter, they should not be taught those. Dewey's child-centered pedagogy led to the creation of the Progressive Education Association (PEA) in 1919. The problem with the child-centered pedagogy was that it ignored social realities because it focused entirely on a child's individual development. Without a connection to political progressivism, the progressive education movement lost its momentum as a reform movement and became merely a pedagogical approach to education.[48]

EDWARD L. THORNDIKE: MEASURING STUDENT PERFORMANCE

Another influential educator of the time was Edward L. Thorndike, whose work with animals led to his ideas on intelligence (IQ) testing.

A major part of Edward L. Thorndike's work centered on measuring student performance, for example, in measuring handwriting skills. An important part of the elementary curriculum during the period from 1890 to 1930 was to teach students handwriting skills so that they could write quickly but legibly. Thorndike collected samples of children's handwriting and asked experienced judges to "grade" or rank these samples according to quality, from best to worst. A child's handwriting was evaluated by comparing it with the ranked samples and giving the handwriting the same grade as that on the closest matching sample.[49]

Similarly, standardized oral reading paragraphs and silent reading tests were used to measure students' ability to read out loud. Students were given a set of 12 paragraphs, arranged in order of difficulty from easiest to hardest. As the students read, the teacher recorded the time needed to read each paragraph and the number of mistakes made. Six different types of mistakes were identified: gross mispronunciation, minor mispronunciation; omission of words; omission of important syllables; insertion of words that were not there; and substitution of a word or group of words for another. With such specific criteria, evaluators knew exactly what to look for, *before* the student read out loud, which helped them to grade the student on a more objective, and supposedly scientific, basis.[50]

Thorndike recommended using standardized criteria to evaluate students according to grade level and age, to determine how well they are progressing. He believed these benchmarks would also protect teachers from accusations of unfairness, because specific criteria would be used to judge students' work, rather than personal bias.

Spotlight On ◄——————————————————————————————

EDWARD L. THORNDIKE (1874–1949)

Thorndike's work with chickens, whose "instinctive and intelligent behavior" intrigued him, led him to breed two of the chickens to whom he had taught various things, to find out whether acquired traits could be passed on to offspring. The idea of stimulus-response (S → R) connections came from his work in animal behavior, and he applied it to teaching. He thought that a given stimulus would evoke a certain response. An important area in which this theory can be applied is that of classroom management, referred to by Thorndike and other scientists of education as "social management." Conditions can be manipulated to avoid certain situations in which it is expected students may behave badly, and appropriate rewards and punishments can be determined.

Thorndike was affiliated with Teachers' College at Columbia University for 31 years.

Thorndike also contributed to the IQ testing movement. The idea of testing became so popular that during World War I intelligence tests were used to determine which men were suitable for Army service. The intelligence testing movement arose because of the belief that mental ability was inherited and could not be changed by schooling. Intelligence testing was developed by the French psychologist Alfred Binet and brought to the United States by Henry H. Goddard, who worked in special education. The idea was that intelligence testing could be used to sort people into the social roles that matched their intellectual abilities. Mental tests would determine the course of study for children, thus making education more efficient. For instance, a low IQ score could be taken to mean that a child should not attend college but should attend a vocational or technical program instead.

Thorndike himself held the elitist view that many people were not smart enough to make their own decisions, and that more intelligent individuals in society should be the ones to do so. He stated, "In the long run, it has paid the masses to be ruled by intelligence."[51]

Intelligence tests were used to evaluate children in the Detroit public schools in 1922 in a massive testing program in which 60 percent of students were classified as average, 20 percent as backward, and 20 percent of superior intelligence. Different courses of study were developed to suit the needs of these different groups; those classified as "backward" were given a simpler curriculum. Factors such as English as a second language do not appear to have been considered in these decisions. Unfortunately, intelligence tests were used to bolster the argument that the poor were poor because they lacked intelligence and that the blacks had not progressed very far in American society because their race was genetically inferior.[52]

The testing movement continues to be an issue in American education, especially because of the No Child Left Behind Act of 2001. Furthermore, state departments of education have their own assessments that are used to make educational decisions about children. Unfortunately, the tests often ignore external factors of culture, race, and language that are unrelated to intelligence and may affect a student's performance on the tests.

THE ESTABLISHMENT OF KINDERGARTEN EDUCATION

William Torrey Harris, superintendent of the Saint Louis, Missouri, public school system, had studied the German kindergarten system and reported on it to the St. Louis Board of Education in 1873, to convince the board members to expand the kindergarten program. Harris's contributions are summarized in the "Shaper of Education" feature on page 205.

Friedrich Froebel had established the German kindergarten system of education in his native country, and had written extensively about his work and methods. Harris studied these reports to learn more about the value of early childhood education. Harris's intentions to adapt and expand the kindergarten system to the Saint Louis school system were helped by the work of Susan Blow, who had written a report on the role of early childhood education in preventing children from becoming involved in street crime.[53] By the time Harris resigned as superintendent in 1880, 7,828 children were enrolled in the kindergarten classes of the Saint Louis,

Missouri, school district. Kindergarten education in the city was very successful, and other school districts began to include it as well; 29 years after kindergartens began in Saint Louis, 189 cities had established the kindergarten system, and by 1897–98, the total number of kindergarten pupils was 95,867.[54]

Susan Blow quoted teachers who gave positive recommendations regarding kindergarten training, especially before students entered the first grade. These evaluations came from a study in which 163 first grade teachers in Boston were polled about the value of kindergarten education. One teacher who had taught first grade for 2 years commented that "the kindergarten child is methodical in thought, and, consequently, in all expression, oral, written, and manual."[55] Another first grade teacher wrote that kindergarten children were "much more industrious, interested, and observant, and have more general information."[56] This first grade teacher also added that "the training they have received is a great help in number, language, expression in reading, drawing, and all manual work."[57]

Today, first grade teachers who encountered a child who was not enrolled in kindergarten the previous year would be very skeptical of that student's ability to do first grade work without prior preparation, for as Harris stated, the work would be "beyond the average child's powers." Kindergarten classes teach children how to follow directions and develop skills such as the ability to identify colors, numbers, and shapes; to write their names; and color, which requires manual dexterity. These same skills were taught in the early days of kindergarten training. Encouraging self-reliance and independence, and teaching better concentration and a good work ethic are common goals for kindergarten educators today.

TEACHERS' UNIONS: PROTECTION FOR TEACHERS

Women were seen as the most desirable teachers for youth, particularly young children. Since women possessed natural "nurturing" abilities, the teaching force became feminized, particularly after 1870, in the Northeast. Even the famous educators Emma Willard and Catherine Beecher commented that women made the best teachers because they were designed by God to be the best teachers of small children, because women possessed greater patience and the ability to understand young minds.

Women represented a majority of the teaching force in the middle decades of the twentieth century.[58] The national statistics of 1870 revealed that about 60 percent of teachers nationwide were female. By 1900, this number had increased to 70 percent, and by 1920 it was 86 percent.[59] Male teachers did exist but were usually found in the upper grades and high schools, while women teachers preferred to teach in primary grades. Today, a large percentage of teachers are still female. The similarities and differences of the teaching force in the year 1900, compared to today, are found in Table 9-2.

These young women teachers were supervised by older males, who were usually white, middle-aged, Protestant, and more experienced in education than they. The younger female teachers stayed in education rather than moving up to positions of higher pay. Male teachers often found administrative posts, which paid more money and offered more prestige than teaching.

SHAPER OF EDUCATION

William Torrey Harris

- Believed in the value of early childhood education.
- Traveled to Germany to study the German kindergarten system and reported on this system to the Saint Louis, Missouri, Board of Education (1873).
- Recognized that children who had not completed kindergarten would probably have difficulty with reading, writing, geography, and arithmetic as they were taught in the typical elementary classroom.
- Was a member of the Committee of Ten, which debated the curricula for the American high schools (1890).
- Served as the U.S. Commissioner of Education (1889–1906).

Although school board members desired individuals of high moral character to train youth, they did not want to pay them well. Teachers had to be of middle class appearance, have middle class habits such as being punctual and diligent, be reasonably literate and well-versed in the so-called three R's, and be of native birth.[60] Immigrants were not usually hired as teachers, because school board members believed that teaching should remain a white-collar occupation, although the wages paid to teachers corresponded to those of railroad workers and canal builders. The place to find honest, moral, upright, and middle class individuals who would work for low wages was among the labor pool of single, literate, white, middle-class young women.[61]

As the public educational system expanded, to include immigrant children, and the cities took on the task of accommodating larger classes, problems with teacher welfare surfaced. Teachers, mostly women, were concerned about their wages and pension plans. This concern led to teacher unions, the AFT, or **American Federation of Teachers,** and the NEA, or National Education Association, both of which still exist. The NEA, which had established the Committee of Ten, did not have a woman president until 1910 and did not welcome women to the organization. Therefore, women in the large cities decided to form their own women-only organizations to push for equal pay in the early twentieth century. This move was met by resistance by male educators, who complained that women teachers

Table 9-2 **Characteristics of the Teaching Force: 1900 Versus 2005**

1900	2005
Teachers came from the labor pool of white, single, literate, middle class women.	More men are entering the teaching profession and are especially needed in the elementary grades.
Teachers had to possess good moral qualities.	Teachers have to pass a criminal record check in all states.
Teacher pay for women educators became an issue starting in 1904, with Margaret Haley and the AFT.	Unionized teachers have higher salaries than non-unionized teachers.
Women teachers organized against bureaucratic policies and strict control of their personal lives.	The NEA was recently called a "terrorist" organization by Secretary of Education Rod Paige.
Report of Joseph Mayer Rice in *Forum* cited teachers as ill-prepared and illiterate.	Carnegie Foundation has called for complete reform of teacher education programs in colleges and universities.

feminized the male students! Determined women educators such as Margaret Haley of Chicago, however, pushed for higher salaries, pensions, and more autonomy and decision making power in the classroom in 1904. Women teachers also organized against what they saw as oppressive bureaucratic politics, as instruction and supervision became centralized. They chafed at the strict control of their personal lives; as mentioned earlier in this section, the rules for women teachers' personal conduct, especially in small-town America, were very strict.[62]

Women teachers also revolted over the Harper Report. The president of the University of Chicago, William Raney Harper, read the reports of Joseph Mayer Rice, a physician turned progressive educator and educational scientist. Rice had written a series of articles in *Forum,* a national magazine, on the poor quality of schoolteachers, stating that he had visited schools in Chicago, Saint Paul, Philadelphia, and New York City and found most schoolteachers to be poorly prepared to teach and barely literate. He also alleged that they appeared to know little about teaching methods other than rote memorization. Critics of the schools, including Nicholas Murray Butler, president of Teachers' College at Columbia University, were interested in Rice's findings, and Harper took action by assigning a commission to study Rice's findings and propose a new organizational structure for the schools.[63]

The Harper Report called for all teachers to have a college education and also stated that there should be special procedures to hire and fire teachers. Finally, the report recommended centralized control, with one superintendent of schools and a smaller board of education, with only 11 board members.

Margaret Haley, the sixth-grade teacher at the Hendricks School in Chicago, was infuriated. She directed a campaign to mobilize women schoolteachers against the Harper Bill and the school reorganization policies. Chicago schoolteachers had previously organized in 1895 to ask for pensions, and again in 1897 to ask for a raise.

However, they met with resistance from the wealthy women's clubs, who opposed the idea of pensions for teachers because pensions would make teachers overly dependent on others. Margaret Haley was so incensed by this that she told them they took better care of their maids than their schoolteachers. Another issue was educational benefits; the Harper Bill called for women teachers to take college courses, but the bill did not raise their pay enough to cover tuition costs. Chicago schoolteachers were told they had to take courses at the University of Chicago, Northwestern University, or the Cook County Normal School, but few of them could afford to attend on their pay scale.[64]

The Harper Bill was defeated in 1899, but reformers tried to pass it again in 1901, 1903, and 1909; however, each year, teachers grew more vocal in their protests, and centralization efforts did not succeed until 1917.[65]

The leadership of the NEA gradually changed from male administrators to newly organized teachers' groups, but it was still very hard to eradicate the gender bias that was prevalent from the early days of the NEA. Nicholas Murray Butler blocked the growing power of local teacher delegations and refused to provide any more funding for the study of salaries, tenure, or pensions.[66] Although the NEA got tired of the issue of teacher unionism and began to disassociate itself from this issue, the AFT (American Federation of Teachers) did not. The AFT had risen from a general suffrage movement among women schoolteachers and believed that teachers, like other workers (such as carpenters and bricklayers), were entitled to appropriate compensation, working conditions, and benefits. Margaret Haley traveled to Baltimore, Philadelphia, and Boston, to convince teachers' organizations to join the American Federation of Labor (AFL) to get better pay. Between 1902 and 1910, at least eleven of these teacher organizations joined the AFL. The cities of Baltimore, Philadelphia, Boston, Saint Paul, Atlanta, and Toledo became the operating centers for the AFT.[67]

Unions for teachers are still important today, for they have much in common with their counterparts in 1900 (see Table 9-2). Teachers are still paid less than physicians, lawyers, accountants, and many other professionals. Teachers' unions continue to fight for improved benefits, better pensions, and better working conditions. New teachers have to join the local branch of the union that covers the school district in which they are hired. This union provides new teachers with insurance coverage against lawsuits, much as physicians have coverage against malpractice. The union also will negotiate for benefits, job security, and even professional advancement opportunities, such as the opportunity to take college courses for credit, to further their knowledge base. At present, the National Education Association (NEA) is now the largest union in the world. Although union membership is not mandatory, teachers join because they realize the benefits, which include *collective bargaining*. This refers to the union's role in setting up terms and conditions of employment for individual teachers, including pay scale, based on factors such as years of experience and education, benefits, evaluation procedures, leaves, and adjunct duties. All teachers benefit from an increase in pay when a new contract is negotiated with the school board. This unified approach certainly is more effective than if each teacher had to negotiate his or her own pay and benefits.

The AFT still represents teachers, and about 65 percent of the AFT's members are K to 12 school personnel.[68]

EDUCATION IN THE DEPRESSION: NO SHOES, NO SCHOOL

During the 1920s many people had invested money in the stock market and had become very wealthy; however, the stock market plunged the country into the Great Depression in 1929 and many people suffered profoundly. Education was affected; families who could not afford to put food on the table certainly could not afford to send their children to school.

You will learn more about the effects of the Depression in the next chapter; however, they are mentioned here so that you can understand that curriculum development was affected by economic concerns. Students were unable to go to school because they lacked clothes or shoes; in 1932, people learned to put newsprint under their shirts to keep warm when the shirts wore thin or to put cardboard inside their children's shoes to replace the worn out soles. The Depression brought attention to the plight of the rural poor and their schools, revealing the inequalities in school finance and educational opportunity in these areas. Only about 50 percent of American rural schoolchildren attended school, even before the Depression, because their families did not have the resources to send them. Property taxes were insufficient to support many rural schools even at the most basic level.[69]

Teachers saw firsthand the effects of the Depression on their students: Detroit teachers collected shoes so that their students could attend classes. When the New York City teachers found out that one fifth of the school children were malnourished they contributed funds for school lunches from their own poor salaries. Teachers in Chicago observed that Mexican and black children were coming to school in rags and lived in cold tenement buildings. In San Jose, California, teachers gave up 5 percent of their salaries to provide schoolchildren with clothing, blankets, medicine, and food. The sight of so much suffering convinced many teachers that something was drastically wrong with the entire social order and that real reform was necessary.[70]

Teachers today are still very much aware of the discrepancies in the lives of rich and poor children, and try as much as they are able, to provide their students with an education that will help change their lives.

BRIDGES FROM THE PAST TO THE PRESENT: CONTRIBUTIONS FROM THE PERIOD 1890–1930, TO THE PRESENT

A major contribution from this time period to the present is the "curriculum wars"; that is, whether a student should pursue a vocational (industrial) education in high school, or a college-preparatory one. Overall, parents, teachers, and guidance counselors want students to be involved in a curriculum that meets all their needs. The type of curriculum pursued is also affected by socioeconomic concerns.

The concept of tailoring or adjusting a curriculum to students' needs arose with John Dewey's Progressive movement, or the child-centered education movement. Teachers follow his ideas on education, for instance, when they try to find out what kind of home life a child has if the child does not turn in his or her home-work, or often comes to school late. Dewey himself commented on the importance of living conditions in determining how best to help children learn.

Although Edward L. Thorndike's scientific education movement and its emphasis on testing has been more influential than Dewey's emphasis on democratic education for the individual, educators still recognize the importance of Dewey's work. In our society, in which high-stakes testing, corporate involvement in education, and increased government surveillance are prevalent, students should be prepared to become full, active citizens in a democratic society.[71] It has been suggested that teachers should model a humanistic, student-centered approach in which connections are made with the community as a whole.[72] The curriculum wars include the debate over testing; today the No Child Left Behind Act of 2001 mandates testing for all students in grades K through 12.

Although both Thorndike and Dewey were considered progressive educators, Thorndike's work was more to the liking of those who were in centralized administration, such as school superintendents and principals. They needed to measure student progress and achievement, and testing became a way of doing this on a large scale as school districts became bigger.[73]

Another contribution from the period is the concept of teacher unions, which promote professionalism and protect teachers by providing job security and help in negotiating benefits. Critics have accused teacher unions of hindering educational reform efforts. Teachers' unions are still recovering from a scathing remark made by Secretary of Education Rod Paige in 2004, in which he called the NEA a "terrorist organization."[74] Although Paige subsequently apologized for the remark, the damage was done, and the NEA president urged President George W. Bush to replace the secretary.[75]

The point for the future teacher to remember is that despite any criticisms of teacher unions, they exist for an important purpose: to protect teachers' rights. Although it is certainly true that teachers are often not well-prepared to teach, the fact remains that teachers are at a disadvantage in society. Society does not regard teaching as a profession and teachers are still paid less than lawyers, physicians, and other professionals. In 2003 an AFT survey revealed that the average teacher salary was $45,771, an increase of 3.3 percent over the previous year. The survey also showed that average beginning teacher salaries rose 3.2 percent, to $29,564.[76] However, the salary increases are being offset by much higher health-care costs.[77] With regard to whether unions actually help teachers or not, the *AFT Public Employees Compensation Survey* reveals that union-represented state employees, including public school teachers, earn significantly higher salaries than those employees who are non-unionized.[78]

Teachers' unions have taken stands on crucial issues such as early childhood education. A statement on the NEA's website states that early childhood education "is a common sense investment we can't afford to pass up."[79] Just as William Torrey Harris declared in his work with kindergartens in the Saint Louis, Missouri, public school system, the NEA believes that "children in quality preschool programs are less likely to repeat grades, need special education, or get into future trouble with the law."[80] Unfortunately, a survey of state preschool programs revealed that ten states spend nothing on preschool, and the level of funding in other states is also lower than expected.[81]

The issue of poverty and its effect on education was noted during the Great Depression. Today, teachers are very much aware of the connection between economics and education. Unfortunately, many of the teachers in struggling districts are often poorly paid. They leave for better paying jobs in wealthier districts. The students in poor districts thus have poorer paid teachers, who have been criticized for being less qualified. One solution to reducing this discrepancy in the quality of education that rich students and poor students receive is performance pay.

Union leaders are aware that teacher quality is very important in increasing student achievement and decreasing the achievement gap between rich and poor students.[82] Traditionally, unions have been averse to the idea, but are now rethinking it. The idea of performance pay, however, always raises the question of peer evaluations or principal evaluations, which can involve favoritism, so the question is how to develop a way to evaluate teachers that uses rubrics and multiple classroom visits.[83] If a fair, non-biased method of evaluating teachers for performance pay can be developed, it will help decrease the gap between rich and poor students, because poorer students will have access to better qualified teachers.[84] The problem of poverty and education is a very complex one, however; so putting better qualified teachers who are compensated more fairly in the struggling districts is only part of the answer to such a complicated problem.

SUMMARY

This chapter described various influences upon today's curriculum, including the work of the Committee of Ten, and John Dewey, the progressive educator who tried to adjust the curriculum to the needs of the child, and Edward L. Thorndike, an educational psychologist who believed in standardizing criteria to measure achievement. The debate between progressivism and the use of measurement to evaluate a child's progress continues today. The No Child Left Behind Act is an example of how federal policy has utilized the concept of measurement to standardize education and teaching while ignoring factors such as poverty, which can adversely affect a child's ability to learn.

In Chapter 10 you will learn more about how poverty affects education, and how various social programs have been developed to alleviate poverty.

QUESTIONS FOR DISCUSSION

1. John Dewey discussed the developmental needs of children and the issue of relevance in education so that pupils could relate what they learned to their own environment. Think back to your own educational experiences from elementary school, through high school. How often did your teachers use this method? If not, why do you think they did not?

2. Of John Dewey and Edward L. Thorndike, which do you believe made the greater contribution to education and why? Provide evidence for your answer.

3. The Committee of Ten issued a report on the subjects that secondary school students should study to prepare for college. Think back to your high school curriculum. Do you believe that those subjects prepared you well for college level work? If not, why not?

4. How important is it that high schools include manual or vocational training in their curriculum? What types of vocational training were offered in the high school you attended?

5. Do you believe that unions will help you become a better teacher? Why or why not?

6. Poverty adversely affects children's ability to learn. In your opinion, what steps can you take as a teacher to encourage children of poverty to learn?

SUGGESTED ACTIVITIES

1. Review the college-preparatory curriculum of a local high school in your area. As a mock Committee of Ten, present the curriculum to your class. Divide up the work so that one person introduces the topics and eight persons present one subject each, and one person will summarize. For example, subjects might include:

   English

   Latin

   mathematics

   chemistry

   biology

   foreign languages (French, German, Spanish)

   Physical education

   Physics

   (Note to instructor: A rubric could be used to grade this assignment).

2. Interview the principal of a high school in your area to find out the percentages of students who are enrolled in a vocational curriculum versus the percentage of students who take the college preparatory or other curriculum. Determine the principal's position regarding the importance of vocational education in his or her school. Write up your interview and present the findings to your classmates in a 15 minute presentation. Provide a handout with the data.

3. Interview a teacher who teaches in a vocational education program, to find out his/her philosophy of teaching and how he/she prepares vocational students for the job market. Write up your interview and present the findings to your classmates in a 10 to 15 minute presentation.

4. Research your local school districts and the unions they belong to: NEA or AFT. Contact the local union representative and interview him or her about problems the teachers have had and how they have been resolved. Write a letter to the representative telling him or her what you need, and specify that you seek general information and that no names of individual teachers will be used. Write up your interview and present it to the class in a 15- to 20-minute presentation.

5. Research the No Child Left Behind Act (NCLB) of 2001. What are the consequences of failing the tests for poor children in your state? Present your findings to the class in a 15-minute PowerPoint presentation.

6. Interview both a kindergarten teacher and a first grade teacher, in the same school. Determine each teacher's expectations for his or her students, and how the curriculum for kindergarten prepares students for first-grade work. Ask each teacher to recommend how the curriculum might be improved. Present your findings in a 15-minute PowerPoint presentation.

7. Research *one* of the following educators who was important in developing education programs to benefit African Americans: Booker T. Washington, Mary McLeod Bethune, or W.E.B. DuBois. Explain this individual's philosophy of education, major contributions, and the effects of these contributions today. Present your findings in a 15- to 20-minute PowerPoint presentation, or write up a five-page report. Use at least two primary sources, that is, writings of the educator himself or herself.

Bibliography

Blair, J. (January 30, 2002). Gen-xers apathetic about union label. *Education Week* p. 5.

Blow, S. E. (1910). Kindergarten education. In N. M. Butler (Ed.). *Education in the United States: A Series of Monographs*. New York: American Book.

Carlson, R. A. (1975). *The quest for conformity: Americanization through education*. New York: Wiley.

Cohen, S. (1968). The industrial education movement, 1906–1907. *American Quarterly, 20*(1), 95.

Cremin, L. A. (1964). *The transformation of the school: Progressivism in American education, 1876–1957*. New York: Vintage Books.

Dewey, J. (1900). *The school and society, being three lectures*. Chicago: University of Chicago Press.

Dillon, S., & Schemo, D. J. (2004, February 25). Union urges Bush to replace education chief over remark. *New York Times*, p. A15.

Eliot, C. W. (1971). *A late harvest: Miscellaneous papers written between eighty and ninety*. Freeport, NY: Books for Libraries Press. (Reprint ed.)

Good, H. G. (1962). *A history of American education* (2nd ed.). New York: Macmillan.

Gumbert, E. H., & Spring, J. H. (1974). *The superschool and the superstate: American education in the twentieth century, 1918–1970*. New York: Wiley.

Gursky, D., Rose, M., & Moss, D. (2004). Banding together. *NEA Today, 22*(8), 31.

Herbst, J. (1967). High school and youth in America. *Journal of Contemporary History, 2*(3), 165–82.

Judd, C. H. (1918). *Introduction to the scientific study of education*. New York: Ginn.

Karier, C. J. (1986). *The individual, society, and education: A history of American educational ideas.* (2nd ed.). Chicago: University of Illinois Press.

Levin, R. A. (1991). The debate over schooling: Influences of Dewey and Thorndike. *Childhood Education 68*(2), 71–75.

Mayhew, K. C., & Edwards, A. C. (1965). *The Dewey school: The Laboratory School of the University of Chicago, 1896–1903.* New York: Atherton Press. (Originally published 1936, New York: D. Appleton).

Murphy, M. (1990). *Blackboard unions: The AFT and the NEA, 1900–1980.* Ithaca, NY: Cornell University Press.

National Education Association (1969). *Report of the Committee on Secondary School Studies.* New York: Arno Press and the *New York Times.* (Reprint; originally published 1893.)

O'Brien, L. M. (2003). Teacher education for a democratic society. *Childhood Education, 79*(6).

Perkinson, H. J. (1991). *The imperfect panacea: American faith in education, 1865–1990* (3rd ed.). New York: McGraw-Hill.

Ravitch, D. (2000/01, Winter). A different kind of education for black children. *Journal of Blacks in Higher Education,* no. 30, 98–106.

Security threat? (2004). *NEA Today, 22*(8), 12.

Sizer, T. R. (1964). *Secondary schools at the turn of the century.* New Haven, CT: Yale University Press.

Smith, I., & Johnson, R. E. (2003, Spring). To attend or not to attend: Guiding all students in the right direction. *Journal of College Admission,* pp. 2–5.

Solmon, L. C. (2004, January). What's fair about performance pay? *Phi Delta Kappan 85*(5).

Spring, J. (1986). *The American school, 1642–1985.* New York: Longman.

Tyack, D. B., Lowe, R. & Hansot, E. (1984). *Public schools in hard times: The Great Depression and recent years.* Cambridge, MA: Harvard University Press.

Tyack, D. B., & Strober, M. B. (1981). Women and men in the schools: A history of the sexual structuring of educational employment. National Institute of Education (ED), Washington DC.

Why children leave school. (1913, April). *Manual Training Magazine, 14.*

Suggestions for Further Reading

In addition to the works cited in the bibliography, the following are suggested for further reading.

The Committee of Nine (1969). Reorganization of secondary education. In Raubinger, F. M., Rowe, H. G., Piper, D. L., & West, C. K. *The development of secondary education.* London: Collier-Macmillan.

Joncich, G. M. (Ed.). (1962). *Psychology and the science of education: Selected writings of Edward L. Thorndike.* New York: Bureau of Publications, Teachers' College, Columbia University.

Horst, S. L. (1987). *Education for manhood: The education of blacks in Virginia during the Civil War.* Lanham, MD: University Press of America.

Monroe, P. (1971). *Founding of the American public school system; From the early settlements to the close of the Civil War period:* Vol. 1. New York: Hafner.

Relevant Web Sites

American Federation of Teachers *http://www.aft.org* Home page of the American Federation of Teachers. Includes salary scales for teachers, by state, and reports on educational issues.

National Education Association *http://www.nea.org* Home page of the National Education Association, with information on NCLB, ESEA, teacher preparation, and more.

Center for Dewey Studies *http://www.siu.edu/~deweyctr/* Home page of the Center for Dewey Studies, established in 1961 at Southern Illinois University at Carbondale, Illinois. Contains videos of Dewey and copies of his papers and other memorabilia.

Edward L. Thorndike: Human Intelligence *http://www.indiana.edu/~intell/ethorndike.shtml* Great site with biographical information on Thorndike as well as current information on research in human intelligence and testing.

John Dewey and Informal Education *http://www.infed.org/thinkers/et-dewey.htm* Information on John Dewey's life and work and his pedagogic creed.

The Pragmatism Cybary John Dewey *http://www.pragmatism.org* Lists educators such as John Dewey who are classical pragmatists and explains their contributions to education.

National Center for Education Statistics *http://www.nces.ed.gov* Information at the federal and state level relating to all topics in education.

U.S. Department of Education *http://www.ed.gov* Home page of the U.S. Department of Education, to research federal and state educational policies.

Endnotes

[1] Lawrence A. Cremin, *The Transformation of the School: Progressivism in American Education, 1876–1957* (New York: Vintage Books, 1964), 15.

[2] Diane Ravitch, "A Different Kind of Education for Black Children," *Journal of Blacks in Higher Education,* no. 30 (Winter 2000/01), 98–106.

[3] Clarence J. Karier, *The Individual, Society, and Education: A History of American Educational Ideas,* 2nd ed. (Chicago: University of Illinois Press, 1986), 71.

[4] Irving Smith & Robert E. Johnson, "To Attend or Not To Attend: Guiding All Students in the Right Direction," *Journal of College Admission,* Spring 2003, pp. 2–5.

[5] Cremin, *Transformation of the School,* 15.

[6] H. G. Good, *A History of American Education,* 2nd ed. (New York: Macmillan, 1962), p. 242.

[7] Joel Spring, *The American School, 1642–1985* (New York: Longman, 1986), 193.

[8] Good, *History of American Education,* 240–41.

[9] Ibid., 242. See also Lucy Larcom, *A New England Girlhood* (Boston: Houghton Mifflin, 1920; orig. 1889), for a firsthand description of life working in the cotton mills.

[10] Spring, *American School,* 195.

[11] Karier, *Individual, Society, and Education,* 71–73.

[12] Ibid., 74.

[13] Ibid., 75.

[14] National Education Association, *Report of the Committee on Secondary School Studies* (1893; repr., New York: Arno Press and the *New York Times,* 1969), 5.

[15] Ibid., 8–11. It is worth noting that all the individuals participating in the conferences to determine the secondary school curriculum were men; women did not participate.

[16] Ibid., 11.

[17] Ibid.

[18] Ibid., 13.

[19] Ibid.

[20] Ibid.

[21] Ibid., 90–91.

[22] Theodore R. Sizer, *Secondary Schools at the Turn of the Century* (New Haven, CT: Yale University Press, 1964), 122. See also *Report of the Committee,* pp. 34–35 (Table I) and p. 37 (Table II).

[23] Sizer, *Secondary Schools,* 142.

[24] *Report of the Committee,* 51.

[25] Sol Cohen, "The Industrial Education Movement, 1906–1907," *American Quarterly, 20,* no. 1 (1968), 95.

[26] Ibid., 97.

[27] Ibid.

[28] Ibid., 98.

[29] "Why Children Leave School," *Manual Training Magazine, 14* (April 1913), 360. See also Cohen, "Industrial Education Movement," 98.

[30] Cohen, "Industrial Education Movement," 99.

[31] John Dewey, *The School and Society, Being Three Lectures* (Chicago, IL: University of Chicago Press, 1900), 42.

[32] Cohen, "Industrial Education Movement," 101. See also Jurgen Herbst, "High School and Youth in America," *Journal of Contemporary History, 2,* no. 3 (1967), 165–82.

[33] Cohen, "Industrial Education Movement," 104.

[34] Ibid., 105. See also Ellwood P. Cubberley, *The Portland Survey: A Textbook on City School Administration Based on a Concrete Study* (New York: 1916), 274–78.

[35] Cohen, "Industrial Education Movement," 109–10.

[36] Ibid., 104. See also Charles W. Eliot, *A Late Harvest: Miscellaneous Papers Written Between Eighty and Ninety* (1924; repr., Freeport, NY: Books for Libraries Press, 1971). See pp. 93–110, "Needed Changes in Secondary Education."

[37] Sizer, *Secondary Schools,* 200.

[38] Ibid., 201.

[39] Ibid., 201–202.

[40] Robert A. Carlson, *The Quest for Conformity: Americanization Through Education* (New York: Wiley, 1975.) See chapter 5, "Purifying the 'New Immigration': The 'Humanitarian Americanizers.' "

[41] Ibid. The outcome of these "American breakfasts" was that Italian mothers stopped tying bags of salt around their children's necks. This was a practice meant to ward off the "evil eye," which they believed was the cause of rickets.

[42] Carlson, *Quest for Conformity,* p. 83.

[43] Ibid.

[44] Ibid., 8.

[45] Ibid., 42–43. These are Dewey's own words, translated from stenographic notes taken at the time.

[46] Ibid., 44.

[47] Ibid., 45.

[48] Henry J. Perkinson, *The Imperfect Panacea: American Faith in Education, 1865–1990,* 3rd ed. (New York: McGraw-Hill, 1991), 198–99.

[49] Charles Hubbard Judd, *Introduction to the Scientific Study of Education* (New York: Ginn, 1918). See p. 216 in chapter 15, "Standardization."

[50] Ibid., 224.

[51] Edgar H. Gumbert & Joel H. Spring, *The Superschool and the Superstate: American Education in the Twentieth Century, 1918–1970* (New York: Wiley, 1974), 88. See chapter 3, "Intelligence Testing and the Efficient Society."

[52] Ibid., 100.

[53] Susan E. Blow, "Kindergarten Education," in *Education in the United States: A Series of Monographs,* ed. Nicholas Murray Butler (New York: American Book Company, 1910), 9.

[54] Ibid.

[55] Ibid., 19.

[56] Ibid.

[57] Ibid.

[58] David B. Tyack & Myra B. Strober, "Women and Men in the Schools: A History of the Sexual Structuring of Educational Employment," National Institute of Education (ED), (Washington DC, 1981), 3.

[59] Ibid., 4.

[60] Ibid., 5.

[61] Ibid., 6.

[62] Ibid., 22.

[63] Marjorie Murphy, *Blackboard Unions: The AFT and the NEA, 1900–1980* (Ithaca, NY: Cornell University Press, 1990), 25.

[64] Ibid., 30.

[65] Ibid., 31.

[66] Ibid., 59.

[67] Ibid., 65.

[68] Julie Blair, "Gen-Xers Apathetic About Union Label," *Education Week,* January 30, 2002, p. 5.

[69] An excellent source for understanding the impact of the Depression on education is David B. Tyack, Robert Lowe and Elisabeth Hansot, *Public Schools in Hard Times: The Great Depression and Recent Years* (Cambridge, MA: Harvard University Press, 1984).

[70] Ibid., 24.

[71] Leigh M. O'Brien, "Teacher Education for a Democratic Society," *Childhood Education. 79,* no. 6 (2003), 376.

[72] Ibid.

[73] Robert A. Levin, "The Debate Over Schooling: Influences of Dewey and Thorndike," *Childhood Education, 68,* no. 2, (1991), 71.

[74] "Security Threat?" *NEA Today, 22,* no. 8, (2004), 12.

[75] Sam Dillon and Diana Jean Schemo, "Union Urges Bush to Replace Education Chief Over Remark," *New York Times,* February 25, 2004, p. A15.

[76] AFT Salary Surveys, "2003 Survey & Analysis of Teacher Salary Trends," *http://www.aft.org.*

[77] Ibid.

[78] Ibid.

[79] See the NEA Web site, *http://www.nea.org/earlychildhood*

[80] Ibid.

[81] Ibid.

[82] Lewis C. Solmon, "What's Fair About Performance Pay?" *Phi Delta Kappan 85,* no. 5, (2004), 407.

[83] Ibid.

[84] Ibid.

PART 4

Modern Educational Problems and Reform Movements (1930–Present)

Chapter 10

Education from the Depression to the War on Poverty (1930–1960)

Learning Objectives

1. Describe the social, economic, and political forces in American society that led to the expansion of the American public school system from 1930 to 1960.
2. Discuss the curriculum changes that occurred after World War II and how they have affected curriculum today.
3. Discuss the increased federal involvement in education from 1950 to 1960.
4. Explain the significance of the National Defense Education Act (NDEA), and the *Brown v. Board of Education* decision of 1954 and their implications for education today.
5. Describe the history of business involvement in education and the positive and negative aspects of business involvement in education.
6. Discuss the beginnings of school violence.
7. Describe the criticisms of the public schools from 1930 to 1960, and compare them with those of the present.

INTRODUCTION

The U.S. educational system continued to expand during the period from 1930 to 1960. Urban public schools became very large, and funding issues, especially during economic crises such as the Great Depression, became increasingly important. Superintendents, principals, and teachers were concerned about being able to provide adequate services for students. As the immigrant population in America increased, the issue of bilingual education became another problem; teaching students whose native language was not English required special accommodations, which schools often were unable to provide.

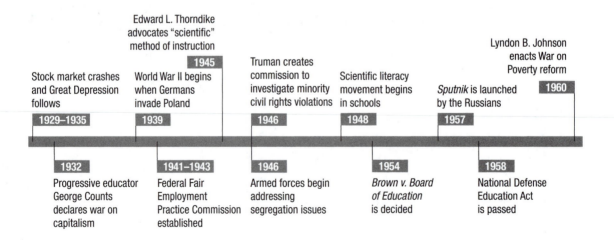

Edward L. Thorndike advocates "scientific" method of instruction — **1945**

Stock market crashes and Great Depression follows — **1929–1935**

World War II begins when Germans invade Poland — **1939**

Truman creates commission to investigate minority civil rights violations — **1946**

Scientific literacy movement begins in schools — **1948**

Sputnik is launched by the Russians — **1957**

Lyndon B. Johnson enacts War on Poverty reform — **1960**

1932 — Progressive educator George Counts declares war on capitalism

1941–1943 — Federal Fair Employment Practice Commission established

1946 — Armed forces begin addressing segregation issues

1954 — *Brown v. Board of Education* is decided

1958 — National Defense Education Act is passed

World War II and the space race prompted many curriculum changes, and also led to widespread changes in the area of civil rights. Several U.S. Supreme Court decisions had a great impact on education in this period.

The American public became increasingly aware of the discrepancies between the achievements of students in other countries and those of American students. Criticisms of U.S. education were voiced in many sectors, and various curriculum movements arose in answer to these criticisms.

Also in this period the federal government began to play an increasingly powerful role in an attempt to equalize the gap between education for the rich and poor. One federal program was Operation Head Start, which provided early childhood education to poor children.

Keep in mind as you read this chapter that many of the characteristics of the American educational system changed as the country grew and became industrialized and as immigrants came to America in search of jobs.

THE 1930S: SCHOOL FUNDING

Chapter 9 alluded to some of the effects of the Great Depression on education, especially relating to children of poverty. School funding, and the discrepancy between the financing available to rural schools versus those in wealthier areas, became an issue of concern during the Great Depression. Lack of funds made it impossible to hold school for an entire year; from 1933 to 1934, 21 states had school terms shorter than six months, particularly in the Southern and Great Plains states. Nearly 300,000 rural teachers earned less than $650 per year and 85,000 of the rural teachers earned less than $450 per year.[1]

President Franklin D. Roosevelt's New Deal programs of the 1930s, which offered education for adults and youth, provided the necessary economic recovery; however, implementing these programs took time, and results were not seen immediately. The 1930s were a time of struggle for most Americans, even those who had been wealthy before the stock market crashed in 1929.

Before the Depression, Americans had lost interest in reforming society through education. After the Depression, however, this concept was revived because of the belief that education can help produce a certain type of social order, by teaching literacy skills, moral behavior, and citizenship skills. The Great Depression, as teachers saw firsthand, produced a lot of suffering among students and caused teachers to question the wisdom and virtue of economic leaders.[2] Teachers became angry when the business sector became involved, as when the finance committee of the U.S. Chamber of Commerce drafted a letter calling for eliminating kindergarten classes and evening classes and increasing class sizes.[3] George S. Counts, a progressive educator from Teachers College, Columbia University, declared war on capitalism in a meeting of the Progressive Education Association (PEA) in 1932.[4] He believed teachers had a mission to develop a new kind of educational culture, based on scientific planning, where true character education, intellectual and aesthetic development would occur, and told teachers to fight the capitalist injustices.[5] Unfortunately, he ignored the fact that many school board members are businessmen or professional people in the cities and wealthier districts. Counts had documented the inequalities in the governance of school boards, showing that they were dominated by members of the elite. The poor were disproportionately underrepresented on school boards.[6]

Ultimately, the Great Depression played a very important role in the socioeconomics of schools. It made teachers and those who wanted education to play a role in social reconstruction aware that the business sector would make decisions that would affect education. Superintendent Harold Campbell of the New York City public school system had the opinion that members of the "business civilization" were "nothing more than gentlemen who bought things as cheaply as they could and sold them for as much as they could with little regard for the fairness of their dealings."[7]

EFFECTS OF WORLD WAR II ON CIVIL RIGHTS

As the 1930s drew to a close, the United States became involved in World War II.

When the concentration camps were liberated by U.S. soldiers in 1945, Americans got a firsthand look at the side effects of "efficiency." Six million Jews and individuals with physical and mental handicaps were exterminated in concentration camps in a methodically chilling manner. Americans saw the effects of this ideology, which was supposed to represent progress, and it led them to enact laws to protect the rights of minorities and others in disadvantaged positions in society.

In 1941 and 1943 President Franklin D. Roosevelt prohibited discrimination on government contracts because of race, creed, color, or national origin. The Federal Fair Employment Practice Committee was subsequently established to make sure that his orders were followed.[8] In 1946, President Harry S. Truman created a blue-ribbon commission to investigate civil rights violations, and the committee reported its findings in 1947. In 1946 the armed forces began making changes that led to the elimination of segregation practices in the armed forces by 1954, which was the year of the landmark ***Brown v. Board of Education*** decision.[9] Changes in American society led to an increased emphasis on school desegregation.

THE 1940S: EFFECTS OF WORLD WAR II ON MATH AND SCIENCE CURRICULA

World War II also caused changes in school curricula and in methods of instruction. In 1945, articles in the *Journal of School Science and Mathematics* proposed that the "scientific method" of instruction, advocated by Edward L. Thorndike was the best way to instruct students. Furthermore, recognition of the products of science during the war, such as the atomic bomb, radar, codes, computers, and communications, made science an important topic for instruction.

How to teach science, however, was the question. David Aptekar of Mackenzie High School in Detroit, Michigan, wrote an article for the *Journal of School Science and Mathematics* in January 1945, questioning whether science courses could actually be taught scientifically. He proposed that rather than learning facts straight from the textbook, and learning to answer questions based on laws, theories, and facts, students in science courses should hear guest speakers describe how science was used in industry.[10]

The idea of scientific literacy for the public also arose. It was said that because science had been so important in the war, the teaching of science should be the best in the world.[11] It was thought that science had to be demystified because to the American public "science is magic. A scientist is a man in a white coat who stares at the light through a test tube and solves any problem quickly—as in the movies."[12] The scientific literacy movement in schools thus became an important goal for educators after World War II. In 1948 the principal of Harper High School in Chicago, Butler Laughlin, wrote that "only a small part of our people get enough science to react intelligently to the problems which they meet every day."[13] In describing how science should be taught to future teachers, Gordon Mork of the State Teachers College in Bemidji, Minnesota, wrote in 1947 that "science reaches its greatest heights when its findings are utilized for better living and greater happiness for the individual among all men."[14] Mork described how the scientific method should be taught so that the ordinary citizen would understand that science was something to be used in everyday life, rather than feared. The steps included: (1) recognition, definition, and statement of a problem; (2) development of a hypothesis for the solution of the problem; (3) planning a course of action and testing the hypothesis; (4) carrying out the plan; (5) organizing and analyzing facts collected; (6) drawing conclusions and inferences with respect to the hypothesis; and (7) applying the generalizations to new situations.[15]

Science was not the only subject area of concern after World War II. Mathematics was also said to be poorly taught, and educators were blamed because they had spent time creating a curriculum that related science and math to everyday concerns, problems, and interests of students, particularly those students who were not college bound.[16] This curriculum was part of the progressive education movement.

The high school physics curriculum also came under scrutiny during the period from 1930 to 1960. Starting about 1937 a study of physics education found that the physics curriculum was being updated more slowly than any other curriculum in the high school.[17] High school textbooks concentrated on classical physics, so that students would be prepared for college. The 1937 study found that teaching methods were mainly lectures and demonstrations. Students did not have the opportunity to experiment or formulate their own questions.[18] Teachers appeared to experience difficulty in teaching because they were unfamiliar with classroom materials and equipment. The study concluded that the level of instruction was tailored to the "mythical average pupil whose weaknesses are often such as to preclude much effort on the behalf of those who have real capacity and inclination for serious science study."[19]

The progressive education movement had emphasized practical arts, home and family living, and civic competence to those students who were not enrolled in either college or vocational tracks during the Depression years. Enrollment in physics classes during this period declined. To make physics courses more attractive to non-college-bound students during the 1940s, it was suggested that math be eliminated and that physics topics in everyday life, such as the electricity of battery rechargers and how tire jacks worked, would pique students' interest in physics.[20]

During World War II, attitudes about science, especially physics, changed as the social implications of physics achievements such as radar were realized; however, these attitudes were not reflected in the school curricula until 10 years after the War ended.[21] Enrollment in physics courses did increase slightly, but by 1947, it was only 5.49 percent.[22] Girls were seldom present in physics classes. Those who took it were taught what one teacher referred to as "kitchen physics," to learn how refrigerators work or how to tell if an egg was hard boiled or fresh.[23]

An apparently universal problem in physics teaching was inadequate training in science as well as a deplorable lack of equipment. In Pittsburgh, Pennsylvania, most physics high school classrooms lacked labs, and teachers had no time to hold them anyway. In northwestern Missouri, rural high schools had no facilities to teach physics, so field trips to garages and power plants had to be substituted for lab work.[24]

Despite the lack of equipment for science and a scarcity of science teachers, military personnel held educators responsible for making sure that students knew enough science to function. Brehon B. Somervell, commanding general of the Services Supply Department, at a meeting of the National Institute on Education and the war in 1942 told the audience that every classroom was "a citadel" and that they were personally responsible for making certain students were adequately trained. He stated that they should ascertain that "no American soldier is ever killed or injured because you failed to do your part to provide adequate training."[25] Somervell ignored the actual developments in education while making this statement. Although he held educators responsible for teaching science, he did not take into account the fact that there was a teacher shortage. During World War II it was common for administrators to issue emergency teaching certificates because of the low teaching salaries and the teacher shortage.[26]

THE 1940S: STATUS OF TEACHING

One might suppose that with the new recognition that science and mathematics were important for the welfare of the United States, more money would be given to teachers to encourage them to teach these subjects; however, this was not the case. For one thing, there were few students in colleges and schools of education who were being prepared to teach science and math. An article in the 1947 issue of the *Journal of School Science and Mathematics,* by Professor Raleigh Schorling of the University of Michigan, stated that in the previous semester "there were about 200,000 students enrolled in 24 prominent colleges and universities that educate teachers."[27] He further stated that "there were last semester only about 2200 students doing practice teaching."[28] Schorling further explained that at his own school only 26 students would "qualify in physics, chemistry, biology, general science, or mathematics. The total number of student teachers in physics and chemistry for the year is four."[29] Schorling also stated that "we do not have a single student with a major in physics who is planning to teach in high school."[30]

Finding teachers who could teach math and science was only one area of concern. In addition to suffering from low salaries, teachers were struggling for citizenship rights.[31] They were disciplined for being outspoken or for questioning the policies of the districts in which they taught.

The status of teachers on the socioeconomic scale in the 1940s was still low. For instance, teacher salaries in Wilmington, Delaware, had not shown any improvement in 25 years.[32] The local union of the Wilmington public schools was chartered in 1943. The condition of teacher welfare was also alarming in other states. In Connecticut, teachers in 1944 found that the salary schedule was completely being disregarded, and membership in teachers' unions increased as a result. In 1947, at the biennial session of the state legislature of Connecticut, an expanded state subsidy program of $10,000,000 per year was passed.[33]

With regard to citizenship rights, a noteworthy case occurred in 1949. Arthur Symond, the executive secretary of the Tri-Cities Local 580 in the cities of LaSalle, Oglesby, and Peru, Illinois, was present at a hearing to defend a dismissed teacher from Oglesby. In the hearing Symond commented that the courts of Illinois could not be trusted to adequately protect a teacher under the state teacher tenure law. His comment was heard by members of the Oglesby school administration, who were present at the hearing and used the comment to attack Symond's loyalty to the district.[34] Although the district itself never complained, Symond was summoned to appear in Springfield, Illinois, in November 1949, for a hearing to determine whether his teaching license should be suspended. This incident led the Illinois Federation of Labor and the American Federation of Teachers to offer him their support.[35]

Teachers had to use caution while teaching so they would not be accused of promoting communism. In 1949 the Illinois legislature introduced the Broyles Bills, which required dismissal of teachers for teaching any doctrine that would appear to subvert the Illinois state government or the government of the United States. The AFT successfully opposed these bills as being dangerous to the civil liberties of teachers.[36] In 1953, however, an amended version of the Broyles Bills, which mandated that teachers file an oath of loyalty, was approved by the Illinois Legislature but was vetoed by Governor William G. Stratton.

The fight for teachers' citizenship rights extended even to their private lives. In Everett, Washington, married women were not allowed to teach before World War II, but during the war the teacher shortage forced the district to hire some married women teachers temporarily. The local teachers' union of Everett, Local 772, supported this move, and these teachers were given the same pay and conditions of employment as other teachers in the system.[37]

THE 1950S SPACE RACE: *SPUTNIK* AND MATH AND SCIENCE IN SCHOOLS

During the 1950s the federal government began to formulate educational policy. The teaching of science and math in the schools intensified in 1957 when the USSR launched *Sputnik,* triggering the space race for superiority in space flight. This event focused the U.S. public's attention on the state of science and math teaching in the public schools and on the quality of education in general. The federal government passed the National Defense Education Act (NDEA) in 1958, which resulted in fellowships and loans to students studying mathematics, foreign languages, and science, and payments for equipment and building construction.[38] The NDEA also set a precedent for federal involvement in education that persists to this day.

THE 1950S: SCHOOL SEGREGATION: *BROWN V. BOARD OF EDUCATION*

At the same time that the federal government was worrying about U.S. students' poor preparation in math and science, racial and socioeconomic inequalities were becoming greater. Although the total national wealth was increasing, not everyone was becoming wealthy. Members of minority groups, immigrants, and those of lower socioeconomic status were suffering.[39] The common school that Mann envisioned as providing an equal education for all had not materialized. American blacks, Native Americans, and girls were not receiving the type of education to which they were entitled.

Although all segregation practices had been eliminated in the armed forces by June of 1954, they had not been eliminated in the American public school system. Despite the nondiscrimination policies for citizens passed by both Presidents Truman and Eisenhower in 1954 and 1955, American schools were still segregated. Black children simply were not found in white schools.

Many whites were unhappy about the large numbers of blacks who moved north to find jobs after World War II. Blacks settled in the large cities, leading to the so-called white flight to areas outside the city because they did not want to live in the same neighborhoods as black people, or send their children to the same schools. Between 1950 and 1960, the population of the central area of New York City decreased by 1.4 percent while the population around the central city grew by 75 percent. In Chicago, the area around the central city grew by 71.5 percent, and in Boston 13 percent of the population of the central city left for the suburbs. The white middle and upper middle classes fled the central areas of these cities to avoid mixing with the poor and "culturally deprived" members of society.[40]

The extent of segregation was revealed in a study of the Columbus, Ohio, public school system. During the 1950s enrollment increased by 87 percent, despite the fact that the schools were in poor physical condition owing to years of wartime neglect.[41] The school district's growth remained off limits to blacks, although 100 schools were built from 1951 to 1964. By 1964, more than 50 schools were either 100 percent black or 100 percent white.[42] In Columbus during this period, blacks were prohibited from attending white schools or movie theaters, restaurants, hotels, or hospitals used by whites.[43]

The "separate but equal" doctrine, in which separate facilities were provided for blacks and whites, originated with the *Plessy v. Ferguson* case of 1896, in which Homer Plessy, a black man, insisted on riding in the white section of a train that went from New Orleans to Covington, Louisiana. Despite being fined and physically removed from the train, he appealed to the U.S. Supreme Court, citing the Thirteenth Amendment, which had freed the blacks. The Court, with the exception of Justice Harlan, ruled against Plessy because the justices believed Plessy was indeed treated fairly since facilities were provided for him on the train, even though they were separate. The idea that separate inherently meant unequal was apparently not understood. This doctrine was used in public schools to justify having separate educational facilities for blacks and whites.

The U.S. Supreme Court had to rethink its "separate but equal" doctrine in *Brown v. Board of Education of Topeka* in 1954, when the Court was forced to look at the issue of segregation in public education. The Court believed that it was the responsibility of state and local governments to provide an education for youth to train them to be productive and useful citizens and to teach them to be civilized and cultured. The justices thus decided that segregated schools left black children feeling inferior, an emotion that would destroy their motivation for learning. The ultimate conclusion was that segregation approved by law would slow the educational and mental development of black children. Thus, the ruling ended what is known as *de jure segregation,* or segregation caused by law.[44]

The *Brown v. Board of Education of Topeka* case is a testament to those who stood up against racism and school segregation. The lead plaintiff in this case was Reverend Oliver Brown, who joined with 12 other plaintiffs whose children were forced to attend a segregated black school 30 or 40 blocks from their home, even though a public elementary school was only 4 to 5 blocks away. Elementary schools in Kansas were segregated at that time, although other schools were integrated.[45] The plaintiffs in this case were all asked to join in the fight against segregated schools by the National Association for the Advancement of Colored People (NAACP), which was challenging the law that upheld segregation in the elementary schools of Kansas.[46]

When the *Brown* case went to the Supreme Court it was combined with four other school segregation cases from the District of Columbia, and the states of Delaware, South Carolina, and Virginia.[47] Some of the plaintiffs in the other cases were in fear for their lives after they took a stand against racism and school segregation. Cheryl Brown Henderson, the daughter of the Reverend Oliver Brown, the lead plaintiff in the case, is now the executive director of the Brown Foundation. In an article commenting on the fate of those who were courageous enough to stand up against school segregation, she points out that the problems with educational equity are still just as real today as they were in 1954. She states, "the educational agenda of the civil rights movement remains unfinished."[48]

Despite the order to desegregate schools beginning in 1955, people resisted it. Some parents still objected to having their children attend the same schools as black children. People found ways to get around the law; for example, setting geographic boundaries for attendance areas made it easier to keep black children out of certain schools in a district. This practice is known as *de facto segregation.* Discussions have abounded for years about how to reverse this practice. One solution to the problem has been busing, which involves transporting some black students from city schools with a high percentage of black students to schools outside their neighborhoods that have a high percentage of white students, to integrate students. Some members of the black community favor this solution, whereas others dislike it.[49]

Teachers were aware of the impact of segregation on students, and the AFT issued a statement that segregation "deprives children of their right to enjoy full association with their fellows of different creed and color," which the federation felt was "a loss of one of the major privileges of democratic education."[50]

It was not until the mid-1960s, with the passage of the Civil Rights Act and the Elementary and Secondary Education Act (ESEA) that school desegregation began to occur more seriously; however, segregation is still seen in the U.S. public school system today. Cheryl Brown Henderson has commented that "the goal of equal educational opportunity for our children remains elusive."[51]

In the following section you will learn more about how the federal government became involved in school desegregation as the nation became increasingly aware of the adverse effects of poverty on a child's education.

THE 1960S: INCREASED FEDERAL INVOLVEMENT IN EDUCATION

With the passage of the NDEA, the federal government had begun to play an important role in the nation's educational system. In the 1960s the government became increasingly involved in educational policy making. Although each state controls its own educational system, all states increasingly had to follow the mandates of the federal government.

The Civil Rights Act of 1964 and the War on Poverty were direct responses by the federal government to the concerns of the period. During the period 1950–1960, the federal government became involved in everything from using the schools to reduce or eliminate poverty to establishing high schools and college preparatory schools on a massive scale. Not only were schools expected to solve the problem of poverty, which is an overly ambitious undertaking in itself, but they were also expected to deal with social problems ranging from juvenile delinquency to eliminating traffic accidents through driver's education courses. Concern over escalating drug use and venereal disease was translated into health education programs to teach students about the dangers of unprotected sex and the risks of drug use. These non-academic programs, however, took time away from the teaching of academic material, which was one of the criticisms of them.[52]

The progress of American public school students continued to be scrutinized and various curriculum movements were adopted to improve students' performance. In addition to teaching students how to overcome poverty, teachers were also expected to try out new curricula to raise student achievement levels to match or better those of students in other countries.

The passage of the 1964 Civil Rights Act cleared the way for the Elementary and Secondary Education Act (ESEA) in the following year. The key provision of ESEA, signed by Lyndon B. Johnson on April 11, 1965, was Title I, a compensatory education program that offered grants to schools, to help them reduce the effects of poverty on children's academic progress.[53] The federal government was becoming aware of the adverse effects of poverty on a child's cognitive and emotional functioning. It was believed that poverty led to "anti-intellectual" behavior such as a dislike of school and a dislike of reading and that these behaviors and attitudes would prevent children from reaching their full potential. The second role of ESEA was to determine that children could be taught the skills to succeed, and be motivated to do well in school, and it was the federal government's responsibility to do so.[54] One of the most important aspects of ESEA was financial help for children who were considered to be "culturally deprived."[55]

Presidents Kennedy and Johnson were well aware of the economic inequalities that existed in society at this time and tried to address them. In 1964, Johnson signed the Economic Opportunity Act, to eliminate poverty by providing training for people who could not find work. The act also provided for retraining of people with outdated skills and created the Job Corps, to assist a maximum of 100,000 youth whose background made them "unfit for useful work."[56]

Presidents Kennedy and Johnson increased the minimum wage, made changes to housing legislation, and applied welfare and training approaches to the problem of poverty, and President Johnson signed the Medicare Act of 1965. Operation Head Start was set up to establish nursery schools in deprived areas so that disadvantaged children could acquire the skills necessary to compete with those from wealthier backgrounds. Using schools to solve the problem of poverty is a neutral approach. Suggesting that if teachers do a good job of educating children and youth, they will grow up to be productive and successful adults with good jobs is considered to be easier than undertaking real economic reform measures.[57]

Evidently the American public did not believe that schools alone could solve the problem of poverty or joblessness. Many people, including black Americans, were angry that the government had not kept the promises it had made. These promises included better jobs and more education. The best jobs at that time were in government, in the professions, in service industries, and in clerical positions, but these required an education and credentials from a formal training program, which were often denied to black Americans. Riots broke out in New York City, parts of north central New Jersey, and in Philadelphia and Chicago. Between June and August of 1967 there were riots in 67 cities.[58] Conditions did not improve in 1968, the year Martin Luther King, Jr., the civil rights leader, was assassinated. Although the civil rights movement was said to have ended with King's death, the struggles of blacks to achieve equality are evidence that the movement has continued.

Although Public Law 94-142, or the Education of All Handicapped Children Act, was not passed until 1975, education for special-needs students gained more attention. Training programs were established for special education teachers because the U.S. Department of Education had begun its first program of support for research in education, called the Cooperative Research Program.[59] The type of education that gifted students should receive was also investigated.[60]

STUDENTS' ACADEMIC PROGRESS AND NEW CURRICULUM MOVEMENTS

The criticism that U.S. students did not make satisfactory academic progress in the public schools arose with the space race and never died away. In the mid-1960s, Scholastic Aptitude Tests (SATs) were given, and the scores were interpreted to mean that American educational programs were ineffective.[61]

One reason for the mediocrity of students' academic progress may have been the hodgepodge of curriculum movements that arose between 1960 and 1975, which U.S. educators embraced in turn. Rather than having formal education goals that could be applied to every student in every grade, regardless of gender or socioeconomic status, teachers had education goals that were connected to these various reform movements. For instance, the alternative education movement, exemplified by the radically child-centered English boarding school Summerhill run by A.S. Neill, recommended that textbooks, grades, and a formal curriculum be discarded. The educational philosophy of A.S. Neill is highlighted in the "Shaper of Education" feature on page 233.

Methods used in the Summerhill school led to the concept of the open classroom (no walls) and instruction based on the English method. However, American teachers had not been formally trained in the British method, and they took a system that worked in a country with a different governmental system (a monarchy) and a different system of school organization and adopted the method anyway.

During the late 1960s the open classroom movement and progressive education for students meant that formal lesson plans, curriculum guides, grades, textbooks, and tests, could be disregarded, and often were. Workstations for children with planned activities such as artwork, sand and water play, and reading were popular at this time. The idea of an open classroom was supposed to reduce the "mindlessness" of a set curriculum and make the classroom a more joyful place for children. Many educators, such as Max Rafferty, the conservative superintendent of schools in California, hated this concept. Referring to Summerhill, in which students had the freedom to design their own curriculum, and sexual behavior was tolerated as long as students did not become pregnant, Rafferty said that he would just as soon enroll a child of his in a brothel as enroll him or her there. He further stated that "a school isn't a school unless it offers organized knowledge in some systematic way."[62]

One high-profile critic of the progressive movement in education was Admiral H.G. Rickover, of the U.S. Navy. In 1964 he berated the U.S. educational system for its failure to provide adequate math and science programs for its students. Rickover noted that students entering the Navy were not prepared in math and science, and in an age in which national defense was a priority, this could not be tolerated.[63] He made unflattering comparisons between the achievement levels of U.S. students and those of students from other countries, including Denmark, Germany, and England. Blaming this partly on the practice of allowing "children to study only what pleases and interests them,"[64] Rickover berated the progressive educators. He said that progressive education was good for students who wanted the easy way out in school and wanted to "have a good time in school, dabble in trivia, and choose easy courses."[65] Instead, he recommended that students had to be made to understand that "if they choose the good time they will have to resign themselves to the certain prospects of life on the fringes of American society."[66] Rickover believed that schools should focus on teaching basic subjects and should eliminate instruction in any area(s) that did not contribute to the intellectual development of American students.

SHAPER OF EDUCATION

A.S. Neill
(1883–1973)

- He was a Scottish educator who began the private school Summerhill in England in 1921.
- Premise of Summerhill is Rousseau's educational philosophy that the school should fit the child and that lessons should be optional. If children want to avoid formal lessons, they can.
- There is no set curriculum, time for studying, and there are no textbooks, formal lessons, or schedule. Tests are not given at Summerhill.
- Students cannot be forced to do anything. When they are ready to do something or learn something, they will.
- Finding happiness is the aim of education.
- Students investigate what they want to learn and set their own schedule.
- Neill had faith in all children to reach their potential, relying on their own ability to sense when they were ready to learn.
- Democracy is important at Summerhill. Students have meetings, make the rules for the school, and enforce them.
- Neill said that "heterosexual play" was healthy and encouraged exploration.
- Low student-teacher ratio encourages closeness of teachers and students, and a mentoring relationship.

Rickover's other objection to the way U.S. schools were run focused on moral education. He stated that the separation of church and state made it impossible to teach anything with religious undertones in the public schools.

Rickover stated that American teachers depended more on textbooks than did teachers from other countries, resulting in lessons that were bland, uninteresting, and uninspiring. He stated: "the boring pablum fed our children in the

Dick and Jane series of textbooks would discourage anyone from ever again opening a book."[67]

Rickover's criticisms of the failure of the public schools to interest students in their work and to motivate them to succeed, and their lack of academic progress in math and science, are echoed by critics today. There are still too many students who struggle with literacy and who drop out of school. Also, the results of the Third and Fourth International Math and Science Studies (TIMSS) reveal that American students are still lagging behind students of other countries in their knowledge of math and science. Data from the National Center for Education Statistics (NCES) reveal that eighth-grade students are less likely to be taught mathematics by teachers who majored in mathematics in college. Their teachers, like teachers overseas, usually majored in mathematics education, rather than in the field of mathematics. The number of teachers who majored in science in college was less of a problem, with the exception of physics; U.S. students in the eighth grade were less likely than international peers to be taught science by teachers who had a physics degree.[68]

THE 1960S: BEGINNINGS OF DISCIPLINE PROBLEMS AND SCHOOL VIOLENCE

The radical child-centered open classroom movements, popular in the late 1960s, held that children were innately good and would automatically make the correct decisions about how to behave if given the opportunity to do so.

It is theorized that an unforeseen side effect of the progressive education movement was a dramatic increase in students' misbehavior, as teachers in the 1950s and 1960s noted. This misbehavior was part of the rebellion against the increasingly custodial role of the schools.[69]

One critic of the progressive education movement, James B. Conant, a chemist who became president of Harvard University at age 40, compared the academic progress of high school students in suburban areas with those in urban areas and found that urban students were suffering the consequences of a non-challenging academic program.[70] Conant conducted a study of 55 schools in 18 of the most populated states.[71] He remarked that "I found eight schools which, in my judgment, were satisfactorily fulfilling the three main objectives of a comprehensive high school."[72] These three objectives were as follows: (1) to give all future citizens a good education; (2) to offer elective programs to those students who wished to work right after graduation; and (3) to offer programs to prepare students who wished to attend college to do college-level work.[73] Conant made a compelling statement that is echoed by educators today: "The academically talented student, as a rule, is not being sufficiently challenged, does not work hard enough, and his program of academic subjects is not of sufficient range."[74] He further criticized the finding that girls in high school often avoid math and science classes as well as foreign languages, all of which are subjects that can prepare them for college and university-level study.[75]

Conant's study made recommendations not only for those he characterized as "academically talented" but also gave "special consideration for the very slow readers."[76] Noting that it was difficult for teachers to provide enough instruction for the

10 to 15 percent of the students reading at the fourth-, fifth-, or sixth-grade levels in high school, he commented that "even with the best of instruction, it is very difficult to raise the reading level of these students more than two grades."[77] Today, teachers, administrators, and the American public are very concerned about those with poor reading ability as they frequently get involved in school fights and become discipline problems.[78] Conant himself remarked upon this back in 1961 in his book *Slums and Suburbs,* in which he commented that the schools had taken on an increasingly custodial role, trying to keep youth off the streets and in school; however, youth aged 16 to 21 often dropped out of school and were unemployed. In the 1960s, educators noted that black youth in urban areas had few role models and had low prospects of employment, factors that might lead them to juvenile delinquency.[79] The idea that underprivileged youth in urban areas might not find traditionally "white" subjects appealing was raised, and one suggestion was to offer vocational programs tailored to inner city youth that would interest them.[80] The idea arose that juvenile delinquency could be prevented if the appropriate types of educational programs that would lead to productive jobs in the community were provided.[81]

BRIDGES FROM THE PAST TO THE PRESENT: CONTRIBUTIONS FROM THE PERIOD OF 1930 TO 1960, TO THE PRESENT

The issues in public education that arose during the period from 1930 to 1960 are all still very much alive today. Table 10-1 compares the issues in public education from 1930 to 1960, versus today.

Table 10-1 **Public Education in 1930 to 1960 Compared with Education Today**

1930 TO 1960	TODAY
Schools were segregated until *Brown v. Board of Education* in 1954 made school desegregation illegal.	Schools are desegregated by law, but communities have found ways to segregate schools by geographical boundaries and other methods—*de facto segregation.*
The progressive education movement of the 1960s and 1970s was criticized for student misbehavior and poor student academic performance.	Standards are set by states and the federal No Child Left Behind Act specifies subjects to be learned and acceptable levels of performance.
Financial conditions during the Great Depression caused schools to close early; in 1933–1934, 21 states had school terms less than 6 months long.	Financial problems in 2003 and 2004 and state budget issues caused some states, such as Oregon, to close schools early because not enough money was left to keep them running.
After World War II, schools were criticized for poorly teaching math and science.	Many schools, especially those classified as "high minority" schools, lack certified science and math teachers.

Since 1930 there has been an increasing amount of state and federal control legislation. States today have academic content area standards, all of which must be covered by teachers when they develop their lesson plans. These standards come from state departments of education, and are published on the Internet. States also are mandated to follow federal legislation such as the No Child Left Behind Act.

It is troubling that there are still not enough certified math and science teachers, particularly in "high-minority" schools, or schools where 75 percent of students are members of minority groups.[82] For instance, statistics show that 16 percent of teachers in high minority schools lack certification in science. The percentages for other subjects are also troubling; 14 percent of teachers are not certified to teach mathematics, 12 percent are not certified in English, and 8 percent are not certified in social studies. Compare these data with figures for low-minority schools: 5 percent for science teachers, 7 percent for mathematics teachers, 4 percent for English teachers, and 6 percent for social studies.[83]

American public school students still score below their international peers in math and science achievement, according to the Third and Fourth TIMSS studies. The 2000 National Association of Educational Progress (NAEP) report revealed that 82 percent of American 12th graders performed below proficiency level on the 2000 NAEP science test. The TIMSS study in 1995 showed similar discouraging results; by 12th grade students ranked 16th in the world, scoring above only Cyprus and South Africa. It appears that the longer students stay in the system, the worse they do in science.[84] This situation is eerily similar to that in 1958, when the National Defense Education Act was passed by the federal government to ensure national security. Today, the U.S. Commission on National Security in the Twenty-First Century has reported that "the inadequacies of our systems of education pose a greater threat to U.S. national security over the next quarter century than any potential controversial war that we might imagine."[85] The No Child Left Behind Act of 2001 does support paying math and science teachers more money to attract them. It is a requirement of this law that states had to have teachers who were certified in math and science by 2005.[86] It is theorized that students in high minority or high poverty schools perform poorly on math and science tests because they are taught by teachers who are not certified in math and science; however, that may be only *one* of the reasons for poor achievement.

Although teachers' rights have expanded since 1960, teachers still have to fight for adequate pay, benefits, and working conditions. One proposed solution to the problem of teacher compensation is a knowledge- and skill-based pay system, in which teacher knowledge and skills must be judged to be beyond the levels shown by beginning teachers to be eligible for better pay.[87]

Today, the involvement of the business community in education is still one of real controversy. For instance, the entrepreneur Chris Whittle, who began the Channel One program, and who also started the Edison Project, which runs troubled schools in the city of Philadelphia for profit, has been criticized as being more concerned with making money than with students' welfare. Operating schools for profit is an idea that inextricably links schools with the business sector. Channel One began in 1990, and is viewed in 12,000 schools across the country, with an average viewership of 6 million students.[88] The network programs are delivered via satellite. A new 12-minute segment is broadcast daily for 40 weeks a year. This 12-minute segment consists of 10 minutes of news and two 60-second ads.[89] Schools sign up with Channel One for 3 years and receive free television sets, VCRs, and satellite-receiving systems as part of the deal. However, now that DVD technology is replacing the standard VCR, Channel One will be forced to upgrade its technology to stay current, something it is struggling with at the present time.[90] Just as in the 1940s–1950s, the business community's motives in educational involvement are questioned.

School desegregation is still a major concern. Many schools, especially in poor urban areas, are segregated. Students in segregated schools are more likely to receive free lunches and be enrolled in Title I reading programs for compensatory education.[91] The psychological effects on children enrolled in segregated, high-poverty schools are examined by Jonathan Kozol in his recent book *Ordinary Resurrections,* which portrays the lives of children in an after-school program in Mott Haven, a high-need section of the South Bronx, New York.

Today, educators are still investigating the best ways to teach those who come from families who live below the poverty level or who are otherwise considered to be "underprivileged." Schools classified as "high poverty" are those in which 75 percent or more of students are eligible for federal free or reduced-price lunch programs.[92]

Teachers and administrators are concerned about discipline problems and violent behavior in schools. The problem of violence is often blamed on the progressive education movement, because it encouraged teachers to adapt subject lesson plans to students' interests rather than forcing them to study a set curriculum and develop academic discipline. The 1999 Columbine incident in a Colorado high school, in which two students killed 12 of their classmates and a teacher, and wounded others before shooting themselves, apparently was a reaction to extreme bullying by other students and is but one of many recent examples of school violence. Schools have had to adopt a zero-tolerance policy, meaning that students' lockers are searched regularly for weapons, and students who threaten others in the school, including teachers, may be suspended or expelled. Schools have also been forced to install improved security systems, often including metal detectors, to check for weapons that students may smuggle into a building. In 1996, 94 percent of schools reported a zero tolerance policy for firearms, and 1 percent had a zero-tolerance policy for weapons such as razor blades or knives.[93] Statistics show that the percentage of students being bullied increased from 5 percent in 1999 to 8 percent in 2001.[94]

The poor academic abilities and achievement records of many students have caused increasing concern, prompting passage of the No Child Left Behind Act in 2001. This law mandates that all public school students take federally funded tests each year. They must pass the tests to be promoted to the next grade. Schools in areas with families living below the poverty line may not be receiving enough funding to offset the poor home lives of these children, who often come to school sick, cold, and hungry.[95] World War II and the space race and NCLB and its implications for public education will be explored more fully in the next chapter.

SUMMARY

In this chapter you learned how the Great Depression adversely affected the lives of American citizens and schools, many of which could not hold classes for a full year because they ran out of money. The chapter also discussed the increasing criticism of the public schools from many sectors. Admiral Rickover, for example, worried that schools did not teach enough math and science to properly prepare students to enter the military and go into war. The issue of "separate but equal" education arose in the 1950s, and the *Brown v. Board of Education* case finally mandated school desegregation. The 1960s saw the rise of the progressive education movement and the growth of alternative schools such as Summerhill, run by the Scottish educator A. S. Neill.

Chapter 11 continues the discussion of federal involvement in education, started with the National Defense Education Act.

QUESTIONS FOR DISCUSSION

1. Students' academic achievement in math and science, as measured by the NAEP and the TIMSS, is compared with that of students in other countries in the same subjects. It is theorized that U.S. students do so poorly because they are taught by teachers who are not certified in math and science. In your opinion, will increasing the number of teachers certified in those areas improve the academic performance of students in high-minority schools? In low-minority schools? Give evidence for your answer.

2. This chapter described how the War on Poverty legislation, signed by President Lyndon B. Johnson, was used to help reduce poverty through education. In your opinion, is there anything the federal government should do TODAY to reduce poverty rates in America so that children from poor families get a better education and can lead better lives? Give evidence for your answer.

3. From your own school experiences, ask yourself whether teachers depended on the textbook to be the curriculum. How do you believe this affected your educational experiences (both positive and negative)? Be prepared to share with your classmates. In the future, when you teach, how will you decide to supplement the textbook, so that the curriculum is not *just* the book?

4. In your opinion, do American schools do enough to help those whose second language is English, get an education? Is there still prejudice against those who are ESL and a "sink or swim" mentality with regard to learning the language? Be sure to have evidence for your answer.

5. Why do students in other countries (Japan, Singapore) score higher in math and science than American students? Do you believe our culture, school organization,

curriculum, or parental involvement in education is responsible for the poor outcome? Give evidence to back up your answer.

SUGGESTED ACTIVITIES

1. As a future teacher how will you incorporate science and mathematics into your curriculum? Choose a or b.

   a. You are a third-grade teacher in a school with a high percentage of students from homes at or below the poverty line. More than 75 percent of the students qualify for free lunch, and your entire third-grade class gets free breakfast and lunch daily. Your students have no science class. Many students have poor dental hygiene; they have chipped teeth and poor gum health. They don't seem to know how to brush their teeth. How could you use this situation to promote scientific knowledge?

   b. You are a high school teacher whose students don't seem to enjoy math or science; however, you find out that they are upset about the landfill nearby and ask you about its effects. One student says the smell constantly gives him a headache. How could you use this opening to stimulate scientific interest among these students?

2. The progressive education movement included the curriculum theories and educational philosophy of A.S. Neill, whose school, Summerhill, was highly criticized. Read a biography of A.S. Neill, and summarize the book to your classmates, explaining Neill's philosophy, and giving examples from the book of the pros and cons of this type of education in a 15- to 20-minute PowerPoint presentation.

3. Interview an elementary or secondary-grade teacher and ask him or her to analyze the science and math curriculum taught in that school district. Ask the teacher his or her opinion about the science and math curriculum and how it could be improved. Also look through the curriculum materials. Write a one- to three-page summary of your visit, including the types of equipment used to teach math and science and the hours per day or week teaching these subjects. Also include information from the teacher on students' interest levels and obtain general information on the students' achievement in science and math.

4. Interview a social worker or member of a nearby school district's staff (guidance counselor, school psychologist) to find out how he or she feels about the influence of poverty in the home on students' behavior, including misbehavior (if any). Present your findings to your classmates in a 15- to 20-minute PowerPoint presentation and include information and a class handout on how poverty can influence students' behavior and how future teachers can help students.

5. Research information on dropout rates for blacks, Native Americans, and Latinos, and write an opinion paper on whether you believe U.S. education offers equal opportunity for these individuals to succeed. Give evidence to back up

your opinion. Use at least one current newspaper article, such as from the *New York Times* or another valid source. Tabloid newspapers are unacceptable. You may also use scholarly peer-reviewed journals, such as *Educational Leadership* or *Phi Delta Kappan.*

6. Research information on gender and education. Do you believe girls receive the same type of education as boys in today's schools? If not, why not? Provide evidence to back up your answer. Utilize sources from peer-reviewed journals such as *Educational Leadership,* or *Education Digest.* Newspapers may also be a valuable source of information. Share your findings with the class in a 15- to 20-minute PowerPoint presentation. Distribute a handout with references at the end of the presentation.

Bibliography

American Federation of Teachers. (1955). *Organizing the teaching profession: The story of the American Federation of Teachers by the Commission on Educational Reconstruction.* Glencoe, IL: Free Press.

Angus, D., & Mirel, J. (1995). Rhetoric and reality: The high school curriculum. In D. Ravitch & M. A. Vinovskis (Eds.), *What history teaches us about school reform: Learning from the past.* Baltimore: Johns Hopkins.

Aronson, E. (2000). *Nobody left to hate: Teaching compassion after Columbine.* New York: Worth.

Bates Ames, L. (1970). In H. W. Hart (Ed.), *Summerhill: For and against.* New York: Hart.

Casella, R. (2001). *At zero tolerance: Punishment, prevention, and school violence.* New York: Peter Lang.

Conant, J. B. (1959). *The American high school today.* New York: McGraw-Hill.

Conant, J. B. (1961). *Slums and suburbs.* New York: McGraw-Hill.

Crews, G. A., & Reid Counts, M. (1997). *The evolution of school disturbance in America: Colonial times to the modern day.* Westport, CT: Praeger.

Donahue, D. M. (1993). Serving students, science, or society? The secondary school physics curriculum in the United States, 1930–65. *History of Education Quarterly, 33*(3), 321–352.

Garrett, A. W. (2003). Teaching with fanfare and military glamour. *Educational Forum, 67*(3), 225–34.

Gumbert, E. B., & Spring, J. H. (1974). Youth and the custodial role of the schools. In *The superschool and the superstate: American education in the twentieth century, 1918–1970.* New York: Wiley.

Herbst, J. (1967). High school and youth in America. In W. Laqueur & G. L. Mosse (Eds.), *Education and social structure in the twentieth century.* New York: Harper and Row.

Jacobs, G. S. (1998). *Getting around Brown: Desegregation, development, and the Columbus public schools.* Columbus: Ohio State University Press.

Karier, C. J. (1986). *The individual, society, and education: A history of American educational ideas* (2nd ed.). Chicago: University of Illinois Press.

Kirst, M. W. (1995). Who's in charge? Federal, state, and local control. In D. Ravitch & M. A. Vinovskis (Eds.), *What history teaches us about school reform: Learning from the past.* Baltimore: Johns Hopkins.

Krug, E. A. (1966). 1954: *Brown et al. v. Board of Education of Topeka et al.* In *Salient dates in American education, 1635–1964.* New York: Harper and Row.

LaGumina, S. J., & Cavaioli, F. J. (1976). *The ethnic dimension in American society.* Boston: Holbrook Press.

Mork, G. M. A. (1947). The scientific method as a teaching procedure. *School Science and Mathematics, 47*(6), 526–530.

National Center for Education Statistics. *Trends in International Mathematics and Science Study: Highlights from the Third International Math and Science Study—Repeat (TIMSS-R).* Retrieved 2005, from *http://www.nces.ed.gov/timss*

National Center for Education Statistics (2003, May 29). "Commissioner's Statement—The Condition of Education 2003," pp. iii–xi. Retrieved May, 2004, from *http://www .nces.ed.gov*

National Center for Education Statistics. (2004). Out of Field Teachers: Percentage of public high school students taught selected subjects by teachers without certification of a major in the field they teach, by minority concentration and school poverty, 1999–2000. Retrieved 2005, from *http://www.nces.ed.gov/programs/coe/2004/charts/chart24.asp*

These appear to be the most recent statistics on this subject.

Oliver, J. S., & Kim Nichols, B. (2001). The method of science in the middle of the century. *School Science and Mathematics 101*(7).

Pounds, R. L., & Bryner, J. R. (1967). *The school in American society* (2nd ed.). New York: Macmillan.

Rafferty, M. (1970). In H. W. Hart (Ed.), *Summerhill: For and against.* New York: Hart.

Reynolds, M. C. (1985). The special education of a drummer. *Journal of School Psychology, 23*(3).

Rickover, H. G. (1963). *American education; A national failure: The problem of our schools and what we can learn from England.* New York: E. P. Dutton.

Spring, J. (1988). *Conflict of interests: The politics of American education.* New York: Longman.

Taglianetti, T. J. (1975). Reading failure: A predictor of delinquency. *Crime Prevention Review, 2*(3), 24–30. Available through National Criminal Justice Reference Service (NCJRS).

Thompson, R. (1984, August 24). Status of the schools. *Education report card: Schools on the line.* Washington DC: Congressional Quarterly.

Tyack, D. B., Lowe, R. & Hansot, E. (1984). *Public schools in hard times: The Great Depression and recent years.* Cambridge, MA: Harvard University Press.

Urbanski, A., & Erskine, R. (2000). School reform, TURN, and teacher compensation. *Phi Delta Kappan, 81*(5), 367–70.

Suggestions for Further Reading

In addition to the works cited in the bibliography, the following are suggested for further reading.

AUW Report. (1995). *How schools shortchange girls: A study of major findings on girls and education.* New York: Marlowe.

Drew, D. E. (1995). Class, race, and science education. In S. W. Rothstein (Ed.), *Class, culture, and race in America's schools: A handbook.* Westport, CT: Greenwood.

Drew, D. E. (1996). *Aptitude revisited: Rethinking math and science education for America's next century.* Baltimore: Johns Hopkins.

Kozol, J. (1991). *Savage inequalities: Children in America's schools.* New York: Crown.

Kozol, J. (2000). *Ordinary resurrections: Children in the years of hope.* New York: Crown.

Lusi, S. F. (1997). *The role of state departments of education in complex school reform.* New York: Teachers College.

Lynch, J. (1983). *The multicultural curriculum.* London: Batsford Academic and Educational.

Sadker, D. & Sadker, M. (1994). *Failing at fairness: How our schools cheat girls.* New York: Simon and Schuster.

Sykes, C. J. (1995). *Dumbing down our kids: Why America's children feel good about themselves but can't read, write, or add.* New York: St. Martin's Press.

Relevant Web Sites

American Association of University Women (AAUW) *http://www.aauw.org* Home page of AAUW, which encourages and promotes educational equity for women and girls in schools, colleges, and universities across the country.

American Federation of Teachers *http://www.aft.org* Home page of the American Federation of Teachers. Includes salary scales for teachers, by state, and reports on educational issues.

National Education Association *http://www.nea.org* Home page of the National Education Association, with information on NCLB, ESEA, teacher preparation, and more.

Summerhill *http://www.summerhillschool.co.uk/* Home page of the school Summerhill, founded by A. S. Neill. The school has moved to Leiston in Suffolk, England, but is still in operation.

National Center for Education Statistics *http://www.nces.ed.gov* Information at the federal and state level relating to all topics in education.

The National Center for Public Policy Research's Constitution and the Courts Archive *http://www.nationalcenter.org/brown.html* Original appeal from the U. S. District Court of the District of Kansas on the *Brown v. Board of Education* case.

No Child Left Behind Act *http://www.nclb.gov* U.S. Department of Education site explaining NCLB.

Journal of American Indian Education *http://jaie.asu.edu/* At Arizona State University, information pertaining to education of Native Americans.

Questia online *http://www.questia.com* Books, journals, and articles on many topics, including progressive education, the Great Depression, and World War II and education.

U.S. Department of Education *http://www.ed.gov* Home page of the U.S. Department of Education for research on federal and state educational policies.

Wikipedia, the free encyclopedia *http://en.wikipedia.org/wiki/Hyman_Rickover* Great biography of Admiral Hyman Rickover. Look up any topic or educator using this Web site.

Endnotes

[1] David B. Tyack, Robert Lowe, & Elisabeth Hansot, *Public Schools in Hard Times: The Great Depression and Recent Years* (Cambridge, MA: Harvard University Press, 1984), 7–8.

[2] Ibid., 58.

[3] Ibid.

[4] Ibid., 19.

[5] Ibid.

[6] Ibid., 19–22.

[7] Ibid.

[8] Ralph L. Pounds & James R. Bryner, *The School in American Society,* 2nd ed. (New York: Macmillan, 1967), 320. See also Clarence J. Karier, *The Individual, Society, and Education: A History of American Educational Ideas,* 2nd ed. (Chicago: University of Illinois Press, 1986).

[9] Ibid., 320 in chapter 9, "Problems of Intergroup Relations."

[10] J. Steve Oliver & B. Kim Nichols, "The Method of Science in the Middle of the Century," *School Science and Mathematics, 101,* no. 7 (2001), 390–91.

[11] Ibid.

[12] Ibid., 392.

[13] Ibid., 393.

[14] Gordon M. A. Mork, "The Scientific Method as a Teaching Procedure," *School Science and Mathematics, 47,* no. 6 (1947), 530.

[15] Oliver & Nichols, "The Method of Science," 393.

[16] David M. Donahue, "Serving Students, Science, or Society? The Secondary School Physics Curriculum in the United States, 1930–65," *History of Education Quarterly, 33,* no. 3 (1993), 321.

[17] Ibid., 323.

[18] Ibid., 324.

[19] Ibid. This quote comes directly from the author of the survey, Alexander Efron of Teachers College, Columbia University, New York City.

[20] Ibid., 325–26. See also p. 333.

[21] Ibid., 328.

[22] Ibid., 331.

[23] Ibid., 333.

[24] Ibid., 324.

[25] Alan W. Garrett, "Teaching with Fanfare and Military Glamour," *Educational Forum, 67,* no. 3 (2003), 227. See also B. B. Somervell, "Military Needs for Trained Manpower," *National Association of Secondary School Principals (NASSP) Bulletin, 26,* no. 108 (1942), 3–6.

[26] American Federation of Teachers, *Organizing the Teaching Profession: The Story of the American Federation of Teachers by the Commission on Educational Reconstruction* (Glencoe, IL: Free Press, 1955), 187.

[27] J. Steve Oliver & B. Kim Nichols, "Early Days: The Alarming Threat to the Welfare of Our Children," *Journal of School Science and Mathematics, 99,* no. 8 (1999), 457.

[28] Ibid.

[29] Ibid.

[30] Ibid.

[31] See chapter 2, "The Teacher's Struggle for Citizenship Rights," in American Federation of Teachers, *Organizing the Teaching Profession.*

[32] American Federation of Teachers, *Organizing the Teaching Profession,* 47.

[33] Ibid., 48.

[34] Ibid., 73.

[35] Ibid.

[36] Ibid., 65.

[37] Ibid., 57.

[38] Karier, *Individual, Society, and Education,* 320.

[39] Edgar B. Gumbert & Joel H. Spring, *The Superschool and the Superstate: American Education in the Twentieth Century, 1918–1970* (New York: Wiley, 1974), 116–20.

[40] Ibid., 136.

[41] Gregory S. Jacobs, *Getting Around Brown: Desegregation, Development, and the Columbus Public Schools* (Columbus: Ohio State University Press, 1998), 15.

[42] Ibid.

[43] Ibid., 7.

[44] Edward A. Krug, "1954: *Brown et al. v. Board of Education of Topeka et al.,*" in *Salient Dates in American Education 1635–1964* (New York: Harper and Row, 1966), 136–39.

[45] Cheryl Brown Henderson, "*Brown v. Board of Education:* Fiftieth Anniversary of the Supreme Court Ruling," *College Board Review,* no. 200 (Fall 2003), 7–11. See p. 8.

[46] Ibid.

[47] Ibid.

[48] Ibid., 11.

[49] Joel Spring, *Conflict of Interests: The Politics of American Education* (New York: Longman, 1988), 150.

[50] American Federation of Teachers, *Organizing the Teaching Profession,* 193.

[51] Henderson, "*Brown v. Board of Education,*" 11.

[52] Gordon A. Crews & M. Reid Counts, *The Evolution of School Disturbance in America: Colonial Times to the Modern Day* (Westport, CT: Praeger, 1997), 80.

[53] Roger Thompson, "Status of the Schools," August 24, 1984, *Education Report Card: Schools on the Line* (Washington DC: Congressional Quarterly), 14.

[54] Crews & Counts, *Evolution of School Disturbance,* 81.

[55] Ibid.

[56] Gumbert & Spring, "Youth and the Custodial Role," in *The Superschool and the Superstate,* 45.

[57] Crews and Counts, *Evolution of School Disturbance,* 80.

[58] Karier, *Individual, Society, and Education,* 331.

[59] Maynard C. Reynolds, (1985). The special education of a drummer. *Journal of School Psychology, 23*(3).

[60] Ibid. The term *mentally advanced* is used by Reynolds.

[61] Crews and Counts, *Evaluation of School Disturbance,* 82.

[62] Max Rafferty, in *Summerhill: For and Against,* ed. H. W. Hart (New York: Hart, 1970), 17.

[63] H. G. Rickover, *American Education; A National Failure: The Problem of Our Schools and What We Can Learn from England* (New York: E. P. Dutton, 1963), 72–73.

[64] Ibid.

[65] Ibid.

[66] Ibid, 68.

[67] Ibid., 323.

[68] National Center for Education Statistics, *Trends in International Math and Science Study: Highlights from the Third International Math and Science Study—Repeat (TIMSS-R),* *http://www.nces.ed.gov* (retrieved 2003). These data are from the February 22, 2002 report. More recent findings are explained in the "Bridges" section.

[69] Gumbert & Spring, "Youth and the Custodial Role," 115.

[70] Jurgen Herbst, "High School and Youth in America," in *Education and Social Structure in the Twentieth Century,* ed. Walter Laqueur & George L. Mosse (New York: Harper and Row, 1967), 165.

[71] James B. Conant, *The American High School Today: A First Report to Interested Citizens* (New York: McGraw-Hill, 1959), 14.

[72] Ibid., 22.

[73] Ibid., 17.

[74] Ibid., 40.

[75] Ibid.

[76] Ibid., 55.

[77] Ibid., 56.

[78] T. J. Taglianetti, "Reading Failure: A Predictor of Delinquency," in *Crime Prevention Review, 2,* no. 3 (1975), 24–30. Available through National Criminal Justice Reference Service (NCJRS).

[79] Gumbert & Spring, "Youth and the Custodial Role," 137. See also James B. Conant, *Slums and Suburbs* (New York: McGraw-Hill, 1961).

[80] Ibid.

[81] Ibid., 138.

[82] National Center for Education Statistics, "Out of Field Teachers: Percentage of Public High School Students Taught Selected Subjects by Teachers Without Certification of a Major in the Field They Teach, by Minority Concentration and School Poverty, 1999–2000," *http://www.nces.ed.govprograms/coe/2004/charts/chart24.asp* (retrieved 2003). These appear to be the most recent statistics on this subject.

[83] Ibid. A bar graph is used to represent these statistics.

[84] "Proven Methods: The Facts About Science Achievement," U.S. Department of Education, (*http://www.ed.gov* (retrieved 2003–2004).

[85] Ibid.

[86] Ibid.

[87] Adam Urbanski & Roger Erskine, "School Reform, TURN, and Teacher Compensation," *Phi Delta Kappan, 81,* no. 5 (2000), 367–70.

[88] Jim Cooper, "Channel One on the Move," *Mediaweek,* March 14, 2005, p. 12.

[89] Ibid.

[90] Rhea R. Borja, "Channel One Struggling in Shifting Market," *Education Week,* July 27, 2005, p. 3.

[91] National Center for Education Statistics, "Commissioner's Statement—The Condition of Education 2003," May 29, 2003, pp. iii–xi, *http://www.nces.ed,org* (retrieved 2004).

[92] National Center for Education Statistics, *Violence and Discipline Problems in the United States, 1996–1997 (NCES 90-030).* Based on data from the 1996–1997 Fast Response Survey System (FRSS) Principal/School Disciplinarian Survey on School Violence, *http://www.nces.ed.org* (retrieved 2000–2001).

[93] National Center for Education Statistics, "Indicators of School Crime and Safety, 2003," *http://www.nces.ed.org* (retrieved 2004).

[94] National Center for Education Statistics, "Commissioner's Statement," iii–xi.

[95] Ibid.

Chapter 11

Reforms in Modern Education 1960–1983: From the War on Poverty to *A Nation at Risk*

Learning Objectives

1. Describe the expanded federal role in education from 1960 to 1983.
2. List and discuss the federal laws protecting the educational rights of women, African Americans, and persons with handicaps.
3. Describe the reports that criticized the performance of public schools, such as *A Nation at Risk*, and the federal responses to these reports.
4. Explain the major concerns in education in the 1960s and 1970s.
5. Discuss the major concerns in education in the 1970s and the 1980s and their significance.
6. Discuss the involvement of American business in education.

INTRODUCTION

Chapter 10 profiled the expansion of the American public school system in the years 1930 to 1960.

This chapter continues the discussion of the expanded federal role in education from 1960 to 1983, the year in which *A Nation at Risk*, a report citing the deficiencies of American public schools, was released under President Ronald Reagan. The 1960s were notable for the War on Poverty, a government program begun under President Lyndon B. Johnson, which tried to reduce poverty through education. Civil rights legislation in the 1950s to 1960s focused attention on social and economic inequalities of blacks, Native Americans, and women. It also led to the passage of federal laws protecting the educational rights of women, blacks, and persons with handicaps.

In this chapter, you will learn about the concerns of educators during the 1970s and 1980s, during which the "Back to Basics" movement arose in response to

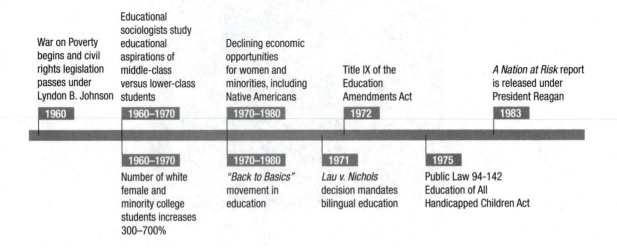

War on Poverty begins and civil rights legislation passes under Lyndon B. Johnson — **1960**

Educational sociologists study educational aspirations of middle-class versus lower-class students — **1960–1970**

Declining economic opportunities for women and minorities, including Native Americans — **1970–1980**

Title IX of the Education Amendments Act — **1972**

A Nation at Risk report is released under President Reagan — **1983**

1960–1970 Number of white female and minority college students increases 300–700%

1970–1980 "Back to Basics" movement in education

1971 *Lau v. Nichols* decision mandates bilingual education

1975 Public Law 94-142 Education of All Handicapped Children Act

declining SAT scores. The open education movement of the late 1960s and early 1970s had failed, as educators began to see that this type of education did not adequately prepare students for college or the job market and led to poor achievement on the Scholastic Aptitude Test (SAT). The 1970s also saw the passage of Title IX, which focused on gender equality, as well as the passage of Public Law 94-142, or the Education of All Handicapped Children Act, to provide free public education to children with physical or mental disabilities.

The first section of Chapter 11 explores the problems of race, gender, education, and work.

THE 1960S: RACE, GENDER, JOBS, AND EDUCATION

The 1960s were marked by an emphasis on education for members of minority groups. Even though 65 percent of non white males with 4 or more years of college were employed in technical or professional positions, compared with only 4 percent of high school graduates, concern about discrimination against blacks in the job market persisted.[1]

In 1962 the mean occupational status score for whites was almost twice as high as the score for non-whites.[2] Racial discrimination in hiring and promotion practices was to blame for this discrepancy. It has been theorized that as the percentage of blacks enrolled in college increases, the level of discrimination rises to cope with the competition that capable, well-educated blacks pose to whites in the job market.[3]

In the 1960s, an educational sociologist, Murray Milner, stated that one of the most important solutions to the educational and occupational discrepancies between blacks and whites was to ensure that blacks finished high school as they could not enter college unless they had earned a high school diploma.[4] Another recommendation was to improve job skills training for white and black men, with 1 to 4 years of high school, and to enforce antidiscrimination laws in the industries that usually employed men with these levels of education.[5]

During the 1960s, educational sociologists compared the educational aspirations of students from lower-class families to those of middle-class families. A study conducted in White Plains, New York, found that 52 percent of students classified as being from lower socioeconomic status declared that they would continue their education through college; however, only 37 percent of those students were enrolled in college-preparatory courses. In contrast, 95 percent of the middle-class students intended to finish college, and 100 percent of them were taking college-preparatory courses.[6]

The sociologists conducting this research concluded from their findings that there are two major factors related to race or ethnicity and educational levels: discriminatory hiring practices used by companies, and the aspirations of members of minority or other ethnic groups themselves. Future teachers often wonder why students from families who are struggling financially have lower than expected educational aspirations. Although these students may indeed want to attend college or finish high school, they may doubt whether this will be possible, because it requires an amount of money they do not have and are not sure they will ever be able to obtain.[7]

During the 1960s the percentage of white males enrolled in college more than doubled and the number of white females and minority students increased between 300 and 700 percent in that decade. In 1960, 62 percent of female college graduates were employed in teaching or nursing.[8] Fifty percent of these graduates went into teaching in 1960. Increased governmental support of education during the 1960s made more teaching jobs available. Few opportunities existed for women in other professional areas or even in clerical areas.[9]

During the 1970s those working in teaching and other areas found fewer opportunities as it was a time of declining economic opportunity for women. White and black females earned less than white males, even those white males who had no college education.[10] This was also the case for Native Americans, whose economic and social status steadily worsened during the period from 1940 to 1970. In 1969 the income of male Indians was only one third the income of white males.[11]

Today, black males, particularly in the inner cities, have lower levels of education. Native Americans live on reservations, where poverty is rampant and where educational opportunities may be almost nonexistent. Table 11-1 compares the educational opportunities available to African Americans and Native Americans.

Women also still find themselves economically disadvantaged; although increasing percentages of women are attending college and graduate school, their earning potential is still below that of white males.

THE 1970S: BACK TO BASICS

The late 1960s and early 1970s were a time of curricular innovations and exploration. By the mid 1970s, educators had given up on the alternative education movement. Donald A. Myers, who participated in a team effort to evaluate the

Table 11-1 **Educational Opportunities for Disadvantaged Groups: African Americans and Native Americans**

AFRICAN AMERICANS	NATIVE AMERICANS
African Americans often attend segregated schools and live in inner-city communities which have few opportunities for employment.	Native Americans are rarely found in integrated public schools; they are more likely to be on remote reservations with great poverty and few employment opportunities.
African Americans in inner cities often felt that they did not belong and questioned whether it was necessary to give up their culture to become "successful" in the white world.	Native Americans were put in boarding schools at the turn of the century and were required to cut their hair, wear Western clothing, and give up native customs, language, and food.
U.S. schools for African Americans are often underfunded and lack supplies and certified teachers.	Schools for Native Americans on reservations have poor resources and supplies and lack teachers.

open classrooms of this movement in New York State, stated that educators should not make the mistake of adopting every educational fad under the sun, especially those that were implemented without careful and thorough research.[12] SAT scores were declining, and it was believed that the open classrooms and lack of a formal curriculum were to blame.

The Back to Basics movement was developed in response to this situation. This movement reached its peak in 1975 because of public demand for instruction in traditional academic subjects.[13] President Richard M. Nixon launched the Career Education Program in the early 1970s, a federally subsidized program to introduce students to the workplace by acquainting them with career opportunities and preparing them for jobs while they were still in school.[14]

Teachers noticed a deterioration in students' behavior, which was thought to be due, in part, to the open education movement. Increasing student disrespect for teachers and authority figures was noticeable and was thought to be due to decreased expectations of students and even to the elimination of the dress code.

High schools had cut back on graduation requirements, and fewer courses in math, English, foreign languages, and the sciences were required for graduation. In California it was reported that high school students were enrolling in twice as many electives as in English or composition courses. The amount of homework had been reduced, and absenteeism was more leniently tolerated. It was said that regardless of absenteeism, students still received A and B grades.[15] The poor academic achievement and the behavioral problems led to more federal involvement to improve public education.

By the middle of the 1970s, schools were financially troubled because of a recession, and educators were demoralized.[16] In fact, the 1970s have been characterized as an unhappy time for American public education. Budget cuts were necessary because of the recession, and these eliminated some of the programs thought necessary for students' well-being. The cuts also made it necessary to eliminate staff, such as guidance counselors, who provided much-needed psychological and academic support services for students. As federal funding for education was cut by 25 percent, school buildings had to be closed.[17] It was in the middle of this period, during the cutbacks, that the passage of P.L. 94-142 occurred.

TITLE IX: PROMOTING GENDER EQUALITY (1972)

Title IX of the Education Amendments Act of 1972 was a federal initiative to improve gender equality. It required colleges to initiate affirmative action so that females would be just as likely as males to be admitted to college. This law made it illegal to discriminate against females in college admissions, classes, employment, or financial aid, or sports.

Female student athletes were traditionally not given appropriate locker or playing facilities or provided with coaches. Title IX ruled that schools that sponsored either intercollegiate or intermural sports had to provide the same types of opportunities for students, regardless of gender.[18] Despite this law, however, discriminatory practices still exist in education, from the elementary school through graduate school. We will examine this topic further in the "Bridges" section at the end of the chapter.

PUBLIC LAW 94-142 (1975)

Before the federal government intervened to ensure that children with disabilities or handicaps would be allowed to attend public schools and have their needs met, students with conditions such as spina bifida, cerebral palsy, or mild mental retardation did not attend public schools. If they went to school at all, they attended a private school or they were taught at home. Families who could afford to do so sent their children to special schools.

The civil rights movement of the 1960s contributed to the consideration of the rights of students with special needs to obtain a free public education. In the late 1960s, the Pennsylvania Association for Retarded Citizens (PARC) campaigned to overturn the laws that prohibited mentally retarded children from being in school because they were traditionally considered uneducable and untrainable.[19] The landmark case that drew attention to the rights of retarded children was the case *PARC v. Commonwealth of Pennsylvania.* Conditions at the Pennhurst State School and Hospital, which housed mentally retarded children and youth, were investigated. The Council for Exceptional Children, along with PARC, researched the possibilities of educating children with special needs. The result of the case was that the Commonwealth of Pennsylvania withdrew its objections to educating retarded children in the public schools. Subsequently, other lobbying groups filed cases against other state governments, and these suits led to the passage of Public Law 94-142 in 1975.

Known as the *Education of All Handicapped Children Act,* P.L. 94-142 was a milestone in special education legislation. It guaranteed a free appropriate public education for all children with all types of physical or mental disabilities. Public schools are required to provide free public education for children regardless of their disability.

The emphasis today is on what a student *can* do, not what he or she *cannot do.* The curriculum is intended to make the most of a child's abilities and helps him or her learn to read and write, to do simple arithmetic, to dress him- or herself, and so on. A group of educators, including a school psychologist, classroom teacher(s), principal, special education teacher(s), guidance counselor(s), and parent(s) or guardian(s), decides on the curriculum for an individual classified as a special-needs student. This team assembles an Individualized Education Plan (IEP), which specifies the goals for the student and how he or she will achieve them. Parent(s) or guardian(s) must attend these IEP meetings and agree to the placement of their child before any intervention can begin. Increasing numbers of students have IEPs, so as a future teacher you should be knowledgeable about the origins of special education, special education legislation, and your role in educating a student with special needs. You will learn more about IEPs and the 1997 amendments to P.L. 94-142 in chapter 12.

THE 1980S: SOCIOLOGICAL EFFECTS ON EDUCATION

Sociologists noticed and studied many changes in American society during the 1980s. For example, they researched whether the influence of peers had an adverse effect on school achievement, and they found that such influence was greater for adolescents of lower-class families. Factors such as a larger proportion of single-parent families and less parental supervision may lead to more involvement with peers who have negative influences, such as gang members.[20] Such involvement may translate to failing performance in school as students become tied up with gangs or others who do not encourage them to be successful in school.

Sociologists also identified parental socioeconomic status as a primary influence on adolescent educational and occupational aspirations and attainment.[21] The effects of poverty are more significant than the effects of family structure, which includes factors such as birth order and family size.[22]

During the 1980s, sociologists also addressed issues such as the rise in adolescent childbearing and its negative effects on maternal and infant health as well as the effects of child sexual abuse and family violence on the stability of the family. They noted the serious social-psychological consequences of child sexual abuse.[23] Family violence and child abuse and neglect received much attention during the 1980s.[24] Research also began on the diversity of families. With increasing immigration a growing population of Hispanic children were entering the public schools and sociologists recognized that the educational aspirations of other ethnic groups might differ from those of the mainstream.

Today, this is an important topic for teachers to know about when communicating with parents or guardians of various ethnic groups. The traditional academic model, in which individual achievement is most important, may not be the model with which other ethnic groups identify. In some ethnic groups cooperation with others is more important than individual success.

REVISITING *SPUTNIK* IN THE 1980S

You will recall that the 1957 Soviet launch of *Sputnik* spurred the development of educational programs in science, mathematics, and foreign languages in public schools and colleges, through the National Defense Education Act of 1958.[25]

During the 1980s there was renewed interest in funding programs in mathematics, science, foreign language instruction, and in promoting technological innovations.[26] In the 1980s, however, U.S. students' lack of preparation in these areas was linked to America's economic decline. Congress responded by providing funding in an effort to develop more programs in these areas, so that Americans could eventually compete on an equal playing field with other countries.[27]

Business leaders also took an interest in the state of U.S. education and called for reform in the public schools, comparing the type of education in America with that given in Japan. A report commissioned by the New York Stock Exchange stated that one of the most important reasons for Japan's success was the quality of its educational system. The report stated further that Japan educates its population to a higher level than that in the United States. The report concluded that if America were to become economically competitive with other countries, its educational system would have to be overhauled so that American students were made to achieve at the same high levels as Japanese students.[28]

The 1980s was seen as the most recent period when the nation became aware that its public schools drastically needed to be improved. Although increased federal funding was called for, President Reagan proposed to cut federal spending on education by almost one third.[29] The president wanted the states and local school districts to take charge of the schools, rather than relying on the federal government to overhaul them. In fact, he wanted to abolish the U.S. Department of Education because he felt so strongly that the federal government should stay out of educational policy. From 1980 to 1986 an additional $4.2 billion was made available by the states and local school districts for elementary and secondary education.[30] At the same time, federal spending for education decreased by $4.2 billion. Whereas President Reagan and his supporters believed in limiting the role of the federal government in funding education, others disagreed, such as the National Commission on Excellence in Education, appointed by the president. The commission recommended that the federal government continue to support and fund American educational programs.[31]

One result of the federal cuts was that programs for gifted and talented children, as well as the Chapter 1 program to provide remedial education for poor and minority children, were adversely affected. The Chapter 1 program was cut by 23 percent, which meant that 500,000 students were affected. Funding for the Education of All Handicapped Children Act was also cut by 7 percent.[32] Overall, the federal spending for all levels of education decreased by 11 percent between 1980 and 1986. Ironically, at the same time, the *A Nation at Risk* report was issued by the commission, and Americans worried that their educational system was not making their students competitive with those in other countries.

A NATION AT RISK

The report *A Nation at Risk* focused on the improvement of educational reform standards so that the United States could compete effectively in the global marketplace.[33] Educators recognized that utilizing the schools to solve the nation's problems such as poverty and other social issues had conflicted with providing high educational standards and that schools could not effectively do both.[34]

The National Commission on Excellence in Education had synthesized data collected by university based administrators, professors, corporate officials, and politicians, all of whom were concerned with educational achievement of public school students.[35] It has been pointed out that although the data were gathered by social scientists, their interpretation was highly influenced by the business-oriented and conservative viewpoint of those involved with the commission. The report was subsequently followed by the Regents' Action Plan of New York State, and others. These all focused on the high schools, said to be the "weak link" in the American educational system.[36]

The report concluded that all subjects that could be considered frills, such as home economics, music, and art, should be eliminated from the curriculum. First, the schools should focus on mathematics and science, keeping in mind the aim of preparing American students to be competitive in the global market.

Second, teachers must be better paid, have increased autonomy, and be of better quality. Teacher education programs were said to be doing a substandard job of preparing the nation's teachers. It was recommended that colleges and universities revise their programs to remedy this situation.

Third, the school curriculum needed to be redesigned to meet the needs of the labor market.

Fourth, foreign language instruction should be a high priority for a global marketplace and should begin in elementary school, to help students more easily learn to become bilingual in a global economy.

Finally, the report recommended that students spend more hours in school, but on instruction only, not on any "frills." Debates persist to this day on whether the school day should be lengthened or if the school year should be longer, with a shorter summer vacation, or if it should be year-long.

THE CARNEGIE FOUNDATION REPORT

The Carnegie Foundation report appeared shortly after *A Nation at Risk* was released. Ernest Boyer, president of the Carnegie Foundation, stated that the high school curriculum needed to be redesigned in many ways. For example, science was to be taught so that all students understood how scientific discoveries can enhance and enrich their lives. Boyer stated that high school educators should stop "offering material intended for future scientists and engineers, which touches only a handful of our students."[37]

William Bennett, secretary of education under President Reagan, had expressed the view that students should study only Western cultures, because they represent the roots of our present culture. Boyer explained that social studies should be taught so that students could learn to integrate history, civics, geography, and economics.[38] Boyer expressed concern that if students studied only Western culture, it would not help them understand the global interdependence of the future and how the world would be different.[39]

Boyer addressed the issue of student behavior in his report by recommending mandatory community service as a part of the high school curriculum.

Boyer's predictions that testing would become increasingly important in education have come true with NCLB. He stated that "testing will suffocate school reform."[40] Rather than leave educational reform to what he called "the experts on leave from Mt. Olympus," Boyer recommended the school-based management movement, which emphasizes teacher-driven reform efforts.[41] Boyer's contributions to education are summarized in the "Shaper of Education" feature on page 256.

LEGISLATIVE POLICIES: RESPONSES TO *A NATION AT RISK*

Although Boyer's report received widespread attention, it did not lead to increased federal intervention in public education, unlike *A Nation at Risk*. President George H. W. Bush, the father of our current president, George W. Bush, took on the role

SHAPER OF EDUCATION

Ernest Boyer
(1928–1995)

- Seventh president of the Carnegie Foundation for the Advancement of Teaching
- Believed that learning could liberate people
- Stated that the high school curriculum needs reform but questioned certain aspects of *A Nation at Risk*
- Believed students need to understand how the subjects they are studying relate to their world
- Advocated that the needs of high school students be clarified—do they need material that is more appropriate for scientists and engineers, or more general knowledge?
- Recommended that social studies should be integrated with history, civics, geography, and economics
- Thought that students should study non-Western cultures, to understand the global interdependence of the future
- Stated that community service should be a required part of the high school curriculum, to increase responsibility and encourage good behavior
- Predicted that testing would become increasingly important, but would "suffocate school reform"

of the "education president" and formulated the Goals 2000 plan, which created national goals for education. To achieve these lofty goals, which began with "all children in America will start school ready to learn," the federal government had to start and maintain several programs, including Project Head Start, the Maternal and Child Health Block Grant Program, and Medicaid. These programs allow children of poor mothers to receive appropriate medical care and nutrition in infancy and early childhood.[42]

Whereas President Bush felt that parents should have the option of choosing between private and public schools for their children, President Clinton limited school choice to public schools. Clinton's rationale was that if parents took their children out of public school, it would create a system of failing public schools for the poor, and successful private schools for the rich. Parents could transfer their children out of a failing public school, into a public school with a higher success rate. Clinton's 1992 presidential campaign platform also tied the educational issue to economic concerns.

From 1993 to 2001, Clinton continued his predecessor's plan. The Goals 2000: Educate America Act was signed into law on March 31, 1994. It created the National Education Standards and Improvement Council to equalize education for the rich and the poor and also to negate the role of geography. Schools in states that spent less on education per child would have to teach the same standards as those that spent more per child. Thus, for instance, a child in one of the poverty-stricken Appalachian states would be able to achieve the same standard of learning as the richest child in the Central Park area of New York City.

National standards also make it necessary to specify exactly what students should know by a certain age or grade, which has political and legal implications, since students are not allowed any input into what they are learning. Thus, national standards may have the unintended effect of increasingly alienating students and distancing them from education.

The increasingly authoritarian and conservative views on public educational reform were highlighted in an important Supreme Court decision during the 1980s. In the 1982 case *Board of Education, Island Trees Union Free School District No. 26 v. Pico*, students from the Island Trees Union Free School District of New York complained that their First Amendment rights to free expression were violated when their board of education removed certain books from the junior and senior high school libraries.[43]

BRIDGES FROM THE PAST TO THE PRESENT

As Table 11–2 shows, the issues from the 1960s through the 1980s are still important today. Poverty and school segregation issues are still very much in the forefront, and the U.S. public school system continues to be criticized for poorly preparing students, particularly in math and science. The academic achievement of students in other countries is still said to be superior to that of American students, particularly in those subject areas.

From the *Trends in International Math and Science Study* results from 2003, some definite problem areas can be pinpointed. In high-poverty schools, eighth-grade students had lower average mathematics and science scores compared with eighth-grade students in public schools in more prosperous areas.[44] International comparisons with five Asian countries (China-Taipei, Hong Kong SAR, Japan, Korea, and Singapore) found that Asian eighth graders performed better than American eighth graders in science and mathematics in 2003.[45] Equally disturbing to those who believe that American students should be scoring higher in math and science

Table 11-2 **Comparison of Educational Issues in 1960–1983 and the Present**

1960 TO 1983	MODERN EDUCATION
In the 1970s and 1980s, schools were said to poorly prepare students for outside work.	Today, students do not score as well in math and science as students from other countries.
School segregation, especially in high-poverty schools, was an area of concern.	Schools are still segregated, and students in high-poverty schools do not score as high in math and science as students from wealthier schools.
Reports blamed "frills" in high school curricula for students' poor achievement.	More time is spent today on making sure students score high on the state standardized assessments than is spent on optional subject matter.
War on Poverty in the 1960s attempted to use schools and education to eliminate or reduce poverty in America.	Schools continue to struggle with the issue of poverty and its adverse effects on a child's ability to learn.
School funding was cut by 25 percent in the 1970s.	School funding is still a concern.

was the finding that eighth graders in Estonia and Hungary also did better than American eighth graders in those areas.[46]

SUMMARY

Chapter 11 focused on the educational reforms from 1960 to 1983. Each decade was marked by increasing federal intervention in education, which continues today with the No Child Left Behind Act.

QUESTIONS FOR DISCUSSION

1. Describe the pros and cons of the educational reforms of presidents George H. W. Bush in the 1980s and Bill Clinton in the 1990s.
2. Title IX of 1972 was supposed to prevent gender discrimination in educational institutions and in hiring practices. Do you believe Title IX has been effective? Why or why not? Provide evidence for your answer.
3. In your opinion, did the decreased student expectations and the more informal school climate contribute to student misbehavior and violence in schools? Why or why not? Give evidence to back up your answer.
4. In this chapter, you learned that William Bennett stated that students should study only Western culture, because it is the roots of our present culture. Do you agree with the statement? Why or why not?

5. In your opinion, what are the advantages and disadvantages of studying non-Western culture?

6. As a future teacher, what are your recommendations for reforming the high school curriculum? How do these compare with those of Boyer and the recommendations of the *A Nation at Risk* report of 1983?

7. Is it appropriate to compare American students' performance with that of students from other countries, when the cultures differ so widely? Give evidence for your answer.

8. Think of an experience you had with someone in your school years (elementary or high school) who had a physical or mental handicap. How was that individual treated by other students? Do you believe that the school and teacher(s) did the best they could to help that student, or could they have done more? Give evidence for your answer.

SUGGESTED ACTIVITIES

1. Interview two teachers, one with more than 20 years of experience, and one who has been teaching less than 10 years, to gain two perspectives on the reasons for student misbehavior in the classroom. Tabulate your findings and make a 20-minute PowerPoint presentation to your classmates.

2. Interview a principal who has been in education for at least 20 years to obtain his or her perspective on the reasons for the decline in student behavior. Does he or she agree with the idea that the lack of student expectations is partly to blame? Present your findings in either a three to five page report or a 15- to 20-minute PowerPoint presentation.

3. Interview a teacher who would likely be involved in exposing high school students to a study of non-Western culture such as a high school English or literature teacher, or a social studies teacher. Ask how he or she would plan a new curriculum for studying non-Western cultures. What materials would the teacher include and reject? Present the results of the interview to your classmates in the form of a 15- to 20-minute PowerPoint presentation, and also provide a handout.

4. Prepare a chart, using either PowerPoint or easel paper, illustrating the differences between Japanese and American culture, and explain why, in your opinion, it is (or is not) appropriate to compare American students' achievement levels to those of Japanese.

5. Interview a student with a handicap and his or her parent(s) or guardian(s) about the role they think the school is doing to help that student. Describe the student's disability (do not give any names), the effects of the disability on his or her daily life, and the school's response to the student. If the response is less than satisfactory, find out how the parents plan to resolve this situation. Write up the interview in question-and-answer format.

6. Interview a store manager or other personnel manager concerning that person's expectations of an employee, and also his or her opinion regarding the adequacy of the school system in preparing students for a responsible position in the business world. Ask the manager for his or her recommendations for improving the high school curriculum to meet the needs of business. Relate your findings to the class in a PowerPoint presentation or using other media.

7. This activity allows you to work together with your classmates. Assume you are part of a committee which is working to evaluate high school curricula. The task of each person on the "committee" is to evaluate the status of a subject area in a local high school, for instance, mathematics, or English, by answering the following questions:

   a. When was the subject matter curriculum last revised, and who revised it?

   b. What specific topics are included in each area?

   c. How were the revisions decided upon?

   d. What are the advantages and disadvantages of the revisions?

   e. When will the curriculum in that area be revised again?

   f. What recommendations do the teachers have about revising that curriculum area?

   g. How have the students responded to the curriculum revisions?

   Each person will present a summary of his or her answers to the set of questions to the class. Each presentation should take approximately 10 minutes and should include a one- to two-page handout.

8. Read the book *Our Guys* (see Suggestions for Further Reading in this chapter), and present a summary of the book to your classmates in a 20-minute PowerPoint presentation. Conclude your presentation with a list of recommendations for teachers to help them teach students how to appropriately treat others, specifically those with a handicap or disability.

Bibliography

Altbach, P. G. (1986). A nation at risk: The educational reform debate in the United States. *Prospects: Quarterly Review of Education, 16*(59), 337–47.

Angus, D., & Mirel, J. (1995). Rhetoric and reality: The high school curriculum. In D. Ravitch & M. A. Vinovskis (Eds.), *What history teaches us about school reform: Learning from the past.* Baltimore, MD: Johns Hopkins.

Berardo, F. M. (1990). Trends and directions in family research in the 1980s. *Journal of Marriage and the Family, 52*(4), 809–17.

Bishop, J. H. (1990). The productivity consequences of what is learned in high school. *Journal of Curriculum Studies, 22*(2), 101–26.

Bonner, T. N. (1958). Sputniks and the educational crisis in America. *Journal of Higher Education, 29*(4), 177–84, 232.

Brandt, R. (1988). On the high school curriculum: A conversation with Ernest Boyer. *Educational Leadership 46*(1), 4–9.

Burnham, M. (1989). Legacy of the 1960s: The Great Society didn't fail. *Nation, 249*(4), 122–24.

Carnegie Foundation for the Advancement of Teaching. (1988). *An imperiled generation: Saving urban schools.* Princeton, NJ.

A Conversation with Ernest Boyer. (1982, January/February). *Change,* pp. 18–21.

Dinkelman, T. (1990, Spring). Critical thinking and educational reform in the 1980s. *Illinois Schools Journal, 69*(2), 5–14.

Gecas, V., & Seff, M. A. (1990). Families and adolescents: A review of the 1980s. *Journal of Marriage and the Family, 52*(4), 941–58.

Giroux, H. (1988). Educational reform in the age of Reagan: Schooling for less. *Democratic Left, 16*(2), 7–9.

Hyman, R. T. (1980). Educational beliefs of the Supreme Court justices in the 1980s. *West's Education Law Reporter, 59*(2), 285–95.

Jarvis, P. S. (1990). A nation at risk: The economic consequences of neglecting career development. *Journal of Career Development, 16*(3), 157–71.

Jennings, J. F. (1987, October), "The *Sputnik* of the eighties. *Phi Delta Kappan,* pp. 104–9.

Milner, M., Jr. (1973). "Race, education, and jobs: Trends 1960–1970. *Sociology of Education, 46*(3), 280–81.

National Commission on Excellence in Education. (1983). *A Nation at Risk: The Imperative for Educational* Reform. U.S. Department of Education, Washington, DC.

Plisko, V. *The Condition of Education Report, 2003.* National Center for Education Statistics. Retrieved 2004, from *http://www.nces.ed.gov*

Plotnick, R. D. (1990). Welfare and out-of-wedlock childbearing: Evidence from the 1980s. *Journal of Marriage and the Family, 52*(3), 735–36.

Ravitch, D. (2000). *Left back: A century of failed school reforms.* New York: Simon and Schuster.

Reynolds, M. C. (1985). The special education of a drummer. *Journal of School Psychology, 23*(3), 205–16.

Rumberger, R. W. (1984). The job market for college graduates, 1960–1990. *Journal of Higher Education, 55*(4), 436–44.

Schreier, R. (1980). Parents, teachers and back to the basics. *Clearing House, 53*(6), 186–285.

Sorkin, A. L. (1976). The economic and social status of the American Indian, 1940–1970. *Journal of Negro Education, 45*(4).

Spring, J. (2000). *American education* (9th ed.). New York: McGraw-Hill.

Thompson, R. (1984, August 24) Status of the schools. *Education Report Card: Schools on the Line.* Washington DC: Congressional Quarterly.

Weber, M., & Murray, W. (1963). Another look at the culturally deprived and their levels of aspiration. *Journal of Educational Sociology, 36*(7), 320–21.

Wishnetsky, D. H. (2001). *American education in the 21st century.* Bloomington, IN: Phi Delta Kappa Educational Foundations.

Suggestions for Further Reading

In addition to the works cited in the bibliography, the following are suggested for further reading.

Lefkowitz, B. (1998). *Our guys*. New York: Vintage Books. A spellbinding true-life account of the rape of a retarded high school girl enrolled in special education classes in Glen Ridge, New Jersey, in 1986.

National Center for Education Statistics. (2003). *Highlights from the Trends in International Math and Science Study (TIMSS)*. Retrieved 2004 from *http://www.nces.ed.gov* This is a large report that can be downloaded in .pdf format.

Wilson, W. J. (1997). *When work disappears: The world of the new urban poor*. New York: Vintage Books.

Relevant Web Sites

American Association of University Women (AAUW) *http://www.aauw.org* Home page of the AAUW, which promotes educational equity for women and girls. Describes programs and initiatives for achieving educational equity in schools.

American Federation of Teachers *http://www.aft.org* Home page of the AFT. Includes salary scales for teachers, by state, and reports on educational issues.

Carnegie Foundation for the Advancement of Teaching *http://www.carnegiefoundation.org/* Home page of the Carnegie Foundation for the Advancement of Teaching, founded in 1906. Describes reform initiatives in K–12, undergraduate, and graduate education.

National Center for Education Statistics *http://www.nces.ed.gov* Information at the federal and state level relating to all topics in education.

National Education Association *http://www.nea.org* Home page of the National Education Association, with information on NCLB, ESEA, teacher preparation, and more.

Journal of American Indian Education *http://jaie.asu.edu/* At Arizona State University, information pertaining to education of Native Americans.

National Indian Education Association *http://www.niea.org/* Home page of the NIEA, which was founded in 1969 and is the oldest Indian education organization in the United States. Its goal is educational equity for all those of Native American ancestry.

No Child Left Behind Act *http://www.nclb.gov* Web site from the U.S. Department of Education explaining NCLB.

U.S. Department of Education *http://www.ed.gov* Home page of the U.S. Department of Education, for researching federal and state educational policies.

Endnotes

[1] Murray Milner, Jr., "Race, Education, and Jobs: Trends 1960–1970," *Sociology of Education, 46,* no. 3 (1973), 280–81.

[2] Ibid.

[3] Ibid., 295.

[4] Ibid., 297.

[5] Ibid.

[6] Max Weber & Walter Murray, "Another Look at the Culturally Deprived and Their Levels of Aspiration," *Journal of Educational Sociology, 36,* no. 7 (1963), 320–21.

[7] Ibid., 320.

[8] Russell W. Rumberger, "The Job Market for College Graduates, 1960–1990," *Journal of Higher Education, 55,* no. 4 (1984), 436–44.

[9] Ibid., 444.

[10] Ibid., 448.

[11] Alan L. Sorkin, "The Economic and Social Status of the American Indian, 1940–1970," *Journal of Negro Education, 45,* no. 4 (1976), 433.

[12] Diane Ravitch, *Left Back: A Century of Failed School Reforms* (New York: Simon and Schuster, 2000), 391–401.

[13] David Angus and Jeffrey Mirel, "Rhetoric and Reality: The High School Curriculum," in *What History Teaches Us About School Reform: Learning from the Past,* ed. Diane Ravitch & Maris A. Vinovskis (Baltimore, MD: Johns Hopkins, 1995), 300.

[14] Ibid.

[15] Ravitch, *Left Back,* 403–4.

[16] Roger Thompson, "Status of the Schools," August 24, 1984, *Education Report Card: Schools on the Line* (Washington DC: Congressional Quarterly), 14.

[17] Philip G. Altbach, "A Nation at Risk: The Educational Reform Debate in the United States," *Prospects: Quarterly Review of Education, 16,* no. 59 (1986), 340.

[18] Ibid., 340–41.

[19] Joel Spring, *American Education,* 9th ed. (New York: McGraw-Hill 2000), 136–37.

[20] Viktor Gecas and Monica A. Seff, "Families and Adolescents: A Review of the 1980s," *Journal of Marriage and the Family 52,* no. 4 (1990), 945.

[21] Ibid.

[22] Ibid., 946.

[23] Felix M. Berardo, "Trends and Directions in Family Research in the 1980s," *Journal of Marriage and the Family 52,* no. 4 (1990), 815.

[24] Ibid, 814.

[25] John F. Jennings, "The *Sputnik* of the Eighties," *Phi Delta Kappan* (October 1987), 104.

[26] Ibid.

[27] Ibid.

[28] Ibid., 105.

[29] Ibid.

[30] Ibid.

[31] Ibid., 106.

[32] Ibid.

[33] John H. Bishop, "The Productivity Consequences of What Is Learned in High School," *Journal of Curriculum Studies, 22,* no. 2 (1990), 101.

[34] Altbach, "A Nation at Risk," 340.

[35] Ibid.

[36] Ibid., 341.

[37] Ibid, 5.

[38] Ibid., 6.

[39] Ibid.

[40] Ibid., 8–9.

[41] Ibid., 9.

[42] Dan H. Wishnetsky, *American Education in the 21st Century* (Bloomington, IN: Phi Delta Kappa Educational Foundations, 2001), 108.

[43] Ronald T. Hyman, "Educational Beliefs of the Supreme Court Justices in the 1980s," *West's Education Law Reporter, 59,* no. 2 (1990), 286.

[44] National Center for Education Statistics, *Highlights from the Trends in International Math and Science Study (TIMSS), 2003, http://www.nces.ed.gov* (retrieved 2004).

[45] Ibid.

[46] Ibid.

Chapter 12

Solutions to the Problems of Public Education: Reform Movements After *A Nation at Risk* (1983–present)

Learning Objectives

1. Understand and analyze modern problems of education since the 1983 *A Nation at Risk* report.
2. Describe educational reform movements since *A Nation at Risk* report, especially No Child Left Behind.
3. Examine the advantages and disadvantages of homeschooling, charter schools, alternative schools, and privatization.
4. Analyze whether civil rights legislation has improved educational opportunities for women, girls, African Americans, and Native Americans.
4. Understand societal changes such as increased immigration, increased divorce rate, and increased single-parent families and the effects of these changes on children and schools.
5. Discuss reasons for the problem of disruptive and violent behavior in schools, including the furious child syndrome.
6. Describe ways to recruit qualified teachers to poorly performing schools.

INTRODUCTION

This chapter analyzes modern problems of public education, since the 1983 *A Nation at Risk* report was released and describes the ensuing educational reform movements. Problems of modern education include teaching highly disruptive children; attracting more qualified teachers to poorly performing schools; teaching bilingual students; gender discrimination issues; school segregation; and school funding issues.

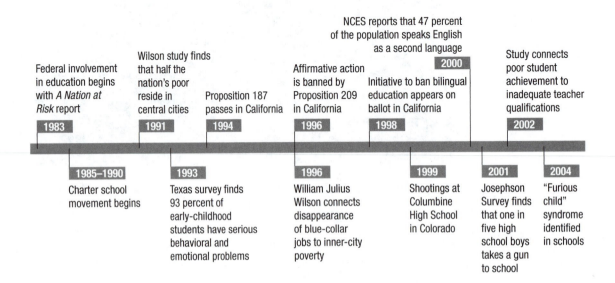

Studies during the 1980s concluded that reform efforts such as the Back to Basics movement prior to 1983 had not been successful.[1] Instead, schools focused on teaching math and science so that students could begin to catch up to students from Japan and other countries, who had higher scores on international measures of academic achievement. The issue of improving math and science education in public schools persists to this day.

This chapter analyzes issues pertaining to women's education and the problem of gender discrimination, which persists today despite the passage of Title IX in 1972. Furthermore, segregation still exists in America, despite the civil rights laws of the 1950s.[2] Schools in high-poverty areas are segregated both racially and economically.

Increased immigration has caused an increase in bilingual student enrollment in large city schools. Although these students speak many languages, Spanish is the most commonly spoken language. With more bilingual students, schools have had to implement bilingual education programs.

Reform movements since 1983 have emphasized more federal accountability. In this chapter, you will learn about the most recent federal legislation, the No Child Left Behind Act, which emphasizes testing of all students and holds schools and teachers accountable for student achievement. This puts pressure on those failing public schools to improve. Those schools that do not improve may be taken over and run for profit.

This chapter concludes with a look at current popular alternatives to public education: homeschooling, charter schools, alternative schools, and privatization.

As you read this chapter, you should be asking yourself: What solutions are the best for reforming the American public school system? A more troubling question is whether the American public school system can *be* reformed.

THE CURRENT STATUS OF AMERICAN PUBLIC EDUCATION

Individuals who want to pursue a teaching career may be discouraged from doing so by parents, relatives, and friends. Despite the teacher shortage, and as many teachers approach retirement age and decide to retire, teaching continues to be poorly regarded by many. John Goodlad, a renowned teacher educator at the University of Washington, has commented on the lack of respect that the American public has for teachers and has declared that the reform of teacher education is only one piece of a very complicated puzzle. His work is summarized in the "Shapers of Education" feature on page 273.

Why do we continue to hear that American public schools fail to teach students the basics, that teachers are not respected, that students fight in school and bully each other, that shootings occur in schools, that students leave without learning to read and write, and that U.S. students score poorly on the same tests that Japanese students pass? Critics of the American public educational system harshly evaluate the schools, and many believe that the system is hopelessly flawed and cannot be fixed. Consequently, alternatives to public education such as home schooling and charter schools have developed.

Table 12-1 **The Facts Behind School Criticisms**

ASSERTIONS	FACTS
Public education is beyond repair.	Only schools with inadequate funding are failing.
Teachers have poor grades and criteria for state certification is minimal.	States have raised the grade point average needed for certification from a 2.5 to a 3.0.
Schools lack resources to teach bilingual education and do not start teaching other languages to English-speaking students early enough.	Bilingual education is required by law, according to the Bilingual Education Act of 1968, and *Lau v. Nichols* decision of 1974. Some elementary schools teach a foreign language.
States vary too widely in evaluating students.	The federal government is attempting to develop national curriculum and national evaluation standards (NCLB).
Teacher wages do not match wages offered in the private sector.	There are efforts to increase pay, but the public does not often agree.

Although the analysis in this chapter cannot possibly be comprehensive enough to answer all aspects of this question, Table 12-1 summarizes the major criticisms of American public schools.

PROBLEMS OF PUBLIC SCHOOLS: DISCIPLINE AND VIOLENCE ISSUES

Discipline problems in classrooms and schools are very serious for teachers today. Societal changes in the last 20 years are thought by some to be responsible for this phenomenon. Critics cite the increase in single-parent families and an increased divorce rate as reasons for such behavior in schools. Critics also believe that the unavailability of parents or guardians, because they are busy with their own careers and financial problems, may be a major cause of frustration and anger among students who misbehave or are violent in school.

The behavior in schools mirrors what is occurring in our society. In the news, missing person reports abound, and domestic abuse is common.[3] Violence is seen by some individuals as a way to solve problems to which they cannot otherwise find solutions.

Neil Postman has described the "disappearance of childhood," or an increase in behaviors in children that were formerly seen only in adults. The demarcation between adulthood and childhood has gradually eroded, making it easier for children to emulate adult criminal activity.[4] Children and youth engage in activities once off-limits to them. For example, Postman cites the increased early sexual activity of American youth. He refers to the spread of venereal diseases; between 1956 and 1979, the percentage of 10- to 14-year-old youth diagnosed with gonorrhea increased from 17.7 per 100,000 population to 50.4 per 100,000 population.[5] In youth aged 15 to 19, the incidence of venereal disease has climbed from 415.7 per 100,000 to 1,211.4 per 100,000.[6]

Just as adults use violent means to solve their problems, so do American youth. They have become accustomed to violence through watching violent movies or playing graphically violent video games. Manufacturers have been criticized for marketing such games to impressionable youth. Some music today even suggests violence as a method of problem resolution. For impressionable teens, this message can be very dangerous, particularly if the adults in the home have no idea what is going on. That video games and other forms of media violence do indeed influence youth was dramatically demonstrated in the 1999 shootings at Columbine High School in Colorado. The two teenagers involved had repeatedly viewed violent video games and movies. Viewed as loners at school, they did not participate in any of the popular activities, such as sports. They spent a lot of time listening to violent music at home and watching violent media. These teenagers felt scorned by their classmates and alienated by the peer culture of Columbine, which centered on the popularity of athletes. After several years of this alienation, the two outcasts deliberately planned the shooting with the intent to commit harm. The definition of violence, in fact, is "a deliberate use or threat of physical force, against another person." The key word is *deliberate*. Some type of harm is intended; it is not accidental.[7] In fact, violent acts against strangers have increased for the first time since 1970.[8]

THE "FURIOUS CHILD PROBLEM": A NEW DISCIPLINE ISSUE IN SCHOOLS

In her recent book, *Home Alone America: The Hidden Toll of Day Care, Behavioral Drugs, and Other Parent Substitutes,* Mary Eberstadt, a research fellow for the Hoover Institution of Stanford University, describes the "furious child" problem.[9] Eberstadt states that the individuals involved in school violence, such as the Columbine teens, all had very little parental supervision. Eberstadt remarks that the parents of the Columbine teens did not know that their children were building war weapons at home. One of the boys had weapons concealed in his bedroom, although investigators found them easily when they searched them.[10]

The parents of both these boys did not know that their sons tortured animals, spent time on the Internet on questionable sites, and even threatened some of the neighbors.[11] The warning signs were there, but it seems few adults were paying any attention.

The students involved in the Columbine massacre did not appear to have had much emotional nurturing from their parents. Parental inattention and school violence or disruptive behavior in school are closely linked. Material comforts and luxuries do not make up for emotional distancing from parents.

Eberstadt's book also describes the alarming increase among violent behavior in kindergarten children. A 2003 survey of child-care centers, pediatricians, and elementary schools in the Fort Worth, Texas, area found that 93 percent of kindergarten children have significantly more severe behavioral and emotional problems than were apparent 5 years ago.[12] Day-care students bite, hit, and kick one another and these behaviors are fairly common.[13]

Bullying is a frequently occurring outward manifestation of anger. In a survey of 15,686 public and private school students, a third of them reported having been bullied. Approximately 30 percent of children reported that they had been involved in bullying. More students in the middle-school grades (grades 6 through 8) reported being bullied more often than students in the ninth and tenth grades. Bullying has been linked to poor grades and to abuse of alcohol or nicotine.[14]

Finding teachers who will tolerate a school climate in which bullying and disruptive behavior occur so frequently is difficult. One source for finding teachers to staff schools with discipline problems is the organization Teach for America, which hires new college graduates to teach in beleaguered inner-city schools; however, this approach often does not work well because the organization does not always provide these new teachers with the training they need to be successful in managing disruptive and unruly students. The example of Joshua Kaplowitz, a recent Yale graduate with a degree in political science, sounds a cautionary note about the consequences of this lack of training.

Kaplowitz was placed as a fifth-grade teacher at Emory Elementary School in Washington, D.C., and began teaching in September 2000. Some children there were so difficult to control that it was almost impossible for him to teach. These children displayed the behaviors consistent with the "furious child" syndrome, even as young as second grade. The preparation Teach for America provided in classroom management was completely inadequate. A great deal of time was spent on "sensitivity" training. Ultimately, the program did not simulate the training necessary to become an effective teacher.[15]

Ultimately, Kaplowitz was sued for $20 million by the mother of a boy who told his mother that Kaplowitz has pushed him out the classroom door, injuring his head and back. According to Kaplowitz, he merely let the student out of the classroom door so he could go to the restroom. Subsequently, the case was thrown out of court. This case underscores the need for children with behavior disorders to be either handled differently to reduce disruptions or placed in a school that specializes in the treatment of such problems.

As research continues on the "furious child," and doctors and scientists learn more about the physiological and psychological components of this problem, more information will become available to educators. Not enough information currently exists about how to treat children with these problems. Meanwhile, school districts are developing policies so that nondisruptive students are protected against violent confrontations by those students who routinely disrupt class and act out in anger and frustration.

DISCIPLINE ISSUES AND INDIVIDUALIZED EDUCATION PLANS (IEPS)

School administrators and teachers must consider what to do about students whose disruptive behavior has repeatedly been cause for concern. This question is especially crucial for students who have an Individualized Education Plan (IEP), owing to a learning disability or other problem. If a student is disruptive because of a disability, and he or she brings a gun to school, can the student be suspended or expelled, if that behavior is due to the disability? Many school administrators hesitate to expel students with IEPs because they believe that the student is protected under the 1997 IDEA amendments.[16] However, this interpretation of the IDEA amendments is incorrect, as they *do* permit schools to suspend or remove students with disabilities for weapons and drug offenses.[17]

It is important to understand the provisions of the IDEA amendments to prevent disruptive students with disabilities from harming themselves or others. Ultimately, the administrators in schools where there are large numbers of disruptive students, including students with IEPs, must develop zero-tolerance policies with regard to bullying, fighting, and bringing weapons to school. Those students with IEPs who have special needs but engage in this type of behavior will have two choices: They can be removed from the regular school and placed in a special educational setting, as Kaplowitz suggested, or they can be allowed to remain in the regular educational placement, but stricter policies for all students will need to be developed and enforced.

PROBLEMS OF PUBLIC SCHOOLS: ATTRACTING QUALITY TEACHERS

Although overall crime in schools has decreased, reports from the National Center for Education Statistics and other sources reveal that violent crime in schools has increased.[18] A report from the Josephson Institute of Ethics in 2000 found that in a study of 15,877 middle- and high school students, one in five high school boys took a weapon to school.[19]

In schools with high rates of crime, fighting, bullying, and poverty, it is difficult to retain well-prepared and certified teachers. This section looks at one of the difficulties in reforming American public schools: the crucial issue of attracting and retaining qualified teachers.

A report from the *Washington Times* states that students attending high-poverty schools are likely to be taught by poorly trained or uncertified teachers.[20] A 2002 study found that in schools where more then 20 percent of students scored at the lowest level on the fourth-grade English Language Arts (ELA) exam, 35 percent of the teachers failed the general-knowledge portion of the certification exam at least once.[21] The correlation between the percentage of students who obtained the lowest scores and the proportion of that school's teachers who are not certified to teach any of their current courses was 0.63.[22]

Studies also reveal that teachers prefer to work in schools close to where they grew up. They also prefer to work in areas with characteristics similar to those of their hometowns.[23] The geographic scope of labor markets is an often-ignored factor in recruiting qualified teachers for schools, particularly schools in urban areas with higher numbers of poor, non white, and low-performing students.[24] From 1999 to 2002, 61 percent of teachers in New York State began their teaching careers in schools only 15 miles from their hometowns, and 85 percent chose schools within 40 miles of their hometown.[25] A 1999 study found that about 40 percent of Pennsylvania teachers get teaching jobs in the same districts where they attended high school.[26] Overall, studies have shown that approximately 34 percent of new teachers begin their teaching careers in the school districts where they themselves were pupils.[27] Further, 87 percent of elementary school teachers find jobs less than 40 miles from home. The statistic for math and special education teachers is 84 percent, and for science teachers, 81 percent.[28]

These data mean that schools that are poorly funded, lack resources, and are located in impoverished urban areas will often be overlooked by new teachers seeking a first public school teaching job. Urban schools frequently have to bring in teachers from suburban or rural districts to staff their schools. For instance, in Buffalo, New York City, Rochester, and Syracuse (all of which are major metropolitan areas in New York State), school districts have had to import teachers to fill vacancies. It is often especially difficult to fill vacancies in special education, math, and science.[29]

Analysts in educational policy state that urban schools, which historically have graduated less qualified individuals who are less likely to attend college and become teachers, will have to take steps to break this cycle. Urban schools must offer prospective teachers the salaries and working conditions that are at least as good as, if not better than, those provided by the suburban districts that usually hire them, or these schools will continue to have difficulty hiring qualified teachers. One proposed solution has been to offer increased compensation to students enrolled in teacher education programs if they will agree to teach in urban areas.[30] Developing partnerships between the colleges and universities in urban areas and the schools in urban areas, may increase the number of available candidates for teaching in schools that have traditionally been difficult to staff.[31]

PROBLEMS OF SCHOOL FUNDING AND SCHOOL SEGREGATION

Schools in urban areas, as was mentioned earlier, often lack resources, including chalk, paper, and books. Schools with inadequate funding may lack computers and Internet access. With so many jobs today requiring at least rudimentary competence on the computer, students who attend these schools and infrequently use computers are not obtaining the type of education that will lead to well-paying jobs.

Schools in urban areas often tend to be segregated. Despite the 1954 *Brown v. Board of Education* desegregation decision, school boards have continued to find ways to erect barriers to equal educational opportunity. Inadequately funded urban schools often tend to enroll large numbers of minority or immigrant children and are more likely to be classified as high- poverty schools. The achievement record of Latino and African American high school seniors is dismal; their average reading and math skills are identical with those of eighth graders.[32]

In ethnographic studies of inner-city children, the educational critic Jonathan Kozol has pointed to the disastrous effects of inadequate school funding and school segregation on minority children in the urban areas. Kozol has interviewed children attending poorly performing, segregated schools in the communities of Mott Haven, a district in the South Bronx, New York City, and in East Saint Louis, Illinois. In both these settings, Kozol found that many children suffer from asthma, possibly caused by environmental pollution. These children, who often suffer from depression and may cry without any apparent reason, are acutely aware of their living conditions and have very mature insights on their situations.

John Goodlad

- Renowned teacher educator and advocate of teacher reform efforts at the University of Washington; now President of the Institute for Educational Inquiry.
- Author of more than 30 books on education, including *A Place Called School* (1984) and *In Praise Of Education* (1997).
- Believes that reform of teacher education programs is only one piece of a very complicated picture.
- Discusses the need for teachers to have true professional standing in American society.
- Believes that teachers need to have time to meet together and plan curricula, and there is no time for this during the school day or school year.

Jonathan Kozol

- Former teacher turned educational critic and author. He has written extensively about segregation and poverty in the public school systems, particularly in the Mott Haven section of the South Bronx, New York City, and East Saint Louis, Illinois, and their effects on children.
- Schools in these communities are deteriorating. In East Saint Louis, Illinois, Kozol noted that one school was located next to a sewage marsh, and the roof was caving in.
- In *Amazing Grace* and *Ordinary Resurrections,* Kozol describes the psychological and emotional impact of the living conditions of children in Mott Haven and how their parents or guardians cope with the grueling realities of everyday life. Concerns such as rats, broken elevators, and rundown apartment complexes with gangs and graffiti are all normal occurrences in Mott Haven.
- Kozol describes the outreach services in the community, most notably those available through St. Ann's Church, a nearby Episcopal parish. The dynamic young pastor, known as Mother Martha, has been instrumental in setting up an after school program for children in this school district. They receive help with homework, and the women of the church make sure they have enough to eat.
- Children in Mott Haven and other poor urban areas often have to visit their fathers "upstate," which is a euphemism for visiting them in prison.
- Kozol discusses the changes that have to be made in American society for children who are attending poorly performing, highly segregated urban schools to become successful. The recommendations are many, as the solution to this problem is highly complex and will take decades to achieve.

The work of Jonathan Kozol, as well as that of John Goodlad, is summarized in the "Shapers of Education" feature on page 273.

WHY ARE INNER-CITY SCHOOLS SEGREGATED AND POOR?

In his book *When Work Disappears: The World of the New Urban Poor,* William Julius Wilson explains that the problems of inner cities, including poorly funded schools, are directly due to the disappearance of blue-collar jobs with the globalization of the economy.[33] Recent news reports have focused attention on the disappearance of American jobs as companies find it cheaper to use labor overseas for many jobs. For instance, Dell Computer now operates its technical support service from Ireland rather than the United States.

When inner-city areas lose their economic support as factories close and fewer and fewer opportunities exist for employment, the schools in these areas also suffer. Wilson vividly describes the problems of public schools in economically troubled urban areas. In addition to being segregated, they are overcrowded, have poorly maintained physical facilities, and are staffed by teachers who often hold few expectations for their students.[34] The curricula are not relevant to the students' needs, and because these students are so familiar with an environment in which joblessness is endemic, they do not think outside of their immediate environment. Their social networks are concentrated in the ghetto areas, thus not allowing them any exposure to other socioeconomic groups with different values or ways of living.[35]

Elderly residents in poor urban areas reminisce about when department stores were open in their neighborhoods, grocery stores were available, and the streets were clean and safe.[36] Wilson interviewed one mother who said that she sent her 13-year-old son away, to live with his father out of town, because the gang members beat her son and threatened him. It was safer for him to leave the area.[37]

In 1991 about half of the nation's poor resided in central cities. The rapid population expansion in the central cities has occurred primarily in African American neighborhoods.[38] Racial segregation in the inner-city ghettos is due to racial practices such as zoning and the creation of massive public housing projects in low-income areas. Racially segregated ghettos are less conducive to employment, because residents of these ghettos are socially isolated and lack the education that would allow them to find jobs and move out of the area.[39]

Work for low-skilled workers has disappeared in many urban areas, making unemployment for low-skilled men a particularly acute problem. For instance, from 1987 to 1989, a low-skilled male worker would go without a job for nearly 9 weeks, whereas in 1967–1969, a low-skilled male worker could find a new job fairly quickly.[40] Table 12-2 summarizes statistical information on the job market for low-skilled workers.

In such urban areas as parts of Philadelphia, New York City, Chicago, and Detroit, jobs requiring less education have disappeared. Without work that they can do, poorer people in the inner cities will continue to be poor, and their schools will reflect the lack of nearby resources provided by manufacturing companies and other businesses that formerly provided employment for those who did not intend

Table 12-2 **Employment Opportunities for Low-Skilled Men in Urban Areas**

1967–1969	1987–1989	2005
Low-skilled male workers could find a new job fairly quickly.	Low-skilled male workers could spend nearly 9 weeks without a job.	Many jobs today require training in technology, which low-skilled workers may lack.
Many factories still existed in the inner cities, where low-skilled workers could find jobs.	Philadelphia lost 64% of manufacturing jobs, Chicago lost 60%, New York City lost 58% and Detroit lost 51%.	Work for less educated African American female workers in hospitals, child care, nursing care, and elementary schools has grown, with the growth of the social services industry.

to go on to college. The new work opportunities for those with limited training and education in the inner cities are in the service sector, including the health field, education, and welfare services. These jobs are traditionally held by women rather than men.[41] The social service industry has provided many less educated black female workers with employment in hospitals, elementary schools, child care, and nursing care. Without the growth of the social service industry, economists have concluded that inner-city poverty, and the state of inner-city schools, would be even worse than it is today.[42]

It is thought that federal and state governments will have to invest money to help deteriorating urban neighborhoods and schools; but without government incentives to start businesses in poorer neighborhoods that can provide jobs for people living there and the needed capital for the neighborhood public schools, this solution will probably not work in the long run.

GENDER DISCRIMINATION: IT'S NOT DEAD!

Minority groups, including immigrants, African Americans, and Native Americans, have traditionally been afforded fewer educational and economic opportunities than individuals from wealthier, Caucasian groups. In general, women, regardless of color, also have suffered from discrimination. Overall, women still earn less than men, are subject to sexual harassment on the job, and are often targeted by criminals, especially when traveling alone.[43] Girls and women frequently complain about sexual harassment in schools as well. This is completely unacceptable, because schools, whether public or private, are supposed to function as gender-neutral institutions dedicated to education without regard for other factors, such as sexual orientation or handicapping condition or disability.

Unfortunately, this utopian vision is seldom achieved. Females reading this section may recall being harassed in high school and feeling powerless, because nobody would take them seriously. This phenomenon is documented in Mary Pipher's book *Reviving Ophelia: Saving the Selves of Adolescent Girls*. Pipher, an experienced clinical psychologist who has interviewed many girls and their parents about the problems their daughters are experiencing in school, finds that girls and boys take different courses in schools. Fewer girls than boys take courses in physics or chemistry, and fewer girls than boys take advanced courses in mathematics. The math and science scores of girls drop, as do their IQ scores. Furthermore, girls may suffer from depression, eating disorders, and a lack of self-esteem that may lead them to self-mutilation and even such drastic steps as running away from home.[44] Pipher points out that American culture leads girls to focus on what she calls "lookism," which is defined as evaluating someone strictly on the basis of that individual's appearance.[45] Girls may worry more about their body image than their career plans or their school studies. Furthermore, adolescent girls (and adolescents in general) may turn away from their parents for guidance and focus on their peers instead, who encourage them to participate in the values of the mass culture. Some knowledge of this developmental phenomenon is required for teachers to be able to understand adolescent behavior.

It is helpful for future teachers to think about how gender discrimination has affected them or someone they know. Suggestions for further research on gender discrimination are found at the end of this chapter, as are Questions for Discussion. Educational equality cannot be achieved without adequate attention to gender discrimination issues or the needs of individuals with disabilities or special needs, which are discussed next.

SPECIAL EDUCATION LEGISLATION: IDEA OF 1997

The Individuals with Disabilities Education Act (IDEA), which is administered by the Office of Special Education Programs, was passed in 1997. IDEA is the amendment to the 1975 Education of All Handicapped Children Act, which mandated an appropriate, free public education for all children in the least restrictive environment possible. The phrase "least restrictive environment" means that students with special needs such as learning problems, emotional difficulties, or physical limitations, are supposed to be placed in the most normal environment possible, which is the regular classroom.

Although learning disabilities appear to be the most common problem plaguing students today, other conditions also cause students to be referred for special education services. These conditions include orthopedic problems such as cerebral palsy or spina bifida, both of which can severely limit mobility or the ability to perform certain psychomotor activities; visual problems, including low vision or partial blindness; hearing problems, such as partial or complete deafness from a variety of causes; and physical limitations such as cystic fibrosis or juvenile diabetes.

Although students with disabilities are supposed to be included in the public school educational system whenever possible, difficulties with special education placements remain. Increasing numbers of students require special education services, but inadequately funded school districts may be unable to provide such services. Despite funding difficulties and a shortage of special education teachers, students with disabilities are placed in regular education classrooms for at least 80 percent of the day. This is especially true for students with specific learning disabilities, as these students make up 20 to 45 percent of the population of students with disabilities.[46]

One of the problems faced by educators, especially now that the No Child Left Behind Act requires annual testing, is testing students with disabilities. Students with disabilities are supposed to be tested to ascertain that their education has successfully prepared them to pass the tests, regardless of their format. Both NCLB and IDEA emphasize providing appropriate instructional and statewide assessment accommodations. Students with disabilities are supposed to be included in school, district, and statewide accountability systems.[47] However, according to a two-part study investigating the extent and focus of statewide training to help teachers learn accommodations practices, states lack the staff development training programs needed to help school personnel understand the need for, as well as the implications of, the statewide assessment accommodations.[48]

One of the difficulties identified by this study, conducted by the State Collaborative on Assessment and Student Standards (SCASS), was that students with disabilities need to have instructional accommodations linked to the statewide assessment accommodations. States are working toward an agreement on what the accommodations should include, and so far they have described setting (lighting, furniture, location) and presentation (Braille, large print, audio prompts, visual magnification devices, markers to keep one's place).[49]

The SCASS found that although all states have policies that specify that assessment accommodations for students with disabilities are to be used, these assessment accommodations may not be used correctly, or the accommodations themselves may be incorrect.[50]

A report by Thurlow, Wiley, and Belinski, published in 2003, analyzed state reports from 2000–2001 to determine the extent to which states publicly report information about students with disabilities in statewide assessments. This report found that the number of states reporting both participation and performance results for students with disabilities on *all* tests increased from 16 to 28.[51] The study also found that 16 states reported test results for students with disabilities on at least *some* of the state assessments.[52] It is clear that although IDEA mandated that all states publicly report participation and performance information for students with disabilities, states appear to have had problems following these requirements. Suggestions for more effective data reporting include (1) providing data no more than 6 months after the test is administered and (2) reporting data for the performance of general education students as well as performance on alternative assessments.[53]

Directors of special education and directors of assessment in school districts are responsible for reporting participation rates of students with disabilities to their state. States vary in the ways they report participation rates to the government, because the methods used to calculate participation rates vary. Some states report enough numerical information to calculate participation rates, whereas others simply report the number of students with disabilities who were tested.[54]

States now must report on the participation rates and the performance results of students who cannot take the general assessment, even with accommodations.

Such students, who require the alternative assessment, are supposed to be represented in the reports. In the 2000–2001 alternative assessment data for students with disabilities, half the states did not report their performance. States are required to define minimum subgroup sizes for reporting and accountability according to the reporting requirements of No Child Left Behind.[55]

Because NCLB is still in effect, concerns over reporting performance and participation rates for students with disabilities will likely continue. Clearly, the issue is one that needs to be carefully studied so that the students receive the best type of instructional modifications as well as the best form of assessment device.

Students with limited English proficiency are also affected by the new testing requirements because English is their second language. How does the American public school system serve these students?

BILINGUAL EDUCATION IN THE PUBLIC SCHOOLS

At the turn of the century, bilingual education was unknown. Studies of immigrant education, as reported in sources such as the *Pittsburgh Survey,* in the early 1900s, describe the approach to teaching children as "immersion." Students were put in regular classrooms with children who did speak English, and they had to "pick it up" little by little. They did not have special services to help them, as is commonplace today. In the 1960s, students dropped out of school because they could not understand their instruction, which was in a foreign language. In 1968, the *Bilingual Education Act* was passed, mandating instruction in two languages for non-English-speaking students. However, many school districts still did not provide their students with limited English proficiency with instruction appropriate for their needs until 1974 and the *Lau v. Nichols* decision. The San Francisco school district was sued because it did not provide remedial instruction in English to high school students, which violated their civil rights. Subsequently, bilingual education was taken more seriously. Today, school districts have to provide students with LEP with English instruction as well as instruction in their native language.

The National Center for Education Statistics provides information on the number of students in U.S. public schools with limited English proficiency. According to the NCES report of 2001–2002, 47 states and the District of Columbia reported the number of students classified as English Language Learners (ELL). In Texas and California, both of which have large Spanish-speaking populations, the number of LEP students receiving remedial instruction in English is very high. In California, 1.5 million ELL students were receiving English language services. This amounted to approximately one fourth of all students in the state of California. In Texas, more than half a million, or one in seven students, received ELL services.[56]

NCES reported that in 1990, 32 million people over age 5 spoke a language other than English in their home. This figure increased to 47 million by the year 2000, meaning that nearly 18 percent of the total U.S. population was speaking a language other than English.[57] Most of the students who are classified as ELL are found in the western states; schools in the West identified 1.7 million students as being ELL in 1999–2000, compared with 1.1 million students in 1993–1994.[58] In

1999–2000, the Midwest still had the lowest percentage of ELL students in the public schools, compared with the western states and the southern states. The Northeast actually experienced a decline in the percentage of ELL students enrolled in public schools.[59]

The U.S. Department of Education has established the Office of English Language Acquisition, Language Enhancement, and Academic Achievement for Limited English Proficient Students (OELA to promote high-quality education for America's population of English language learners). The emphasis of this office is on high academic standards, school accountability, professional development, family literacy, early reading, and partnerships between parents and communities.[60]

The No Child Left Behind Act of 2001 gives states and school districts a strong reason to participate in the National Assessment of Educational Progress (NAEP).[61]

NATIONAL ASSESSMENT OF EDUCATIONAL PROGRESS (NAEP) AND NCLB

Since 1969 the NAEP has assessed students' performance in various subject areas and evaluated the conditions and progress of the nation's and individual states' student education at grades 4, 8, and 12. These tests measure only academic achievement and only public school students take them.[62]

NAEP is now strongly connected with NCLB as well as with other federal legislation. States applying for Title I grants from the federal government must administer the biennial tests to fourth and eighth graders in reading and mathematics. These tests are paid for by the federal government.[63] Past assessments have included tests in science, mathematics, reading and writing, but as of 2002–2003, only the long-term trend in students' reading and mathematics performance will be assessed.[64] NAEP scores are reported in two formats: scale scores and achievement levels. Scale scores give a numeric summary of students' knowledge and performance levels in a particular subject, by groups and subgroups. Achievement levels categorize students' achievement as basic, proficient, and advanced based on a set of criteria.

The results of the 2003 NAEP are far too comprehensive to address in one chapter; suggestions for further research into this topic appear at the end of the chapter. Results for the 2003 assessment for Hispanic students are summarized in Table 12-3.[65]

African American or Native American students also scored below the basic level on the 2003 NAEP reading assessment. Poverty and proficiency in English affect these results. Suggestions for further research into this topic appear at the end of the chapter.

Educators are concerned not only about the performance of ELL students and others who score poorly on the NAEP assessments; they are also concerned about the general performance of students in math and science, particularly in relation to that of their international peers in these same areas.

Table 12-3 **NAEP Assessments for Hispanic Students**

- Fifty-seven percent of the nation's Hispanic students are reading at or below the basic proficiency levels.
- Only 14 percent of the nation's Hispanic students are at or above the proficient level.
- In nearly all states the percentage of Hispanic students who read below the basic proficiency level is higher than the percentage of white students who read below the basic proficiency level.
- In 1999, Hispanic students had higher reading, mathematics, and science scores on the NAEP than they did in the 1970s, but the NAEP performance was lower than that of white students.
- Hispanic students are the fastest growing population in the schools today. As of 2005 the Hispanic population in the schools exceeded the African American population.
- States have to test students who are identified with a disability and those who are English Language Learners (ELL).
- In 2002, NAEP started to report results for all students, including those who are ELL and those who need special education services.[66]

OVERVIEW OF MATH AND SCIENCE EDUCATION ACHIEVEMENT: THE TIMSS

The Trends in International Math and Science Study (TIMSS) in 2003 was the third comparison of math and science achievement carried out by the International Association for the Evaluation of Educational Achievement (IEA). IEA is an international organization of international research institutions and governmental research agencies.[67] The TIMSS was developed to assess students' understanding of math and science concepts, based on their school curricula.[68] TIMSS surveyed fourth graders in 1995 and 2003, and eighth graders in 1995, 1999, and 2003.[69]

In 1999, American eighth graders achieved an average score of 502 in mathematics, and 515 in science, whereas Singapore outperformed the United States in mathematics with a score of 604. Chinese Taipei, Singapore, Korea, Japan, Australia, the Netherlands, and the Slovak Republic also scored higher than the United States in both math and science assessments on TIMSS.[70] In 2003 Singapore scored 594 on the TIMSS, whereas the United States scored 518. Fourth graders in Singapore, Chinese Taipei, Japan, Hong Kong Special Administrative Republic (SAR), and England all outperformed American fourth graders. Thus, although American fourth graders did score higher than the international average, they still did not score as high as the top three countries on the list.[71]

Table 12-4 gives statistical data on the TIMSS.

A COROLLARY TO TIMSS: TRENDS IN SCHOOL VIOLENCE

TIMSS sampling data were used to report incidences of school violence during 1995 to 1999. The types of violence listed by school principals as areas of concern for their schools were vandalism; theft; weapon use or possession; inappropriate sexual behavior; intimidation or verbal abuse of teachers/staff; physical injury to other

Table 12-4   **Third Trends in International Math and Science Study Results (1995, 1999, 2003)**

1995	1999	2003
Fourth and eighth graders were surveyed.	Eighth graders were surveyed.	Fourth and eighth graders were surveyed.
Black fourth graders in 1995 scored 457 in math. The average fourth-grade score for U.S. students was 542.	Average score was 502 in math and 515 in science.	Average for fourth graders in math was 495, black fourth graders scored 472. Fourth graders in highest poverty schools scored 96 points lower than fourth graders in wealthier schools.
White and Hispanic fourth graders had no measurable difference in scores in 1995 or 2003.	Singapore students scored 604 in math.	Singapore scored 594, the highest in 2003.
Boys and girls had no statistically significant difference in math scores.	Sixty-five percent did science experiments, thought to contribute to higher scores.	Math and science scores improved among boys and girls and all racial groups since 1995.

students; physical injury to teachers or staff; alcohol use/possession; illegal drugs use/possession. The first four (vandalism, theft, weapon use or possession, and inappropriate sexual behavior) were reported with the same frequency for eighth graders in both 1995 and 1999. Offenses reported less often by 1999 were intimidation or verbal abuse of other students, teachers, or staff, and physical injury to other students, teachers, or staff.[72] From grades 4 to 8, vandalism was reported more frequently than physical threats to other students. By eighth grade, alcohol use or possession and illegal drug use or possession are reported more frequently than for twelfth graders. TIMSS data reveal that as students get older, problems with drug and alcohol use and possession become more prevalent than interpersonal conflict issues.[73] Students thus appear to try to resolve their problems by using mood-altering and illegal drugs or drinking alcohol to increase their self-esteem and to deal with stresses at school and at home.

Students who score poorly on the TIMSS and the annual assessments required by NCLB may become very frustrated, particularly if they are enrolled in schools without the funding necessary to sufficiently prepare them for these tests. The problem is that all states must conform to the NCLB Act, even if there is not enough funding for them to do so.

FUNDING OF PUBLIC EDUCATION: THE EFFECTS OF NCLB

In January 2003, the Bush administration celebrated the first anniversary of the NCLB. Five states: Colorado, Indiana, Massachusetts, New York, and Ohio had submitted their school accountability plans to the U.S. Department of Education with specific written guidelines for ensuring that students in public elementary and secondary schools make yearly progress in reading and math.[74] States are allowed some flexibility and variety in implementing the requirements of NCLB into their accountability systems. The Department of Education has given states the guidelines on how to implement such programs as Teacher Quality, Supplemental Services, Public School Choice, Transferability, Reading First, 21st Century Community Learning Centers, Technology, and English Language Acquisition Programs.[75] States have also implemented the concept of public school choice as they have adapted to the policies specified in NCLB. This concept means that parents of students in low-performing schools have the option of transferring to better public schools if they choose to do so.[76]

NCLB requires all states to annually test all children in grades 3 through 8 in reading and mathematics, beginning in fall, 2005. Current law requires that students be tested only three times in these same subjects.[77] Although critics have been complaining since 2002, when the law was signed into action, that there is not enough funding for testing, the Bush administration maintains that enough money was allotted ($387 million in the 2003 budget). President Bush has stated that schools should be accountable for the money they spend. Instead of spending money on educational fads, they should spend money on what works, and they should demonstrate results.[78]

The 2004 budget proposal increased funding for the Reading First and Early Reading First programs by $75 million over the first year of NCLB, to a total of over $1.1 billion, so that children will learn to read by the end of third grade. The Early Reading First program is intended to help children learn to improve their pre-reading skills while they are enrolled in preschool programs. The 2004 budget also was to provide an additional $1 billion, a 9 percent increase, for the Title I program, which helps support educational programs in the neediest public schools.

In 2003, $412 million in funding was distributed among 20 states so that they could fund the Reading First program. These grants will be used by school districts to support scientifically based strategies to improve pre-reading skills of children in early childhood development programs, by focusing on the development of verbal skills, phonological awareness, and letter knowledge.[79]

State legislators and educators continue to declare that they do not have enough funding to make all the changes needed to fulfill the requirements. The NEA reported in 2004 that per-pupil spending for education would have to increase by 3.6 percent through 2004 if all the requirements of NCLB were to be achieved.[80]

People for the American Way, a liberal group that monitors political funding policies for public education, has reported the administration's funding plans for NCLB are inadequate. In 2002 the programs were underfunded by $4.2 billion, and in 2004 the fiscal appropriations for NCLB fell short by $8 billion. The 2004 budget proposed the elimination of 46 public education programs, including Rural Education, the National Writing Project, Arts in Education, Native American Education programs, and dropout prevention programs. About $75 million of federal money was diverted into voucher programs, and $226 million was given away in revenues to fund tax-credit vouchers for public schools.[81]

One criticism of NCLB is that funding inequalities may contribute further to school segregation. Dr. Christopher Edley, professor of law and co-director of the Civil Rights Project at Harvard University, has criticized the NCLB budget because it will cut funding for a large percentage of poor and minority students.[82]

Ultimately, the success of NCLB in improving the performance of failing schools and helping students learn better will be directly related to funding the required reforms. In 2004 President Bush requested a "massive increase" in funding for this law; however, many Democrats have criticized the funding for NCLB and have stated that states cannot possibly implement the required reforms with so little funding.[83] As of April 20, 2005, the NEA and eight school districts in Michigan, Texas, and Vermont had sued the U.S. Department of Education over NCLB. In their lawsuit they allege that NCLB violates a passage in the law stipulating that states cannot be forced to spend their own money to meet educational requirements, yet that is clearly what is happening.[84] The Utah state legislature has also challenged this law.[85]

Wealthier parents who can afford to pay as much as $1997 per child are now electing to hire tutors from the federally financed tutoring industry to prepare their children for the required NCLB tests. These companies are offering gift certificates and computers to encourage parents to sign up their child for tutoring. However, they do not guarantee that the child will receive a quality tutor; in some cases, the tutors they send have not yet graduated from high school![86] The lack of regulation among these tutoring industries means that they will make a lot of money but will not necessarily be required to follow any guidelines. This unforeseen growth of the private tutoring industry appears to be directly connected to NCLB and the new annual testing requirements.

Some parents have chosen to deal with this situation by opting out of the public school educational system and turning to other alternatives, such as homeschooling and charter schools or using the voucher plans to send their children to schools of their choice.

HOMESCHOOLING: BACK TO THE FIRESIDE?

Homeschooling, in which parents teach their own children at home, dates to colonial America, as described in earlier chapters. There are many reasons why parent(s) or guardian(s) may want to teach their children at home. One frequently cited reason is that the public schools do not promote values such as courtesy, listening to adults, and not fighting with each other.

Data from the National Household Education Surveys Program (NHES), collected in 1999 and 2003, reveal that the number of homeschooled students increased from 850,000 in 1999 to 1.1 million students (1,096,000) in 2003, or about 2.2 percent.[87] Homeschooled students are defined as those who are enrolled in school only part-time or not more than 25 hours a week. Students who were being taught at home because of a temporary disability, such as a broken leg, are not counted as homeschoolers. Students who have been taught at home for at least part of their education are also considered to have been homeschooled.[88]

The 2003 survey requested that parents give reasons for homeschooling their children. Thirty-one percent said the major reason for homeschooling was concern about the environment of public or private schools; 30 percent cited religious or moral instruction; and 16 percent cited poor academic instruction at public or private schools.[89]

Is homeschooling the only venue in which values can be taught? Some educators, particularly those who subscribe to progressive educational beliefs, think that public education can and should teach students how to become good citizens as well as moral human beings. These educators, including John Dewey, point out that merely imparting academic knowledge is not enough; educators have to know how students' character traits, such as perseverance, accuracy, honesty, courage, and thoroughness, interact with students' understanding of the academic material. Dewey gave the example of teaching the chemical properties of dynamite to two different individuals. One will become a chemist, whereas the other will embark on a career as a safecracker![90] Although the same academic knowledge is transmitted to each individual, how that individual absorbs that knowledge is related to his or her aims, goals, and habits. Home schooling, with its one-on-one attention to students, allows more time to be spent assessing the student's personality and character traits to individualize the academic content and ensure that the student uses any acquired knowledge for constructive rather than destructive purposes.

Although critics argue that the public schools are not the proper places to teach values and moral education, because it is so difficult to precisely define what values should be taught, they do wonder if morals might not be a prerequisite to intellectual knowledge. Such morals include temperance, courage, honesty, fairness, and friendship.[91]

MORALS OF AMERICAN YOUTH

In 2004 the Josephson Institute of Ethics, a nonprofit corporation in Los Angeles, California, surveyed 24,763 high school students and found that nearly 62 percent had cheated on exams, 27 percent had stolen something from a store within the past year, and 40 percent said they had lied to save money.[92] Despite such dismal findings, 74 percent rated their own ethics as being higher than those of their peers.[93] The study revealed that high school students, particularly males, believe that "in the real world, successful people do what they have to do to win, even if others consider it cheating."[94] With regard to ethics and character, 98 percent of high school students agreed that it was important for them to be "a person of good character," and 97 percent reported that "it's important to me that people trust me."[95]

In the Josephson Institute survey, 82 percent of students admitted lying to a parent within the past 12 months, and 62 percent admitted lying to a teacher within the past year. Cheating was widely reported; 62 percent reported that they had cheated during a test at school in the past year, and 38 percent had done so at least twice. This figure was a decrease from the 74 percent who said they had cheated on an exam in the 2002 survey.[96] The researchers concluded that public schools need to spend more time instilling better attitudes toward integrity so that honesty and integrity become lifelong habits for students.[97]

So what happens if parents or guardians disagree with the type of values that a public school is imparting to their children? Under NCLB, parents or guardians can move their children to schools of their choice under a voucher plan.

VOUCHERS

Vouchers have existed since the 1700s to help students in remote areas attend public or parochial schools.[98] Today, vouchers are used as a means of educational reform. In the voucher plan, the typical per-student state allotment goes to the school of the student's choice, rather than to the local public school district. Whatever money is not funded by the voucher has to be paid by the student's family. Vouchers are also funded by state, local, and/or private funding sources.[99]

The Compulsory Education Act, passed by the State of Oregon in 1922, required all children from ages 8 to 16 to attend a public school. Students who did not attend a public school would be charged with a misdemeanor. The Society of Sisters challenged this law, and in the 1925 *Pierce v. Society of Sisters* case, the U.S. Supreme Court agreed that it was acceptable for parents to send their children to private schools if they chose. In the 1930 case *Cochran v. Louisiana State Board of Education,* the Supreme Court declared that the state of Louisiana could provide free secular textbooks for all students, even those students enrolled in religious schools.[100] In 1955 the conservative economist Milton Friedman introduced vouchers for education. He said that in schools that were part of an educational market, resources would be used more efficiently than in schools run by the government (that is, public schools). Friedman argued that if parents were able to apply the money used to send their children to public school to the school of the parents' choice instead, it would greatly improve educational efficiency.[101]

Vouchers have also been used to get around school desegregation attempts. In 1956 the Virginia state legislature's response to the *Brown v. Board of Education* decision was to create a tuition grant, so that students in the state of Virginia could attend any nonsectarian school in the state and thus avoid attending the newly integrated schools if they chose. The idea of vouchers continues to be popular because schools have continued to fail. If schools were all succeeding at graduating students who could read and write, and if schools had no incidents of violence, then vouchers would not be an issue. That they remain under consideration as an alternative indicates that public education has failed to improve to the point where all Americans feel safe putting their children in public schools.

The U.S. Supreme Court put the voucher concept permanently on the map when it upheld the June 2002 decision of *Zelman v. Simmons-Harris* in Cleveland, Ohio.[102] This case revolved around the pilot program of the state of Ohio to provide educational choices to families with children who lived in the Cleveland City School District. Judge Rehnquist of the U.S. Supreme Court ruled that this pilot program did not violate the establishment clause of the U.S. Constitution because the 75,000 children enrolled in the Cleveland City School District were attending school in a district that had been cited as among the worst performing public schools in the country.[103] In fact, the federal district court had placed the entire

Cleveland school district under state control in 1995. The district had not met any of the 18 state standards for minimal acceptable performance.[104]

In 1990, John Chubb and Terry Moe advocated school choice in their book *Politics, Markets, and America's Schools.* Chubb and Moe reiterated that if schools had to operate in a marketplace where parents had a choice, the better performing schools would automatically be selected, leaving the poorer performing schools to close.[105]

NCLB provides for school choice. Parents can transfer their children out of failing schools and into better performing schools and can also use part of the Title I federal funds to obtain tutoring, after-school help, or weekend classes. The federal E-rate program provides funding for private and religious schools to implement computer technology and online learning programs.[106]

The "child benefit theory," which states that the welfare of the child should take precedence over all other concerns, has greatly helped the voucher plans. If it benefits a child to transfer to a parochial school, then the child should transfer if it is in his or her best interests.

Table 12-5 summarizes the status of the voucher plans in use in Milwaukee, Wisconsin, Cleveland, Ohio, the state of Florida, New York City, and Washington, DC.

The positive note about vouchers is they provide children attending failing public schools with the choice to attend another school. On the negative side, vouchers may do nothing to improve the conditions of failing urban schools, which already lack necessary resources for education, including technology. Instead, these schools will be shut down, and schools may well become even more economically and racially segregated. More research is necessary in order to determine the long-term effectiveness of voucher programs across the United States. One question in the research is how to define a child's race, especially for children of mixed race, which has led to some statistical debate.

An early type of school choice program was known as the *magnet school.* Magnet schools are still in existence today and are very attractive to many parents and students. Magnet schools and charter schools and their place in today's educational system are described next.

MAGNET SCHOOLS AND CHARTER SCHOOLS

In 1968 the first magnet school, McCarver Elementary in Tacoma, Washington, allowed students from anywhere in the city of Tacoma to enroll. The second magnet school opened in Boston in 1969. These magnet schools were designed to use market forces to desegregate public schools peacefully.[107] By offering a certain type of curriculum, magnet schools would attract students of all ages and races, no matter where they were located or which type of students they usually enrolled. These curricular offerings can include performing arts, Montessori, advanced math, science, and technology. Such schools have included the Thomas Pullham Creative and Performing Arts magnet school, in Prince George County, Maryland, and the School 59 Science magnet in Buffalo, New York, also known as the "Zoo School."[108]

Table 12-5 **Overview of Voucher Plans in Use**

PROGRAM	REQUIREMENTS	RESULTS
Milwaukee, Wisconsin; Parental Choice Program (MPCP), is the most established. Grew to 10,882 students at 106 schools in 2001–2002.	Vouchers are given to low-income families so they can enroll their children in sectarian private schools.	Harvard researchers found students had statistically significant gains in reading and math; Princeton researchers found gains in math, not reading.
Cleveland, Ohio; Ohio Pilot Project School Program, started in 1995 by the Ohio General Assembly	Scholarships are given to children who attend school districts under state control. Preference is given to families with incomes below 200% of the poverty level, with a charge of $2,500 per child.	Peterson and Howell report significant positive results for African American students after 2 years in Dayton, Ohio: an increase of 7 percentile points on the math portion of the ITBS.
Florida; The entire state uses vouchers in the A+ Opportunity Scholarship program, begun in 1999.	Vouchers are given to students who have attended schools designated as failing for 2 years, in a 4-year period. Schools are graded from A to F.	Evaluations conducted by Florida State, Harvard, and the Manhattan Institute have concluded that the program has forced failing schools to improve
New York City; Begun in February 1997 by School Choice Scholarships Foundation, a private foundation.	Children of low-income families attending public schools in grades K–4 are awarded $1300 scholarships, each worth up to $1400 per year for 3 years.	Peterson and Howell found significant positive gains after 1 to 3 years.
Washington, DC; First federally funded program	Grants of at least $7500 each for use at private or religious schools in next 5 years.	Legislation signed June 2004, so data are still being collected.

By 1981 there were 1000 magnet schools in the United States, and in 1991, more than 2,400 magnet schools were in operation. These schools were successful at attracting white students if the school structure and racial composition had certain characteristics. The most popular magnet school structure was the *dedicated magnet,* in which all those enrolled wanted to be there and had signed up to attend. Most of these students were white. Parents and students searching for this type of magnet school would be less likely to find it than the other type of magnet school, in which a magnet school has been developed and is housed within a regular school building. This second type of magnet school was less popular and was usually found in black neighborhoods. The population involved in the magnet school curriculum was usually 50 percent white, while the remainder of the school population not in the magnet curriculum was minority.[109]

Magnet schools represent an alternative for parents who wish to enroll their children in schools with special curricula. Enrolling children in schools with curricula that emphasize certain skills, such as musical or scientific ability, can be very attractive to many parents who are advocates of school choice.[110] Today, magnet schools receive help from the federal government. The Magnet Schools Assistance Program (MSAP), which was included in the Education for Economic Security Act of 1985, is now administered by the Office of Innovation and Improvement in the U.S. Department of Education.[111] As of 2000–2001, the latest year for which statistics appear to be available,[112] according to the National Center for Education Statistics, Los Angeles Unified School District had 124 magnet schools (18.8%), and Puerto Rico Department of Education had 151 (9.8%). The Chicago School District had 280 magnet schools, or 46.5%, with 50.4% of students in magnet schools.[113] These school districts have the largest numbers of magnet schools in the United States.

Charter schools are another alternative to poorly performing public schools. Charter schools are public schools of choice.[114] These schools are chosen because of the makeup of their student population and their location. A higher percentage of African American fourth grade students attend charter schools than other public schools in central cities.[115] Although public funds are used to operate charter schools, they are run independently and are not required to follow many of the state laws and school district policies with regard to curriculum and hiring practices. According to the most recent information (2004–2005), charter schools are supposed to be "held strictly accountable for their academic and financial performance."[116] The charters of these schools can be revoked if the schools do not meet satisfactory academic progress. Funding for these schools can be discontinued if inappropriate educational results are shown.[117]

The first charter school legislation was passed in Minnesota in 1991. As of January 2004, approximately 3,000 charter schools were operating in the United States, with 750,000 students enrolled under various charter laws.[118]

PRIVATIZATION OF EDUCATION: THE EDISON PROJECT

The concept of running public schools for a profit was implemented in 1991 with the Edison Project. This private corporation, founded by Christopher Whittle, an entrepreneur who also started Channel One, is partnering with public school districts to raise student achievement. Currently, Edison serves more than 250,000 public school students in more than 20 states, and in the United Kingdom through whole-school management partnerships with public school districts as well as charter schools.[119] Edison's schools are operated using research principles, from research conducted by the University of Chicago and Johns Hopkins University.[120] Students are taught in academies, or multigrade groups of 100 to 180 students taught by four to six teachers. These academies include the Primary Academy (K–2), Elementary Academy (3–5), Junior Academy (6–8), Senior Academy (9–10), and Collegiate Academy (11–12).[121] The academic school year is 200 days long, rather than 180, as in most public schools, and is based on a 7-hour class day divided into 90-minute classes.[122] Graduation requirements are strict; students are mandated to master basic math and reading skills before graduating from the Primary Academy (grades K–2).[123] The concept of FLES (Foreign Language in the Elementary Schools) is used at Edison; students are mandated to take Spanish courses and learn to speak Spanish.[124]

According to Edison's *Seventh Annual Report on School Performance 2003–2004*, the percentage of students who achieved higher standards increased by 7.4 percentage points from the 2002–03 to 2003–04 school year. The survey points out that this increase was approximately twice the gain of the states and districts in which these schools are found.[125] Edison also states that African American students in their schools are achieving at rates comparable to those of Caucasian students. The report cites that in schools with predominantly African Americans, there has been a yearly gain of 9.2 percent in achievement, and a 2-year increase of 17.8 percent, which Edison states is two to three times the gain of the districts and states in which these schools are found.[126]

Edison reports that the parents of students enrolled in Edison schools are extremely satisfied and rate the Edison schools highly; 84 percent of parents who answered surveys gave their child's school grades of A or B. Teachers apparently voice a similar level of satisfaction, with 85 percent of teachers rating their level of career satisfaction as A or B, with A being the predominant grade or level.[127]

Technology is an accepted and established part of the operating principles of Edison Schools. All students attending Edison schools are connected via "The Common," which is an intranet system, and students are given access to computers and the Internet as needed for their work.[128]

As of April 25, 2005, the Philadelphia public school district expanded its partnership with Edison Schools. Edison will now operate the Huey Elementary School, which serves grades K–6 in the Southwest Region, and the K–8 Hartranft Elementary School, located in the Central Region.[129] The Philadelphia School Reform Commission requested that Edison operate these two additional schools owing to what Edison reports as "stunning gains" in previously low-performing schools.[130]

According to the Edison Web site, the reason for Edison's success in Philadelphia is a focus on managed instruction and partnerships with private companies, universities and community groups to increase student achievement in low-performing schools.[131] Philadelphia began its partnership with Edison in 2002–2003. The district CEO, Dr. Paul Vallas, states that in the 20 schools that Edison operates within the District of Philadelphia, student achievement increased 10 percentage points under Edison's leadership. Before Edison's involvement in these same schools, achievement had increased less than 1 percentage point a year.[132]

Despite such claims of success, the Edison Project remains highly controversial. Claims of mismanagement and inappropriate behavior on the part of Edison staff have surfaced. On April 7, 2005, an article in the *Philadelphia Inquirer* reported that an Edison school, the Chester High School, which enrolls a high percentage of African American students, had hired a 28-year-old male principal, who seduced a 16-year-old female student in March 2005. The 17th principal in 35 years, Dr. Eboni Wilson had made significant improvements in school conditions, according to teachers at the school, which has been under Edison management since September 2001.[133] Wilson has been charged by Delaware County, Pennsylvania, authorities with two counts each of corrupting a minor and indecent exposure.[134] A member of the state-appointed board said that Edison should go, because "this is just one more black mark on Edison's record with Chester-Upland School District."[135]

The Philadelphia Public School District's effort to privatize its schools by using Edison, Kaplan, and the Princeton Review is costly; in 2005 the district spent $80 million to hire private companies to run its public schools.[136]

BRIDGES FROM THE PAST TO THE PRESENT: WHERE ARE WE HEADED?

Education today is in a state of flux. Families want education to be relevant, with curriculum encompassing AIDS and drug abuse awareness, fitness, career and consumer education, multicultural topics, and environmental concerns. Public schools are required to follow the rules of No Child Left Behind, and school districts are beginning to question the wisdom of this law. The states of Utah, Texas, Michigan, and Vermont are suing the U.S. Department of Education over the perceived inequalities of this law. This appears to be an unsettling, troubling time for many educators, who question the wisdom of NCLB and wonder, with decreases in funding, how they will be able to fulfill its requirements.

Educators today are accountable to many parties (state departments of education, the U.S. Department of Education, school boards, parents) in their quest to prove that they are adequately providing an appropriate public education. With the increased emphasis on testing required by NCLB, teachers wonder if they will end up "teaching to the test" and exactly how they will accomplish this. Teachers are also concerned with how students will learn to verify and evaluate the facts on which to make choices if they are taught only how to memorize answers to pass the required tests.

Schools today have school boards that demand that school expenditures be cut because community residents balk at paying high property taxes to fund the community's public schools. Teachers become stressed dealing with discipline problems and inadequate resources. Many teachers spend their own money for supplies for their students. In an NEA survey of March 2005, nearly 700 NEA teachers revealed that they spent $254.00 for books and videos, $214.76 for lesson materials, and $103.59 for school supplies such as pencils and crayons.[137] This online NEA survey found that the average teacher spent $1,180 in unreimbursed expenses for their students. An elementary teacher in California revealed that she spent $3,000 in 2003 for supplies for her students. Two teachers bought copy machines so they could make copies for their students. A teacher in Buffalo, New York, put $1000 on her credit card so that a student's mother, a recent widow, could have her car repaired and continue to work so she did not lose her home.[138]

Stories of social and economic inequalities abounded in the United States in 2004–2005. Black students increasingly attend failing inner-city schools with low graduation rates and high levels of illiteracy, drug use, and teenage pregnancy. Native Americans suffer from a similar fate. A recent school shooting in Minnesota on a reservation provided new insights into the fates of Native Americans in this country. The old ways of living, which fostered tribal bonding, are no longer being taught, contributing to their children's feelings of isolation and depression.

White students who live in poor areas also find it difficult to overcome poverty. This author has taught in higher educational institutions in Appalachia and spoken with many first-generation college students who reported that they struggled to overcome feelings of inadequacy on a regular basis. They were attending an institution of higher education to obtain a job or start a career with earning potential and increased job security, in contrast with their parents, who may not have had job security while they were working in the coal mines or oil fields.

President George W. Bush, the U.S. Department of Education, and others involved in federal educational policy making, appear to view school choice as the solution to economic inequality, which underlies many of the problems of students in today's public schools. Although it is certainly important to allow students and parents to be free to choose which schools they want to attend, it is also just as important to address the underlying socioeconomic inequities in society. The lack of affordable health care and dental care causes some children to attend school with poor health and toothaches caused by poor dental hygiene and lack of access to dentists. Deplorable housing conditions in deteriorating urban and rural areas lead to disease and often cause students to drop out of school to work and to ease economic tensions in the family.

Ultimately, federal policies will be necessary to assist lower-income families and families in depressed urban and rural areas in obtaining jobs and securing adequate housing and health care. With inadequate health care, for instance, families can end up filing for bankruptcy and losing their homes. If families' basic needs are not met, then education becomes the least of their worries. Parenting classes also need to be made available, perhaps through community organizations, to help parents cope with the stresses of modern life and daily parenting crises.

Although personal responsibility, accountability, and a strong work ethic are necessary for success in today's society, there is no denying that many schools with few resources cannot adequately educate students for today's jobs and careers. Schools with inoperative bathrooms due to outdated sewage systems, a shortage of qualified teachers, and lack of access to the Internet and other technology cannot do an adequate job of educating students.

SUMMARY

This chapter focused on the problems of modern education since the *A Nation at Risk* report and the reforms that have been attempted since that report was released. It is clear that, although the American educational system certainly does graduate many students every year who go on to higher education, graduate from college, and become very successful in a career, the educational system also has many failings that need to be addressed. Teachers often have trouble disciplining students who have special needs, and these students, who can become very frustrated and unhappy in school, may drop out and never return. They end up settling for minimum-wage jobs that do not allow them to save for retirement. Owing to the growing Hispanic population in this country, the issue of bilingual education continues to be of concern. Improved methods of teaching large numbers of non-English-speaking children must be developed so that these children can retain their native language while learning English. Multilingualism is an advantage in the global economy.

Teachers need better training in classroom management skills, instructional methods, and strategies to control students with behavioral and emotional problems. Schools need policies specifying the types of behaviors that will not be allowed in schools, and these policies must apply to all students and be enforced. In addition, the educational system must provide better vocational programs for those students who dislike school and have no desire to attend college. More guidance counselors and school psychologists are needed to ensure that students suffering from low self-esteem, abuse at home, eating disorders, and other problems receive the help they need at a young age. Currently, the Carnegie Foundation estimates that the average student-to-counselor ratio in the United States is 319 students per counselor. Interviews with guidance counselors reveal that the figure is actually much higher; in one interview, the counselor revealed that she had a caseload of 576 elementary school students.[139]

If American students are to perform better on the TIMSS and other standardized achievement tests, then the system of public education must be evaluated carefully to assess what it needs to achieve these necessary goals. At present it does not appear that public support for teachers or public education is very high, which is a contributing factor to the problem of finding qualified teachers willing to tolerate the lack of parental support in their schools. Teachers who lack basic resources for teaching and are forced to purchase them out of their own salaries will become increasingly frustrated and bitter and will leave the field of teaching. If the American public school system is to succeed, increased public support for public education, both in terms of emotional and psychological support and appreciation of teachers, as well as financial support, is mandatory.

QUESTIONS FOR DISCUSSION

1. The "furious child" syndrome was discussed in this chapter as an explanation of student misbehavior. Do you believe this is an actual phenomenon, or is it "just an excuse"? Give evidence for your answer.

2. Do you believe that gender discrimination is still an issue in schools today? Why or why not? Provide at least two examples to back up your answer.

3. Consider how you would deal with this situation: You are an elementary school teacher in a parochial school and your principal will not give you any more money for school supplies, but the children have little paper to write on and you can't afford to purchase these items yourself on a salary of $13,000 per year. With a group of your classmates, brainstorm how you would resolve this situation.

4. Do you believe that charter schools are the answer to the problem of poorly performing public schools? Why or why not? Be sure to provide evidence for your answer.

5. Describe the academic, personal, and professional qualifications you believe are necessary to be an effective teacher today.

6. In your opinion, what are the major reasons for violence among students in schools today? Provide evidence for your answer.

7. Describe how as a teacher you would encourage ESL students in your class to become fluent in English. Consider that these students may speak English in school but then go home and speak their native language the rest of the day.

8. Is No Child Left Behind the answer to the problems of public education today? Be prepared to defend your answer with at least two reasons.

SUGGESTED ACTIVITIES

1. Interview a teacher of a primary grade and a teacher of a secondary grade to get their opinions about the causes of disruptive and/or violent behavior in school. Find out the *strategies* these teachers use to deal with such students. Share your findings with your classmates in a 20-minute PowerPoint presentation.

2. Interview the principal of a charter school and the principal of a public school about the differences in teaching philosophies and administrative policies. Research the latest test scores of students in both schools. Present your findings to your classmates in a 20-minute PowerPoint presentation, and state the reason(s) for your findings.

3. Interview a principal and a teacher (any grade, any school) about their perceptions of No Child Left Behind and the type of accommodations they have had to make to fulfill this law. Write a short paper (three to five pages), on your findings, or present them to your classmates in a PowerPoint presentation of at least 15 minutes.

4. Ask a teacher to survey a group of at least 25 high school students (any school). Develop a survey of at least two pages relating students' values on cheating, stealing, lying, shoplifting, and the like. Analyze the data and report your findings to your classmates in a PowerPoint presentation of at least 20 minutes. Share your survey instrument and summarize your data findings with a class handout. How do your findings compare with those of the Josephson Institute of Ethics survey discussed in this chapter?

5. Interview a guidance counselor to find out how much time he or she spends on the following each day:
   a. career preparation for students
   b. personal/psychological counseling

    c. testing for special education students

    d. college entrance counseling and preparation

Report your findings to your classmates in a presentation using a handout with a bar graph to illustrate the amount of time the counselor spends on each of these tasks.

6. Interview a special education teacher about the teaching methods she uses to meet her students' needs. Ask for recommendations for new teachers addressing the needs of such students in a regular classroom setting. Present your findings to your classmates using a handout, such as a chart, or PowerPoint.

7. Interview a parent who sends his or her child to a charter school, and find out why he or she chose that school. Why did the parent find public education inappropriate for the child? Summarize your findings in a report of at least five pages, and include a list of recommendations for teachers and administrators in public schools, based on your findings.

8. Write a report of at least four pages on the issue of property taxes and school funding in American education, using statistics from the National Center for Education Statistics (NCES) as well as other current sources. Conclude with a list of recommendations for funding schools other than with property taxes.

Bibliography

Austin, V. L. (2003). Fear and loathing in the classroom: A candid look at school violence and the policies and practices that address it. *Journal of Disability Policy Studies, 14*(1).

Bush plans $1 billion boost to public schools. *Philadelphia Inquirer* (Education), 2003 January 9.

Chubb, C., Linn, R., Haycock, K., & Winner, R. (2005, Spring). Do we need to repair the monument? Debating the future of No Child Left Behind. *Education Next* (Forum), (2), 8–19.

Costa, A. Sr., Elseginy, S., Lusco, E., & Pinney, J. (2003, November). *Vouchers: A school choice (ED482515).* Paper presented at the annual meeting of the Mid-South Educational Research Association, Biloxi, MS.

Cromwell, S. 1998. *Education World administrators.* Schools combat violence. Retrieved 2004, from *http://www.educationworld.com/a_issues/issues032.shtml*

Curl, J. (2003, January 9). Bush OKs 5 state plans on education reform. *Washington Times.*

D'Andrea, M. (2004). Comprehensive school-based violence prevention training: A developmental-ecological training model. *Journal of Counseling and Development, 82*(3).

Eberstadt, M. (2004). *Home alone America: The hidden toll of day care, behavioral drugs, and other parent substitutes.* New York: Sentinel.

Ferraiolo, K., Hess, F., Maranto, R., & Milliman, S. (2004). Teachers' attitudes and the success of school choice. *Policy Studies Journal, 32*(2).

Gonzales, P., Guzman, J. C., Partolow, L., Pahlke, E., Jocelyn, L., Kastberg, D., & Williams, T. (2004). National Center for Education Statistics. *Highlights from the Trends in International Math and Science Study (TIMSS) 2003 (NCES 2005-005).* Washington, DC: U.S. Government Printing Office.

Josephson Institute of Ethics. (2001). *Report card on the ethics of American youth 2000: Report #1: Violence, guns, and alcohol.* Retrieved 2003. Updated information is available at: *http://www.charactercounts.org*

Kaplowitz, J. (2003, Winter). How I joined Teach for America—And got sued for $20 million. *City Journal,* pp. 1–7. Retrieved Spring 2004, from *http://www.manhattan-institute.org/cfml*

Kozol, J. (1996). *Amazing grace: The lives of children and the conscience of a nation.* New York: Crown.

Krueger, A. B., & Zhu, P. (2004). Another look at the New York City School voucher experiment. *American Behavioral Scientist, 47*(5).

Langan, D., and Malico, M. (2003, January 8). President Bush celebrates one-year anniversary of No Child Left Behind Act. U.S. Department of Education. Retrieved 2004, from *http://www.ed.gov/PressReleases*

Langley, J., & Olson, K. (2003, September). *Training district and state personnel on accommodations: A study of state practices, challenges, and resources.* Assessing Special Education Students project of the State Collaborative on Assessment and Student Standards. Washington, DC: Council of Chief State School Officers.

Lankford, H., Loeb, S. & Wyckoff, J. (2002). Teacher sorting and the plight of urban schools: A descriptive analysis. *Educational Evaluation and Policy Analysis, 24*(1), 38–62.

Murphy, J. B. (2003, Fall). Tug of war. *Education Next,* (3), 70–76.

Nansel, T., Overpeck, M., Pilla, R., Ruan, W., Simons-Morton, B., & Scheidt, P. (2001, April). Bullying behaviors among U.S. youth: Prevalence and association with psychosocial adjustment. *Journal of the American Medical Association, 285,* 2094–2100.

National Center for Education Statistics. International Outcomes of Learning in Mathematics Literacy and Problem Solving; PISA 2003 Results from the U.S. Perspective, Issue 4, Vol. 6, Lemke, Mariann, Anindita Son, Erin Pahlke, Lisette Partolow, David Miller et al. (Retrieved 2004–5) from *http://www.nces.ed.gov*

National Center for Education Statistics. (2002–2003). Contexts of elementary and secondary education: Inclusion of students with disabilities in regular classrooms. Retrieved 2004, from *http://www.nces.ed.gov*

National Center for Education Statistics. Issue Brief: 1.1 Million homeschooled students in the United States in 2003. Retrieved 2004, from *http://www.nces.ed.gov/nhes/homeschool/*

National Center for Education Statistics. (2003). NAEP Reading: Percentage of students, by race/ethnicity, and reading achievement levels, grade 4 public schools (by state). Retrieved from *http://www.nces.ed.gov*

National Center for Education Statistics. (2004 August). Issue Brief: English language learner students in U.S. public schools: 1994 and 2000. Retrieved 2003 from *http://www .nces.ed.gov/pubs2004/2004035.pdf*

National Center for Education Statistics. (2004, December). Program for International Student Assessment (PISA): PISA 2003 results from the U.S. Perspective. Washington, DC. Retrieved 2005, from *http://www.nces.ed.gov*

National Center for Education Statistics. (updated 2005, 4 March). The nation's report card: National Association of Educational Progress. Retrieved 2003 from *http://www.nces.ed.gov*

National Center for Education Statistics. (n.d.) *TIMSS USA: Trends in International Math and Science Study.* Retrieved 2004-5, from *http://www.nces.ed.gov*

National Center for Education Statistics. (n.d.) *Trends in International Math and Science Study: Highlights from the Third International Math and Science Study-Repeat* (TIMSS-R). Retrieved 2005, from *http://www.nces.ed.gov/timss/highlights.asp*

People for the American Way on Capitol Hill. (n.d.) Full funding for public education; Federal education legislation: Elementary and Secondary Education Act. Retrieved   , from *http://www.pfaw.org*

Pipher, M. (1994). *Reviving Ophelia: Saving the selves of adolescent girls.* New York: Random House.

Postman, N. (1994). *The disappearance of childhood.* New York: Vintage Books.

Saulny, S., & Beller, P. (2005, April 4). A lucrative brand of tutoring goes unchecked. *New York Times,* p. 1.

Sorokin, E. (2003, January 8). High poverty schools report fewer qualified instructors. *Washington Times.*

Strauss, R. (1999). Who gets hired to teach? The case of Pennsylvania. In M. Kanstroom & C. Finn (Eds.). *Better teachers, better schools.* Washington, DC: The Fordham Foundation.

Thurlow, M., Wiles Ivey, H., & Bielinksi, J. (2003). *Going public: What 2000–2001 reports tell us about the performance of students with disabilities.* Technical report. National Center on Educational Outcomes. Minneapolis: University of Minnesota.

U.S. Department of Education. (2005, January 21). National clearinghouse for English language acquisition & language instruction educational programs. Retrieved 2005, from *http://www.ncela.gwu.edu*

Weisenberger, A. (2001). Cleveland program could lead to definitive Supreme Court precedent on school vouchers. *Journal of Law and Education, 30*(3).

Wilson, W. J. (1996). *When work disappears: The world of the new urban poor.* New York: Vintage Books.

Yu, L. (2003, April 21–25). Trends of school violence across years: What do TIMSS and TIMSS-R tell us? Paper presented at the Annual Meeting of the American Educational Research Association (AERA), Chicago, IL. (Available through EDRS; document number ED481654).

Suggestions for Further Reading

In addition to the works cited in the bibliography, the following are suggested for further reading

Fusarelli, L.D., "Will Vouchers Arrive in Colorado?" *Education Next* (Fall 2004), 51–55. Available from the Education Next Web site at: *http://www.educationnext.org.*

Llgas, C. and T.D. Snyder, "Status and Trends in the Education of Hispanics" (April 2003). Available from National Center for Education Statistics Web site at *http://www.nces.ed.gov.*

NCES Working Paper series, NAEP Validity Studies: "Reporting the Results of the National Assessment of Educational Progress," working paper 2003–11, April 2003.

Relevant Web Sites

American Association of University Women (AAUW) *http://www.aauw.org* Home page of the AAUW, which promotes educational equity for women and girls. Describes programs and initiatives for achieving educational equity in schools.

American Federation of Teachers *http://www.aft.org* Home page of the AFT. Includes salary scales for teachers, by state, and reports on educational issues.

Carnegie Foundation for the Advancement of Teaching *http://www.carnegiefoundation.org/* Home page of the Carnegie Foundation for the Advancement of Teaching, founded in 1906. Describes reform initiatives in K–12, undergraduate, and graduate education.

National Center for Education Statistics *http://www.nces.ed.gov* Information at the federal and state level relating to all topics in education.

National Education Association *http://www.nea.org* Home page of the National Education Association, with information on NCLB, ESEA, teacher preparation, and more.

Journal of American Indian Education http://jaie.asu.edu/ Based at Arizona State University. Information pertaining to education of Native Americans.

National Indian Education Association *http://www.niea.org/* Home page of the NIEA, founded in 1969 and the oldest Indian education organization in the United States, which is working toward educational equity for all those of Native American ancestry.

No Child Left Behind Act *http://www.nclb.gov* U.S. Department of Education site explaining NCLB.

U.S. Department of Education *http://www.ed.gov* Home page of the U.S. Department of Education for research on federal and state educational policies.

Endnotes

[1] These studies include *High School,* by Ernest Boyer; and *An Imperiled Generation: Saving Urban Schools,* by the Carnegie Foundation.

[2] For a first-hand look at the personal effects of segregation on the lives of children, read Jonathan Kozol's *Amazing Grace: The Lives of Children and The Conscience of a Nation* (New York: Crown, 1996).

[3] As this chapter was being written, a 9-year-old girl, Jessica Lunsford, went missing in Homosassa, Florida. She was abducted, sexually molested, and strangled by a crack-addicted pedophile in her neighborhood. Her body was found in a shallow grave at the back of the trailer home of John Couey, a previously convicted pedophile and sexual predator who had failed to register in the state of Florida. The trailer home was only 150 yards from Jessica's home.

[4] Neil Postman, *The Disappearance of Childhood* (New York: Vintage Books, 1994), 134–36.

[5] Ibid., 137.

[6] Ibid.

[7] Michael D'Andrea, "Comprehensive School-Based Violence Prevention Training: A Developmental-Ecological Training Model," *Journal of Counseling and Development, 82,* no. 3 (2004), 277–78.

[8] Ibid., 277.

[9] Mary Eberstadt, "The Furious Child Problem," chap. 2 in *Home Alone America: The Hidden Toll of Day Care, Behavioral Drugs, and Other Parent Substitutes* (New York: Sentinel, 2004), 23–26.

[10] Ibid.

[11] Ibid.

[12] Ibid., 32. See the wonderful section on "Savage Schoolkids."

[13] The author once had a student describe an incident in which his daughter, who attended day-care, was bitten on the ear by another child at the day-care center. The bite became badly infected, causing the little girl to be hospitalized. The child who bit this little girl had previously acted aggressively toward other children in the day-care center, showing a clear preference for violent confrontation even at such a young age.

[14] T. Nansel, M. Overpeck, R. Pilla, W. Ruan, B. Simons-Morton, & P. Scheidt, "Bullying Behaviors Among U.S. Youth: Prevalence and Association with Psychosocial Adjustment," *Journal of the American Medical Association, 285* (April 2001), 2094–2100.

[15] The story of Joshua Kaplowitz provides a warning to those who think they can take a few courses in education and be prepared to teach. Clearly, there is more to preparing effective teachers than this.

[16] Vance L. Austin, "Fear and Loathing in the Classroom: A Candid Look at School Violence and the Policies and Practices That Address It," *Journal of Disability Policy Studies 14,* no. 1 (2003), 17

[17] Ibid., 17.

[18] Sharon Cromwell, Education World Administrators, "Schools Combat Violence," 1998, *http://www.educationworld.com* (retrieved 2001).

[19] Josephson Institute of Ethics, "Report Card on the Ethics of American Youth 2000: Report #1: Violence, Guns, and Alcohol," 2001 (most recent study available), *http://www .charactercounts.org* (retrieved 2002).

[20] Ellen Sorokin, "High-Poverty Schools Report Fewer Qualified Instructors," *Washington Times,* January 8, 2003.

[21] Hamilton Lankford, Susanna Loeb, and James Wyckoff, "Teacher Sorting and the Plight of Urban Schools: A Descriptive Analysis," *Educational Evaluation and Policy Analysis 24,* no. 1 (2002), 38–62.

[22] Ibid.

[23] Donald Boyd, Hamilton Lankford, Susanna Loeb, and James Wyckoff, "The Draw of Home: How Teachers' Preferences for Proximity Disadvantage Urban Schools," *Journal of Policy Analysis and Management 24,* no. 1 (2005), 113.

[24] Ibid.

[25] Ibid., 117.

[26] R. Strauss, "Who Gets Hired to Teach? The Case of Pennsylvania," in *Better Teachers, Better Schools,* ed. M. Kanstroom & C. Finn (Washington, DC: The Fordham Foundation, 1999).

[27] Boyd, Lankford, Loeb, & Wyckoff, "The Draw of Home," 118.

[28] Ibid., 119.

[29] Ibid., 126–27.

[30] Ibid., 127–28.

[31] Ibid.

[32] John Chubb, Robert Linn, Kati Haycock, & Ross Weiner, "Do We Need to Repair the Monument? Debating the Future of No Child Left Behind," *Education Next,* no. 2 (Spring 2005), 10. This article is a dialogue/discussion among the authors.

[33] William Julius Wilson. *When Work Disappears: The World of the New Urban Poor* (New York: Vintage Books, 1996). See the introduction.

[34] Ibid., xv.

[35] Ibid.

[36] Ibid., 3.

[37] Ibid., 4.

[38] Ibid., 11.

[39] Ibid., 23–24.

[40] Ibid., 25.

[41] Ibid.

[42] Ibid.

[43] See the Doe Network case files at *http:/www.doenetwork.us* More women than men are reported missing, abducted, and killed in this country. See also the National Center for Missing Children (NCMC) at *http://www.ncmc.org*

[44] Mary Pipher, *Reviving Ophelia: Saving the Selves of Adolescent Girls* (New York: Random House, 1994), 19–21.

[45] Ibid., 23.

[46] National Center for Education Statistics, "Contexts of Elementary and Secondary Education: Inclusion of Students with Disabilities in Regular Classrooms," (2002–2003) *http://www.nces.ed.gov* (retrieved 2005).

[47] Jennifer Langley & Ken Olson, "Training District and State Personnel on Accommodations: A Study of State Practices, Challenges, and Resources," Assessing Special Education Students project of the State Collaborative on Assessment and Student Standards, 2003. Available through the EDRS. See the abstract, p. 6.

[48] Ibid.

[49] Ibid., 7.

[50] Ibid., 8.

[51] Martha Thurlow, Hilda Ives Wiley, & John Bielinksi, "Going Public: What 2000–2001 Reports Tell Us about the Performance of Students with Disabilities," technical report (National Center on Educational Outcomes, Minneapolis: University of Minnesota, 2003).

[52] Ibid., 4–5.

[53] Ibid., 6.

[54] Ibid., 6.

[55] Ibid., 17–28.

[56] National Center for Education Statistics, "Bilingual Education/Limited English Proficient Students," *http://www.nces.ed.gov* (retrieved 2004).

[57] National Center for Education Statistics, "Issue Brief: English Language Learner Students in U.S. Public Schools: 1994 and 2000," August 2004, *http://www.nces.ed.gov* (retrieved 2005).

[58] Ibid.

[59] Ibid.

[60] U.S. Department of Education, "National Clearinghouse for English Language Acquisition and Language Instruction Educational Programs," January 21, 2005, *http://www.ncela.gwu.edu* (retrieved 2005).

[61] National Center for Education Statistics, "The Nation's Report Card: National Association of Educational Progress," updated March 4, 2005, *http://www.nces.ed.gov* (retrieved 2005).

[62] Ibid., 2.

[63] Ibid., 3.

64 Ibid.

65 Charmaine Llagas and Thomas D. Snyder, "Status and Trends in the Education of Hispanics," National Center for Education Statistics, April 2003, *http://www.nces.ed.gov* (retrieved 2004).

66 Ibid., 6.

67 Patrick Gonzales, Juan Carlos Guzman, Lisette Partolow, Erin Pahlke, Leslie Jocelyn, David Kastberg, & Trevor Williams (2004). *Highlights from the Trends in International Math and Science Study (TIMSS) 2003* (NCES 2005–005), National Center for Education Statistics (Washington, DC: U.S. Government Printing Office), 1.

68 Ibid.

69 Ibid.

70 For further information on these figures, see the National Center for Education Statistics, "TIMSS USA: Trends in International Math and Science Study," *http://www.nces.ed.gov*

71 Ibid. See Table 8, "Average science scale scores of fourth-grade students, by country: 2003."

72 Lei Yu, "Trends of School Violence Across Years: What Do TIMSS and TIMSS-R Tell Us?," Paper presented at the Annual Meeting of the American Educational Research Association (AERA), Chicago, IL, April 21–25, 2003. Available through EDRS. Document number ED481654. See pp. 3–10.

73 Ibid.

74 Dan Langan and Melinda Malico, "President Bush Celebrates One-Year Anniversary of No Child Left Behind Act," January 8, 2003, U.S. Department of Education, *http://www.ed.gov/PressReleases* (retrieved 2004).

75 Ibid.

76 Ibid.

77 Joseph Curl, "Bush OKs 5 State Plans on Education Reform," *Washington Times*, January 9, 2003.

78 Ibid., 2.

79 Ibid.

80 Ibid.

81 People for the American Way on Capitol Hill, "Full Funding for Public Education: Federal Education Legislation: Elementary and Secondary Education Act," *http://www.pfaw.org* (retrieved 2005).

82 "Education Left Behind," *Boston Globe,* January 8, 2003, editorial, *http://www.boston.com* (retrieved 2004).

83 "Bush Plans $1 Billion Boost to Public Schools," *Philadelphia Inquirer* (Education), January 9, 2003.

84 Sam Dillon, "Districts and Teachers' Union Sue Over Bush Law," *New York Times*, April 21, 2005, *http://www.nytimes.com* (retrieved 2005).

85 Ibid.

86 Susan Saulny & Peter Beller, "A Lucrative Brand of Tutoring Goes Unchecked," *New York Times*, April 4, 2005.

87 National Center for Education Statistics, "Issue Brief: 1.1 Million Homeschooled Students in the United States in 2003," *http://www.nces.ed.gov/nhes/homeschool* (retrieved 2004).

[88] Ibid.

[89] Ibid.

[90] James B. Murphy, "Tug of War," *Education Next,* no. 3 (Fall 2003), 74–75.

[91] Ibid., 76.

[92] 2004 Report Card: Ethics of American Youth: The Josephson Institute of Ethics, 2004, (The report card 2004 was on the 2001 statistics, available at that time) *http://www.josephsoninstitute.org/Survey2004/* (retrieved 2005).

[93] Ibid.

[94] Ibid.

[95] Ibid., 2.

[96] Ibid., 5.

[97] Ibid., 5.

[98] Alicia Sr. Costa, Siham Elseginy, Ellen Lusco, & Jean Pinney, "Vouchers: A School Choice," (ED482515) paper presented at the Annual Meeting of the Mid-South Educational Research Association, Biloxi, MS, November, 2003. See p. 4.

[99] Ibid.

[100] Ibid., 10.

[101] Ibid., 7.

[102] Ibid., 5.

[103] *Zelman, Superintendent of Public Instruction of Ohio, et al. v. Simmons-Harris et al., http:// caselaw.lp.findlaw* (retrieved 2005).

[104] Ibid.

[105] Ibid., 9. See also John Chubb and Terry Moe, *Politics, Markets, and America's Schools* (Washington, DC: The Brookings Institution, 1990).

[106] Ibid.

[107] Ibid., 10.

[108] Christine H. Rossell, "No Longer Famous but Still Intact: Magnet Schools," *Education Next,* no. 1 (Spring 2005), 44–45.

[109] Ibid.

[110] Ibid., 46.

[111] Ibid., 47.

[112] Ibid.

[113] National Center for Education Statistics, "Characteristics of the 100 Largest Public Elementary and Secondary Districts in the United States, 2000–2001," *http://www.nces.ed.gov* (retrieved 2002).

[114] National Center for Education Statistics, "America's Charter Schools: Results from the NAEP 2003 Pilot Study," *http://www.nces.ed.gov* (retrieved 2004).

[115] Ibid.

[116] "Innovations in Education: Successful Charter Schools," *http://www.uscharterschools.org* (the U.S. Charter Schools Web site, operated by the Charter School Leadership Council (CSLC), National Association of State Directors of Special Education (NASDSE), and

WestEd (web maintenance)). This site was operated until September 18, 2004, with support from the U.S. Department of Education. Currently it is no longer sponsored nor endorsed by the U.S. Department of Education.

[117] Ibid., 1.

[118] Ibid.

[119] Edison Schools: Overview, *http://www.edisonproject.com/home* (retrieved 2005).

[120] "EMO's: Edison Project," *http://www.edwebproject.org* (retrieved 2005).

[121] Ibid.

[122] Ibid.

[123] Ibid.

[124] Ibid.

[125] Ibid. See "Student Achievement Data."

[126] Ibid.

[127] Ibid.

[128] Ibid.

[129] "Edison Schools: Philadelphia School District Expands Historic Partnership With Edison Schools," *http://www.edisonproject.com/news* (retrieved 2005).

[130] Ibid.

[131] Ibid.

[132] Ibid.

[133] "School Reeling Over Sex Charges: A 16 Year-Old Says She Twice Had Sex With Chester High's Acting Principal," *Philadelphia Inquirer,* April 7, 2005.

[134] Ibid.

[135] Ibid.

[136] "Schools $80 Million Bet," *Philadelphia Inquirer,* April 24, 2005.

[137] National Education Association, "Classroom Supplies," March 2005, *http://www.nea.org* (retrieved 2005).

[138] Ibid.

[139] Interview with Beth Ann Fahr, Altoona, Pennsylvania, who formerly was a guidance counselor in the elementary schools of Juniata Valley, Alexandria, Pennsylvania.

Glossary

Abacus Device with beads, used to help children learn to count.

Abbaco Math skills—term used in Renaissance Florence.

Act of Supremacy King Henry VIII named himself Head of English Church so as to be able to divorce his first wife.

Aeneid Work of Virgil, studied in Roman grammar schools.

Aesop's Fables Tales told by the Ancient Greek philosopher Aesop, formerly a slave, who served the monarch Croesus at Sardis, and who told stories to get the inhabitants of Athens and Corinth to accept their rulers.

Age of Pericles Age of great achievement in Ancient Greece under King Pericles.

Alcuin Established schools in cathedrals and monasteries in AD 789, under Charlemagne.

Almonry schools Charity schools, for those who could not pay.

Almshouses Housing for the destitute.

American Federation of Teachers (AFT) Teachers' union which began as part of the American Federation of Labor (AFL).

Apprenticeships Pre-professional training, common in the Renaissance, for children ages 8 and over.

Aristotle Scientist and tutor of Alexander the Great.

Athens City-state of Ancient Greece and major cultural center.

Augustus (Emperor) Last Roman Emperor, who was deported AD 476.

Barbarians Strangers who invaded ancient Rome when the Roman Empire fell. They spoke other languages.

Barnard, Henry Secretary of the Connecticut Board of Education.

Bede Monk who wrote *Church History of the English People*.

Benedictines Members of the Order of St. Benedict, who farmed, preserved literature, and ran schools in England and Ireland.

***Bill for the More General Diffusion of Knowledge* (1779)** Proposal for a three year system of free public education in Virginia.

Black Death Fatal flu-like illness, caused by fleas which were carried by rats.

Blow, Susan Early childhood educator who documented the need for kindergarten education in Saint Louis, Missouri.

Boyer, Ernest Former president of the Carnegie Foundation.

***Brown v. Board of Education of Topeka* (1954)** Desegregation of U.S. schools was ordered by the Supreme Court.

Calvinism Religious movement founded by John Calvin.

Cathedral schools Schools established in cathedrals, such as Chartres in France.

Catherine of Aragon First wife of King Henry VIII.

Central and High Middle Ages Period when cathedral schools were established.

Chantries Chapels where Masses were said for the souls of the dead.

Chantry Schools Schools attached to chantries, where children were taught to sing *plainsong*, assist at Mass, basic reading, and writing, and sometimes the rudiments of Latin grammar.

Charlemagne   Emperor who passed law in 802 mandating that children had to be sent to school to learn to read.

Charter schools   Public schools established by local school boards and run as public schools of choice.

City States   Different geographical areas in ancient Greece, each with its own system of education and government.

Collegiate schools   Type of *grammar school* run by secular clergy in Tudor England. Examples are Eton and Winchester.

Comenius, John Amos   Advocated early-childhood education.

Committee of Ten   Evaluated high school curricula in 1892 to determine methods of improvement.

Communal schools   Educated professionals in Renaissance Italy.

Commune of Treviso   Law of 1475 which stated that Florentine teachers had to be capable and well-trained.

Condotta   Renewable teaching contracts in Renaissance Florence.

Corporal punishment   Use of physical force to discipline students.

Cromwell, Thomas   King Henry VIII's minister of affairs.

Da Feltre, Vittorino   Wanted liberal-arts education for girls.

Dark and Early Middle Ages   From AD 500 to 962, period of great social, economic, and educational turmoil.

Delian League   Athens and Sparta joined together in a defensive league which incorporated the lower classes into society.

Demesnes   Plots of land worked by peasants in the Middle Ages (see *estates*).

Dewey, John   Progressive educator who began the Laboratory School at the University of Chicago.

Dissolution of monasteries   Henry VIII abolished monasteries.

Ecclesiastical schools   Schools in Renaissance Italy sponsored by bishops.

Elyot, Thomas   Made educational recommendations for wealthy children in *The Book Named the Governour.*

Estates   Large plots of land owned by nobility and worked by peasants (serfs).

Fourth Annual Report   Horace Mann's report on teacher qualifications.

Franklin, Benjamin   Enlightenment inventor, printer, and educator. Founded the Academy of Pennsylvania (now the University of Pennsylvania).

Gensfleisch zur Laden zum Gutenberg, Johannes   Inventor of printing press.

Gentry   Elite or wealthy individuals.

Gerbert, Bishop   Teacher at Rheims Cathedral who used manipulatives to teach young children numbers.

Grammar schools   Schools, which were actually for students from the ages of 7 or 8, to 14 or 15, in Tudor England.

Grammaticus   Higher school in ancient Rome, where Latin was taught.

Guild schools   Grammar schools established by craft or merchant guilds, which picked chaplains to run the schools.

Haley, Margaret   Influential union organizer in turn of the century Chicago.

Harper Report   Report citing poorly prepared teachers as a major problem in U.S. schools.

Harris, William Torrey   U.S. commissioner of education and member of the Committee of Ten; also Superintendent of Saint Louis, Missouri public schools.

Hellenistic culture   Height of achievement in Ancient Athens.

Helots   Name for slaves in ancient Greece and Rome.

Honestiores   Ancient Rome's highest social class of senators and knights, and veterans with children.

Hornbook   Piece of wood with alphabet and verses attached to it, used to teach the alphabet and basic reading in colonial America.

Hospital schools   In Tudor England, schools connected with almshouses, to provide charity for the poor.

Humanism   Philosophy of learning not only for learning itself, but to apply knowledge to real-world problems.

Humiliores   Another name for plebeians, a poor social class.

Idealism   Plato's philosophy about sensory input and reality.

Indulgences   Selling prayers for forgiveness in the Church.

Inns of Court   Law schools in London, in Tudor England.

Jefferson, Thomas   Enlightenment educator and politician, and founder of the University of Virginia.

King Charles I   English monarch who tried to prevent Puritans from immigrating to America.

King Henry VIII   Tudor-Age monarch who dissolved the monasteries.

Lancaster, Joseph   Founder of the monitorial school movement.

Lilly's Grammar   Used to teach English grammar.

Ludimagister   Schoolmaster in *ludus* (see below).

Ludus   Primary school in Ancient Rome, for children 6 to 12.

Luther, Martin   German Reformation leader who wrote *95 Theses*.

Mann, Horace   Founder of the U.S. public school system, and secretary of the Massachusetts Board of Education.

Manorial economy   Medieval economic system.

Manuscript books   Long manuscripts rolled up in a container.

Mather, Cotton   Puritan leader in Massachusetts.

Melanchthon, Philipp   Educator in the German Reformation.

Minerva   Roman goddess of education.

Monastic education   Medieval education, provided by monks.

Moral education   Educating children so they know the difference between right and wrong, and how to live a Christian life.

Mulcaster, Richard   Headmaster at St. Paul's and Merchant Taylors' Grammar schools in London.

National Education Association (NEA)   Influential teachers' union, which is very powerful today, that started the Committee of Ten.

Neill, A.S.   Founder of Summerhill, an English alternative school still in operation.

Nepotism   Practice of awarding jobs (positions) to relatives or friends regardless of qualifications for the position.

New England Primer   Used to teach reading in colonial America.

No Child Left Behind (NCLB)   Federal legislation passed in 2001 to mandate annual federal testing for all students.

Normal schools   Teacher training institutions, meant to train future teachers in the patterns and standards (norms) of teaching.

Oblati and externi   Two types of monastic schools.

Old Deluder Satan Act   Mandated school attendance in Massachusetts in 1647.

Original Sin   Children were born sinful and had to be baptized.

Orphan Court   In Colonial Virginia, a court which met to make sure that orphaned children were being cared for properly.

Otto the Great   Crowned Emperor of the Holy Roman Empire in 962.

Outside school   School associated with a monastery, in Tudor England, in which the endowment was held in trust.

Owen, Robert Dale   Founder of the infant school movement.

Pagus   District in Ancient Rome, in which families worshipped.

Petrarch   Founder of humanism.

Petty schools   For children aged 4, in 16th c. Tudor England.

Plainsong   Religious chanting done without music.

Plato   Wrote the *Republic* and founded the Academy in Athens.

Plebeians   Regular citizens (not aristocrats), in Ancient Rome.

***Plessy v. Ferguson* (1896)**   Led the way for the "separate but equal" doctrine to justify segregated schools.

Pluralism   Clergyman could hold more than one office at a time.

Puritans   English dissenters who broke with the Church because of its extravagances.

Quintilian   Roman educator who prohibited corporal punishment.

Renaissance   From AD 1150–1517, a time of renewed interest in learning. Literally means "rebirth."

Rockfish Gap Report   Established the need for the University of Virginia (1814).

Rush, Benjamin   Philadelphia physician and Enlightenment educator.

Serfs   Peasants who farmed for lords or nobility of the estates.

Seven Liberal Arts   Study of grammar, rhetoric, logic, and dialectic, (Trivium) and arithmetic, music, geometry and astronomy (Quadrivium).

Smith-Hughes Act (1917)   Restricted federal aid to schools that offered vocational training to students over age 14.

Socrates   Ancient Greek philosopher.

Song Schools   Type of school found in Tudor England, where young children learned reading and writing and singing, and to assist at Mass.

Sparta   City-State of Ancient Greece which emphasized training for war.

Sputnik   Satellite launched by the U.S.S.R. in 1957.

St. Augustine   Writer and teacher in Roman North Africa (AD 354–430), who wrote *Confessions* and *The City of God*.

St. John Chrysostom   Recommended to Christian parents that their children should be educated after age 10 by monks.

Sunday schools   Function was to teach working children on their free day in the week, hence the name.

Third International Math and Science Study (TIMSS)   Compares academic performance of U.S. students in math and science with those of students in other countries.

Thorndike, Edward L.   Educational psychologist who focused on standardizing grading practices and the scientific study of education.

Title IX   Federal initiative to improve gender equality.

Tudor England   England during the reign of Henry VIII (Henry Tudor).

Twelfth Annual Report   Horace Mann's 1848 report explaining the effects of poverty on children and their education.

12 Tables   Romans inscribed their laws in the Twelve Tables in 450 BC.

Universitas   A guild, formed by schoolmasters in the cathedral schools.

Vernacular   In someone's regular language, not in Latin.

Vespasian (Emperor)   Founded the University of Rome.

Vives, Juan Luis   Spanish educator who wrote educational plan for Mary Tudor, daughter of Henry VIII.

Vocational education   Training for a trade or occupation such as carpentry, millwork, plumbing, etc.

Wet nurses   Women hired during the Middle Ages, Renaissance, and Reformation, to breastfeed children of the upper classes.

Winthrop, John   City lawyer and Puritan activist who was elected the new Governor of the Massachusetts Bay colony in America.

Index